CAPITALISM WITHOUT DEMOCRACY

Capitalism without Democracy

THE PRIVATE SECTOR IN CONTEMPORARY CHINA

Kellee S. Tsai

Cornell University Press ITHACA AND LONDON

First published 2007 by Cornell University Press
First printing, Cornell Paperbacks, 2007

Printed in the United States of America

Library of Congress Cataloging-in-Publication Data
Tsai, Kellee S.
  Capitalism without democracy : the private sector in contemporary
China / Kellee S. Tsai.
      p. cm
  Includes bibliographical references and index.
  ISBN 978-0-8014-4513-2 (cloth : alk. paper)—ISBN 978-0-8014-7326-5
(pbk : alk. paper)
  1. Free enterprise—China.   2. Entrepreneurship—Political aspects—China.
3. Businessmen—China—Political activity.   4. Informal sector (Economics)—China.
5. China—Economic policy—2000.   6. China—Economic policy—1976–2000.   I. Title.
  HC427.95.T73 2007
  338.6'10951—dc22
2007013551

Cornell University Press strives to use environmentally responsible
suppliers and materials to the fullest extent possible in the publishing
of its books. Such materials include vegetable-based, low-VOC
inks and acid-free papers that are recycled, totally chlorine-free, or
partly composed of nonwood fibers. For further information, visit
our website at www.cornellpress.cornell.edu.

Cloth printing   10 9 8 7 6 5 4 3 2 1

Paperback printing   10 9 8 7 6 5 4 3 2 1

For Felix and Kirby

Each new generation of scientists or social researchers furthers its predecessors' understanding of the world of reality. If one day we look back at our present findings . . . and find that this understanding was superficial and naïve, this will only be evidence of progress in our understanding.

Fei Xiaotong, "Small Towns, Great Significance:
A Study of Small Towns in Wujiang County" (1984)

Contents

Preface

When I first visited China in 1992, I remember marveling that for an authoritarian country dominated by a Communist party, people seemed to get away with a lot at the ground level. To be sure, there were—and still are—serious restrictions on freedom of speech and assembly when it comes to practices that could threaten the party-state's legitimacy. But ordinary people were finding ways around midlevel rules and regulations that were anachronistic or impractical. A few years later when I was conducting research on informal finance, the evasive capacity of China's private entrepreneurs impressed me further. Despite numerous obstacles, China's business owners raise capital through innovative and often illegal means, and in the process the private sector has boomed.

Is this transformative potential of private entrepreneurs limited to economic issues? What are the political implications of private sector development in China? This book's title, *Capitalism without Democracy*, summarizes the broad contours of the conclusion. To date, the spread of markets has not brought democracy to China, and my research shows that private entrepreneurs are not likely to demand regime change. A venture capitalist in Beijing predicted, "Things would quickly become chaotic if China became a democracy. What I worry about the most is maintaining social stability so the economy will continue to do well." But that is only part of the story. Regardless of whether China ultimately makes a transition to democracy, dramatic changes in the country's paramount political institutions have already occurred. Moreover, those changes have favored private entrepreneurs—the Chinese Communist Party now welcomes capitalist members, and at least on paper the Constitution of the People's Republic of China protects private property rights. How did these institutional changes occur in the absence of regime transition or political mobilization by private entrepreneurs?

My explanation is similar in logic to what I found in the veiled, yet expansive, world of informal finance: in discrete collaboration with local officials, private entrepreneurs have devised a host of what I call "adaptive informal institutions," which are routinized adaptations to the constraints and opportunities of various formal institutions. In turn, these adaptive informal institutions have undermined and contributed to the transformation of the formal institutions that once endeavored to constrain the activities of business owners. Private entrepreneurs have indeed had an impact on Chinese politics, but this influence has occurred through indirect means. That this is possible in an authoritarian party-state helps us understand endogenous institutional change. As a middle-aged hotel owner put it, "I have already experienced two revolutions in my lifetime—the Cultural Revolution and a market revolution—and somehow, the Chinese Communist Party has managed to survive both."

Because this book explores both the origins and the consequences of adaptive informal institutions, it is fitting that many of the contributions to this project occurred through informal means—impulsive late night e-mails, pontifications during happy hour, cab driver chats, interminable banquets, dank massage parlors, delays at public transportation hubs, and, yes, even interactions by the water fountain outside my office in Mergenthaler Hall. Recounting those encounters would make a colorful narrative about the anthropology of fieldwork and life in the ivory tower.

Less colorful, but more central to resolving the practical challenges facing academics in social science, is another book-length tribute that I could write about the kindness of friends, colleagues, institutions, interviewees, and students who took the time to support various dimensions of this project over the years.

First, this book would not have been possible without the multiple sources of institutional support that I received. A two-year grant from the International Research Fellowship Program of the National Science Foundation (NSF INT-0107326), administered by Program Manager Susan Parris, enabled me to design and implement a national survey based on multistage area probability sampling, as well as to conduct field interviews with hundreds of entrepreneurs and officials in various parts of China. Any opinions, findings, and conclusions or recommendations expressed in this book are those of the author and do not necessarily reflect the views of the NSF.

The Private Economy Research Center and the Institute of Sociology of the Chinese Academy of Social Sciences proved to be professional hosts. In this regard, I thank Zhang Houyi and Chen Guangjin for their diligence and patience as research collaborators; I also thank Dai Jianzhong, Huang Ping, and Wang Xiaoyi for their friendship and assistance along the way.

My institutional home, the Department of Political Science at Johns Hopkins University, generously allowed me to spread the NSF grant over five years, which meant that I was able to conduct the fieldwork, analyze the data, have two babies, and write this book, while students and colleagues dealt with my staggered absences from campus.

Sage Publications permitted me to use some of the material that originally appeared in my article, "Capitalists without a Class: Political Diversity among Private Entrepreneurs in China," *Comparative Political Studies* 39 (November 2005): 1130–1158.

I am also grateful for access to data from the East Asia Barometer Project (2000–2004), which was co-directed by Professors Fu Hu and Yun-han Chu and received major funding support from Taiwan's Ministry of Education, Academia Sinica, and National Taiwan University.

For superb research assistance, I thank Mary Akchurin, Shirley Chen, Daniel Slater, and Jack Yeung. Li Jianjun, Wang Juan, and Zeng Jin helped to clarify many queries in a timely manner. Graduate students in my seminar on comparative democratization—Renny Babiarz, Michael Becher, Kersten Hoenig, Michael McCarthy, Mariam Mufti, and Jeff Pugh—also deserve credit for critically reading key portions of the manuscript, and Mariam Mufti assisted diligently with indexing.

In the course of shaping and completing this book, I have benefited greatly from sound advice, thoughtful comments, tough questions, and fruitful exchanges with Howard Aldrich, Joel Andreas, Giovanni Arrighi, Richard Baum, Eva Bellin, Thomas Berger, Thomas Bernstein, Kathy Chen, Chen Yongjun, Erin Chung, William Connolly, Sarah Cook, Richard Doner, Mary Gallagher, Merle Goldman, Stephan Haggard, Lingxin Hao, Jonathan Hartlyn, He Daming, Yasheng Huang, Richard Katz, Margaret Keck, Scott Kennedy, Melvin Kohn, Cheng Li, Davin Mackenzie, Gerald McDermott, Tobie Meyer-Fong, Ethan Michelson, Kin Moy, Andrew Nathan, Jean Oi, William Parish, Albert Park, Margaret Pearson, Minxin Pei, Elizabeth Perry, Benjamin Read, Elizabeth Remick, William Rowe, Ben Ross Schneider, Adam Sheingate, Tianjian Shi, Matthew Shum, Beverly Silver, Aseema Sinha, Daniel Slater, Sidney Tarrow, Lily Tsai, Andrew Walder, Andrew Watson, Martin Whyte, Ezra Vogel, Dali Yang, Madeleine Zelin, and Elke Zuern.

I also enjoyed input from audiences at annual meetings of the American Political Science Association and the Association for Asian Studies, as well as seminars or conferences held at the following institutions (in several cases, more than once): Columbia University, Cornell University, Georgetown University, Harvard University, Indiana University–Bloomington, the International Food Policy Research Institute, Jiang Han University, Johns Hopkins University, Luce Foundation, Stanford University, University of Chicago, University of Havana,

University of North Carolina–Chapel Hill, University of Michigan–Ann Arbor, and University of Pennsylvania.

I owe an intellectual debt and special thanks to the three readers who offered constructive feedback on the entire manuscript—Bruce Dickson, Kevin O'Brien, and Dorothy Solinger; indeed, their scholarship influenced my own thinking on the topic before I even started this project. Mark Blyth and Davis Bookhart read multiple versions of certain sections with characteristic care and without complaint. At Cornell University Press, Candace Akins expertly guided the book through production, and Roger Haydon deserves a medal for his editorial magic, ongoing attention, and friendship.

None of the people mentioned above bears any responsibility for remaining errors, unsubstantiated claims, or other embarrassing shortcomings in the final product.

Above all, I acknowledge the unreciprocated generosity of all the entrepreneurs and other interviewees, who should remain anonymous and who are identified by pseudonyms in the text. I wouldn't have much to write about without them. At the same time, most of the interviews are not even mentioned in this book—like a photographer who shoots countless rolls of film to capture a particular image, I have presented only a sliver of the material gathered from very busy people in the course of my conducting a national survey and extensive fieldwork.

Finally, I am fortunate to have a family that offers absolute confidence and support in me and my research. My parents, especially my mother Katherine, my sister, Linda, my in-laws Betty and Sam, and my husband, Davis, have all helped out in a multitude of thankless but very much needed ways—*thank you*. The contribution of my two young sons was more oblique: their impending births, at the beginning and the end of the writing process, respectively, helped to keep things on schedule. I dedicate this book to them with love. Without them, I might still be rewriting the introduction or wandering around dusty markets in China, transcribing the details of other people's lives rather than living my own.

KELLEE S. TSAI

Baltimore, Maryland

Abbreviations

ABS	Asian Barometer Survey
ACFIC	All-China Federation of Industry and Commerce
CASS	Chinese Academy of Social Sciences
CBA	China Brilliance Automotive Holdings Limited
CCP	Chinese Communist Party
CEO	Chief executive officer
CPPCC	Chinese People's Political Consultative Committee
FDI	Foreign direct investment
FIC	Federation of Industry and Commerce
FIE	Foreign-invested enterprise
GDP	Gross domestic product
HITIC	Hunan International Trust and Investment Corporation
ICMB	Industrial and Commercial Management Bureau
ILA	Individual Laborers Association
IPO	Initial public offering
LLC	Limited-liability company
NGO	Nongovernmental organization
NPC	National People's Congress
PEA	Private Entrepreneurs Association
PLA	People's Liberation Army
PPS	Probability proportionate to size
PRC	People's Republic of China
PSU	Primary sampling unit
RCC	Rural credit cooperative
SAIC	State Administration for Industry and Commerce

SEZ	Special Economic Zone
SHC	Shareholding cooperative
SHE	Shareholding enterprise
SME	Small and medium enterprise
SOE	State-owned enterprise
SSU	Secondary sampling unit
TVE	Township and village enterprise
UCB	Urban commercial bank
UCC	Urban credit cooperative
UFIC	United Front for Industry and Commerce

Note on Conversion of Key Measures and Romanization

The conversion of key measures is as follows:

1 *mu* of land = 0.0667 hectare or 1/6 acre
1 *jin* = 0.5 kilograms or 1.123 pounds
1 *wan* = ten thousand
1 *yi* = 100 million

$1.00 = 8.28 renminbi (RMB) or yuan during the 1998 to 2004 period

Selected historical exchange rates are as follows:

Year	Rate	Year	Rate
1975	1.86	1987	3.72
1976	1.94	1988	3.77
1977	1.86	1990	4.78
1978	1.68	1991	5.32
1979	1.56	1992	5.52
1980	1.50	1993	5.76
1981	1.71	1994	8.62
1982	1.89	1995	8.35
1983	1.98	1996	8.31
1984	2.33	1997	8.29
1985	2.94	2005	8.19
1986	3.45		

Sources: Rates for 1975 to 1980 are from *China Financial Statistics 1952–1991*; rates for 1981 to 1984 are from the *China Financial Yearbook 1986*; and rates for 1985 to 2005 come from the *China Statistical Yearbook 2006*.

Note on Romanization

The pinyin system of romanization is used throughout the text, except in cases where the Wade-Giles term is more familiar.

CAPITALISM WITHOUT DEMOCRACY

Areas in which author conducted research:
Beijing, Hebei, Shandong, Jiangsu, Zhejiang, Fujian,
Guangdong, Hubei, Jiangxi, Henan, Shaanxi, and Chongqing.

Map of China

1

The Myth of China's Democratic Capitalists

> The biggest problems in China are corruption and absence of the
> rule of law. But democracy wouldn't solve these problems because the
> Chinese masses are too ignorant to participate in politics.
>
> Private entrepreneur in Shanghai, 2005

The Myth

In the summer of 1989, when college students were squatting in Tiananmen Square, demanding democracy, Beijing's street vendors donated food and water to the students. Private copy shops operated their fax machines around the clock to spread the word. A brigade of private entrepreneurs on motorcycles dubbed the "Flying Tigers" spontaneously formed to deliver messages and patrol the perimeters of Beijing for signs of troop movement toward the square (Li et al. 1989, 189–193).[1] The privately owned Stone Corporation provided computer equipment and cash donations to the students. To domestic and international audiences, these accounts were quite moving. The idea that China's new capitalists were altruistic and supportive of the spontaneous student-led democracy movement, the idea that China's bourgeoisie were also becoming democrats like their historical counterparts in Europe and North America, was encouraging.[2]

Even a decade after the Tiananmen crisis, Jonathan Adelman boldly asserted, "It is hard for the great majority of Americans who have not visited China or followed it closely to realize that China is in the middle of a historic transition to capitalism and ultimately democracy" (Adelman 2001, 41A).[3]

---

1. Cited in Gong and Walder 1993, 11, n. 36.
2. On other myths associated with 1989, see Esherick and Wasserstrom 1994.
3. Those who expect democratization in China usually mean a liberal democracy, including competitive and fair elections, and protection of civil and political liberties by rule of law.

The global business community soon added its euphoric prognostications that encouraging private sector development would ensure a democratic transition in China. The American Society for Competitiveness instructed its corporate readers that "global entrepreneurs must continue to invest in corporate infrastructure to help insure stability, success and the inevitable attainment of full democracy there" (*Global Competitiveness*, January 2002, S183). A number of political scientists have gone as far as pronouncing that democratization is inevitable in China and will be brought about by its growing economy. Larry Diamond (1999) asserted that "sooner or later, economic development will generate growing pressures (and possibilities) for China to make a definitive regime change to democracy."[4] Hu Shaohua elaborates on this general logic in *Explaining Chinese Democratization* (2000):

> China is one of the fastest-growing economies in the world, and its economy probably will continue to expand in the foreseeable future. The growing economy will bring higher living standards, a higher level of education, and a more complicated socioeconomic structure in its wake. Under these circumstances, more people will demand more freedom and democracy. (155)[5]

Other scholars have devoted their energies to identifying the economic benchmarks for regime transition. Stanford economist Henry Rowen predicted that if China maintained a 5 percent per capita growth in gross domestic product, then by 2015 it will reach a critical threshold of $7,000–8,000 per capita GDP and become democratic (Rowen 1996, 61, 68–69).[6] Xia Li Lollar (1997) not only finds evidence for "a positive correlation between a market economy and democracy" (4) but contends that

---

See Zhao 2000 and the special issue, "Will China Democratize?" *Journal of Democracy* 9, 1 (January 1998). Examples abound around the world, however, of so-called illiberal democracies, electoral/procedural democracies, and hybrid regimes that lie somewhere between the ideal types of authoritarianism and liberal democracy. See Collier and Levitsky 1997, Diamond 2002, and Zakaria 1997.

4. In a 2004 talk at Hong Kong's Asia Society, Diamond further honed this prediction: "I'm 53 years old and I will make you a bet that before I die, China will be a democracy." "Analysis: Is China Inching toward Democracy?" United Press International, September 18, 2004.

5. In addition to applying the logic of modernization theory, Hu (2000) also offers a functionalist explanation: "Sooner or later, China will adopt a democratic system, because democracy is the most feasible system in modern society" (156). Other China scholars have advanced variations on this general prediction. For example, over a decade ago, Ronald Glassman (1991) announced, "[China's] new middle classes have become the ardent 'carrying class' of modern democracy" (8). Gordon White (1994) similarly referred to the economic foundations for a "new form of 'civil society,'" which "provides the basis for political democratization in China" (81). And Bruce Gilley (2004) speaks of "the inevitability of such a transition" (251).

6. A critique is Zweig 1999. Also, note that Thomas Rawski (2000) disputes the assumption of ongoing growth.

China has already commenced a dual-step transition to democracy such that "China has gone through its first stage of transition from totalitarianism to authoritarianism and is on the verge of starting the longer-term, second transition toward democracy" (83–84). Using a resource distribution index, Tatu Vanhanen (2003) finds that China has already reached the "transition level" for democracy.

Such predictions are inspired in part by the stunning expansion of China's private sector since the late 1970s. In 1977, China did not even keep official statistics on private enterprises because they were illegal and negligible in number. By 2005, there were 29.3 million private businesses, employing over 200 million people and accounting for 49.7 percent of the GDP (*China Daily*, December 14, 2005).[7] Yet private property rights are not protected consistently by rule of law, private entrepreneurs lack access to most conventional sources of credit, and business owners are denied the opportunity to vote for political leaders who will defend their material interests. Hence, based on the evolution of democracy in a handful of Western countries, many observers expect that China's growing population of capitalists will naturally agitate for democracy in the spirit of "no taxation without representation." They will strategically leverage their economic resources to acquire political ones. As Zheng Yongnian puts it, "Chinese business classes are likely to play a role that their European counterparts did in the past. Capitalism is generating a Chinese bourgeoisie. It is a class with teeth" (Zheng 2004, 311).

The Reality behind the Myth

The 1989 images of private business owners helping democracy activists are outdated and misleading.[8] Today most private entrepreneurs are not donating resources toward building a democratic People's Republic of China (PRC) in their spare time. Instead, most are working eighteen-hour days and struggling to stay in business. Others are saving their profits to educate their one child, pay for medicine, buy a house, or retire. Some are planning to leave the country. Quite a few entertain local officials as necessary business expenses, and many are members of the Chinese Communist Party (CCP). Remarkably, most entrepreneurs think that the system generally works for them. One told me in 1996, "Even though I spend about 70 percent of my

7. A 2006 report issued by the Chinese Academy of Social Sciences estimated that in five years the nonstate sector would account for three quarters of China's GDP and that 70 percent of the country's firms would be privately owned (*China Daily*, September 22, 2006).

8. Moreover, most business owners were not supportive of the 1989 student demonstrations because they disrupted the business environment. See Guo 2003, 152–154; He 1996, 184; Wank 1995, 67–69.

profits on fees and bribes, running this restaurant still gives me a better life than what I had as a state factory worker."[9] This entrepreneur's loyalty to the regime was especially apparent when he voluntarily expressed strong approval for the way that the central government dealt with student protestors in 1989. He believed that the crackdown "maintained the social stability necessary for continued economic growth."

Rather than assuming that Chinese entrepreneurs are going to demand democratic reforms, I suggest that it is more instructive to assess whether members of the current generation of capitalists share a common identity and definition of interests—which would be necessary for constituting a politically assertive class or even part of a class (Thompson 1966; cf. Katznelson 1986). China's business owners are diverse. Most do not fall into the income and lifestyle strata that we regard as constituting the "middle class."[10] Because of their diversity, entrepreneurs deal with the government in different ways and have different political views—if they have any. And to the extent that China's capitalists are politically assertive, they are not inclusive in their demands. Existing studies and my own research demonstrate that class formation, to the extent that it results in a common identity, has not occurred among private entrepreneurs and is unlikely to in the near future.[11] This is not to say that private sector development is politically irrelevant or that China will never develop some form of democracy but, rather, that the sequence of events leading to capitalist demands for democracy in a handful of other countries is distinctive and unlikely to be replicated. China's private entrepreneurs should be analyzed on their own terms to understand how and to what extent they are politically consequential. Based on hundreds of in-depth interviews and an original national survey of business owners, in this book I demonstrate that China's capitalists are pragmatic and creative but they are not budding democrats.

9. Field notes, Kaifeng, Henan Province, July 23, 1996.

10. The very definition of the middle class varies according to different economic, political, social, and cultural contexts, and even within a particular country, one cannot assume that members of a middle income group or an emerging strata of "new rich" will share similar political views or engage in similar types of activities. For example, Hagen Koo (1991) has observed that South Korea's middle classes may be divided into four distinct categories—of which the petty bourgeoisie are only one; furthermore, during the country's democratic transition, each subgroup had different preferences about the type of democracy that should be implemented. The other three categories identified include managerial and professional workers, lower-grade white-collar workers, and intellectuals, respectively. Cf. Goodman and Robison 1996; Howe 1992; Walkowitz 1999. Moreover, various Marxist-influenced scholars generally agree that by virtue of its structural position, middle-class politics is variable, inconsistent, and, ultimately, indeterminate (Koo 1991, 492–493): Abercrombie and Urry 1983; Mills 1951; Poulantzas 1975; Wright 1985.

11. China scholars who have focused on particular subsets of private entrepreneurs have reached similar conclusions about the absence of class-based yearnings for democracy. See Dickson 2003; Hong 2004; and Pearson 2002.

Why, then, do general observers continue to have high democratic expectations of China's toiling entrepreneurs? Whether voluntarist or structuralist in orientation, few scholars propound a simple linear model of political development based on an overgeneralization of Barrington Moore's famous quotation "no bourgeois, no democracy" (Moore 1966, 418).[12] Yet a number of vocal observers remain influenced by a handful of classic works in political science that can be summarized by Joseph Schumpeter's declaration that "modern democracy is a product of the capitalist process" (Schumpeter 1976 [1942], 296–297).[13] Post–cold war notions of convergence toward capitalist democracy as a global norm have also revived the logic of modernization theory, which associates economic prosperity with political liberalization (Fukuyama 1992; Lipset 1959; Pye 1990). As Bruce Gilley asserts in *China's Democratic Future* (2004), "The laws of social science grind away in China as they do elsewhere, whether people like it or not" (xiii). But in reality, the path to democratization is not nearly so simple.[14] The belief that capitalists must demand democracy is a myth, not a law of social science. Historically, the processes that lead to democratization are highly contingent and involve a multiplicity of actors and institutions. China is no different in this regard, so debunking this popular myth is not difficult. In this book I do not predict whether China will someday become a liberal democracy. I do, however, assert with a high level of certainty that should democratization occur in China, it will not be led by a disgruntled horde of private entrepreneurs.

Private entrepreneurs may not be clamoring for democracy, but they are influencing Chinese politics. In the course of their day-to-day interactions—with one another and with local officials—entrepreneurs are changing the country's formal political institutions in ways that reflect their needs and interests. Although liberal democracies permit many direct forms of political expression, what China's entrepreneurs are doing is more subtle and possibly more effective in conveying their policy concerns than voting, lobbying, and protesting. In this book I thus engage the more complex issues of what it really means to be a private entrepreneur in China, how entrepreneurs actually perceive themselves, and, most fundamentally, how they get things done. We will see that business owners must navigate a myriad of political

12. Indeed, Moore's oft-cited "no bourgeois, no democracy" was not intended to apply to countries other than those he analyzed.

13. Charles Lindblom elaborated on "this great historic fact": "The association between liberal constitutional polyarchy and market is clearly no historical accident. Polyarchies were established to win and protect certain liberties: private property, free enterprise, free contract, and occupational choice" (Lindblom 1977, 162, 164).

14. Political scientists writing about the "third wave" of democratization in the late 1970s and early 1980s identified multiple paths for authoritarian breakdown and democratic consolidation. See Collier 1999; Diamond 1999; Diamond and Plattner, eds. 1996; Huntington 1991; O'Donnell, Schmitter, and Whitehead 1986; Rueschemeyer, Stephens, and Stephens 1992.

and regulatory restrictions—and in doing so, how they have fundamentally altered the formal political landscape. We will also see that the private sector's political influence has unfolded in an indirect and incremental manner. In examining these issues, I explain why China's private entrepreneurs are not out on the streets demanding democracy and why significant institutional transformations have occurred in China's political economy in the absence of regime change. The answers to these apparent paradoxes are grounded in the daily practices of business owners and their official regulators. Local economic and state actors have evaded, exploited, and appropriated formal institutions through a variety of informal adaptive strategies. Ultimately, the adaptive informal institutions of private entrepreneurs have had a structural impact on the formal institutions governing China's political economy.

The Broader Implications of China's Experience

These claims have broader implications for theoretical debates concerning political and institutional development as well as implications for the study of democracy. China does not fit preexisting models of political economy, and indeed it defies the expectations of many familiar explanations in the study of comparative politics. Analyzing the process of private sector development in reform-era China does, however, yield insights into the dynamics of endogenous institutional change. Despite ongoing regime durability, a number of the country's political, economic, and even social institutions have undergone momentous transformations since the late 1970s. Rather than confirming prevailing theories of political development, the causal mechanism underlying many of these transformations lies in the informal interactions among local state and nonstate actors. Conventional explanations of democratic development and regime change generally overlook the causal potential of informal practices and institutions to change or sustain formal institutions.[15] Meanwhile, studies of transitions from socialism have been more attentive to the relevance of informal institutions and socialist-era legacies, but they have focused more on how deep-rooted informal institutions undermine formal ones rather than how they may contribute to the resilience of formal institutions.

The best-known comparative historical theories of democratic development predict capitalist class formation and democratic mobilization on the basis of structural transformations in the economy and society.[16] Instead of

---

15. Key exceptions include Helmke and Levitsky, eds. 2006; Lauth 2000; and O'Donnell 1996.

16. Bellin 2002; Koo 2001; Moore 1966; Rueschemeyer, Stephens, and Stephens 1992.

focusing on classes and social structure, voluntarist approaches to regime transition expect that disgruntled business elites will join forces with other elites to promote fundamental political changes.[17] Yet thus far evidence for both the structural and the voluntarist explanations of democratization and regime change is absent in China. In the macrolevel sweep of traditional structural approaches, social groups or classes are defined in overly broad terms, which obscures the possibility that various members of those groups may have widely varying identities and interests—and, of particular interest to this study, varying formal and informal resources for interacting with state agents. Even in areas as geographically small as Hong Kong and Taiwan, private capital is segmented along socioeconomic, territorial, and ethnic lines (e.g., Wu 2005). By the same token, China's business owners have different backgrounds and different ways of dealing with their concerns, including the strategic decision to maintain a low profile. Because of this, coherent class formation and collective action have not occurred.[18] Meanwhile, voluntarist explanations overemphasize bargaining among elites and the role of formal associations. In China the wealthiest businesspeople generally have little trouble gaining access to local officials, some of whom are unofficially on their payrolls. And most business associations are either organized or co-opted by the state in a noncontentious manner (Chan and Unger 1995; Dickson 2003; Kennedy 2005; Nevitt 1996; Unger 1996).

The socialist transition literature points out that historical legacies and informal institutions continue to shape political and economic dynamics even after the collapse of Communism and deliberative democratic institutional design on the part of elites. As a result, studies concerning the rapid economic and political transitions of former socialist countries have reached indeterminate conclusions about the post-transition sustainability of liberal democracy, as well as their economic performance under newly installed market institutions.[19] In contrast to the post-Communist countries of the former Soviet Union and East Europe, China has experienced piecemeal, gradualist economic transition over the last two decades, while political reforms have been even more limited. Most of the existing comparative literature therefore focuses on explaining either the institutional endurance of the Chinese Communist Party (Solnick 1996; Walder 1994) or the reasons for China's impressive economic growth (McMillan and Naughton 1992; Woo 1999). Unfortunately, these efforts do not explain the coexistence of political continuity and rapid industrialization in China.

17. Colomer 2000; di Palma 1990; Diamond 1999; Hagopian 1990; Kirchheimer 1969; O'Donnell et al. 1986; Przeworski 1991; Rustow 1970.

18. Of course, not every member of an aggregate "class" needs to be in agreement for class to have political implications. But when classes are disaggregated to a more detailed level of analysis (e.g., occupation) the impact of class is more apparent. See Grusky and Wedeen 2001.

19. See Bunce 2000, 2003; Frye 2002; King 2000; McFaul 2002; Przeworski 1991, 1995.

The "developmental state" model has attracted much attention in Beijing due to its ability to explain the rapid postwar economic growth of China's East Asian neighbors under conditions of political stability.[20] In Japan, South Korea, Taiwan, Hong Kong, and Singapore, the state played a leading role in promoting export-oriented industrialization, while ensuring the political quiescence of its citizens. But efforts to extend the developmental state model to China have not been convincing, largely because they tend to ascribe developmental state qualities to a party-state that has not been nearly as coherent, bureaucratically disciplined, or supportive of the private sector as the original developmental state model requires (Tsai and Cook 2005).[21]

Despite these deviations from existing political and economic models, it is important to recognize that major institutional changes relating to the private sector have occurred since the late 1970s. State-owned enterprises are undergoing privatization, the financial sector is undergoing commercializing reforms, and, perhaps most significantly, the Chinese Communist Party has done something that would have been unthinkable just a few decades ago—broadened its membership base to include private entrepreneurs. Neither political elites nor private entrepreneurs are bursting with liberal democratic sentiments, but the latter are now encouraged to join the CCP as well as corporatist-style consultative and associational bodies. By the same token, even though the PRC does not possess many of the attributes of a developmental state, the policy environment for private capital accumulation has improved significantly over time. As the founder and chief executive officer of a leading telecommunications software company put it in 2005, "Ten years ago the status of the private sector was still vague and uncertain, but now private businesses enjoy many favorable policies. Today if you are educated and have technical skills, you can not only be successful but extraordinarily successful [like me]" (Interview 301). How can these changes be explained?

Most theories of institutional change rely either on the presence of external shocks or on highly motivated political leaders to explain the causal mechanism underlying major institutional reforms and institutional design.[22] As of this writing, China has weathered serious exogenous shocks on

20. On the developmental state, see Amsden 1992; Johnson 1982; Wade 1990; Woo-Cummings 1999.

21. While some scholars have ascribed developmental qualities to the local state (Blecher and Shue 2001; Oi 1992; Remick 2004), others have highlighted the "entrepreneurial" business activities of China's local governments and agencies (Blecher 1991; Duckett 1998; Lin 1995). Meanwhile, other studies emphasize the local state's predatory qualities (e.g., Bernstein and Lü 2003; Gao 1999; Peng 1996). For typologies of China's local state, see Baum and Shevchenko 1999; Tsai 2003.

22. For example, Krasner 1984; Levi 1990; Tsebelis 1990. On ideational explanations, see Blyth 2002.

most sides of its borders, including the fall of European communism in 1989–91 and the Asian financial crisis in 1997–98. In the interim, Beijing has promulgated a number of significant economic and political reforms, including a fundamental ideological reorientation of the most powerful political institution in China, the CCP. Taken together, these reforms could be interpreted as indicating elite-level responsiveness to mitigate potentially catastrophic exogenous shocks.

I argue, however, that most of China's formal institutional reforms have been in reaction to endogenous pressures—that is, to dynamics in the private sector that were already occurring on the ground level *within China.* This does not dispute the relevance and symbolic importance of major international events or official national policies. Instead, I am suggesting that the actual causal dynamics leading to elite-level decisions arise from grassroots interactions among entrepreneurs and between entrepreneurs and officials. These exchanges have facilitated business practices that are usually informal, if not explicitly illegal. More important, in the aggregate they have had a structural impact on the political economy. They facilitated private sector development before central state policies sanctioned these practices. In the course of their everyday interactions, China's local officials and business owners devised novel ways for local enterprises to operate, which in turn attracted elite-level attention in sanctioning, post hoc, changes in the country's economic and political institutions. To put it in comparative terms, even in an authoritarian regime with a unitary political system, the process of formal institutional change has been an adaptive and reactive one on the part of state and economic actors, at both the local and national levels.

Some China scholars focus on elite-level dynamics—and, as a result, tend to have a more top-down view of the country's reform process.[23] However, a growing number of studies have documented instances of institutional innovations originating at the local level and then later being sanctioned or adopted by the center. For example, in a manner evocative of James Scott's (1995) notion of "weapons of the weak," Daniel Kelliher (1993), Andrew Watson (1983), Dali Yang (1996), and Kate Xiao Zhou (1996) have argued that farmers spontaneously reverted to household farming well before the state permitted decollectivization.[24] Barry Naughton (1994), Jean Oi (1999), Kristin Parris (1993), Jonathan Unger (2002), and others have studied how collective enterprises that were supposed to be run by township and village governments effectively served as an organizational disguise for private enterprises with more than eight employees before they were legally

---

23. See Fewsmith 2001; Huang 2005; C. Li 2001; Shirk 1993; Unger 2002.
24. Key critics of this interpretation of peasant power from below include Bianco 2001; Unger 2002; and Zweig 1997.

permitted. And Lynn White (1998) offers numerous examples from Shanghai of local economic and political practices that preceded their formal approval by higher levels of government.

In chapters 3 and 6 I present additional cases of similar dynamics within the private sector from the perspective of local officials and business owners. Although private entrepreneurs do not vote for leaders in Beijing, the latter have nonetheless proven to be quite receptive to formalizing many of the informal practices that entrepreneurs have relied on to run their businesses and local officials have tolerated to develop their economies. As will be seen, when these informal coping strategies become routinized as adaptive informal institutions, they transcend Scottian forms of passive resistance. For example, the systematic violation of national licensing and financing regulations in the form of fake foreign-invested enterprises and disguised private banks, respectively, involves local economic and political elites, not just hapless peddlers and peasants. Adaptive informal institutions are not merely weapons of the "weak."

At the same time, adaptive informal institutions do not always lead to officially sanctioned changes in formal institutions. The scholarship on reform-era China offers manifold instances of local innovation that have not resulted in formal institutional reform but have involved the appropriation of formal institutions to serve the particular interests of various state and nonstate actors. X. L. Ding (1994) refers to this phenomenon as "institutional amphibiousness," because formal institutions are used in ways they were not intended.[25] In one case, he examines the Institute of Marxism and Leninism in Beijing: over the course of the 1980s the state-supported institute unexpectedly evolved into a center for nonconformist, counter-elite liberal intellectuals—or, as the senior CCP ideology boss Deng Liqun put it, "the anti-Marxism base camp" (Ding 1994, 305). Although such distortion of the formal mandate of state institutions could be interpreted as indicating weakness in state capacity, it is overly simplistic to reduce this dynamic to a zero-sum conflict between state and society. The type of "institutional manipulation and conversion" that Ding and others have observed typically requires the complicity of state actors within those very institutions.[26] Moreover, in a cognate process that Kevin O'Brien (1994) refers to as a strategy of "entwinement," new social interests may actually "seek proximity to existing centers of power (i.e., entwinement) rather than distance . . . [because] they realize that independence at this point means irrelevance and that

25. The concept of "institutional conversion" (Thelen 2002; cf. Selznick 1949) is discussed in chapter 2.

26. Note that the notion of institutional amphibiousness contrasts from what Xiaobo Lü (2000) calls "organizational corruption" and Andrew Wedeman (1997) calls "institutional corruption." The latter two terms refer to when state agencies exploit their authority to generate extra income or material gains.

future development demands sensitivity to existing power relations" (101).[27] Andrew Nathan aptly describes this dynamic as the "mutual infiltration" between the party-state and society, whereby conventional state-society boundaries become blurred (Nathan 1990, 5–6).[28] Indeed, the durability of adaptive informal institutions—ranging from institutional conversion of official organizations to the cultivation of legitimate appearances by potentially subversive societal actors—depends on the effective obfuscation of formal rules, regulations, and definitions by the local enforcers (and even leaders) of formal institutions.

Taken together, the findings that official reform policies have lagged behind local practices and that formal institutions often do not operate as expected provide valuable insight into China's reform-era dynamics. In particular, they help to dispel the notion that private sector development has mainly been a top-town process led by enlightened reformers in Beijing (e.g., Yang 2004). They also show how grassroots actors may appropriate formal institutions to promote their own interests even in a nondemocratic setting. The secondary issue of when and whether adaptive informal institutions will eventually have a transformative impact on formal institutions is fundamentally political and requires in-depth empirical research.

Private Entrepreneurs in China

This book offers the following observations about the current generation of China's private entrepreneurs.[29] First, business owners generally rely on informal, nondemocratic means to pursue their economic interests. They have had to do so from the outset of the reform era when the official status of the private sector was still extremely politically controversial. The Chinese government did not permit the existence of private businesses with

27. This example is based on O'Brien's (1994) study of Chinese people's congresses. Individuals who have sought to promote legislative development in China have pursued "legislative embeddedness, as measured by clarified and expanded jurisdiction and increased capacity" (86) because "an embedding legislature often benefits from association with strong individuals who bring it prestige when it has little prestige to confer" (100).

28. Nathan 1990 cited in Ding 1994, 314.

29. In this book the term "private entrepreneur" refers to an individual who undertakes the risk of engaging in private business, which can range from self-employment to larger ventures. This definition does not assume the success of entrepreneurs. Note also that the definition excludes proprietors of foreign-owned firms, managers in state-owned enterprises, and cadres who use governmental units for income-generating purposes, even though these types of individuals may act in an "entrepreneurial" manner. Throughout the text "private entrepreneurs" will be used interchangeably with "entrepreneurs" and "business owners." However, the terms "individual entrepreneur," "individual household," "individual businesses," and *getihu* are reserved for businesses with fewer than eight employees, in contrast to "private enterprises" or *siying qiye*, which are businesses that are permitted to have more than eight employees.

more than eight employees until 1988, a decade after the commencement of reform. To date, entrepreneurs face a wide range of other operational and financing restrictions. They have worked around these legal barriers through innovative arrangements, often in discrete collaboration with local officials.

Second, most business owners do not act as if they were part of a unified class. Due to the relative youth of the private sector, the current cohort of entrepreneurs identifies more with their previous form of employment and class background than the fact that they are running businesses on their own. The observation that conflicts often break out among private entrepreneurs themselves further attests to the tenuous nature of their sector-specific ties. As a former sheepherder who is now an antiquities vendor from Tibet explained, "After my business partner stole from me, I thought that the commercial environment at home was too uncivilized, so I traveled alone by train for four days to get to this market [in Beijing], only to find that businesspeople here are even more competitive and difficult to endure" (Interview 284). Looking out across the vast market of petty traders, the former shepherd added, "I have nothing in common with them."

Third, China's entrepreneurs do not share similar political concerns. Their self-defined interests vary according to the nature of their social and political networks, industrial sector, income level, and geographic location. Indeed, to the extent that entrepreneurs are attuned to political issues, their attitudes and opinions vary substantially even within a particular locality. On a day-to-day basis entrepreneurs are more concerned with issues that do not seem to have overt political solutions (e.g., difficulties with increasing sales volume and hiring reliable workers).

Fourth, for a variety of reasons, the upper tier of capitalists that possesses the most economic clout is not active in forming autonomous organizations that could become the basis for an oppositional force or political party. Some of the wealthiest entrepreneurs have been politically incorporated by the party-state. Others have been prosecuted on charges of "economic crimes," meaning corruption. A number have diversified their assets and moved abroad. And the media outside of China occasionally reports on exceptional cases of politically subversive entrepreneurs who have been arrested.[30]

The "private sector" includes all businesses that are managed and de facto owned by Chinese citizens within China. This includes individual entrepreneurs (*getihu*), as well as private enterprises (*siying qiye*) registered under various organizational forms, including sole proprietorships (*duzi*), partnerships (*hehuo*), limited liability companies (*youxian zeren gongsi*), and shareholding corporations (*gufen youxian gongsi*) in which private individuals hold dominant ownership stakes. This book also discusses businesses that are falsely registered as other types of firms (e.g., collective or foreign-invested ones), but are in fact privately invested and managed.

30. For example, Edward A. Gargan, "Detoured on His Road to Democracy: Chinese Businessman Jailed after Speaking Out," *Newsday*, August 10, 2003.

Covered farmers' market in Hechuan, Chongqing Municipality

Fifth, even though most private entrepreneurs have not engaged in collective action to defend their interests, the operating conditions for private businesses have improved significantly. In the last few decades, dramatic reforms in the PRC's formal institutions—namely, official national ideology, the Chinese Communist Party, and the PRC Constitution—have enhanced the private sector's political legitimacy and economic security. The key point is that these institutional changes occurred in the absence of political mobilization on the part of business owners.

None of these conditions adds up to a unified prodemocratic capitalist class that holds the potential to effect liberal regime change. Hence, my analytic tasks are to explain why private entrepreneurs are not mobilizing to demand democracy and what the case of capitalism without democracy in China can tell us about the dynamics of endogenous institutional change.

The Research and the Logic

On looking more deeply into the above observations, we can see the processes of institutional manipulation and change in China through examining the informal interactions between local state agents and business owners that structure private sector transactions. Because these informal interactions and agreements contribute to defining institutional reality, they have the potential to transform formal, state-level institutions. This causal potential of informal interactions explains why China's capitalists have not mobilized to demand democracy. Formal institutions can be remarkably flexible and accommodating when elites are concerned about their survival.

To establish the causal and constitutive links between everyday practices and macrolevel phenomena, I use a combination of quantitative and qualitative research methodologies. The quantitative data presented in chapters 4 through 6 are drawn from national surveys based on multistage area probability sampling, including one that I designed and conducted in 2002–03. The surveys establish that the overarching empirical conclusions are not idiosyncratic or unrepresentative. The bulk of this book, however, relies on the over three hundred interviews that I conducted with Chinese entrepreneurs, officials, intellectuals, financiers, and local bureaucrats in twelve provinces. Most of the cases cite interviews that took place over the course of 2001 to 2005, but a few come from unpublished field notes dating back to 1996. (More details about the research methodology and a numbered list of the interviews are presented in appendix A and B, respectively.)

In analyzing the theoretical implications of these statistical and case-oriented findings, I start from the premise that institutional existence and change is fundamentally relational. In other words, institutions derive their causal relevance through reflexive human interactions—or absence thereof. The methodological value of this relational approach is that examining the contextual logic underlying human interactions yields insight into causal processes that would not otherwise be apparent.[31] Intrinsic to this approach is the expectation that even though actors behave in a consequentialist manner, their actions may yield unintended outcomes. In brief, examining the microfoundations of China's institutional flexibility shows why private entrepreneurs have not organized themselves to demand representation in formal political institutions, much less demanded a transition to democracy. Informal interactions and adaptive strategies at the local level have contributed to the elasticity and durability of China's formal institutions at the national level.

Going Forward

Why does China remain authoritarian despite the expectations of classic theories of democratic development? How can regime durability be explained

31. This relational approach resonates with that of Jessop (2001) and Tilly (1998).

in light of significant political and institutional changes since the late 1970s? Although China has not experienced a democratic transition, substantial transformations in the country's political economy present an opportunity to examine the dynamics of endogenous institutional change. We shall see that the etiology of formal institutional change lies in the informal coping strategies devised by local actors to evade the restrictions of formal institutions. With repetition and diffusion, these informal coping strategies may take on an institutional reality of their own. I call the resulting arrangements "adaptive informal institutions" because they represent creative responses to formal institutions that local actors find too constraining. In contrast to the full universe of "informal institutions," which includes deep-rooted cultural practices, this study is only interested in adaptive practices that arise in reaction to the limits and possibilities of formal institutions. To complete the argument, I propose that over time, the overt popularity of adaptive informal institutions may motivate political elites to change the original formal institutions.

China's changing policy environment governing the private sector illustrates the causal impact of adaptive informal institutions. The party-state has moved from criticizing private business owners to welcoming them into the Communist Party and other formal political institutions. How did this occur? Despite their relatively low political profile, private entrepreneurs are far from being passive. They have exercised agency by engaging in income-generating activities long before it was legal to do so. In their own voices, entrepreneurs recall the challenges that they faced during the early years—and how things have changed since then. Here is one of the more colorful responses to the question of why larger scale entrepreneurs diversify and disguise their assets: "There's a saying that people are afraid of getting famous, just as pigs are afraid of getting fat . . . and slaughtered (*ren pa chuming, ju pa fei*). It's bad to get too much personal attention" (Interview 307).

Although business owners share certain challenges, private entrepreneurs in China define their interests in widely varying ways because they have different identities and values. As such, they pursue their interests through equally diverse channels. In addition to presenting statistical findings from national surveys, I have developed a typology of entrepreneurs' coping strategies that classifies the strategies into four categories: avoidant, grudgingly acceptant, loyally acceptant, and assertive. Only those in the latter category hold the potential for making direct demands for democracy, but in-depth interviews with business owners show that assertive entrepreneurs are more interested in defending particularistic material interests than in changing the regime. A minority of capitalists possesses the unusual combination of both substantial resources and discontent with the current regime type, but due to fear of political persecution they are more likely to invest in exit options for their families than to advocate political reform.

Just as the microlevel qualities of private entrepreneurs mediate their political activities, the structure of the local economy influences the extent to which business owners may have grievances, the nature of their grievances, as well as how they express their interests. Contrary to the expectations of modernization theory, capitalists in areas with the most developed private sectors are far less likely to act in a politically assertive way—by, for example, conveying their opinions through formal political institutions, writing letters to governmental and media outlets, and using the judicial system—than entrepreneurs in localities where the economy is less developed or dominated by the state, collective, or foreign-invested sectors. Moreover, where local economies are dominated by private ownership, business owners are less likely to identify with one another than in localities where the private sector has been more marginalized. With the spread of both privatization and private sector development de novo, over time private entrepreneurs may be more likely to be internally divided rather than politically cohesive.

Although this book does not supply a comprehensive explanation for the persistence of authoritarianism in China, it does examine a key piece of the puzzle of why Chinese capitalists are not likely to bring down the regime single-handedly. The superficial reason for the absence of political mobilization by business owners is because the operational and political environment for private commerce has gradually improved over the course of the reform era. And the proximate reason for changes in China's formal political and economic institutions may be traced to elite-level decisions. At a deeper constitutive level, however, the causal processes underlying formal institutional change lie in the often informal interactions between economic and political actors, who generally do not dwell on the broader consequences of their actions or inactions on a day-to-day basis. Instead, most entrepreneurs and state agents are busy selling products, building networks, juggling responsibilities, and, as a result, stretching the limits of various institutions. Their lives and interactions are multidimensional, with mixed motives, and lack the ordering quality of myths.

As for why the myth of democratic capitalists persists, Roland Barthes (1972) provided an elegant possibility:

> In passing from history to nature, myth acts economically: it abolishes the complexity of human acts, it gives them the simplicity of essences, it does away with all dialectics, without any going back beyond what is immediately visible, it organizes a world which is without contradictions because it is without depth, a world wide open and wallowing in the evident, it establishes a blissful clarity: things appear to mean something by themselves (143).

By contrast, in the following pages I seek to demythologize both the process and implications of private sector development in China.

2

Bypassing Democracy: Regime Durability, Informal Institutions, and Political Change

> For many political-economic institutions that persist over long periods, one is very often struck simultaneously by how little *and* how much they have changed.
>
> Kathleen Thelen, *How Institutions Evolve*

The political economy of China's reform experience challenges conventional explanations of political development in two ways. First, contrary to the expectations of modernization theory and other classic theories of regime change, the People's Republic of China remains authoritarian.[1] Despite over two decades of rapid growth and private sector development, China has not undergone a democratic transition, and its capitalists show no evidence of mobilizing to demand democracy. Second, the coexistence of significant institutional changes and regime durability presents an informative case of how major institutional transformations may occur in an endogenous manner. While most studies of authoritarian durability derive from neopatrimonial regimes in the Middle East, discussions of institutional development generally focus on democratic countries in Europe and North America. Analyzing China in light of these frameworks bridges different branches of political science, while yielding additional insights into the dynamics of endogenous institutional change.

---

1. In this book I follow O'Donnell and Schmitter's (1986) definition of regime as "the ensemble of patterns, explicit or not, that determines the forms and channels of access to principal governmental positions, the characteristics of the actors who are admitted and excluded from such access, and the resources or strategies that they can use to gain access" (72 n1).

Two complementary questions thus present themselves: Why do observers expect capitalists to demand democracy in China? And how can we explain the authoritarian regime's ability to endure substantial structural and institutional changes in the country's political economy? The answer to the first question is relatively straightforward: those who have democratic expectations of China's capitalists are guided by classic theories of democratic development, which are inappropriate for explaining democratic transitions in late-industrializing countries. Capitalists have at most played a complementary rather than a leading role in the twentieth-century transitions to democracy. At the same time, although contemporary China lacks both the structural and elite-level conditions necessary for democratic development, major political and economic transformations have in fact occurred. That these changes have taken place without destabilizing the regime raises the issue of how China's formal institutions have managed to adapt and, in some cases, change in light of new economic and social conditions.

Explanations for regime durability tend to emphasize familiar variables such as culture, economic performance, coercive capacity, social structure, and degree of political institutionalization. Although the persistence of authoritarianism in reform-era China has been attributed to these factors, analyses of institutional development by historical institutionalists provide greater insight into the processes through which formal institutions may change in the absence of crises or external shocks.[2] The notion of "reactive sequences," for example, draws attention to the manner in which certain events may produce backlash effects (Mahoney 2000). Institutional "layering" draws attention to the potential for different types of institutions to be in conflict with one another or, alternatively, to coexist in a synthetic or mutually transformative manner (Lieberman 2002; Orren and Skowronek 1994; Schickler 2001). Relatedly, the concept of "conversion" refers to the use of institutions in ways that deviate from their intended purpose (Thelen 2004). In both layering and conversion, formal institutions typically retain their superficial defining characteristics, which may disguise the extent to which they have changed in substance.

Building on these insights, I propose that informal institutions can serve a vital intermediate role in explaining the process of endogenous institutional change. Specifically, the case of private sector development in reform-era China demonstrates that the flexibility of formal institutions stems in part from the often informal interactions between various state and nonstate actors at the local level. Despite the proximate causal role of

2. In the study of political economy, major institutional changes are often traced to periods of internal or external crisis, e.g., Gourevitch 1986; Katzenstein 1985; Keller and Samuels 2003; Krasner 1984.

elite politics and decisions, under certain circumstances the etiology of formal institutional change lies in the informal coping strategies devised by local actors to evade the restrictions of formal institutions. Formal institutions
comprise a myriad of constraints and opportunities, which may motivate
everyday actors to devise novel operating arrangements that are not officially sanctioned. With repetition and diffusion, these informal coping
strategies may take on an institutional reality of their own. I call the resulting arrangements "adaptive informal institutions" because they represent
creative responses to formal institutions that local actors find too constraining. Over time, adaptive informal institutions may become more popular in
practice than the formal institutions that stimulated them in the first place.
Depending on the political climate, pervasive reliance on adaptive informal
institutions may motivate political elites to change the original formal institutions. Several empirical examples in the following chapters illustrate the
iterative logic of this contention, as well as the everyday expression of informal interactions that constitute a relational approach to understanding the
dynamics of institutional development. Although the following argument
derives from the specific empirical experiences of reform-era China, these
general claims about the process of institutional development are meant to
travel beyond the case of China as readers see fit. But first, we will consider
the more conventional explanations of democratic development, authoritarian durability, and institutional change to show how these theories res-
onate with popular narratives about the political economy of reform-era
China.

The Sources of Democratic Expectations

Assessing the democratic potential of private entrepreneurs in China requires reviewing the causal logic that underlies these democratic expectations. The literature on democratic development and regime transition is
roughly bifurcated between structural and voluntarist approaches, which
provides us with an opportunity to identify at least two causal pathways that
connect the rise of the private sector to a democratic transition.[3] First,
from a structural perspective, private entrepreneurs may evolve into a
prodemocratic capitalist class. Second, from a voluntarist perspective,
reform-oriented political elites may join forces with private entrepreneurs
to promote extrication from authoritarian rule. Both scenarios require a

---

3. Many accounts of democratization draw on both structural and individual-level variables, e.g., Bratton and van de Walle 1997; Collier 1999; Haggard and Kaufman 1995; Huntington 1991. Helpful reviews include Hagopian 1993; Kitschelt 1993; Munck 1994; Remmer
1991. The applicability of these third-wave explanations to post-Communist societies is ques-
tionable; see McFaul 2002.

certain degree of discontent and collective organization on the part of business owners. But neither approach predicts democratization in China in a determinate manner.

Class-Centric Path to Democratization

Structural or class-based theories of capitalist development vary in their emphasis on the relative contribution of the working versus middle classes and the types of class alliances that lead to democratic outcomes.[4] But they agree with the traditional Marxist logic that industrialization in a capitalist environment gives rise to new relationships among the means of production. This provides the material basis for a different class structure and under certain conditions leads to class formation and class practices.[5] The most frequently cited explanation for the association of capitalism with democracy implies that over time the capitalist class will seek greater access to the political system to protect its property rights and justify its contribution to state coffers in the spirit of "no taxation without representation." The historical precondition for this scenario is the formation of a coherent capitalist class whose collective actions "cause" democracy. The bourgeois revolutions that Barrington Moore observed in England, the United States, and France best illustrate this causal pathway. In each of these cases, the bourgeoisie, meaning the collectivity made up of private merchants, acted collectively in defense of its material interests (Moore 1966). Although various scholars have proposed more nuanced interpretations of the extent to which the bourgeoisie—or newer segments of the bourgeoisie—has agitated for democracy, most concur that in the late nineteenth-century cases of European democracies, private merchants supported parliamentary government over the crown (Brenner 1993).[6]

Because China has experienced rapid growth rates under increasingly market-oriented conditions since the late 1970s, this structural, social class–based explanation is the typical framework invoked by observers who anticipate democratic development in China. Yet even a cursory consideration of twentieth-century transitions to democracy reveals that capitalists have demonstrated neither consistent opposition to authoritarian regimes nor consistent support for democratic ones. As Eva Bellin (2000) has argued, the political preferences of capitalists in late-industrializing countries appear to be contingent on the group's degree of dependence on the state

4. See Bellin 2002; Koo 2001; Moore 1966; Rueschemeyer, Stephens, and Stephens 1992.

5. On the distinction among class structure, class consciousness, class formation, and class practices, see Wright 2000, 185–215. For different critiques of purely objective or materialist definitions of class, see Katznelson 1986 and Thompson 1995.

6. Cf. Stephens 1989. Germany represents the major counterexample to the association of the bourgeoisie with liberal politics and democracy. See Blackbourn and Eley 1984.

for the protection of their material interests, and the extent to which they fear that mass political empowerment would have destabilizing consequences. That is, capitalists are not likely to support democracy if they are highly dependent on the state and fearful about the disruptive potential of democratization. (Conversely, capitalists are more likely to support democracy if they are less dependent on the state and not fearful of mass empowerment.) The cases of Brazil and South Korea are particularly illustrative in this regard.

Brazil's experience with regime change presents two starkly contrasting observations of the apparent preferences of capitalists for authoritarian versus democratic rule. In 1964, business elites were active among the coalition of conservative forces supporting a military coup that ended Brazil's nineteen years of democratic experimentation. Private sector industrialists also supported the subsequent military governments, for the material interests of large capitalists were well served by the bureaucratic-authoritarian regime during the high-growth phase of 1968 to 1973. The second regime transition—authoritarian breakdown and transition to democracy—evolved over the decade from 1975 to 1985. Although economic conditions deteriorated for industrialists, as a group they did not try to stop the transition process—and a segment of them came to support democratization by the late 1980s. Leigh Payne (1994) suggests that this apparent inconsistency in support for different regime types is attributable to Brazilian capital's concern with political stability to protect the value of its members' investments. In other words, business elites do not have inherent preferences for either authoritarian or democratic forms of governance. Instead, their political support for particular governments hinges on their perception of how well the government can provide for a stable business environment.

As in Brazil, South Korea's capitalists were also politically dormant from the outset of bureaucratic-authoritarian governance after World War II.[7] The historian Carter Eckert has observed:

> From its earliest burst of growth in the 1920s to its recent position of economic preeminence, the bourgeoisie has coexisted more or less comfortably with a variety of authoritarian governments, none of which has ever deliberately sought to hinder capitalist growth, and most of which have positively supported it. As a result the Korean bourgeoisie has never had a compelling material incentive to promote democratic politics. (Eckert 1993, 127)

During the 1960s and 1970s, this was certainly the case, as Korean industrialists were dependent on the state for credit and other resources. The

---

7. The term "bureaucratic-authoritarian" was originally coined to describe the regimes in Brazil and Argentina during the 1960s. See O'Donnell 1973.

hospitable and productive relationship between the state and industry led scholars to portray Korea as an enlightened "developmental state" that was adept in promoting economic growth (Woo 1991; cf. Amsden 1992). Yet as Peter Evans (1995) has noted, the very success of the developmental state created economic and social conditions that undermined its original bureaucratic-authoritarian basis. In particular, the growth of the working class—reminiscent of the European pattern of "proletarianization"—led to heightened labor activism, which contributed to South Korea's democratic transition (Koo 2001). Meanwhile, industrialists became less dependent on the state for capital investment and came to advocate less state intervention in the economy (Saxer 2002; Woo 1991).

Although it would not be accurate to say that Korean capitalists as a class became proponents of democracy, at least a portion of industrialists supported the political party that was established by the chair of the Hyundai group in 1991. Ultimately, though, the Korean bourgeoisie's contribution to democratization was more indirect because it led to the rise of civil society, which objected to the apparently privileged status of capital. As Sunhyuk Kim (2000) explains, "Because the bourgeois class and its representative associations in Korea generally partook in the state-corporatist political arrangement and sided with the authoritarian regimes, civil society's political protest for democracy was not only against the state but also against the bourgeoisie" (144). Korean industrialists thus influenced the process of democratization not by mobilizing as a class, but by inspiring resentment against their position in society. To the extent that any "classes" could be singled out as the most consistent supporter of democratization in Korea, it would be the urban middle class (including students) and white-collar professionals, in coalition with blue-collar workers (Koo 1991, 494).

The Brazilian and South Korean cases show how capitalists may become less hostile to democracy over time, but to situate China in comparative perspective it is also relevant to look at countries that have undergone rapid industrialization without accompanying political liberalization. In Asia, the most frequently cited example is Singapore.[8] The political quiescence of Singapore's capitalists continues to illustrate the point that when business elites are essentially incorporated by the regime, they are not likely to initiate major political changes (Lingle 1996; Mak 1999).

As discussed in the next chapter, existing studies of China's private sector have reached similar conclusions about the noncontentious relationship

---

8. Although there is limited practical value in comparing the world's most populous country with a small city-state, Singapore's combination of capitalism and authoritarianism nonetheless serves as a common reference point (verging on role model) for Chinese policymakers and academics. In this respect, India often serves as a negative example of a large developing country with democracy.

between the party-state and capital (Dickson 2003; Pearson 2002). Some scholars have even characterized government-business relations as being symbiotic and mutually dependent (Solinger 1992; Wank 1999). Especially during the early reform years, larger private businesses relied on local governments for political protection and access to state-controlled inputs. Meanwhile, local governments relied on businesses in the nonstate sector to generate fiscal revenue and promote economic development (Oi 1999). The common, if implicit, political implication of these studies is that China's capitalists do not pose a threat to regime durability because they are not truly autonomous from the state itself. To echo Moore (1966), the collective wisdom of these studies suggests that the absence of democracy in contemporary China could be explained in part by the absence of an independent bourgeoisie.

Although this counterfactual assessment is plausible, my book emphasizes a logic different from that of classic structural theories. Private entrepreneurs have indeed had a structural impact on Chinese politics, but not in the class-based manner that structural theories of political development would expect. Rather than imputing structural outcomes through the more familiar lens of class analysis, I examine the macrolevel influence of informal coping strategies at the local level. Ultimately, informal interactions among state and nonstate actors have the causal potential to change formal state-level institutions. Before developing this argument further, we will look at the elite-centric approach to political change, which has gained currency among both China specialists and students of comparative politics more generally.[9] Given how rarely the entire capitalist class mobilizes for political purposes, how might an alternative elite-centric path to democratization involve the upper tier of capitalists?[10]

Elite-Centric Path to Democratization

Voluntarist explanations for democratization generally focus on the bargaining process that occurs between elite factions in the existing authoritarian regime (e.g., hardliners versus reformers) and those in the prodemocratic opposition (e.g., moderates and radicals) (Colomer 2000; O'Donnell and Schmitter 1986; Przeworski 1991). Unlike the structural framework

9. For example, Fewsmith 1994; Gilley 2004; Nathan and Gilley 2003.

10. As Bourdieu (1985) has pointed out, even if we were able to identify a theoretical "class on paper," consisting of agents who share similar positions in the market economy, "it is not really a class, an *actual* class, in the sense of a group mobilized for struggle" (725). In other words, in practice entire classes are not collective actors; instead, classes are represented by groups and organizations that may mobilize people with common interests and make political demands on their behalf.

discussed above, the voluntarist approach distinguishes between different phases in the transition to democracy. In particular, the *initial transition* from authoritarian rule is depicted as an important first stage, during which political elites make the critical decision to commit themselves to building a democratic regime. Dankwart Rustow (1970) has pointed out that, after all, democratic outcomes do not emerge "in a fit of absentmindedness" (355). As such, the final *consolidation* phase of a democratic transition is also a key part of the process to ensure the institutionalization and legitimation of democratic procedures. Despite its undemocratic appearance, the strategic formation of political pacts among different groups of elites may facilitate democratic consolidation because pacts provide a means for contending elites to compromise with one another and negotiate acceptable power-sharing arrangements.[11]

If capitalist elites were to partake in a voluntarist version of democratic transition, their participation would be motivated, at a minimum, by exclusion from the existing political regime and a loss of confidence in the regime's ability to protect its material interests. A related scenario would be if entrepreneurs viewed democratic political institutions as being more likely to protect their material interests. Existing studies of the third-wave democracies reveal that the role of business elites in regime transitions ranges from being marginal during the initial transition to moderately supportive during the consolidation phase. Furthermore, some regional trends are apparent. For example, the strongest statement that one can make about the role of the Latin American bourgeoisie is that they have not blocked the transitions to democracy (O'Donnell 1992). In Argentina, capitalist leaders supported the military coup of 1976, but then disapproved of the ensuing succession of military governments because the generals pursued economic and foreign policies that undermined rather than enhanced the country's social stability and international legitimacy (Smith 1989). Industrialists also resented the military government's intervention in business associations, as it encroached on their autonomy. Despite clear displeasure with the authoritarian regime, business elites did not actively support the new civilian democratic governments. Their contribution to Argentina's democratic consolidation essentially took the form of nonintervention.

Business elites were similarly quiescent in the south European transitions. As in Argentina, industrialists in Spain initially supported the military regime under Franco, but grew increasingly discontented with the country's deteriorating economic conditions and their own exclusion from the policy-making process.[12] Yet when the democratic transition began, business leaders neither

---

11. See Diamond 1999; Di Palma 1990; Hagopian 1990; Kirchheimer 1988 [1941].
12. This section draws from Payne 1994, 143–145.

supported nor thwarted the process. They were not politically apathetic but, rather, internally divided about the pace, direction, and substance of the transition. The cases of Argentina and Spain thus show that even when industrialists are dissatisfied with an authoritarian regime, it does not mean that they will necessarily collaborate with other elites in facilitating a transition to democracy.

The counterfactual corollary to the original voluntarist hypothesis is that if capitalists are not excluded from the existing authoritarian regime and their material interests are not under threat, then it is unlikely that an elite corps of business owners will press for democratic change—even if certain political leaders or other well-organized groups, or both, advocate democratization. During their bureaucratic-authoritarian phases, Brazil and South Korea exemplified this dynamic. In both countries different elements of society pressed for political liberalization years before the formal transition process occurred, but in neither case did business leaders assist or sanction those oppositional activities. If anything, industrial elites were quite loyal to the bureaucratic-authoritarian regimes. It was only when signs of a democratic transition were clear that a faction of business elites became more politically active. In short, capitalist elites have generally played a modest secondary role in voluntarist accounts of democratic transition.

Ultimately, the contemporary association of capitalist development with democracy involves complex processes that extend beyond the mere emergence of private entrepreneurs—as a class or as an elitist vanguard. The development of democracy may stem from a variety of factors, including the rise of civil society, social movements, shifts in elite politics, international pressures, direct foreign intervention, and structural changes in society and the economy.[13] Aside from the British, U.S., and French experiences in democratic development, capitalists have not played a central role in bringing about the establishment of democratic institutions.[14] In late-industrializing countries, the elite layer of capitalists tends to be incorporated by the existing regime and therefore lacks the incentive to demand political liberalization. The lowest tier of business owners may constitute the bulk of the private sector, but it tends to lack the confidence and resources to mobilize politically. Only the middle tier of business owners tends to accumulate both the resources and the desire or material incentives to pose a serious political challenge; but even then, it is often in collaboration with other sectors in society (e.g., Rueschemeyer, Stephens, and Stephens 1992).

13. Anderson 1999; Diamond and Plattner 1996; O'Donnell, Schmitter, and Whitehead 1986; Przeworski 1991.

14. And even in those cases, I would argue that although specific democratizing acts have been associated with capitalists, the causal dynamics of democratic development lie in the evolution of informal practices over time. Maitland's (1997 [1909]) discussion of the evolution of common law in England illustrates this point.

In the following chapters we will see that China's private entrepreneurs are not prone to engage in collective action, much less demand democracy. Meanwhile, the PRC has experienced major political and institutional changes in tandem with—and arguably, in reaction to—rapid private sector development. Moreover, the course of institutional reform has not been linear or smooth. The political crisis of 1989 was the most overt expression of the conflicts that had accumulated at both the elite and societal levels, and the regime resorted to coercive means to end the demonstrations. But disagreement among elites and bureaucrats at different levels of government over the pace, scope, and direction of reform was evident well before, and has persisted well beyond, 1989 (e.g., Baum 1994; Fewsmith 2001a). Conflicts between the central and local governments, or between various bureaucratic agencies, are sometimes expressed by delays in policy implementation or official rhetoric that obfuscates the implications of the policies (e.g., Lieberthal and Lampton 1992; O'Brien and Li 1999). Yet the private sector has thrived, and many of the PRC's most

Family carpentry shop, Zhouzhuang Township, Jiangsu Province

fundamental institutions, including the Chinese Communist Party and the PRC Constitution, have changed substantially. How did this occur without compromising the regime's survival? I propose that part of the answer lies in the responsiveness of political elites to adaptive informal institutions at the local level.

Explaining Regime Stability amid Change

The two literatures that are most relevant for explaining regime durability and institutional change, respectively, have developed in isolation from one another, largely because they derive from the empirical experiences of countries in different regions of the world. First, studies of authoritarian durability emerged out of Middle Eastern studies in political science that tried to explain the persistence of authoritarian regimes in the region despite the third wave of democracy everywhere else. Second, historical institutionalists who have analyzed endogenous institutional change draw from cases in American political development and from that of other industrial democracies. Insights from the latter branch of literature may be used to supplement explanations for authoritarian durability by elucidating the processes of institutional reinforcement and institutional innovation. In addition, examining the informal coping strategies inspired by the formal institutional environment provides a key, yet typically overlooked, dimension in analyses of political and economic change. This is not to say that all informal interactions are causally relevant in explaining formal institutional change but, rather, that under the political circumstances such as those found in reform-era China extensive reliance on adaptive informal institutions may foreshadow the possibility of institutional reforms that bridge the gap between official regulations and everyday practices.

Authoritarian Durability

Explanations for the striking absence of liberal democracies in the Middle East generally rely on cultural, economic, social structural, or institutional variables (Posusney 2004). Although the institutional perspective bears the most potential for theoretical portability beyond the region, I will briefly review all four approaches because they mirror popular narratives about the absence of democracy in China.

First, studies that emphasize the cultural reasons for authoritarian persistence in the Middle East typically point to attributes of Islam that appear irreconcilable with liberal democratic values.[15] The imposition of Islamic law

15. For example, Kedourie 1994; Sadowski 1993; Sharabi 1988.

(*sharia*) in Iran and other countries is often cited as evidence that Islamic regimes are inherently unlikely to adopt democratic procedures. Cultural explanations for authoritarianism in Asia run along similar lines, albeit without reference to religious tradition. Singapore's former prime minister Lee Kuan Yew, for example, has been among the most outspoken proponents of the notion that Asian values are inconsistent with liberal democracy (Barr 2000; Pye 1985). Critics of cultural explanations, however, have pointed out that many countries have developed democratic political systems despite having religions and value systems that have also been cited as being fundamentally inimical to democracy (Stepan 2000). Besides the democratization of Latin American countries dominated by Catholicism, the spread of democracy in the Confucian-influenced countries of East Asia provides strong empirical counterexamples to the expectations of cultural theories (de Bary and Tu, eds. 1998; Diamond and Plattner, eds. 1998).

Second, the availability of major resource endowments and related access to rents has also been associated with the persistence of authoritarianism (Beblawi and Luciano 1987). In rentier states, citizens lack a fiscal basis for demanding democracy, because the state finances benefits to its citizens through natural resource revenues rather than taxes. Rentier states maintain power by distributing rents throughout the population. A related explanation for the authoritarian persistence of rentier states is that they possess the fiscal means to maintain a "robust coercive apparatus."[16] The latter, in turn, inhibits the expression and development of political opposition. Despite some disagreement about the role of repression in the endurance of oil-rich states (Smith 2004), overall the rentier-state argument points to the underlying economic basis for maintaining regime legitimacy and authority.[17]

Although the PRC is not a rentier state, a related explanation for the CCP's continued monopoly of political power is that the country has experienced significant and sustained improvement in its economy since the late 1970s. In other words, one possible reason that the PRC has withstood both the third wave of democracy and the collapse of Communism in the former Soviet bloc is its economic performance. Based on cross-national analysis, Adam Przeworski et al. (2000) have found that economic growth is positively correlated with regime survival; when growth rates are declining, the probability that a regime will die is twice as high as when the economy

---

16. As Bellin (2004) points out, "Democratic transition can be carried out successfully only when the state's coercive apparatus lacks the will or capacity to crush it. Where that coercive apparatus remains intact and opposed to political reform, democratic transition will not occur" (143). See also Ross 2001.

17. A corollary of this is that "fiscal crises quickly become political crises." See Chaudhry 1994. Cf. analyses of the political Dutch disease: Lam and Wantchekon 2003.

is growing (109). Hence, the argument could be made that regime durability in China is simply a function of the economy's high growth rates.

While the material conditions of most Chinese citizens have improved since the Mao era, the commoditization of economic and political life has also been associated with potentially destabilizing effects, such as widespread corruption (Sun 2004; Pei 2006). Indeed, in other contexts rapid economic modernization has been correlated both with political instability and with democratization.[18] As such, especially in the aftermath of the mass demonstrations in 1989, the regime's allocation of fiscal resources to maintaining the robustness of the party-state's coercive apparatus appears to be a more compelling explanation for authoritarian durability than the conventional rentier-state argument.[19] This view is linked to the institutional arguments discussed below.

The third approach to explaining authoritarian persistence in the Middle East is social-structural in the sense that it focuses on the relative political positions and preferences of various social forces in the regime. David Waldner (2004), for example, argues that the political incorporation of rural middle classes before 1980 explains regime durability in both postcolonial democracies and dictatorships. The reasoning is that such incorporation minimizes the intensity of interelite conflicts, while providing the regime with a key source of political support for negotiating relations with other social classes, especially labor and capital. Meanwhile, Bellin (2002) traces the authoritarian preferences of labor and capital in Tunisia (and in other late-developing countries) to their dependence on state sponsorship. This support for authoritarianism is reinforced by labor's privileged status relative to the popular sectors and capital's fear about the consequences of mass empowerment.

Fourth, presenting an institutional twist on structural explanations for authoritarian persistence, Steven Heydemann (1999) attributes the "success," meaning durability, of Syria's populist authoritarianism since 1946 to the Baath Party's strategy of combining state building with populism. As Raymond Hinnebusch (2004, 7) has pointed out, the durability of populist authoritarianism in the Middle East has depended on a number of different variables, including a regime's establishment through a revolutionary coup, the institutional strength of its single-party system, the dominance of a personalistic leader, the distribution of patronage to key groups, and considerable repressive capacity. Both Heydemann and Hinnebusch's arguments

---

18. The classic arguments are Huntington 1968 and Lipset 1959.

19. In a complementary manner, Bueno de Mesquita and Downs (2005) argue that economic growth will not necessarily lead to democracy if the autocratic regime limits the availability of "strategic coordination goods," meaning public goods that facilitate political coordination (e.g., freedom of speech and assembly, freedom of press, access to higher education).

about the endurance of populist authoritarianism emphasize the ability of political and social institutions to incorporate key segments of society while maintaining the institutional capacity to expand the extent of state intervention in the economy for redistributive purposes.[20]

Although my focus is on the post-Mao era, both the social structural and institutional explanations for regime durability are also applicable to post-1949 China more generally. The Communists defeated the Nationalists and consolidated their power on the mainland through a strategy of rural incorporation, and it would not be a stretch to characterize the Mao era (1949–76) as populist-authoritarian based on the qualities enumerated above. Besides rural incorporation, the party-state granted urban labor various privileges in the name of socialism, while private capital was politically persecuted and effectively eliminated.

Since the late 1970s, however, China's reforms have produced a wide range of social and economic tensions, including massive growth in agricultural surplus labor from decollectivization, a rise in urban unemployment due to reform of state-owned enterprises, an increased fiscal burden on farmers, de facto privatization of education and health care, and widespread discontent concerning the rise of both regional and urban-rural inequalities.[21] Arguably, economic reforms have eroded the PRC's original social— and, indeed, socialist—basis for regime durability. At the macro level, private entrepreneurs now appear to be the primary beneficiaries of the regime's market-oriented reforms. As Hinnebusch (2004) has observed with respect to reforms in postpopulist authoritarian regimes, "The key lesson . . . is that in most cases movement away from authoritarianism actually translates *not into more popular power but into privileged class power* and less popular inclusion" (7). Although the following empirical cases show how China's formal institutions have become more accommodating to the private sector over

20. Note that the absence of formal institutionalization does not necessarily portend authoritarian demise. Unlike institutionalized regimes, which operate according to standardized procedures and the rule of law in the rational Weberian sense, neopatrimonial regimes are governed by cronyism and are subject to the personalistic whims of the ruler (Bratton and van de Walle 1997). While neopatrimonial regimes are thus portrayed as being weakly institutionalized, scholars have reached mixed conclusions about their durability. H. E. Chehabi and Juan Linz (1998), for example, view "sultanistic regimes" as prone to breaking down, while Bellin (2004, 149–153) observes that the enduring ones can command significant loyalty in their coercive apparatus. By including counterfactual cases of regimes that have survived crises—not only cases of regime transition—Jason Brownlee's study (2002) of neopatrimonial regimes convincingly finds that, in the absence of foreign intervention, "extensive patrimonialism" may enable regimes to survive serious political challenges and reassert their authority by using force. This suggests that relatively uninstitutionalized or patrimonial regimes are not necessarily at a disadvantage over institutionalized ones in terms of capacity for internal repression.

21. Informative overviews include Goldman and MacFarquhar 1999; Gries and Rosen 2004; Perry and Selden 2003.

time, private capital as a whole has not been dependent on the state in the manner observed by Bellin in Tunisia and others in bureaucratic-authoritarian Korea and Brazil.[22] For example, China's private entrepreneurs lack access to state banks, relying instead on informal finance (Tsai 2002). Moreover, the current generation of business owners cannot be considered a unified class that shares similar identities, interests, resources, and political preferences.[23]

Given the recent tenuousness of the regime's social bases of support, institutional explanations for authoritarian durability may be more appropriate for understanding China's situation. Indeed, if we were to place reform-era China along the spectrum of institutionalized to less institutionalized or neopatrimonial regimes, it would be closer to the institutionalized end (Yang 2004). Since the death of Mao, China has not had a paramount leader with an effective cult of personality, as would be expected in a neopatrimonial or sultanistic regime. Furthermore, post-Mao political elites have not only resuscitated political institutions that stagnated during the Cultural Revolution (1966–76) but have also established a high level of institutionalization in the Huntingtonian sense of adaptability, complexity, autonomy, and coherence of state organizations (Huntington 1968, 12–24). In particular, Nathan (2003) attributes authoritarian resilience in China to four aspects of the regime's institutionalization: the increasingly rule-bound nature of succession politics; the growing use of meritocratic rather than factional criteria for political promotion; the increasing differentiation and functional specialization of the regime's institutions; and the establishment of "input institutions" that give individuals outlets to express their grievances and thus serve to bolster regime legitimacy.

While these indicators of institutionalization contribute to regime durability, here I want to look at the causal mechanisms underlying the relevant institutional dynamics. That is, part of the complexity of the persistence of authoritarianism in China may also be traced to the ability of formal institutions to adapt to innovations that originate from informal interactions between state and nonstate actors at the subnational level. Institutional

22. During the early years of reform, however, the largest private businesses were dependent on the state for access to various resources (Solinger 1992; Wank 1995). Furthermore, as I discuss in chapter 6, there is local variation in the extent of entrepreneurial dependence on the state.

23. Beyond the case of China, I would argue that there are few instances where the full range of private business interests could be considered a "unified class." When structural theories refer to "capital" or "capitalists," they usually only include the top tier of industrialists or financiers. However, the point here is that China's private sector is especially fragmented at this point due to its relative youth. As will be shown, even "red capitalists," meaning Communist Party members who run businesses, have varying identities, concerns, and coping strategies, depending on their backgrounds and local operating conditions.

change is possible in the absence of cataclysmic events or complete institutional breakdown.

Institutional Development

Although revolutions, economic crises, wars, natural disasters, and foreign intervention or occupation provide a readily identifiable context for major institutional transformations, a number of studies have also examined the dynamics of institutional development during "normal" periods.[24] In the literature on historical institutionalism and American political development, two basic approaches to explaining endogenous institutional change may be identified: the "sequencing" approach, which is more structure oriented, and the "layering" and "conversion" perspectives, which are more action oriented. Both draw on the internal logic of formal institutions to explain the origins of change. Incorporating a relational approach clarifies the causal potential of informal institutions in these endogenous accounts of institutional development.

Path Dependence and Sequencing   The sequencing approach to institutional development typically focuses on the self-reinforcing dynamics of path dependency and institutional continuity (Arthur 1994; David 1985; Pierson 2000). As North (1990) explains, "Path dependence comes from the increasing returns mechanisms that reinforce the direction once on a given path" (112). But path dependence does not preclude change over time. In particular, Paul Pierson (2000b, 2004) distinguishes between "self-reinforcing event sequences" and "non-reinforcing event sequences" in path-dependent arguments. A common expression of a self-reinforcing event sequence takes place when certain political actors consolidate power during an early formative period and end up promoting institutions and rules that enable them to maintain their authority over time (Pierson 2004, 73). The moment of institutional genesis is considered a "critical juncture" because once certain options are chosen over others, alternative options are less readily available. The critical nature of these formative periods has been illustrated by a wide range of studies, including how political cleavage structures translate into party systems in various European countries and how differences in state incorporation of labor have influenced electoral politics in Latin America (Collier and Collier 1991; Lipset and Rokkan 1967). In all of these instances, political choices made during critical junctures end up shaping subsequent events in a self-reinforcing manner.

24. Paul Pierson recommends that we focus on the processes of "institutional development" rather than "institutional change" because the "former term encourages us to remain attentive to the ways in which previous institutional outcomes can channel and constrain later efforts at institutional innovation" (Pierson 2004, 133).

not act (Powell and DiMaggio 1991). For example, electoral rules specify the scope, timing, and eligibility of potential candidates in political elections; legislative rules specify the procedure through which legislation is drafted, proposed, approved, and perhaps implemented; while property rights define who has the authority to use, earn income from, and transfer certain assets. In short, formal institutions are intended to provide a certain element of predictability and stability in human interactions.

Assuming that most people accept this proposition, even if they find particular institutions objectionable, it is possible to predict that certain institutions will produce certain outcomes. Even complex multilayered institutional environments can be modeled elegantly to yield convincing explanations for why counterintuitive behaviors or policy choices occur (Tsebelis 1990). But formal modeling is empirically relevant only when formal institutions actually shape and constrain behavior in highly regular and predictable ways. After all, unintended consequences do flow from formal institutions, and cases of institutional failure abound throughout the world, which has thus inspired entire research agendas devoted to explaining the gap between intended and unintended institutional outcomes.

It is in this context that institutionalists have paid greater attention to "softer variables," such as ideas, norms, and culture (Bates 1988; Berman 2001; Blyth 2002)—or what others might call informal institutions. The underlying rationale for turning to less formal variables is relatively straightforward. If formal institutions are expected to produce X outcome, but Y occurs instead, then the noise must stem from exogenous informal variables. The analytic shortcoming of this, however, is that informal institutions effectively become residual variables that are expected to bear the explanatory slack whenever formal institutions can no longer account for the variation in outcomes. And, more typically, informal institutions are blamed for inhibiting the normal functioning of formal institutions. Cultural explanations for why certain countries are neither more developed nor more democratic are often cited as cogent examples of how informal institutions may undermine formal ones.[30] As North (1990) explains, in certain contexts "the formal rules change, but the informal constraints do not. In consequence, there develops an ongoing tension between informal constraints and the new formal rules," which may be attributed to "the deep-seated cultural inheritance that underlies many informal constraints" (91).

This observation leaves us with the analytic conflation of informal constraints, informal institutions, and cultural inheritance—and the vague impression that all three compromise the intended functions of formal institutions. The tendency for explanations to privilege informal institutions only when formal ones have failed at their prescribed tasks ironically

---

30. For example, Harrison and Huntington 2000.

demonstrates the normative power that scholars reflexively ascribe to formal institutions. That is to say, formal institutions implicitly represent the baseline from which we evaluate the desirability of various outcomes. To be sure, constructivists and cultural anthropologists engage in interpretive analyses that take informal processes seriously, but they rarely theorize directly about the causal impact of informal institutions.[31] One of the few works in political science that endeavors to address this analytical lacuna is Gretchen Helmke and Steven Levitsky (2004). In particular, the authors have proposed a typology for classifying the relationship between formal and informal institutions, such that they may be complementary, accommodating, competing, or substitutive.[32] The typology is helpful in clarifying the nature and function of informal institutions relative to formal ones, but it does not develop a theory about the processes of informal institutional emergence and change or about the formalization of informal institutions. And, indeed, a large part of the challenge in inserting informal institutions into causal explanations is where to place them temporally, given that almost no society is devoid of some semblance of formal institutions.

For the purposes of capturing the causal effects of informal institutions at a more manageable intermediate stage, I thus bracket the "deep-seated cultural inheritance" underlying informal institutions and start with the blank slate of formal institutions, which I define as rules, regulations, policies, and procedures that are promulgated and meant to be enforced by entities and agents generally recognized as being official.[33] As in my earlier work (Tsai 2002), in this book I regard formal institutions as being both constraining and enabling. On the one hand, formal institutions limit the range of officially permissible behavior. On the other hand, multilayered institutional environments offer transformative possibilities; in particular, formal institutional contexts with overlapping jurisdiction and inconsistent or unrealistic mandates provide opportunities for actors to adjust, ignore, or evade discrete portions of formal institutions. Initially, many of these adaptive responses may appear to be idiosyncratic or isolated. However, when the adaptive strategies become regularized patterns of interaction that violate or transcend the scope of formal institutions and are widely practiced, they constitute what I call "adaptive informal institutions."

---

31. Possible exceptions include Geertz (1973) and Wendt (1999), but they do not focus on informal institutions as explanatory variables.

32. Five types of informal institutions are identified in Lauth 2000.

33. This definition draws from Helmke and Levitsky (2004, 727), but it also includes public policies because they typically have institutional consequences. Pierson (2004) suggests, "It makes good sense to think of public policies as important institutions. For the individuals and social organizations that make up civil society, public policies are clearly very central rules governing their interactions" (165).

Unlike deeply rooted informal institutions and cultural practices, which exist prior to the establishment of formal institutions, adaptive informal institutions arise within the parameters of a formal institutional context. Actors create and reproduce adaptive informal institutions *in reaction* to the perceived limitations and possibilities of formal institutions. Some adaptive informal institutions may become so prevalent they appear to be long-standing habits or internalized as part of local culture. Yet they should not be confused with primordial practices that predate particular sets of formal institutions. Adaptive informal institutions emerge as adaptive responses to the chasm between formal institutions and practical interests and desires. In addition to the analytic emphasis on behavioral adaptation (versus cultural persistence), recognizing adaptive informal institutions as a specific type of institutional effect also has operational value because it is so difficult to disentangle the relationship between culturally based informal constraints and formal ones. By taking a particular formal institution as a given and then process tracing how various actors interact in dealing with its constraints and possibilities, the analysis yields insights into how formal institutions generate the potential seeds of their own reform: adaptive informal institutions. For this intermediate stage of institutional adaptation to develop, at least the base-level guardians of formal institutions need to be complicit in allowing the institutional distortions to occur over and over again. As such, adaptive informal institutions are more likely to arise and thrive in localities where the enforcers of formal institutions and the creators of informal adaptations have convergent interests. By definition, this means that while local state and nonstate actors benefit mutually from the resulting adaptive informal institutions, those arrangements transgress existing formal institutional mandates. This is the first part of my argument in a longer sequence explaining endogenous institutional development.

The second part concerns what happens after adaptive informal institutions emerge. At the most basic level, the proliferation of adaptive informal institutions may undermine the legitimacy of formal institutions. The relevance of institutions, whether formal or informal, depends on their capacity to guide human perceptions and practices. But do the enforcers of formal institutions discipline, ignore, or incorporate the actors sustaining adaptive informal institutions? The answer to this question is historically and nationally contingent. In the case of China, adaptive informal institutions that threaten to undermine social stability or to compromise the CCP's political monopoly are likely to provoke official censure. Official tolerance for mass mobilization and political dissent remains limited. Meanwhile, crackdowns on adaptive informal institutions in the economic realm are most likely to occur during political campaigns against economic crimes and corruption and other periods when there is heightened political sensitivity to local deviations from national mandates.[34] But if the law enforcers themselves are party to the offending activities, then efforts to curb them are unlikely to be sustainable beyond those priority moments.

Beyond China, we may expect that when adaptive informal institutions constitute flagrant forms of criminal activity, they will elicit the attention of law enforcement entities. Yet even the definition of "flagrant" criminal behavior is contextually variable. In some cases, embezzlement of state assets would constitute flagrant criminal activity, but under other circumstances the same behavior might be so common that it fails to trigger strong official reactions. For present purposes, I will simply define "flagrant forms of criminal activity" as illegal practices that are readily discernable and have immediate social costs that would be difficult to cover up. An example of this would be Ponzi schemes, which usually involve large numbers of enraged people by the time they collapse (Zuckoff 2005). Another example would be violations of food-and-drug safety standards, which endanger lives and motivate regulatory development (Tam and Yang 2005).

In contrast, adaptive informal institutions that merely stretch the limits of formal institutions or create new patterns of interaction not explicitly governed by formal institutions may endure and even thrive unencumbered for some length of time. Most of the adaptive practices discussed in this book fall into these quasi-legal and extralegal gray areas. They are adaptive informal institutions that arise in a context where some local political and economic actors face incentives to promote private sector development but formal institutions lag in adjusting to new businesses and their associated externalities—for example, new licensing and financing needs, changing relations with workers, and new opportunities for generating revenue. In some cases, the adaptive informal institutions may become so widespread that the actors with authority to reform formal institutions choose to incorporate the practices popularized by adaptive informal institutions. In other words, formalization of adaptive informal institutions could occur without jeopardizing the survival of preexisting formal institutions.

Moreover, adaptive informal institutions may have a structural impact on formal institutional development even in the absence of direct demands for institutional reform by those who rely on adaptive informal institutions. This indirect mode of policy influence is more likely to occur when key decision makers recognize both the political and practical value of adaptive informal institutions. More specifically, this means that (1) policy elites

---

34. Distinct cycles of crackdowns on local financial institutions such as trust and investment companies were apparent and corresponded with the broader policy reform cycles through the late 1990s when Zhu Rongji was premier. Correspondence with Yi-feng Tao, November 10, 2006.

must be aware of the existence of adaptive informal institutions; (2) the apparent effects of those adaptive informal institutions should concord with the agendas, whether latent or publicly disclosed, of at least a subset of policy elites (typically reformers); and (3) reform-oriented elites come to view the popularity and performance of adaptive informal institutions as a means to justify changing the formal institutions that gave rise to the informal adaptations in the first place. In the absence of these basic conditions, adaptive informal institutions will either continue to thrive below the radar . . . or face official reproach. Only empirical study of specific political conditions can answer the inevitable question of exactly when and whether adaptive informal institutions are relevant in explaining changes in formal institutions and, indeed, whether the resulting changes enhance regime durability or undermine it.

My focus on the origins and effects of adaptive informal institutions resonates with the logics of nonreinforcing event sequences, layering, and conversion. When adaptive informal institutions arise in response to the dissonance between existing formal institutions and the operational preferences of actors, adaptive informal institutions start to redirect and undermine the previously self-enforcing formal institutions.[35] In this narrative, preexisting formal institutions represent the analytical baseline against which actors devise coping strategies. Indeed, the core of the argument rests on the formal-informal-formal sequence (illustrated in figure 2.1).

Theoretically, this argument may enable institutionalists to deal with the duality of structure in a more operationalizable and dynamic manner. One way to resolve the Giddensian paradox that institutions are simultaneously the medium and the outcome of practices that constitute and reproduce structures is to explore how the practices of everyday actors relate to the mandates of formal institutions.[36] Even when culturally specific informal institutions affect the implementation of formal institutions, it makes operational sense to focus on the actual practices of actors within a formal institutional context. Hence, in this book I hold constant some of the deeper entrenched informal institutions and start with discrete formal institutions to identify how people cope with, adapt to, subvert, and ultimately change institutions that are supposed to be constraining. This is not meant to be a return to the old institutionalism but rather a call for specifying the dynamics and mechanisms through

---

35. Although Greif and Laitin (2004) distinguish between self-reinforcing and self-destructing institutions, Thelen (2004) makes the key point that institutional conversion may occur "rather than either straight reproduction or breakdown" (291).

36. William H. Sewell Jr. (1992) similarly recommends that scholars consider "how the ordinary operations of structures can generate transformations" (16). To facilitate this process,

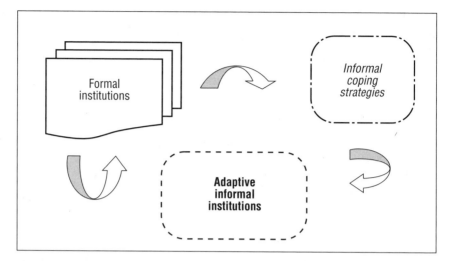

Figure 2.1. Role of adaptive informal institutions in institutional development

which adaptive informal institutions may emerge from and acquire causal influence on formal institutions.

Analytically, the approach is fundamentally relational in the sense that institutions can only be sustained or transformed through human interaction.[37] At the micro level, the empirical cases in the following chapters show that real-life interactions among various actors constitute the causal spaces between formal and informal institutions. Even if they lead to unplanned aggregate outcomes, such as formal institutional change, at a minimum the daily interactions among local political and economic actors are consequentialist in nature. As such, a relational approach is well suited for revealing the empirical processes underlying institutional change. Situating reflexive actors in relation to one another and analyzing how they interact allows us to appreciate the enabling side of both formal and informal institutions. Although most observers focus on the formal institutions governing China's political economy, the emergence of adaptive informal institutions

---

he argues that it is also necessary to transcend Pierre Bourdieu's notion of *habitus* as homologous structures by recognizing that "structures tend to vary significantly between different institutional spheres" (16). Sewell criticizes Bourdieu's concept of *habitus* as being "unrealistically unified and totalized" due to its definition as "a vast series of strictly homologous structures encompassing all of social experience."

37. This resonates with what Bob Jessop (2001) calls a "strategic-relational approach." Cf. Charles Tilly's (1998) discussion of "relational realism."

represents a significant part of the story about how capitalists could thrive in an authoritarian regime that claims to adhere to socialist ideology. Even in nondemocratic contexts where truly representative formal institutions do not exist, state and nonstate actors may collaborate to manipulate the formal rules of the game in a manner that serves their interests and, eventually, leads to more fundamental reform or change of formal institutions that neither of the parties fully intended.

3

The Unofficial and Official Revival of China's Private Sector

What is "market socialism with Chinese characteristics"? It means that powerful government officials can get rich now. They are the ones who are wealthy, not the masses.

Local official in Hebei, 2002

"So much has changed in China that sometimes I find it hard to believe that I have lived in the same country my entire life. Even my friends and family seem like completely different people now that they are fat and rich."

What do you think your friends and family would say about you?

"Oh, well, I haven't changed that much. I'm basically the same person."

Middle-aged entrepreneur in Guangdong, 2002

In 1978, capitalists were official "class enemies" in the People's Republic of China. On July 1, 2001, the eightieth anniversary of the Chinese Communist Party's founding, however, they were publicly invited to join the party. Just a few years later, the National People's Congress amended the PRC Constitution to protect private property rights. What happened? Some observers speculate that it was just a matter of time before China's private entrepreneurs would form autonomous organizations and demand political representation to protect their material interests. But that was not why the most persecuted group in Chinese society was accepted into the country's most powerful political institution, or why the constitution was amended in 2004 to say that "private property legally obtained shall not be violated" and will be "on equal footing with public property." Private entrepreneurs themselves did not pressure the regime to grant them political and economic rights. Instead, these dramatic reversals in the treatment of private capital resulted from elite-level reactions to informal private sector practices at the grassroots level, which preceded official recognition of private sector resurgence and relevance to the national economy.

I will begin with a brief overview of the post-1949 policy environment concerning private capital, followed by a review of existing studies of China's private sector during the reform era. A sampling of interviews with business owners conducted during 2001–05 illustrates entrepreneurs' recollections of the challenges they faced during the early years and how things have changed since then. Both existing scholarship and my field interviews provide mixed assessments of the relationship between the state and business owners, but most analysts would agree that private entrepreneurs exhibit limited signs of political assertiveness. Yet China's business owners are far from being passive. Despite their relatively low political profile, private entrepreneurs have exercised agency by engaging in income-generating activities long before it was legal to do so.

Overall, the empirical observations presented in this chapter reveal two trends that defy the expectations of popular theories of political economy. First, the private sector expanded rapidly during the first two decades of reform, in the absence of formal regulatory institutions to support (much less encourage) such dynamic development. Second, private entrepreneurs have not directly lobbied for the policy and institutional changes that have created increasingly favorable operating conditions for the nonstate sector. These two findings become less puzzling when we take into account the informal norms and practices that private entrepreneurs have relied on in the course of establishing, financing, and expanding their businesses. Informal adaptive strategies by entrepreneurs have both reflected and foreshadowed far-reaching changes in the formal policy environment governing the private sector since the Chinese Communist Party consolidated its power on the mainland. To be sure, reform-oriented elites in Beijing were instrumental in making the official decisions to reform the Communist Party and PRC Constitution. But in this book I argue that the accumulation of informal interactions between local state and economic actors provided both the impetus and the legitimizing basis for these key reforms. Ultimately, both the designers and enforcers of China's formal institutions have proven to be flexible, and even responsive, to the actors driving the country's economic growth: private entrepreneurs.

Building Socialism and Eliminating Capitalism during the Mao Era

In 1949, the CCP inherited a war-torn country whose economy was in shambles. The official economic strategy at the time was "three years of recovery, to be followed by ten years of development." In a manner reminiscent of the Soviet Union's early years under Lenin's New Economic Policy (1921–28), the PRC's official three years of recovery offered a relatively open environment for small-scale private sector activity. In June 1949, on the twenty-eighth anniversary of the CCP, Mao Zedong issued an influential essay, "On the People's Democratic Dictatorship," which declared that the new state would be a "people's republic" led by the working class and based on a national united front that included not only workers and peasants but also the petty bourgeoisie and national bourgeoisie. The essay indicated a pragmatic attitude toward private businesses because they could contribute to the country's economic development. Mao wrote, "China must utilize all elements of urban and rural capitalism that are beneficial and not harmful to the national economy. . . . Our present policy is to control, not to eliminate, capitalism" (1967, 417–421).[1] Unlike the "bureaucratic bourgeoisie," who had been aligned with the Guomindang or foreign economic interests (i.e., "imperialists"), the "national bourgeoisie" were defined as being politically loyal to the CCP and thus permitted to engage in private income-generating activities.

Hence, initially, the CCP confiscated and nationalized the assets of only the bureaucratic capitalists—most of whom had already fled the country—while allowing the over seven million small retailers and self-employed artisans to continue their operations (Gong 1988).[2] Meanwhile, during the three years of recovery the number of larger private industrial enterprises increased from 123,000 to 150,000, and the size of the private industrial labor force grew from 1.6 to 2.2 million workers (Richman 1969, 899).[3] During this phase, the politically acceptable form of national capitalism foreshadowed the subsequent development of state capitalism in the sense that private businesses depended on the state for key inputs, as well as marketing and distribution channels. Access to bank loans, wholesale purchasing of many commodities, and the sale of industrial products, for example, all required collaboration with state agents.

Official toleration for national capitalism proved to be short-lived. In 1951, the CCP launched the Three-Antis political campaign to purge the government of corruption, waste, and bureaucratic tendencies. These "three

1. Cited in Meisner 1986, 67–68.
2. Cited in Malik 1997, 28.
3. Cited in Meisner 1986, 92–93.

evils" were attributed to urban cadres who used their authority in economic and financial departments for personal profit, often in the course of dealing with private entrepreneurs. The Three-Antis campaign merged into the Five-Antis campaign in 1952, which targeted the national bourgeoisie for a variety of economic crimes, including evading taxes, bribing government workers, stealing state property, cheating on government contracts, and stealing state economic secrets. In the course of these political campaigns, both cadres and capitalists were publicly humiliated through mass trials and psychologically terrorized through forced confessions. As Willy Kraus (1991) explains, "The [Five–Antis] campaign generally employed all the available means of mass communications: live reports by local radio stations, loudspeakers on every street corner, wall newspapers and caricatures on the misconduct and crimes of businessmen" (52). Although a relatively modest proportion of cadres were formally purged, the Five-Antis campaign led to the investigation of over 450,000 private businesses (Meisner 1986, 96). The businesses were then categorized according to whether they were law abiding, generally law abiding, partially law abiding, seriously criminal, or completely criminal. Individuals falling into the negative classifications were punished, respectively, by fines, confiscation of property, imprisonment, thought reform in labor camps, and capital punishment (Barnett 1964, 140). Most of the accused business owners were either fined or sent to labor in thought-reform camps, though quite a number were driven to suicide.[4]

The largest private corporations were then converted into joint private-state enterprises. In most cases, the previous owners were given lower-level managerial positions in the joint private-state enterprises, while the state took a controlling interest in the enterprises and compensated the previous shareholders with a small fraction of the dividends. The ideological rationale for joint private-state enterprises was that the national bourgeoisie would continue to contribute to state capitalism, which was considered the initial stage of transition to socialism. But the net effect of the political campaigns and policies of the early 1950s was a dramatic contraction in the scope of the private sector in the economy. For instance, while private operations accounted for 76.1 percent of wholesale trade in 1950, by 1953 their share had shrunk to 30.3 percent. Over the same three-year period, the private sector's share of retail trade declined from 85 to 49.9 percent (Kraus 1991, 54).

By 1953, Beijing declared that the basic tasks of economic revitalization were completed, and thus launched the next stage of socialist construction

---

4. Based on refugee accounts, Chow Ching-wen estimates that more than two hundred thousand people committed suicide during the Three and Five Antis campaigns. See Chow 1960, 133.

based on Soviet-style national economic planning. During the First Five-Year Plan (1953–57), the party-state took an increasingly dominant role in the economy. As part of the "high tide of socialist transformation," joint private-state enterprises were essentially nationalized, private retailers were merged into cooperative teams, and private markets in rural areas were banned (Solinger 1984, 168–192). In practice, private income-generating activities were never completely eliminated and were even revived slightly during the early 1960s in the aftermath of the disastrous Great Leap Forward. Nonetheless, especially during the political turmoil of the Cultural Revolution when petty traders became targets of class struggle and were condemned as the "rat tail of capitalism," the private sector became and remained a marginal part of the Chinese economy for the rest of the Mao era.

The Paradoxes of Private Sector Development during the Reform Era

Reform-era studies by Western scholars have reached varied conclusions about the coping strategies of China's business owners, their relationship to the state, and their impact on legal institutional development. Specifically,

Another busy day for *getihu* in a county seat

existing works have pointed to the illegitimate character of private enterprise during the early reform years; the efforts by larger private business owners to disguise their operations as collective enterprises; the mutually dependent relationship between local entrepreneurs and officials; the corporatist absorption of private entrepreneurs by state-sanctioned mass associations; and the rationalizing influence of marketization and foreign investment on business law and practices. Taken together, these wide-ranging observations suggest that China's private entrepreneurs barely represent, in Marxist terms, "a class in itself," much less "a class for itself" prepared to mobilize politically.[5] In other words, thus far evidence is limited for the expectation of structural theories that China's private entrepreneurs might engage in collective action in defense of their material interests.

The fragmented and relatively quiescent character of the so-called capitalist class becomes less surprising when we take into account the fact that China's policy environment has become increasingly favorable toward the private sector over time, while the country's most important formal institutions—namely, the CCP and the PRC Constitution—have undergone major changes that encourage private sector development. Yet rapid private sector growth has preceded many of the policy and institutional reforms that created more hospitable conditions for private profit. How can these phenomena be explained when entrepreneurs themselves have not lobbied directly for such institutional changes?[6]

As historical institutionalists and scholars of American political development have pointed out, most institutions do not exist in isolation from one another. Instead, instances of "institutional coupling" may be observed among clusters of institutions that are mutually dependent (Pierson 2004, 162–164). The policy and institutional reforms relating to private sector development in China should be viewed in this light. Certain changes in formal institutions may be traced to particular informal practices and adaptive informal institutions. The resulting changes in formal institutions then facilitate complementary adjustments in other formal institutions. Specifically, the empirical cases discussed below show how informal practices at the ground level paved the way for legalization of the private sector, which attracted the participation of party members in entrepreneurial activities. The rise of "red capitalists" then influenced the formal incorporation of capitalists into the CCP. In turn, the preceding adaptive informal

5. In *The Eighteenth Brumaire of Louis Bonaparte*, Marx (1926 [1852]) argued that peasants in nineteenth-century France represented "a class of itself" but not a class that acted "for itself."

6. Business owners have lobbied various bureaucracies for sector-specific concerns in technical areas (e.g., to establish price controls and industry standards), but they have not lobbied the CCP or legislative bodies for changes in the broader public policy environment. See Kennedy 2005.

institutions enabled reform-oriented elites to justify revisions to the PRC Constitution that recognize the existence and contribution of the private economy.

Marginalized Capitalists

As with most of China's economic reforms, policies governing the private sector have evolved in an experimental, incremental, and sometimes contradictory manner; moreover, official policies often trail practices at the ground level. Although the Fifth National People's Congress adopted a constitutional amendment in March 1978 that allowed for "individual laborers" to operate "within the limits permitted by law," the State Council did not formally sanction the revival of the private sector until July 1981 when it issued regulations on the urban nonagricultural individual economy (Young 1995, 16–17).[7] Supported by both Deng Xiaoping and Politburo Standing Committee member Chen Yun, the limited revival of private sector activity had two main purposes: first, to improve economic performance as smaller firms took on the microlevel functions of small-scale production and distribution; and second, to increase employment opportunities, especially for the millions of urban youths who had returned to cities after spending the Cultural Revolution in the countryside.[8] Regulations governing rural individual businesses were then passed in February 1984, but it was not until 1988 that the National People's Congress approved the establishment of "private enterprises" (*siying qiye*) with more than eight employees.[9] Widening the scope of the private sector was ideologically justified by what became known as the theory of the "initial stage of socialism," formally articulated by Premier Zhao Ziyang at the Thirteenth Party Congress in 1987.[10] The logic was that China needed to develop its productive forces at the present time; hence the individual economy would be permitted to facilitate the process until the socialist economy was efficient enough to replace the individual economy. As Susan Young (1995) observed:

7. Cf. Gold 1989.

8. Young 1995, 15. Although Chen Yun is best known for his conservative views on reform and for preserving the planned economy, even in the early 1960s he supported a circumscribed role for private enterprise. On Chen Yun's support for private sector development in Zhejiang Province during the 1980s, see Huang 2005.

9. In *Das Kapital* Marx (1959 [1867]) distinguished between nonexploitive household producing units (with fewer than eight employees) and exploitative capitalist producers (with more than eight employees).

10. The theory of the initial stage of socialism was first debated at a conference on ownership hosted by the Chinese Academy of Social Sciences in April 1981 (Young 1995, 30, nt. 15).

This was a very hard argument for those who opposed the individual economy as a source of capitalist regeneration to refute, as it accepted the assertion that socialized large-scale production was not just the inevitable trend as the productive forces became more developed, but superior to the individual economy. As the productive forces became more developed, socialist enterprises would simply outcompete individual businesses, which would disappear entirely with the arrival of communism.

However, even the combination of ideological rhetoric, economic practicality, and formal legislation governing the private sector has not insulated it from broader shifts in the political environment (Kraus 1991; Young 1989). Particularly during the 1980s, the periodic political campaigns against spiritual pollution (1983–84), bourgeois liberalization (1987), tax evasion, and corruption challenged the legitimacy of private enterprise to varying degrees. Street peddlers, vegetable vendors, and everyday mom-and-pop shops represented readily visible targets for harassment by cadres and tax and fee collectors.

Most accounts of the private sector during the first decade of reform thus focused on the relative marginalization and criminal appearance of petty traders in society (Chan and Unger 1982; Gold 1989; Hershkovitz 1985; Solinger 1984). The earliest generation of individual entrepreneurs (*getihu*) generally lacked alternative, legitimate employment options. They included peasants who had abandoned collective farming before decollectivization was officially sanctioned, unemployed adolescents and intellectuals who had recently returned to urban areas after spending the Cultural Revolution in the countryside, former (political) prisoners, underage retirees, and other types of otherwise idle people who were not fortunate enough to be gainfully employed by the state (Gold 1990). The political and social stigma associated with individual entrepreneurs partly was due to the fact that they (re)emerged well before Beijing had confirmed that private income-generating activities would be permitted. Individual entrepreneurs (with fewer than eight employees) and, to a lesser extent, larger private businesses were already active in a number of areas as early as 1976. For example, as people returned in large numbers from the countryside to Tianjin from 1976 to 1978, the number of private firms increased significantly (Yudkin 1986, 22).[11] During the same period, Ezra Vogel (1989, 313–337) observed a wide range of entrepreneurial activity by local officials, merchants trading with Hong Kong, and petty entrepreneurs in Guangdong.

In the course of my fieldwork, I found that individual entrepreneurs from Wenzhou—a southern coastal municipality in Zhejiang Province—entered

---

11. Cited in Young 1995, 14.

the private sector even earlier, that is, during the 1960s. The owner of a sock factory in Hengtang Village, Bishan Township, Rui'an County, for example, explained that he had no choice but to work for himself from an early age (Interview 113).[12] He was born in 1948 into a family that was classified as a "rich peasant"; his life started out and remained difficult until the reform era. He graduated from elementary school in 1961 when the Great Leap Forward had just ended and his family was struggling to feed his five younger siblings. Because his bad class background prevented him from going on to junior high, at thirteen he started peddling for a living. At first he made homemade candy and went around hauling two buckets of candy balanced on a pole that he carried on his shoulders. He would exchange the candy for scraps of cloth. Then he would take the scraps of cloth and sell them to families who apparently did something else with them.

At the beginning of the Cultural Revolution, he started studying how to make "liberation shoes," that is, cloth shoes that were popularly called "morning-to-evening shoes" (*chunhunxie*) because they were so poorly made that one would put them on in the morning and they would be in shreds by nighttime. In 1980, he started producing liberation shoes himself. To help him start up the business, his family sold two pigs for 100 RMB ($66.66) and he borrowed 200 RMB at 6 percent monthly interest from a loan shark.[13] It cost him eight *mao* ($0.53) to produce one pair of shoes, and he would sell them for one RMB ($0.66). That is how he saved up enough money to run other businesses, by making two *mao* ($0.13) per shoe sale. When I interviewed him in 2001, he was running a sock factory registered as an "individual entrepreneur" (*getihu*), even though the factory employed sixty people, many more than the eight-employee limit for individual households. He explained that he did not want to "show off" by registering as a private enterprise. Even though he lives comfortably now, he will never forget that he started out as an unregistered *getihu* in 1962.

Other entrepreneurs in the Wenzhou area did not become active until the Cultural Revolution. An example of this is a business owner from Jinxiang County, who recounted that in 1971, when he was a teenager, he was sent to work in the northeastern province of Heilongjiang (Interview 121). Shortly after arriving, he and eight other sent-down youths from Jinxiang pooled their limited funds, two RMB ($1.08) each, to start a business that made handles for coal shovels with wood purchased from the Bureau of Forestry. In 1973, the head of the Revolutionary Committee (*geweihui*) ordered the entrepreneurial youths to stop their capitalist activities. They scaled back on the operation, but by then he had already saved up about

12. See appendix B for list of interviews.
13. RMB to USD exchange rates over the period of 1975 to 2005 are listed in the front of the book.

6,000 RMB ($3,226), which was vastly higher than a state worker's average annual salary. When he returned to Jinxiang in 1979, he used this savings to start an aluminum factory to supply the private pin and badges factories that had become popular in his absence. Local officials assumed that he must have engaged in some type of criminal activity to accumulate so much capital, and treated him accordingly. Enduring such negative stereotypes, coupled with abusive treatment by local bureaucrats, was simply part of being an individual entrepreneur in those early years.

Disguised Capitalists

Further evidence of the political inconvenience of operating a private business was the popular strategy of "wearing a red hat" (*dai hongmaozi*), whereby larger private enterprises registered themselves as "collective enterprises." A related disguise was paying a state-owned public enterprise for use of its name in running a private business; those were called hang-on enterprises (*guahu qiye*) because they registered as appendages of established government operations. Red hat operations emerged as an adaptive informal institution during the first decade of economic reform when private enterprises with more than eight employees (*siying qiye*) were not legally permitted. Therefore, until 1988, China's private sector technically consisted of only "individual households" (*getihu*) with fewer than eight employees. Yet, in reality, many of the collective enterprises were larger private businesses wearing red hats (Naughton 1994). One entrepreneur that I interviewed in Huizhou, Guangdong Province, for instance, explained that he was able to open a sizable piglet store as early as 1978 because he ran it under the auspices of the local township's communal supply shop (Interview 191). Another entrepreneur in Nanjing, Jiangsu Province, proudly explained that in 1982 she was able to run a large and lucrative clothing business as a collective enterprise, while running the same business as a private one would have been "impossible" (Interview 166).

By the time that private enterprises were permitted, an estimated half a million businesses were already using the red hat disguise.[14] And in certain localities, it was commonly known that between 90 and 95 percent of registered collective enterprises wore red hats (Parris 1993). Operating within the collective sector offered de facto private entrepreneurs many material advantages, including favorable tax treatment and preferential access to bank credit (Goodman 1995, 12; Naughton 1994; Nee 1992). Government officials now openly acknowledge that the so-called collective sector includes

14. Furthermore, in 1988 the Industrial and Commercial Management Bureau estimated that 115,000 registered *getihu* already had more than eight employees. Young 1995, 112.

everything from quasi-public township village enterprises (TVEs) to truly privately owned businesses.[15]

An example of the mutually beneficial nature of some red hat arrangements is the case of owner Hua who began weaving cloth in a rural township of Jinjiang, Fujian Province, in 1982 (Interview 190). When he first started, he was able to earn an average of 1.4 RMB ($0.74)/day, but soon he began running clothes-making classes for women in the area, which brought in 1,500 RMB ($794)/month. By 1983 he had accumulated sufficient capital to build a garment factory and employ the five hundred or so women that he had trained. Owner Hua registered the factory as a collective TVE even though he was the sole investor and manager. The TVE office at the township level was pleased with the situation because the factory was able to use its assets to guarantee loans from the local rural credit cooperative—not only for the garment factory but also for the township government. As owner Hua explained, "If my factory was not so successful, the township government would have had difficulty securing loans from the local credit cooperative. But if I had been registered as a private enterprise rather than a collective one, then I could not have operated such a large factory back then, and the credit cooperative would not have been willing to lend to a private enterprise."

Although the 1988 regulations allowed businesses with more than eight employees to be registered as "private enterprises" (*siying qiye*), it was only after the politically rooted economic downturn of 1989–92 following the Tiananmen Square crisis that red hats started to come off. In particular, Deng Xiaoping's tour of the southern coastal provinces in early 1992 signaled central approval for continued economic liberalization. The subsequent boom in private sector growth was reflected in official statistics. Between 1990 and 2000, the average annual growth rate in the number of registered private businesses was 10.3 percent; the number of people employed in the private sector grew at an average annual rate of 15.9 percent; their registered capitalization grew at 45.8 percent; their value added to the GDP grew at 58.7 percent; and their volume of retail sales grew at a rate of 56.5 percent.[16] By 2006, the private sector accounted for nearly half of China's GDP and over two-thirds of industrial output. In the interim, a network of formal institutions governing the private sector, namely, the Industrial and Commercial Management Bureau (ICMB), had developed throughout the country. Tables 3.1, 3.2, and 3.3 present the growth of registered private businesses, their capitalization, and number of employees.

15. For example, see Li 1997.
16. *Zhongguo tongji nianjian* (China statistical yearbook), various years.

Table 3.1. Growth of registered private businesses, 1978–2005 [numbers of businesses]

Year	Getihu	Growth (%)	PEs	PE Growth (%)	Total number	Total growth (%)
1978	300,000	n.a.	n.a.	n.a.	300,000	n.a.
1979	560,000	86.7	n.a.	n.a.	560,000	86.7
1980	897,000	60.2	n.a.	n.a.	897,000	60.2
1981	1,827,752	103.8	n.a.	n.a.	1,827,752	103.8
1982	2,614,006	43.0	n.a.	n.a.	2,614,006	43.0
1983	5,901,032	125.7	n.a.	n.a.	5,901,032	125.7
1984	9,329,464	58.1	n.a.	n.a.	9,329,464	58.1
1985	11,712,560	25.5	n.a.	n.a.	11,712,560	25.5
1986	12,111,560	3.4	n.a.	n.a.	12,111,560	3.4
1987	13,725,746	13.3	n.a.	n.a.	13,725,746	13.3
1988	14,526,931	5.8	n.a.	n.a.	14,526,931	5.8
1989	12,471,937	−14.1	90,581	n.a.	12,562,518	−13.5
1990	13,281,974	6.5	98,141	8.3	13,380,115	6.5
1991	14,145,000	6.5	107,843	9.9	14,252,843	6.5
1992	15,339,200	8.4	139,633	29.5	15,478,833	8.6
1993	17,670,000	15.2	237,919	70.4	17,907,919	15.7
1994	21,870,000	23.8	432,240	81.7	22,302,240	24.5
1995	25,280,000	15.6	654,531	51.4	25,934,531	16.3
1996	27,040,000	7.0	819,252	25.2	27,859,252	7.4
1997	28,510,000	5.4	960,726	17.3	29,470,726	5.8
1998	31,200,000	9.4	1,200,978	25.0	32,400,978	9.9
1999	31,600,000	1.3	1,508,857	25.6	33,108,857	2.2
2000	26,710,000	−18.3	1,761,769	17.0	28,741,769	−14.0
2001	24,330,000	−5.8	2,028,548	15.0	26,358,548	−0.08
2002	23,770,000	−2.3	2,435,282	20.0	26,205,282	−0.01
2003	23,531,857	−10.0	3,005,524	23.4	26,537,381	1.3
2004	23,505,000	−0.1	3,651,000	21.5	27,156,000	2.3
2005	24,638,934	4.8	4,300,916	17.8	28,940,916	6.6

Source: Zhang, Ming, and Liang, eds., *Siying qiye lanpi shu: Zhongguo siying qiye fazhan baogao* [Blue book of private enterprises: A report on the development of China's private enterprises], various years.

Note: *Getihu* refers to individual businesses with less than eight employees, while "PEs" refer to private enterprises (*siying qiye*) with more than eight employees.

On the most superficial level, it is tempting to attribute China's remarkable private sector development to official policies and institutions regulating the nonstate economy. However, China's formal institutions have presented local state and economic actors with more of a constraining rather than a permissive environment for private capital accumulation. The center's gradualistic approach to reform has reflected not only a pragmatic experimental attitude toward the economy but also a series of compromises as a result of elite-level disagreement about the desirability of private enterprise (Baum 1994; Naughton 1994; Young 1995). Amid the inevitable

Table 3.2. Registered capitalization of private businesses, 1990–2005 [*yi* or 100 million RMB]

Year	*Getihu*	Growth (%)	PEs	Growth (%)	Total	Growth (%)
1989	347	n.a.	n.a.	n.a.	347	n.a.
1990	397	14.4	95	n.a.	492	41.8
1991	488	22.9	123	29.5	611	24.2
1992	601	23.2	221	79.7	822	34.5
1993	855	42.3	681	208.1	1,536	86.9
1994	1,319	54.3	1,448	112.6	2,767	80.1
1995	1,813	37.5	2,622	81.1	4,435	60.3
1996	2,165	19.4	3,752	43.1	5,917	33.4
1997	2,573	18.8	5,140	37.0	7,713	30.4
1998	3,120	21.3	7,198	40.0	10,318	33.8
1999	3,439	10.2	10,287	42.9	13,726	33.0
2000	3,315	−3.6	13,308	29.0	16,623	21.0
2001	3,436	3.7	18,212	37.0	21,648	30.0
2002	3,782	10.1	24,756	36.0	28,538	32.0
2003	4,190	10.8	37,655	52.1	41,845	46.6
2004	5,058	20.7	49,936	32.6	54,994	31.4
2005	5,809	14.8	61,331	22.8	67,140	22.1

Source: Zhang, Ming, and Liang, eds., *Siying qiye lanpi shu: Zhongguo siying qiye fazhan baogao* [Blue book of private enterprises: A report on the development of China's private enterprises], various years.

Note: *Getihu* refers to individual businesses with less than eight employees, while "PEs" refer to private enterprises (*siying qiye*) with more than eight employees.

ambiguities arising from such a policy environment, local actors have exercised agency in manipulating the resulting formal institutions to their advantage.

Private businesses have been systematically denied access to loans from state banks, prohibited from conducting business in several sectors (e.g., banking, financial services, tobacco, petroleum and chemicals, telecommunications, rail and civil air transportation), and subjected to higher rates of taxation than collective and foreign businesses. Besides these operational challenges, throughout the 1980s and most of the 1990s private entrepreneurs experienced social discrimination for being profit oriented, as well as political persecution. There was considerable political uncertainty about the trajectory of economic reform, and private entrepreneurs were publicly criticized during the national campaigns against spiritual pollution and bourgeois liberalization. At the local level, entrepreneurs were subjected to arbitrary treatment by tax collectors and other bureaucrats. In contrast, state and collective enterprises received favorable treatment relative to private ones in tax breaks, bank loans, and use of land. Those were the operating realities that business owners faced beneath the impressive statistics.

Table 3.3. Number employed in the private sector, 1978–2005

Year	Getihu	Growth (%)	PE's	Growth (%)	Total	Growth (%)
1978	334,000	n.a.	n.a.	n.a.	334,000	n.a.
1979	676,000	102.4	n.a.	n.a.	676,000	102.4
1980	1,658,000	145.3	n.a.	n.a.	1,658,000	145.3
1981	2,274,000	37.2	n.a.	n.a.	2,274,000	37.2
1982	3,200,000	40.7	n.a.	n.a.	3,200,000	40.7
1983	7,464,400	133.3	n.a.	n.a.	7,464,400	133.3
1984	13,510,000	81.0	n.a.	n.a.	13,510,000	81.0
1985	18,323,000	35.6	n.a.	n.a.	18,323,000	35.6
1986	19,214,000	4.9	n.a.	n.a.	19,214,000	4.9
1987	21,483,000	11.8	n.a.	n.a.	21,483,000	11.8
1988	23,050,000	7.3	n.a.	n.a.	23,050,000	7.3
1989	19,414,405	−15.8	n.a.	n.a.	19,414,405	−15.8
1990	20,930,000	7.8	1,700,000	n.a.	22,630,000	16.6
1991	22,580,000	7.9	1,840,000	8.2	24,420,000	7.9
1992	24,680,000	9.3	2,320,000	26.1	27,000,000	10.6
1993	29,390,000	19.1	3,730,000	60.8	33,120,000	22.7
1994	37,760,000	28.5	6,480,000	73.7	44,240,000	33.6
1995	46,140,000	22.2	9,560,000	47.5	55,700,000	25.9
1996	50,170,000	8.7	11,710,000	22.5	61,880,000	11.1
1997	54,420,000	8.5	13,500,000	15.3	67,920,000	9.8
1998	61,140,000	12.3	17,100,000	26.7	78,240,000	15.2
1999	62,410,000	2.1	20,220,000	18.2	82,630,000	5.6
2000	50,700,000	−18.8	24,060,000	19.0	74,765,000	−9.5
2001	47,600,000	−6.1	27,138,644	12.8	74,741,000	−0.0
2002	47,430,000	−0.4	34,093,018	25.6	81,523,018	0.9
2003	46,365,418	−2.2	35,957,684	5.5	82,323,102	1.0
2004	45,871,081	−1.1	40,686,225	13.1	86,557,306	5.1
2005	49,005,412	6.8	47,141,312	15.9	96,146,724	11.1

Source: Zhang, Ming, and Liang, eds., *Siying qiye lanpi shu: Zhongguo siying qiye fazhan baogao* [Blue book of private enterprises: A report on the development of China's private enterprises], various years.

Note: *Getihu* refers to individual businesses with less than eight employees, while "PEs" refer to private enterprises (*siying qiye*) with more than eight employees.

Why, then, were entrepreneurs willing to enter and stay in business? Some simply lacked alternative income-generating options. But others persisted in the private sector—despite having other occupational opportunities and despite all the disincentives associated with running a private business—because they were able to ameliorate many operational disadvantages. In particular, many business owners disguised themselves as managers of collective firms. As suggested above, one way for entrepreneurs to avoid social and political ostracism was to wear a red hat, which became one of the most popular adaptive informal institutions in China's nonstate sector. This adaptive strategy was so widespread that "wearing a red hat" became (and remains) a common term in everyday discourse. The practice became institutionalized as a standard, albeit informal, operating practice for private entrepreneurs.[17] Yet the process through which this occurred was not simply one of entrepreneurs deceiving local bureaucrats; instead, the actions of agents were collaborative and reflexively strategic. Most local cadres knew exactly what they were doing when they accepted, or perhaps extracted, a registration fee from a local entrepreneur to run a collective enterprise. Because of fiscal decentralization and the hardening of local budget constraints, cadres in many rural localities had a vested interest in allowing profitable businesses to operate and contribute to local revenues regardless of their true ownership status.

A number of scholars have also observed such clientelistic dynamics between private entrepreneurs and political cadres.[18] While smaller-scale entrepreneurs tend to suffer more from predatory behavior from state actors,[19] David Wank (1999) points out that owners of larger businesses and cadres are more likely to be mutually dependent in a relationship of "symbiotic clientelism."[20] In other words, private entrepreneurs benefit from bureaucratic protection and favors, while cadres benefit materially (or otherwise) from providing such services. Regardless of whether these relationships are defined as a form of corruption (Manion 1996) or rationalized more innocuously as a practical means to reduce transaction costs in a transitional economy (cf. Zhou, Li, Zhao, and Cai 2003), it is clear that strong ties often exist between cadres and entrepreneurs. In short, hundreds of thousands of both state and nonstate actors were complicit agents in popularizing the red hat phenomenon. Meanwhile, China's collective sector flourished and represented the basis of rapid rural industrialization (Byrd and Lin 1990; Oi 1999).

In the spirit of Deng Xiaoping's dictum to focus on practical results rather than ideology, when central-level elites realized that so many collectives were really private enterprises, it was futile—and indeed, impractical—to insist that the scale of the private sector be limited to household producing units with fewer than eight employees. Although conservative or "leftist" political elites would have preferred to restrict the nonstate sector, both the popularity and the economic effectiveness of wearing a red hat gave reformers concrete evidence and, thus, political support for expanding the scope of China's nascent private economy. Influential scholars, such as Yu Guangyuan and Xue Muqiao from the Chinese Academy of

17. On local variation in the use of red hat strategies and development of private property rights, see Oi and Walder 1999; Whiting 2001.

18. Nee, however, expects increasing marketization of the economy to reduce entrepreneurs' dependence on cadres for resources. For further detail, see Nee 1991.

19. To put it differently, smaller businesses may find themselves in a position of "dependent clientelism" in relation to cadres. See Oi 1985; Walder 1986.

20. Cf. Dickson 2002 and Solinger 1992.

Social Sciences, drew on their observations of local empirical realities to help reformist leaders develop consensus about the appropriate next steps in China's reform process. During a pivotal academic and policy meeting held in Beijing in 1986, they reasoned that since China was still in the initial stage of socialism, first, it would be impossible to avoid private sector development; second, the advantages of developing the private economy would outweigh the disadvantages; and third, under a socialist system the private sector could still be subject to state guidance and control.[21]

Broad-based agreement on these key points about China's "initial stage of socialism" paved the way for shifts in the official guiding principles and policies of the party-state. On the party side, at the Thirteenth National Congress of the CCP in 1987, Premier Zhao Ziyang announced, "Cooperative, individual and private sectors of the economy in both urban and rural areas should all be encouraged to expand. . . . We must formulate policies and enact laws governing the private sector as soon as possible, in order to protect its legitimate interest."[22] Following the party's lead, on the state side the National People's Congress passed a constitutional amendment accepting Zhao's proposal in April 1988, and two months later the PRC State Council issued regulations governing "private enterprises" with eight or more employees. In an acknowledgment that these regulations were really posthoc sanctioning of ground-level realities, official publications disclosed that by then China already had 225,000 private enterprises employing 3.6 million employees with an average of sixteen employees per business—that is, twice the number of workers that individual private businesses were permitted to employ.[23]

In sum, the practice of wearing a red hat is an example of how an adaptive informal institution contributed to the institutional conversion of a formal regulation, the collective registration status. Camouflaging the true ownership structure of a business rendered the formal distinction in nomenclature between collective and private enterprises virtually meaningless. By the same token, as an adaptive informal institution the red hat practice also became an increasingly prominent institutional layer in China's once-limited field of corporate organizational types. Instead of displacing the collective sector, red hat enterprises represented an additional form of collective enterprise; this innovative layer not only expanded the institutional space for private businesses to operate in but also created a politically acceptable rationale for devising a more transparent registration status for larger private enterprises. In this case, the impetus for institutional change stemmed from two strains of "structural friction" in China's political economy: first, there

21. Correspondence with Interviewee 148, November 19, 2006.
22. *Beijing Review*, November 9–15, 1987, cited in Malik 1997, 15.
23. *Beijing Review*, July 18–24, 1988, 6, cited in ibid.

Department store for upwardly mobile consumers in Huizhou, Guangdong Province

was tension between preexisting institutions that privileged the collective sector and policies that sanctioned limited development of the private sector; and second, there was an inconsistency between fiscal reforms that enabled rural localities to retain more revenues and national restrictions on larger private enterprises. Both state and economic actors coped with these institutional incongruencies by popularizing the adaptive informal institution of wearing a red hat. The economic success and widespread use of this adaptive informal institution then provided reformers with the requisite evidence that expanding the scope of the private sector would enhance China's productive forces during the initial stage of socialism. As we will see below, ultimately the adaptive informal institution of wearing a red hat not only influenced the legalization of private enterprises with more than eight employees but also provided the basis for subsequent institutional changes in the CCP and state constitution.

Rationalizing Capitalists

Despite the prevalence of clientelistic relationships between local officials and business owners, some scholars have hypothesized that, in aggregate, the pursuit of private profit promotes more rationalized governing and economic institutions, if not democratization. In particular, Victor Nee

(1989) has suggested that increasing marketization and private sector development will foster a "legal-rational institutional environment," that is, a regulatory state that is not captured by particularistic interests.[24] Doug Guthrie's (1999) research in Shanghai found that interaction between foreign and Chinese firms increased the use of meritocratic hiring and promotion practices and enhanced respect for the rule of law.[25] However, while acknowledging that business elites in the foreign-invested sector are more technocratic than those in strictly Chinese enterprises, Margaret Pearson (1997, 2002) cautions against assuming that foreign sector entrepreneurs may provide the basis for a democratic transition: "Most entrepreneurs in the foreign sector wish to be free of politics, wish for the freedom to be apolitical. This translates not into activism but, rather, into passivity" (Pearson 2002, 146–147). In other words, increased reliance on the rule of law should not be equated with political preference for a particular regime type such as democracy.

Incorporated and Red Capitalists

Although the first generation of reform-era individual entrepreneurs was marginalized and the larger private entrepreneurs tended to be disguised, the political incorporation of business owners represents a countervailing trend in terms of the relationship between the party-state and private capital. Instead of a confrontational or oppositional relationship, some scholars have emphasized that entrepreneurs are tied to the state through a system of state corporatist trade organizations.[26] To preempt private entrepreneurs from articulating their interests autonomously, the party-state has reestablished mass associations as representative bodies. The All-China Federation of Industry and Commerce (ACFIC)—originally established in 1953, but inactive during the Cultural Revolution—was revived in 1977.[27] Local branches of the Individual Laborers Association (ILA) began appearing in 1980, and an umbrella national-level ILA was inaugurated in 1986. Local branches of the Private Entrepreneurs Association (PEA) were established in 1988.

The extent to which these mass associations truly serve the interests of their members varies and depends on the background of individual entrepreneurs, their ties to local elites, and locality. Membership and dues are often compulsory. In many localities, businesses registered with the local

24. Of course, the development of a bureaucratic-rational regulatory state does necessarily entail popular political participation.

25. Cf. Rosen 1999; Santoro 2000.

26. See Schmitter 1974 on the distinction between state and societal corporatism.

27. The CCP's United Front department originally established ACFIC to represent former capitalists. For its 1953–1993 historical record, see Li and Ye 1993.

Industrial and Commercial Management Bureau—the state agency charged with regulating private enterprises—are automatically registered with the local ILA or PEA as well. The offices of the ICMB and ILA/PEA are frequently adjacent to one another in local government complexes, and three quarters of the ILA's budget comes from the ICMB. Given the compulsory membership requirement and the close relationship between the ICMB and ILA/PEA, many entrepreneurs do not find the official associations especially helpful and instead use alternative channels to address their pressing concerns (Foster 2002).[28] Some studies, however, have found that the ILA/PEA or FIC (local branches of the ACFIC, or *gongshanglian*) do serve as state corporatist institutions that represent and protect the interests of their members.[29] Private entrepreneurs may pressure the ICMB to serve their corporate interests (Chan and Unger 1995; Kennedy 2005). Larger-scale entrepreneurs and those who are well connected politically are more likely to have a favorable opinion of the official associations, but, even then, many entrepreneurs have a preference for autonomous business associations.

Besides the strategic incorporation of private entrepreneurs by state-sponsored organizations, some party-state cadres have used their privileged political status to run businesses indirectly or help others run red hat operations. In fact, some cadres are also private entrepreneurs, and some business owners instrumentally pursued party membership even before capitalists were formally permitted to join the party. As Solinger (1992) observed in the early 1990s, "Those most firmly ensconced within the party hierarchy—those with the richest network of cronies—should be best placed to take advantage of the opportunities today's distorted market can offer" (129). Such politically advantaged entrepreneurs are popularly called "cadre entrepreneurs" and "red capitalists" (Dickson 2000, 526; 2003). Even though CCP members were not allowed to operate private businesses, it was apparent throughout the 1980s and 1990s that many were active participants in the nonstate sector.[30] Indeed, official surveys reveal an increasing proportion of self-identified CCP members among private entrepreneurs over time, such that 7 percent of business owners admitted to being party members in 1991 and over one-third of private entrepreneurs identified themselves as party members in 2003 (see table 3.4). It is reasonable to assume that official figures underestimate the true proportion of party members in the private sector due to the politico-ideological sensitivity concerning the appropriate relationship between the CCP and "market socialism with Chinese characteristics." In other words, for many years, the uneasy coexistence

28. Ole Bruun's study (1988) of small businesses in the city of Chengdu also found the local ICMB and ILA to be more extractive than representative of individual entrepreneurs.

29. Nevitt 1996; Pearson 1997, 122–131; Unger 1996; Young 1995, 129–130.

30. The nonstate sector includes collective and private enterprises.

Table 3.4. Political background of private entrepreneurs

Political membership	1991	1993	1995	1997–98	2000	2002	2003
Chinese Communist Party (%)	7.0	13.1	17.1	18.1	19.8	30.2	33.9
Youth League (%)	16.7	7.4	4.5	n.a.	n.a.	n.a.	n.a.
Nonparty members (%)	76.3	79.5	78.4	81.9	80.2	69.8	66.1
Total (%)	100	100	100	100	100	100	100

Sources: China Economic System Reform Committee and National Bureau of Industrial and Commercial Management, *Survey of the Individual and Private Economy 1991. Investigation of Private Enterprises 1993*–data sets from Universities Service Center, Chinese University of Hong Kong; *Zhongguo siying jingji nianjian* [China private economy yearbook], various years; and Zhang, Ming, and Liang, eds., *Siying qiye lanpi shu: Zhongguo siying qiye fazhan baogao* [Blue book of private enterprises: A report on the development of China's private enterprises], *Zhongguo siying qiye fazhan baogao*, 2004.

or "friction" between China's official socialist ideology and the reality of private sector development accounts for the simultaneous growth of business owners among party members and the underreporting of party members in official surveys of private entrepreneurs.

Somewhat counterintuitively, however, when one conducts interviews that are hosted by local officials and bureaucrats, party members are generally overrepresented in the population of officially arranged interviews. During the course of my field research, I found that the easiest way to meet red capitalists was to ask local hosts to select a couple of private businesses for me to interview. In contrast, when businesses were sampled randomly or when I conducted interviews on my own, cadre entrepreneurs were far less prevalent. The reason for the higher occurrence of party members in officially organized interviews is because most local officials are party members and when requested to set up meetings with private entrepreneurs, most of their personal contacts are also party members, that is, red capitalists who interact with local political elites on a regular basis. A typical example of the latter is owner Gong who was introduced to me by a vice general secretary in the Langfang City People's Government in Hebei Province (Interview 153). In 2002, Gong was a forty-seven-year-old red capitalist who was considered well educated because he had a bachelor's degree from the local party school. He worked in a state-owned enterprise for a number of years before joining the party and running his own red hat collective enterprise, a furniture factory, in 1991. In 1995, he decided to take off the red hat and register the factory as a private enterprise. Since then, Gong has also opened a large restaurant and a housing construction business. He clearly has a high profile in the local community. Besides his prominent commercial activities—and the fact that he has donated furniture to four elementary schools in poor villages—Gong is politically active. He is a party member, serves as a deputy in the local People's Congress (which gives him the right to vote for the mayor of Langfang City), and serves as the vice director of the Langfang Chamber of Commerce. Gong is hardly representative of the typical business owner in Langfang, but local government hosts selected him as an interviewee because he is an impressive and upstanding red capitalist. They were proud of Gong's local commercial and political stature, even if he was a cadre entrepreneur who had worn a red hat for several years. Moreover, the ease with which the government hosts were able to set up an impromptu interview suggests that Gong has comfortable working relations with local officials.

In a strategically timed effort to bridge the gap between formal rules and informal practices, on the occasion of the CCP's eightieth anniversary on July 1, 2001, General Secretary Jiang Zemin gave a landmark speech (known as the "7/1 speech") widely interpreted as inviting private entrepreneurs to join the party. The rationale was woven into Jiang Zemin's Theory of the Three Represents, which is supposed to represent the theoretical extension of Marxism-Leninism, Mao Zedong Thought, and Deng Xiaoping Theory, but actually made the controversial recommendation that the party should represent "the most advanced forces of production, the most advanced cultural forces, and the interests of the overwhelming majority of people." The CCP had launched a mass media campaign publicizing the Three Represents leading up to the anniversary, but it was the July 1 speech, followed by the Sixteenth Party Congress in late 2002, that clarified the implication of the "theory," that is, that the CCP should not discriminate against private entrepreneurs and should in fact embrace them because they are contributing (the most) to China's economic development. Official enshrinement of the Three Represents did not occur without objection. A number of the party's old guard disapproved of the sharp ideological turn that Jiang and his supporters were advocating. Even online chat rooms and message boards filled with colorful, passionately argued objections to the selling out of the CCP.[31]

It is remarkable that the CCP agreed to change—and indeed, reverse—its former ideological depiction of capitalists as exploitative "class enemies." Bruce Dickson (2003) suggests that allowing private entrepreneurs into the party was a strategic decision to incorporate a growing, and increasingly wealthy, portion of Chinese society. It was an effort to preempt autonomous political organization on the part of private business owners. Although this strategic interpretation of the party's decision makes sense for explaining regime durability, I would add that the underlying causal mechanisms leading to this decision were rooted in the growing power of the informal rules

31. For example, "Deng Liqun, Others, Criticize Jiang Zemin for Agreeing to Admit Capitalists into the CPC," originally posted on http://www.renminbao.com on July 20, 2001, translated text from FBIS-China, July 28, 2001.

of the game that had evolved over the first two decades of economic reform. Party members were already active in the private sector well before private entrepreneurs were formally permitted to join the party. But how was this possible, given that China remains an authoritarian regime dominated by a Leninist party? As discussed, the adaptive informal institution of wearing a red hat offered Communist Party members an ideologically appropriate cover for participating in for-profit activities. This, in turn, led to the adaptive practice of being a "red capitalist" (*hong zibenjia*). Because private entrepreneurs were explicitly banned from joining the party after 1989, wearing a red hat became a safer way for party members to run large businesses. And local party cadres were willing to look the other way because red capitalists often contributed more to the local economy than ordinary entrepreneurs.

By the early 2000s, the spread of red capitalists presented the party with the critical dilemma of whether to condemn their economic activities or embrace them. Of the entrepreneurs surveyed by official entities in 2000, 19.8 percent indicated that they were already CCP members (SAIC 2005). Should such a large percentage of business owners remain politically marginalized? After consulting with provincial and subprovincial officials throughout China, the party's core leadership decided that it was in the interest of continued economic growth, as well as party rejuvenation and survival, to legitimize the existing red capitalists and co-opt other private entrepreneurs.[32] Shortly after the party lifted the ban on cultivating capitalist members, a party theoretician explained, "If our Party doesn't build more branches [under the circumstances of rapid growth in the non-public economic organizations], then other social forces will attract those people. If the Party doesn't open up its organizations [to private entrepreneurs], then other organizations will hold activities for them" (Li 2005, 107). The report further highlighted the relative underrepresentation of business owners in the party: "By the end of 2002 there were 2.1 million Party members in non-public economic organizations, which accounts for only around two percent of the total membership, and over 80 percent of foreign-invested enterprises and private enterprises do not have Party members."[33]

Within a relatively short period of time, the party line shifted from banning to welcoming capitalists. Such a reversal in party policy would have been difficult to justify in the absence of preexisting grassroots deviations from the party line. Wearing a red hat enabled party members to become red capitalists, which ended up changing the occupational composition of the party from within. As employees of the party-state began running their

---

32. These consultations "took place over a period of perhaps two years." Fewsmith 2002, 3.
33. Ibid., 108.

Dates back to the Ming Dynasty: Hanzheng street market in Hankou, Wuhan Province, 2002

own businesses, albeit disguised as collective ventures, the party's ban on private entrepreneurs became increasingly unrealistic, if not anachronistic. Although Jiang Zemin is generally credited (or blamed) for allowing capitalists into the party, the decision was not the impulsive act of a dictator. The decision did not occur in a societal void, as evidenced by the series of discussions with local officials throughout the country. And at a deeper causal level, all of the informal coping strategies that both state and nonstate actors had reproduced in their daily interactions took on an institutional reality of their own, thereby challenging national leaders to adapt preexisting formal institutions to assimilate these hitherto informal practices. The cumulative effects of this dynamic can also be seen in revisions to the PRC Constitution that have become increasingly favorable toward the private sector.

Private Sector–Friendly Revisions to the PRC Constitution

Revisions to the PRC Constitution have generally lagged behind developments in actual practices. Of the various constitutional changes that have occurred since 1982, the first two revisions represent reactive formalization of local practices and realities. Meanwhile, the more recent revisions put forth ambitious objectives that were inspired by the two adaptive informal institutions discussed above—wearing a red hat and the proliferation of red capitalists.

First, in 1988 the First Session of the Seventh National People's Congress (NPC) revised a paragraph in Article 10 to permit the transfer of land-use rights. In addition, a paragraph was added to Article 11 that "permits the private sector of the economy to exist and develop within the limits prescribed by law." The paragraph also recognizes that "the private sector of the economy is a complement to the socialist economy." This paragraph provided the legal basis for allowing "private enterprises" with more than eight employees (*siying qiye*) to operate, while indicating that the private sector would still be subject to state control, as stated in the final clause of the paragraph: "The state protects the lawful rights and interests of the private sector of the economy, and exercises guidance, supervision, and control over the private sector of the economy."

Second, following the Fourteenth Chinese Communist Party Congress in late 1992, in 1993 the First Session of the Eighth National People's Congress reoriented the economic mission of the country in the preamble to acknowledge that China is "in the primary stage of socialism" and would therefore concentrate on "socialist modernization" to "build China into a strong and prosperous, culturally advanced, democratic socialist nation." (The previous version of that statement did not mention "strong" or "prosperous.") Also, in Article 15, the "state practices a planned economy on the basis of socialist public ownership" was replaced with "the state practices a socialist market economy." Despite the retention of the term "socialist," mention of the market economy marked a clear shift in the regime's definition of its economic mission. It also reinforced the message conveyed in the series of speeches that Deng Xiaoping had delivered during his tour of the southern coastal provinces in 1992—that is, that economic reform would continue despite the political crisis of 1989.

Third, in 1999 the Second Session of the Ninth NPC amended the aforementioned paragraph in Article 11 to say, "Individual, private and other non-public economies that exist within the limits prescribed by law are major components of the socialist market economy." The 1999 revisions also added a provision to Article 5 stating that "the People's Republic of China governs the country according to law and . . . [is] a socialist country ruled by law." The combination of elevating the nonstate sector to a "major component" of the economy and the introduction of the notion that the country is governed by the rule of law signaled a more legitimate and secure status for the private sector.

Fourth, in 2004 the Second Session of the Tenth NPC made the more radical revision of encouraging private sector development and protecting private property rights under the constitution. Article 11 was changed again to stipulate:

> The state protects the lawful rights and interests of the private sector of the economy, including individual and private businesses. The state encourages, supports and guides the development of the private sector, and exercises supervision and administration over the sector according to law.

And Article 13 introduced the statement that "the lawful private property of citizens shall not be encroached upon," while Article 33 added that "the state respects and protects human rights." Meanwhile, the Theory of the Three Represents was incorporated into state ideology alongside "Marxism, Leninism, Mao Zedong Thought and Deng Xiaoping Theory." As mentioned earlier, the Theory of the Three Represents is Jiang Zemin's contribution to official ideology, which makes the controversial claim that the party also represents the "most advanced forces of production," meaning private entrepreneurs. Since the Sixteenth Party Congress in 2002 had incorporated upholding the Three Represents into the CCP's mission statement, it was not surprising that the state constitution would be similarly amended.

Unlike the first two amendments discussed above, however, the constitutional stipulation that private property rights would be protected should be viewed as an objective rather than post-hoc recognition of ground-level realities. Although certain adaptive informal institutions enable economic actors to engage in contractual exchanges as if they were guaranteed by a formal legal system of private property rights (Oi and Walder 1999), the rise of serious disputes concerning asset ownership demonstrates that such arrangements are not immune from government intervention or expropriation. This is, of course, a risk that all adaptive informal institutions face, but the point here is that because the most recent constitutional revisions have more complex systemic implications for China's political economy, lags in actual implementation should be expected. Formal protection of private property rights requires strengthening the institutions that support the rule of law. As Yu An, a Tsinghua University law professor who served on the constitution's drafting committee, commented,

> Some revised articles are an acknowledgement of the current situation, while others are new stipulations. That means adjustments should be made to existing laws, or new laws should be implemented. . . . The Constitution itself can hardly regulate the particular behavior of the government and the people. Without significant adjustment of current common laws, the impact of the constitutional revision may be greatly reduced.[34]

34. Yu An cited in "Constitutional Revision Requires Law Adjustment," *China Business Weekly*, March 8, 2004.

In the interim, various adaptive informal institutions will continue to serve as self-enforcing substitutes for property rights.

Given the opacity of China's political system, it is challenging to prove with definitive data that the spread of adaptive informal institutions used by private entrepreneurs directly influenced the various constitutional amendments. Based on published sources, as well as field interviews with government officials, elite intellectuals, and private entrepreneurs, however, we may infer the plausibility of the counterfactual to my argument. That is, in the absence of the adaptive informal institutions discussed above, it is unlikely that reform-oriented elites would have found the pro–private sector constitutional amendments either desirable or feasible. Both the economic success of private businesses and the popularity of private entrepreneurship among party members offered reformers evidence (against "leftist" or conservative leaders) that enhancing the scope of the private sector would be in the country's political and economic interest. Indeed, various legal scholars were already pushing for the protection of private property rights during the drafting meetings of the 1999 constitutional revision, but their recommendations were shelved due to opposition by more conservative party members.[35] These latter elites also contested the inclusion of the Three Represents in the party constitution on ideological grounds—they questioned how a communist party could also represent the interests of capitalists (cf. Goldman 2005). Only after the party came to terms with red capitalist members in 2002 was it politically possible to revisit the earlier constitutional proposals to protect private property.

While there was still internal debate over the inclusion of protecting private property in the consultative processes leading up to the 2004 constitutional revision, by 2003 and early 2004 proponents of private property rights were able to build their case by implying that there was societal support for constitutional revision along those lines. Even though private entrepreneurs themselves never mobilized from below to lobby for constitutional protection of their assets, reformers strategically solicited input from the ACFIC, the official mass association representing private entrepreneurs. In practice, state-sponsored mass associations in Leninist systems usually serve to transmit official policy to constituent members in a state corporatist fashion, but they are also meant in principle to represent the interests of its members. As such, during the earlier rounds of constitutional revision, ACFIC was charged with convening small-scale forums with entrepreneurs throughout the country to gather their opinions about the upcoming constitutional revisions.[36] Prior to the 2004 revision, however, the official narrative of the process is that ACFIC initiated the consultative discussions

35. Lian Xisheng, former vice chair of the China Constitution Society, cited in "Amendments Protect Private Property," *China Business Weekly*, January 4, 2004.

36. Correspondence with Scott Kennedy, November 2, 2006.

with entrepreneurs and that it played an important role in advocating constitutional protection of private property.[37] In other words, reformers gave ACFIC credit for representing the voice of private entrepreneurs and pushing for the private property clause to create a stronger political case for revising the constitution along the lines that they were hoping for at least five years earlier. In reality, private entrepreneurs themselves were remarkably absent from the actual process, but the cumulative effect of their adaptive informal institutions and the changes that they engendered in formal institutions governing the private sector enabled reformers to justify further protections on their behalf. The causal mechanisms were indirect, informal, incremental, and fundamentally political.

THERE was nothing automatic or predetermined about the transformation and development of various formal institutions—economic regulatory framework, ideological justification, party membership, and constitutional protections—to support the private sector. Even though the present configuration of institutions is mutually reinforcing in various ways, the process of institutional development has been highly contested and incremental.

Yet private entrepreneurs themselves have not been active in articulating their perspectives in the debates that have occurred over the various policy and constitutional reforms. There is scant evidence to suggest that the increasingly favorable policy environment for private sector development in general has resulted from the organized political lobbying efforts of business owners. Indeed, even Scott Kennedy's *The Business of Lobbying in China* (2005) finds that "while firms regularly lobby different parts of the government bureaucracy, they far less frequently interface with Chinese Communist Party organizations on public-policy issues" (164). Certain firms may pressure business associations to provide sector-specific assistance in technical issues such as setting production standards; but due to organizational barriers, they do not make explicitly political demands on formal political institutions or attempt to change them. Individual firms lack the incentive to lobby for collective goods such as constitutional amendments because the latter affects so many firms. Moreover, the process is so formal and opaque that entrepreneurs have limited ability to influence decision-making elites.

Another reason for the limited political assertiveness of business owners—despite certain shared material interests such as the basic right to engage in profit-making activities—is that the current generation of entrepreneurs shares the collective memory of their not-so-distant political persecution by the Communist party-state. Even after the 2004 constitutional revisions

---

37. Correspondence with Interviewee 148, November 12, 2006.

regarding the protection of private property rights, business owners continued to express skepticism about the extent to which changes to a formal document in Beijing would translate into genuine respect for private property and transactions at the local level.[38] In other words, a basic explanation for why entrepreneurs have not been politically active is that they are well aware of what can happen to them, their families, and their businesses when political tides turn against capitalists. Although most observers would agree that it is unlikely that the party-state would reverse the course of market-oriented reforms, these analyses have no bearing on the political challenges that private entrepreneurs faced during the first several decades of the PRC, or the day-to-day realities that they continue to face in the course of running their businesses.

In addition to the historically rooted disincentives for making political demands on the regime, a more immediate reason for the political quiescence of private entrepreneurs is that they lack a common frame of reference for collective organization and action. That is, private entrepreneurs do not constitute a coherent "class" poised to defend their apparently shared material interests through formal political channels. The following three chapters examine national surveys of private entrepreneurs to demonstrate the extent of variation among them in terms of background, resources, and concerns—and, by extension, variation in the likelihood that certain types of business owners would advocate, if not participate in, activities that could lead to democratizing changes in the political system. Private entrepreneurs may engage in similar economic activities and thus appear to share similar interests, but business owners perceive and defend their interests in different ways due to widely varying social and political identities, as well as locally contingent operating conditions. Some are former peasants who have engaged in private commerce since the early years of reform. Others are former state sector employees who have more recently turned to self-employment as an economic survival strategy. Some entrepreneurs retain their formal status as state employees but rely on private enterprise as their primary source of income. Despite these significant differences, all of them are "private entrepreneurs."

---

38. Indeed, the draft Property Law was first submitted to the Standing Committee of the NPC in 2002, but it was not until March 2007, after an "unprecedented seven rounds of debate," that the fifth session of the Tenth NPC passed the draft Property Law. Deliberations over the draft Property Law generated considerable controversy, including accusations that the law is unconstitutional (i.e., inconsistent with socialism) because it seeks to grant equal protection to state, collective, and private property. Xinhua, March 16, 2007.

4

Private Entrepreneurs' Identities, Interests, and Values

> Quietly but steadily, private companies . . . are becoming the
> backbone of China's economy. While thousands of state-owned
> factories still languish with massive debts, red ink, and bloated
> workforces, maverick entrepreneurs are picking up the slack,
> generating badly needed jobs and helping Chinese industry
> approach world standards in sectors ranging from electronics
> manufacturing to Internet services.
>
> *Business Week*, September 27, 1999

> China's entrepreneurs are now a recognized, and even exalted, tribe
> free to roam the nation's vast economic landscape. They invest in
> banks, make aircraft, build cars, control airlines. They have muscled
> into industries, such as steel, aluminum and machinery, which were
> once the stronghold of the state-owned sector.
>
> *China Daily*, March 8, 2004

The revival of China's private sector since the late 1970s has attracted considerable attention from both Western and Chinese observers because it has become an increasingly important part of the Chinese economy. By 2006, the private sector overwhelmingly dominated the retail and light manufacturing sectors, while even the more capital-intensive sectors that state-owned enterprises had monopolized through the 1990s were undergoing privatization. In light of these economic trends, observers tend to focus on the macrolevel effects of the private sector on the Chinese economy. Both existing research and my own, however, suggest that it would be misleading to discuss the social and political attributes of private entrepreneurs in similarly aggregated terms.

This is not to say that private entrepreneurs do not have a structural impact on society but, rather, that differentiating among different types of business owners enables us to understand the nature of their impact in more finely specified terms. Just because political elites and general observers tend to view China's private sector as a collective whole does not mean that the preponderance of its members share similar economic, political, and social attributes.

Based on a combination of official surveys from 1991 to 2000, my 2002–03 national survey, and in-depth field interviews, in this chapter I show that private entrepreneurs vary substantially in terms of their *occupational backgrounds, business size,* and *political networks.*[1] These key differences translate into varying social and political identities, as well as varying access to resources for resolving grievances. As a result, business owners also have varying *policy concerns, public values,* and *political preferences.* Given such diversity, it would not be appropriate to characterize China's private entrepreneurs as a capitalist "class" at this time.[2] Although class formation does not require members of a particular class to be homogeneous or to hold uniform political views, the finding that China's business owners have vastly different identities, interests, and political attitudes reveals multidimensional barriers to class-based collective action (see also Katznelson 1986). The high degree of internal stratification among entrepreneurs limits the likelihood that they would make organized political demands on behalf of a broader class, much less develop consensus on the desirability of democracy. Moreover, to the extent that some business owners indicate that democracy is a good form of government, their definition of democracy is typically conflated with material concerns such as protection of private property rights and rule of law rather than a general emphasis on guaranteeing civil and political liberties. These research findings call into question popular assumptions about the unity of China's capitalists as well as their political interest in rallying for a regime transition to liberal democracy.

Private Entrepreneurs' Diverse Backgrounds

The demographic and political composition of China's private sector has shifted over time. Salient trends include growth in the proportion of business

---

1. See appendix A for details on the data sources and research methodology used in this book.

2. This analysis follows Bourdieu's (1985) distinction between a "class on paper" (where agents share common objective interests based on their position in the social structure) and an "actual class" (where similarly situated agents organize themselves as practical groups for political purposes). While certain types of private entrepreneurs in China might constitute a class on paper because they face similar objective conditions, the political, social, and economic diversity among business owners make it unlikely they will form the types of organizations that would enable them to promote "class" interests.

Table 4.1. Prior occupation of private entrepreneurs, 1991–2002

Prior occupation	1991	1997–98	2000	2002
Professional, technical, skilled[a] (%)	4.6	4.6	10.5	11.3
Government/administrative cadre/officer[b] (%)	11.0	23.5	25.1	5.3
Manager in state or collective enterprise (%)	n.a.	n.a.	22.9	15.7
Worker (%)	8.1	10.7	14.0	17.8
Soldier (%)	2.7	n.a.	n.a.	1.9
Commercial/sales personnel (%)	4.5	n.a.	n.a.	8.7
Farmer/villager (%)	60.9	16.7	9.6	20.3
Self-employed (%)	1.3	38.2	17.4	19.0
Other (%)	6.9	6.3	0.5	n.a.
Total (%)	100	100	100	100
Valid responses	13,142	1,947	3,073	1,465

Sources: All the 2002 data on private entrepreneurs in this chapter comes from my survey. Data from the 1991, 1997–98, and 2000 surveys are available from State Administration for Industry and Commerce (SAIC), *Zhongguo siying jingji nianjian* [China private economy yearbook], 1994, 2000, 2001.

[a] May fall into the "government and administrative officer" category in some cases.

[b] Includes "enterprise manager" cadres in the 1991 and 1997–98 surveys. Understates the actual number of cadres in 2002. See table 4.3.

owners who were previously employed by the state or self-employed and an increase in the proportion of entrepreneurs who are party members. The ongoing fluctuation in entrepreneurs' political and occupational backgrounds provides more evidence of entrepreneurial diversity rather than the emergence of a shared identity and class formation.

As mentioned in the previous chapter, during the first decade of reform the private economy consisted primarily of farmers and others who never had wage employment. These individual entrepreneurs generally turned to private commerce due to a lack of respectable employment options. In 1991, over 60 percent of business owners had been farmers (table 4.1) and in 1991 over 72 percent of individual entrepreneurs lacked previous wage employment (table 4.2). Over the course of the 1990s, however, the proportion of entrepreneurs who were farmers or had "no prior employment" declined markedly (table 4.1 and 4.2). When business owners were asked in 1991 why they left their last positions, 68 percent indicated that they had no formal employment background. By 1993, the proportion of private entrepreneurs who had simply "resigned" from their positions or taken a "leave of absence" was over twice the number of those without prior work experience. Two years later, the 1995 survey revealed that the proportion of entrepreneurs without prior employment had dropped to a mere 8 percent, while 62 percent had either "resigned" or taken a "leave of absence" (table 4.2). But in many cases, respondents who "resigned" or took a "leave of absence" were in fact laid off and lacked alternative employment possibilities (Solinger 2001).

Table 4.2. Terms under which entrepreneurs left previous employment

Status	1991 Getihu*	1991 Siying qiye*	1993	1995
Resigned (%)	7.7	8.8	29.9	31.6
Leave of absence (%)	3.3	4.7	18.9	29.6[b]
Retired (%)	4.1	5.2	6.4	5.6
Illness or Sick leave (%)	n.a.	n.a.	2.2	2.1
Laid off (%)	n.a.	n.a.	0.9	1.3
Not being paid (%)	n.a.	n.a.	13.9	n.a.
Fired or expelled (%)	n.a.	n.a.	0.1	0.4
No prior employment (%)	72.2	68.2	27.8	8.0[c]
Other[a] (%)	11.8	13.1	n.a.	21.4
Total (%)	100	100	100	100
Valid responses	12,474	1,930	1,350	2,564

Sources: Data from the 1991, 1993, and 1995 surveys are available from SAIC, *Zhongguo siying jingji nianjian* [China private economy yearbook], 1994, 1996.

Note: "Retired" might include those forced into early retirement; "illness" may be a face-saving excuse for a "leave of absence." Some take a "leave of absence" because of no pay, low pay, or anticipated lay-offs.

Getihu are "individual entrepreneurs" that employ less than eight employees; *siying qiye* are "private enterprises," which are permitted to employ more than eight employees.

[a] May include entrepreneurs who were laid off, fired, not receiving wages, or on sick leave.

[b] Includes those who took a "leave of absence" (*tingxin liuzhi*) and those who "left work temporarily" (*lizhi*). Some of the workers in these categories may not have been owed back wages.

[c] Of the entrepreneurs who used to work in private enterprises, individual businesses, and rural enterprises, the percentages of those reporting "no prior regular wage employment" are 59.4%, 68.4%, and 77.8%, respectively.

Indeed, since accelerated state sector reform was announced at the Fifteenth Party Congress in 1997, considerable attention has been paid to the ability of the private economy to ease the human impact of the transition. Between 1995 and 2001, over forty-six million workers were laid off from state-owned enterprises (Giles, Park, and Cai 2006). The private sector increasingly consists of former state workers. The 1997–98 survey found that 11.5 percent of all employees in private enterprises were laid-off state workers, and 4.5 percent of all private enterprises were established through mergers with state-owned enterprises, or acquisitions of state enterprises that went bankrupt. Overall, between 1990 and 2003 the private sector accounted for 46.5 percent of the new employment opportunities in urban areas (Information Office of the State Council 2004).[3] By the time of my 2002 survey, 47.2 percent of the respondents had been employed by state,

3. By 2005, the private sector accounted for 80% of new employment opportunities outside of agriculture (*China Daily*, September 22, 2006). From 1996 to 2006, the private sector added almost six million new jobs annually, which accounted for about 75% of the annual total (*China Daily*, July 26, 2006).

Table 4.3. Employment background of entrepreneurs' parents and spouses, 2002

Occupation	Parents/Father	Spouse
Professional, skilled personnel (%)	4.9	6.4
Government/administrative officer/cadre (%)	7.9	4.9
Enterprise manager (%)	7.2	5.7
Administrative staff (%)	4.2	8.0
Ordinary worker (%)	18.7	20.7
Commercial/sales personnel (%)	4.4	9.5
Farmer (%)	42.7	21.5
Soldier (%)	0.8	0.2
Other (%)	4.1	7.8
No occupation (%)	5.1	15.3
Total (%)	100	100
Valid responses	1,133	1,148
Type of work unit		
Party/government organization (%)	6.6	4.5
State-owned enterprise (%)	23.0	15.5
Collective enterprise (%)	12.4	9.5
Foreign enterprise (%)	0.1	1.1
Private enterprise (%)	2.6	19.8
Individual business (%)	3.4	11.1
Rural household or collective (%)	45.2	20.8
Other (%)	3.2	5.8
No unit (%)	3.6	11.8
Total (%)	100	100
Valid responses	1,114	1,132

collective, or governmental organizations, and 23.5 percent were former managers of state-owned enterprises. In brief, over time the private sector has absorbed a large number of state workers and managers, some of whom have become business owners.[4] Later in this chapter we will see that this difference in entrepreneurs' employment background—meaning previous state employment versus lack thereof—is correlated with different operating experiences, policy concerns, and governmental expectations (cf. Wank 2002).

The diversity of private entrepreneurs' previous work experience is mirrored by the diversity in the employment backgrounds of their parents (father) and spouses (see table 4.3). In other words, as of 2002 there were still

4. Houyi Zhang, "Basic Situation of Private Enterprises in China," *People's Daily*, March 20, 1999, 5. Retrieved from FBIS-CHI-1999-0330.

significant inter- and intragenerational differences within the private sector. This finding is consistent with considerable social and economic mobility during the reform era. On the one hand, some formerly impoverished peasants are doing quite well in the private sector; on the other hand, a number of former state employees have lost their jobs, their welfare benefits, and have limited reemployment options. Private entrepreneurs come from all walks of life.

As for the political background of private entrepreneurs, official statistics show an increase over time in the proportion of red capitalists, meaning Communist Party members who engage in profit-making activities. In 1991 only 7 percent of surveyed entrepreneurs admitted to being party members; by 2003 over one-third were party members. Part of this increase is because entrepreneurs were encouraged to join the party after 2001; hence, the pre-2001 statistics may underestimate the true extent of party cadres' involvement in the private sector. Indeed, my 2002 survey found that the average length of time nonparty members had been involved in private business was 16.6 years (i.e., started in 1985), while the average length of time party members had been active in the private sector was 20.4 years (i.e., started in 1981).[5] But due to earlier restrictions on the economic activities of party members, nonparty members were more likely than party members to register their operations as individual or private businesses when they first started operating ($r = -.147$, $p < .001$). Thus, the initial false registration of private firms by party members also contributes to the lower percentage of party members in surveys from the 1990s. Despite the difficulties of estimating the true level of party cadres' involvement in private enterprise over time, what we can surmise from these observations is that since 2001 party members no longer have to conceal their legitimate profit-making activities, while the earlier cohort of red capitalists was either engaging in private enterprise surreptitiously, relatively confident in their ability to withstand potential political trouble, or simply willing to take the risk of violating a widely violated restriction.

Ultimately, both the demographic and political composition of China's private sector has been fluid over the last two decades. Such fluidity in membership suggests that it is premature to conclude that class formation has occurred among the first generation of China's reform-era capitalists. To place these observations in human context, consider the backgrounds of the following two business owners. Both could be considered "typical" of their particular strata, yet the circumstances under which each one entered the private sector differ substantially.

---

5. Independent samples t-tests show that this difference in means is significant at the $p < .001$ level.

When I interviewed owner Xie in late 2002, he ran one of the largest shoe factories in Huangpu Township, Huidong County, Guangdong Province (Interview 196). But in speech and mannerisms, he came across more as a farmer than a big boss. Owner Xie was born in 1948 into a family that was classified as being landlords. During the Communist revolution, his uncle fled to Hong Kong and has remained there ever since. His father ran a small business, but it was merged into the local commune in 1956. Because owner Xie had completed one year of high school when the Cultural Revolution started, he ended up spending seven years working in the countryside as an educated sent-down youth. When he and his family returned to Huangpu in the late 1970s, they survived by working the land, fishing, and raising animals. In the early 1980s, however, his daughter found work in a shoe factory owned by a Hong Kong investor. She worked during the day and then at night taught her father how things were done at the factory. In 1985, owner Xie opened up his own shoe factory using materials from Hong Kong (with some help from his uncle). He initially registered it as a red hat business with the brigade, and all of the workers in his new factory were family members. At the time, there were only five to six other households dealing in shoes. By 1990, there were forty to fifty shoe factories in town, which is when owner Xie took off the factory's red hat and registered it as a private enterprise. Migrants from less-developed rural areas started arriving to work in these factories. This enabled owner Xie to focus on marketing the shoes in Guangzhou, while his wife and brother remained in Huangpu to run the factory. Although he is not a party member, owner Xie is now respected in the local community and makes substantial charitable donations on a regular basis.

While owner Xie entered the private sector relatively early (and willingly), owner Lian did not set up his five-by-eight-foot retail stall in a central market in Wuhan until 2000 when he was laid off from a state-owned enterprise and thirty-eight years old (Interview 226). Lian's wife had left her position in a state firm in 1993 and opened a small underwear stall, so she was able to help him enter a similar line of business. Despite his wife's experience, however, being a laid-off worker and entering the private sector was a bit of an adjustment for Lian. He was accustomed to the comforts of having an apparently stable position in one of the city's largest factories. Moreover, Lian had been active in the factory's Communist Youth League, so he never imagined that he would end up peddling undergarments for a living on the sidewalks of Wuhan. When I interviewed him in 2002, Lian was feeling less embarrassed about having to be an individual entrepreneur (*getihu*). He even considered himself among the luckier laid-off state workers because he lost his job at a time when the local government seemed more active in helping laid-off workers and he had the support of his family and friends in starting his own business. As of late 2002, owner Lian was concerned that economic reforms were proceeding too quickly and that the government would not be as attentive to workers who were laid off from private enterprises later on.

On the surface, both owner Xie and owner Lian might appear to be private sector beneficiaries of reform, but their differing backgrounds and the circumstances under which they entered the private sector fundamentally shaped their identities as "private entrepreneurs." Owner Xie was proud that he gradually built up his business with limited resources, while owner Lian felt he had no choice but to enter private commerce. For both business owners, joining the private economy represented a perceived reversal of fortune from their previous employment situation—one for the better and one for the worse.

Entrepreneurs' Perceptions and Interests

Private entrepreneurs may vary in their occupational and political backgrounds, but do they nonetheless share similar interests by virtue of their pursuit of private profit? Entrepreneurs' perceptions of the main business and policy challenges facing their operations will serve as a proxy for how entrepreneurs define their "interests." When business owners were asked in 1991 to rank fourteen issue areas according to the seriousness of the problem for their operations, no single issue stood out as a unifying concern (table 4.4). The item most frequently identified as a problem, "difficulty in increasing sales volume," was ranked first or second by fewer than 40 percent of the respondents; the next main issue, "competition too intense," was ranked first or second by less than a quarter of the respondents. The remaining issue areas were ranked first or second by a diffuse percentage of respondents.

The 1995, 2000, and 2002 surveys, which sampled larger-scale capitalists (the 2002 survey included both small and large businesses), phrased the question differently and asked additional questions about entrepreneurs' policy concerns (see tables 4.4 and 4.5). Most larger private businesses reported facing obstacles in accessing bank credit, and a substantial portion of entrepreneurs were concerned about corruption, their tax burden, and land policy, including protection of property rights. When the 2002 survey phrased the question in milder terms—that is, whether the policy area could use improvement rather than whether the policy area is a pressing concern—most respondents stated there was room for improvement in almost all the policy areas on the survey. At first glance, this could be interpreted as a growing convergence in political concerns among larger private entrepreneurs and, thus, an increased likelihood that they would support regime change; but on closer examination, this inference is weakened by five additional observations.

Table 4.4. Entrepreneurs' perceptions: Most serious challenges facing their business, 1991–2002

Issue area	1991[a]	2000[b]	2002[b]
Business issues (%)			
Competition too intense	24.4	96.5	n.a.
Difficulty in increasing sales volume	38.5	38.7	n.a.
Difficulty in hiring/managing employees	1.0	27.4	33.7
Instability in inventory supply	12.6	16.0	30.6
Difficulty in collecting account receivables	13.6	n.a.	37.0
Business and policy issues (%)			
Difficulty in getting loans	11.0	63.3	65.4
Difficulty in getting land	8.7	21.3	32.0
Policy issues (%)			
Tax burden too high	17.2	47.0	35.7
Electricity and water supply for production	n.a.	16.2	16.6
Insufficient public security	7.3	12.7	10.0
Too many licenses required	6.1	n.a.	n.a.
Uncertainty about official policies	2.4	n.a.	n.a.
Not earning enough to cover operating expenses	0.9	n.a.	n.a.
Other	0.4	n.a.	0.2

Sources: The 2002 data come from my survey. The 1991 and 2000 data are from SAIC, *Zhongguo siying jingji nianjian* [China private economy yearbook], 1994, 2001.

[a] In 1991, respondents were asked to rank fourteen issue areas in order of significance to their particular business. This column presents the percentage of respondents who ranked the issue as the first or second most pressing challenge.

[b] In 2000 and 2002, respondents were asked whether they experience difficulties in the following areas.

First, when the policy concerns were compared with other business is-sues in 2000 (see table 4.4), the overwhelming majority of respondents (96.5 percent) selected a market issue, "competition too intense," as a dif-ficulty that they face, which vastly outstrips the percentage of entrepre-neurs who expressed concern over issues involving state policy more directly. Even though state policy clearly affects the supply of credit and land to the private sector, their availability also depends on business size in terms of sales volume.

Second, concern over corruption and arbitrary taxation cannot be seen as a purely class-specific or antistatist grievance, given that political cam-paigns were launched on a regular basis throughout the mid-to-late 1990s to combat these problems. Any Chinese citizen who reads the newspaper, listens to the radio, or walks down a main avenue adorned with political banners knows that the state itself presents corruption and arbitrary taxa-tion as serious problems.

Table 4.5. Entrepreneurs' perceptions: Pressing policy areas for private businesses, 1995–2002

Policy area	Most pressing issue (% of respondents) 1995	A pressing issue (% of respondents) 2000	An area in need of further improvement (% of respondents) 2002
Credit policy	31.8	59.0	83.3
Eliminating corruption	n.a.	56.0	92.1
Tax policy	18.8	52.4	83.9
Laws protecting property rights	5.1	39.0	71.0
Reform of the ownership/ political system	5.0	26.6	68.4
Management of industry and commerce	2.6	24.2	78.0
Improving public opinion through propaganda	5.0	20.1	68.7
Stronger macroeconomic controls	23.6	15.6	59.9
Reform of the household registration system	0.6	10.6	57.3
Social security	4.3	n.a.	86.6
Labor management	3.2	n.a.	n.a.
Total	100	n.a.	n.a.

Sources: The 2002 data come from my survey. Data from the 1991, 1997–98, and 2000 surveys are from SAIC, *Zhongguo siying jingji nianjian* [China private economy yearbook], 1994, 1994, 2001.

Third, expressing dismay over structural or central-level policy issues does not necessarily indicate a unified desire for political reform or interest in political participation. A lower percentage of respondents selected "reform of the system of ownership and political system" as a pressing concern relative to concrete issue areas such as credit policy—or in 2002, social security (see table 4.5). Indeed, on a daily basis, business owners face more tangible and perhaps, more resolvable, concerns. For instance, the majority of disputes faced by business owners relate to payment issues (table 4.6).

Fourth, entrepreneurs have different perceptions about their experiences as private business owners, as well as different attitudes toward the need for improvement in various policy areas, depending on their employment background. The ordered logit model based on 2002 data (table 4.7) shows that entrepreneurs who have previously been employed by the state are more likely than those without state employment backgrounds to have complaints about accessing bank loans, securing an adequate production site, taxes, fees, the local allocation of collective funds, and stability in employees. In addition, former state employees are more likely to say that improvements are needed in a wide range of policy issues, including protection of private property rights; intellectual property rights; public attitudes toward the private sector; tax policy; credit policy; macroeconomic

Table 4.6. Disputes encountered by private entrepreneurs, 2002

Nature of dispute	Cumulative Percentage*
With buyers (e.g., delayed payment, not paying)	61.4
With suppliers (e.g., late delivery, poor quality of merchandise)	51.0
With consumers (e.g., product/service quality, pricing)	39.5
With local government agencies and/or officials	22.7
Disputes among internal personnel	12.3
With local residents or other local organizations	15.9
Other	2.6
With news media	1.9

*Indicates the percentage of respondents who chose the dispute area as one of the three most frequently encountered disputes.

management; more equitable treatment of private businesses; fighting corruption; and improving the provision of public utilities, education, and social security. In brief, former state employees are more likely than entrepreneurs with other types of backgrounds to report operational difficulties and to support better policies.[6] Note that these trends remain statistically significant at the .01 level, even when controlling for the profitability of private businesses, as measured by net profit at the end of 2001. In other words, regardless of how successful or profitable a business happens to be, the owner's employment background is a more reliable indicator of her or his level of discontent. This higher level of dissatisfaction among former state employees is also reflected in the finding that they generally expect the government to play a more active role in both the economy and the provision of public goods.

Fifth, even when it comes to a policy issue that affects most entrepreneurs, such as access to credit, respondents are not equally concerned about it. Former state employees are more likely to report difficulties in securing bank loans (table 4.8). And, more generally, when entrepreneurs were surveyed in 2002 about the extent to which they face capital constraints in expanding their operations, 18.9 percent said they experience an extreme shortage of capital, 50.7 percent face a deficiency, 24.9 percent have just enough capital for expansion, and 5.4 percent do not face a shortage. When entrepreneurs

6. This finding contrasts from Wank's (2002) observation that former state employees have advantages over those without state-employment backgrounds. The reason for this divergence in findings is because my sample includes more laid-off state workers, while the private entrepreneurs with public employment backgrounds in his earlier sample (mainly 1988–90 and a few in 1995) were relatively privileged and able to use the social capital accumulated through "prior public employment, be it as a worker, cadre, or technician before the onset of entrepreneurship" to benefit themselves as private entrepreneurs.

Table 4.7. Access to bank loans versus private loans: Ordered logit model (regression coefficients, numbers in parentheses are standard errors)

Variable	Bank loans	Private loans
Gender	−.453*	−.151
	(.201)	(.213)
Education	.061	−.056*
	(.044)	(.047)
Years in business	.013	−.004
	(.008)	(.008)
Net profit (end of 2001)	.000	−.002
	(.000)	(.001)
Number of employees	.001*	.000
	(.001)	(.000)
Previous state employment	−.416**	.320
	(.163)	(.058)
Region East	.092	.129
	(.299)	(.309)
Central	−.659***	.604**
	(.204)	(.205)
West	−.305	.067
	(.172)	(.184)
Member of formal political organization[a]	.567**	.637**
	(.201)	(.198)
Member of business association[b]	.234	.771***
	(.143)	(.148)
Has a party branch in the enterprise	.847***	.048
	(.220)	(.217)
Constant	−.028	−.934*
	(.389)	(.412)
N	974	974
Chi^2	102.45	77.45
Pseudo R^2	.13	.11

*$p<.05$; **$p<.01$; ***$p<.001$
[a] Includes membership in at least one of the following: National People's Congress, Chinese People's Political Consultative Committee, Chinese Communist Party, People's Government, or village committee.
[b] Includes membership in at least one of the following: United Front of Industry and Commerce, Private Entrepreneurs Association, Individual Laborers Association, or trade association.

were then asked about the primary reasons they were unable to access formal bank credit, 62.9 percent said the collateral requirements at banks were too stringent, 45 percent said they lacked a guarantor, 25.8 percent said that bank loans would not be able to satisfy their demand for capital, 24.7 percent said the term of bank loans was too short, 19.8 percent said interest rates were too high, and 15.5 percent said the credit grading requirements were too strict. In other words, most entrepreneurs find that banks have prohibitively rigorous requirements for collateral, but their businesses are also unlikely to rely on bank loans for a variety of other reasons (Tsai 2002).

Furthermore, the business owners who would be in the best position to make demands on the financial system, that is, the larger scale and politically well-connected capitalists, do not face extreme credit constraints. Entrepreneurs who are men with strong political ties (i.e., members of formal political organizations), who run businesses with a larger number of employees, and who have party branches in the enterprise are more likely to have access to bank credit (see the ordered logit model in table 4.7). However, entrepreneurs with state employment backgrounds and those located in central China are less likely to have bank loans (regional and local variation is discussed in chapter 6). Meanwhile, many of the conventional social and economic indicators that one might expect would mediate access to bank credit proved to be insignificant: education level, number of years in business, business profitability, and membership in trade associations are not correlated with access to official bank loans. The regression results also show that members of formal political organizations, members of trade associations, and less-educated entrepreneurs are more likely than other types of entrepreneurs to use informal private loans. To supplement these statistical findings, the following two cases from rural Wenzhou in Zhejiang Province illustrate the variety of ways in which entrepreneurs have raised capital for their businesses.

The experience of individual entrepreneurs (*getihu*) in Zhu Au Village, Ou Bei Township, Yongjia County, shows how limited access to credit is also tied up with other operational challenges. Like most villages in rural Wenzhou, Zhu Au Village has almost no arable land because it is broken up by small tributaries and flanked by mountains dotted with traditional ancestral shrines. As of November 2001, most of the two hundred households ran small garment factories directly out of their homes. Owner Liu's peripatetic peddling before returning to Zhu Au is also typical of Wenzhou's merchants (Interview 55). Born in 1961, owner Liu left school at the age of fifteen, worked the land for half a year, and started selling chalk. By 1978, he was eager to expand his horizons, so he borrowed a total of 1,000 RMB ($595, a large sum at the time) from several different friends. This enabled him to go to Jiangshan City (in Zhejiang, near Jiangxi Province) and sell fake leather shoes for four years. With a couple of thousand RMB saved up, in 1982 he went to Wenzhou City and opened up an industrial glove store. The store did quite well, so in 1985 owner Liu and two partners decided to start a small commodities factory. One partner was responsible for traveling to purchase the inventory, one partner stayed in the village to manage the factory, and owner Liu traveled all over the country selling the products. He reminisced

Table 4.8. Experiences and attitudes of entrepreneurs with state employment backgrounds: Independent samples t-test

(a) *Question: Has your enterprise ever encountered any of the following problem(s) during its operation?* [The numbers in the second column represent the mean of responses, which were measured on a scale of 1 to 3, where 1 indicates "large problem" and 3 indicates "not a problem."]

(b) *Question: In your opinion, do the following systems or policies need further improvements?* [The numbers in the second column in the second half of the table present the mean of a dichotomous variable, where 0 indicates "no need for improvement" and 1 indicates "need for improvement."]

	No state employment (Mean)	Former state employee (Mean)	*t*
Encountered problems with (a):			
Access to bank loans	2.26	2.09	4.53**
Securing production site	2.68	2.56	3.56**
Utilities	2.81	2.77	1.12
Attracting skilled staff	2.62	2.56	1.90
Taxes	2.61	2.55	1.99*
Fees	2.53	2.37	4.37**
Allocation of collective funds	2.57	2.45	3.30**
Government services	2.60	2.54	1.63
Employee stability	2.74	2.66	2.54**
Safety of self/family	2.89	2.88	.47
Need improvement in (b):			
Protection of property rights	.69	.78	−3.66**
Protection of intellectual property rights	.62	.76	−5.25**
Public opinion of entrepreneurs	.65	.78	−4.57**
Tax policy	.82	.90	−4.14**
Credit policy	.81	.88	−3.20**
Macroeconomic controls	.57	.67	−3.66**
Management of private business	.76	.82	−2.54**
Household registration system	.57	.60	−1.21
Equal treatment of different business types	.76	.85	−4.19**
Eliminating corruption	.91	.95	−3.12**
Political system reform	.67	.72	−1.65
Public utilities	.75	.80	−2.10*
Education system	.80	.85	−2.61**
Social security system	.85	.92	−4.30**

**Significant at the $p < .01$ level; *significant at the $p < .05$ level. The n is a minimum of 692 observations for each category.

about how he once went to Lanzhou with only 200 RMB ($58) in his pocket; he stayed in seedy places for 2.5 RMB a night ($0.85), and spent no more than that on food each day. The commodities factory was not profitable for him, so owner Liu left the partnership and opened a rice bag factory. The latter venture did not do well either. Production costs were too high, especially given the high electricity fees, and the product, rice bags, were too cheap. He ended up losing about 300,000 RMB ($62,762) by 1990, but he somehow managed to borrow 300,000 RMB from loan sharks at 36 percent annual interest to open up a small-scale children's pants factory, which I visited (it employed thirty workers), and a floor tile store managed by his wife.

Besides borrowing from loan sharks, owner Liu has also borrowed from rural cooperative foundations, which were grassroots credit institutions that were never sanctioned by the People's Bank and were ultimately forced to shut down in 1999. Owner Liu believes that the rural cooperative foundations really helped small and medium enterprises develop during the early years of reform. Over the course of the 1990s, he borrowed 500,000 RMB from the local rural foundation each of the three times that he needed to purchase equipment for his factory. As of 2001, owner Liu lamented that he could not get loans from either the local rural credit cooperative or the Agricultural Bank of China because it is "not convenient." When asked to clarify what he meant by "not convenient," owner Liu reflected, "Businesses should either get really big or stay small. There is no point in being medium-sized, because you need to be big enough for the government to help out with things like credit." Based on this logic, owner Liu also commented that there is no point in small-business owners joining the Communist Party because the party offers more benefits to large businesses.

Across the river from owner Liu in Zhu Au Village is another household factory that produces children's pants. Like his neighbor, owner Ji also worked as a salesman outside of Wenzhou before returning to his hometown (Interview 56). After graduating from junior high school in 1988, he sold shoes in Nanjing until 1992. Because his father owned a small but relatively well-established printing plant (in operation since 1982), his family was able to borrow 600,000 RMB from the local rural credit cooperative on owner Ji's behalf, which gave him sufficient start-up capital to open the children's pants factory in 1993. It had never occurred to him to borrow from a bank because he does not have any contacts that could give him access to a loan officer; furthermore, he explained, banks do not accept buildings in villages as collateral. Owner Ji said that most people in the village rely on trade credit, whereby suppliers deliver materials to their clients one or two months before being paid. In addition, most households are willing to onlend up to 1 million RMB at a time. Although his small factory seemed to be doing reasonably well with its forty migrant workers in a new building, owner Ji sounded despondent as he delineated the main problems that he faces: first, access to land for expansion and, second, access to credit. He said that the local government is biased against small businesses in both respects. In addition, local taxes on private businesses have been raised at a fixed rate that exceeds their rate of growth. This had posed a particular hardship on household factories in recent years.

The experiences of owners Liu and Ji illustrate the broader finding that smaller businesses face greater challenges than larger ones. Moreover, surveyed entrepreneurs also *perceive* that smaller operations are relatively disadvantaged. In the 2002 survey, 59.5 percent of the respondents agreed that in recent years it has become more difficult for individual businesses to scale up and become "private enterprises" with more than eight employees.[7] Credit scarcity, high taxes, and intense competition are the most frequently cited obstacles to scaling up. At the same time, an overwhelming proportion of the respondents, 88 percent, agreed with the statement on the survey, "The larger a private enterprise becomes, the more local authorities appreciate it." Bivariate correlations show that political elites, politically active entrepreneurs, elites in social organizations, and socially active entrepreneurs are even more likely than less active entrepreneurs to agree that the local government values larger private operations.[8] The next case shows, however, that larger businesses have their share of complaints. Besides the ongoing need for capital, the other credit-related challenges faced by bigger businesses concern juggling multiple sources of formal and informal financing, including interactions with bank officers and repaying friends through expensive means.

While owners Liu and Ji both own small factories that rely primarily on nonbanking sources of capital, by local standards owner Bao would be considered a "big boss," as he runs an export-oriented packaging factory with 105 workers in Tangxia Township, Rui'an County (Interview 99). He could also be considered a red capitalist. Before opening the factory, he joined the Communist Party and worked as the director of a collective factory in the Rui'an County seat for eight years. The collective factory did poorly, so in 1996 owner Bao decided to move back to his hometown in Tangxia, where he established the current factory with the assistance of five shareholders. It was capitalized at 1 million RMB, and he has held 50 percent of the shares from the very beginning. At the time of our interview in late 2001, owner Bao said that he relied on multiple sources of financing.

First, he is now able to obtain loans as large as 1 million RMB from the People's Bank of China. When the factory first started, he was only able to borrow up to 300,000 RMB at a time—and even then, he never received the full amount of his loans. Owner Bao explained, "If you do not have friends in the Industrial Commercial Bank, Agricultural Bank, or Construction Bank, there is no way to get a loan from them. This is a basic problem with the financial system. . . . I was fortunate enough to have contacts in the People's Bank, but when my original application for 300,000 RMB was approved, I only received 200,000 RMB of it because the loan officer held on

---

7. Bivariate correlations show that larger businesses are more likely to disagree that it has become more difficult for small businesses to scale up ($r = -.064$ at the $p < .05$ level of significance).

8. The Pearson coefficients are, respectively, .057*, .061*, .089**, and .081**. * is at the .05 and ** is at the .01 level of significance.

to the remaining 100,000 RMB as his unofficial commission. Of course I had to repay the entire 300,000 RMB." Second, owner Bao has also borrowed about 400,000 RMB from his friends, but the "cost of friendship" (*renqing feiyong*) for these funds runs him about 2 percent of the principal each month. Third, when he needs short-term working capital, he sometimes borrows 300,000 to 500,000 RMB from the village government for three to five days. He just calls his former classmates and they bring the cash right over. Fourth, he also dips into his personal savings for the business; at any given time, about 500,000 RMB of his capital is tied up in the factory. Given that owner Bao is well connected socially and politically, he does not have to turn to the underground money houses (*dixia qianzhuang*), which are illegal. They charge up to 4 percent interest per month and are popular with other businesses in the area. He estimates that at least half of the private factories in Tangxia rely on these underground banks. As he puts it, "From the pre-Liberation days through the Mao era, there have always been underground money houses here." Even though owner Bao has many financing options, he still considers that the factory is capital constrained. When I asked him if he would ever consider lobbying for reform of the banking system, he said that he does not want to interact with officials any more than is absolutely necessary for running his business. "Lobbying," he concluded, "is looking for trouble."

Entrepreneurs' Political Values and Expectations

As indicated by the above tables and cases, private entrepreneurs of varying backgrounds and sizes do have grievances that could be addressed by changes in central and local governmental policies. Entrepreneurs are aware that private businesses have operated at a disadvantage relative to collective and state-owned enterprises, and when it come to credit access even larger-scale entrepreneurs, who are more likely to have access to bank credit, continue to experience difficulties in mobilizing sufficient capital. To evaluate whether business owners are likely to organize politically in light of such challenges, we need to consider the extent of unity versus internal fragmentation in private entrepreneurs' political orientation, including their level of political awareness and trust and their attitudes regarding the nature of government responsibilities and the desirability of various regime types, including democracy.

Political Awareness and Trust

How attentive are different types of private entrepreneurs to newsworthy events? How credible do they find the news? Both political awareness and trust have been used as measures of what Gabriel Almond and Sidney Verba (1963) call "civic culture," which refers to a cluster of attitudinal and behavioral attributes that are associated with citizens in democracies. A political system that has high levels of trust among its citizens enjoys greater support and legitimacy (Easton 1965, 273). This creates a more stable political environment whereby citizens are more likely to comply with rules and regulations, and less likely to engage in disruptive political activities (Muller, Jukam, and Seligson 1982; Paige 1971). Existing analyses of political culture in contemporary China have found that villagers tend to trust the central government more than the local government (Bernstein and Lü 2003; Li 2004), though overall rural residents tend to be less aware of the impact of government on their lives than urbanites (Nathan and Shi 1993). These studies concur that the local government is more likely to be the target of sporadic rural protest, but the analyses do not have specific implications for the political attitudes and behavior of private business owners who live in both rural and urban areas.

My 2002 survey found that, overall, entrepreneurs have relatively high levels of political awareness. Furthermore, surveyed entrepreneurs generally trust the official news media more than they trust cadres, other private entrepreneurs, and other individual entrepreneurs—but less than they trust their friends and family. These findings are consistent with the cases presented thus far: private entrepreneurs usually rely on friends and family members for capital and labor, while cadres and entrepreneurs who do not fall into the friends and family category are viewed with suspicion, if not assumed to be corrupt. Also in line with the present argument, the survey revealed considerable internal variation among the ranks of private entrepreneurs depending on their business size (number of employees), employment background, and political activities.

Cadres, private entrepreneurs (as opposed to individual entrepreneurs with fewer than eight employees), and members of formal political organizations follow the news more closely than other types of business owners (table 4.9).[9] When it comes to perceptions of trust, data from the 2001–02 Asian Barometer Survey (ABS) show that regular Chinese citizens trust the official news media as much as the private entrepreneurs in my sample do.[10] In my survey, however, cadres and members of formal political organizations find the official news media to be less trustworthy than regular entrepreneurs— perhaps because they are more likely to be privy to confidential information that is not reported to the public. Of all the types of entrepreneurs identified

9. Attentiveness to the news is also correlated with educational level ($r = -.075$ at the $p < .01$ level of significance), which in turn is correlated with being a cadre, a member of a formal political organization, and being a private (vs. individual) entrepreneur.

10. In the ABS, 13.8% of the respondents found newspapers to be "somewhat, very, or completely" untrustworthy, as compared with 13.5% in my 2002 sample of entrepreneurs.

Table 4.9. Political awareness and trust: Ordinary Chinese citizens and different types of entrepreneurs

	Percentage who listen to or read the news one or more times/day (%)	Percentage indicating that the category is somewhat, very, or completely untrustworthy (%)					
		Family members	Friends	Cadres	News media	Private entrepreneur	Individual entrepreneur
Ordinary Chinese citizens[a]	n.a.	1.4	13.9	27.4[b] 19.9[c]	13.8	30.7	n.a.
Full sample of entrepreneurs	72.7	1.3	6.4	23.7	13.5	15.3	23.2
Cadres	75.6	0.6	7.1	26.6	15.1	18.6	25.0
Noncadres	70.8	1.3	6.3	21.8	13.1	14.1	22.2
Private entrepreneur	76.0	1.4	5.8	24.6	13.5	13.7	21.5
Individual entrepreneur	66.4	0.8	7.4	21.6	13.1	17.5	24.3
State employment	71.4	0.4	7.4	24.8	13.6	16.6	29.5
No state employment	72.4	1.4	7.4	22.0	13.6	14.4	20.5
Political members[d]	79.0	0.8	6.2	20.7	15.9	15.5	24.3
Nonpolitical members	71.3	1.2	6.5	23.8	12.9	15.4	23.0

[a] Data on ordinary Chinese citizens come from the East Asia Barometer Project (hereafter, Asia Barometer Survey or ABS), which was administered in China over the course of 2001–2.

[b] Refers to trustworthiness of "unit leaders/village officials."

[c] Refers to trustworthiness of "ordinary government officials."

[d] Includes membership in at least one of the following: National People's Congress, Chinese People's Political Consultative Committee, Chinese Communist Party, People's Government, or village committee.

in table 4.9, cadre entrepreneurs are the least trusting of other cadres (26.6 percent of cadre entrepreneurs found other cadres to be "extremely, somewhat, or very untrustworthy"). The ABS survey administered to regular Chinese citizens distinguished between different types of cadres and found that 27.4 percent of respondents regarded unit leaders and village officials to be untrustworthy, while a lower portion of respondents (19.9 percent) found ordinary government officials to be untrustworthy. Given that, on average, 23.5 percent of the entrepreneurs in my sample indicated that cadres are not trustworthy, it seems that business owners are neither more nor less suspicious of party-state officials than ordinary citizens, even while cadres themselves find other cadres to be less trustworthy. Similarly, though to a lesser extreme, individual entrepreneurs also evaluate the trustworthiness of their peers, other individual entrepreneurs, in unfavorable terms. But cadres, former state employees, and members of formal political organizations are even more likely than individual entrepreneurs and the general sample of business owners to indicate that individual entrepreneurs are not trustworthy.

And ordinary citizens in the ABS survey were twice as likely as entrepreneurs in my sample to indicate that private entrepreneurs are extremely, somewhat, or very untrustworthy.

These observations have two main implications for our broader concern with the political orientation of entrepreneurs. First, both cadres and individual entrepreneurs have less favorable reputations than people in other positions. That cadre entrepreneurs and individual entrepreneurs were part of the sample and expressed similar reservations shows that business owners (and, indeed, cadres who are running businesses) do not necessarily view "their own kind" in favorable terms. Second and relatedly, the varying evaluations of trust demonstrate that entrepreneurs with different employment backgrounds and political networks have different attitudes toward the private sector and toward state officials (cadres).

Although I found that entrepreneurs' policy-oriented grievances tend to be directed at local governmental agencies and cadres—which is similar to existing findings about rural discontent—when the 2002 survey asked business owners how concerned they were about major events or policy changes at various levels, they indicated the most interest in national-level developments (table 4.10). Yet, as in the other issues discussed above, different types of entrepreneurs vary in their level of concern. In particular, members of formal political organizations indicated a greater interest than

Table 4.10. Entrepreneurs' concern for major events at various levels, 2002

Question: How concerned are you about major events or policy changes at each of the following administrative levels? [Mean ranking on scale of 1 to 5, with 1 indicating "not concerned at all" and 5 indicating "very concerned"]

	Village	Township	County	Province	National	N[a]
Full sample	2.88	2.93	3.31	3.35	3.81	1,360
Cadres	2.60***	2.80	3.36	3.50*	3.82	283
Noncadres	2.94	2.95	3.29	3.31	3.81	1,017
Private entrepreneur	2.95**	3.04***	3.43***	3.38	3.83	862
Individual entrepreneur	2.73	2.74	3.09	3.30	3.78	473
State employment	2.44***	2.60***	3.32	3.60***	3.99***	936
No state employment	3.04	3.04	3.29	3.25	3.74	367
Political members[b]	3.10**	3.18***	3.68***	3.58***	4.00**	1,112
Nonpolitical members	2.83	2.87	3.23	3.30	3.77	248

***T-test for equality of means significant at the $p < .001$ level; **significant at the $p < .01$ level; *significant at the $p < .05$ level.

[a] Excludes "no comment" and missing responses.

[b] Includes membership in at least one of the following: National People's Congress, Chinese People's Political Consultative Committee, Chinese Communist Party, People's Government, or village committee.

Table 4.11. Perception of government responsibilities, 2002: Independent samples t-test

Question: How do you feel about the following issues: Should the government assume primary responsibility for providing these services, or should individuals be responsible for the services themselves? [Numbers in the second column indicate mean rankings on a scale of 1 to 5, with 1 indicating "entirely the government's responsibility" and 5 indicating "entirely the responsibility of individuals."]

	Ordinary citizens in ABS survey (mean)	Entrepreneurs		
		No state employment (mean)	Former state employee (mean)	*t*
Employment	2.48	2.85	2.68	3.113**
Housing	3.28	3.27	3.21	1.053
Healthcare	2.99	2.85	2.79	1.036
Education	2.62	2.22	1.93	5.305**
Retirement	1.79	2.41	2.14	4.851**
Environmental protection	n.a.	2.39	2.22	3.283**

**Significant at the $p < .01$ level.

nonmembers in major events at all administrative levels; former state employees are more attuned to events at the provincial and national levels than those without state-employment backgrounds; and private entrepreneurs pay greater attention to events at the village, township, and county levels than do individual entrepreneurs. Furthermore, attentiveness does not necessarily translate into action. As I discuss in greater detail in chapter 5, even when entrepreneurs have complaints directed against particular policies or agencies, they are not likely to contact the relevant officials. Instead, they are more likely to contact well-placed individuals in their existing networks for assistance in resolving the problem.

Perception of Governmental Responsibilities

Private entrepreneurs have fairly high expectations of the government when it comes to environmental protection, education, social security, and employment. But those with previous employment experience in state units expect the government to provide more services than entrepreneurs based in rural areas, where individual households are expected to provide for their own housing, health care, and retirement expenses. Specifically, results from the independent samples t-test (table 4.11) show that entrepreneurs formerly employed by the state are more likely to expect the government to bear primary responsibility for employment, education, retirement services, and environmental protection.[11] This may be because

11. But when asked about housing and health care, entrepreneurs in general leaned toward indicating that both individuals and the government share responsibility in their provision.

former state employees are accustomed to receiving more services from the government. But in the areas of employment and retirement, ordinary citizens in the ABS survey had even higher expectations of government responsibility.

Attitudes toward Democracy and Other Regime Types

When asked to evaluate the desirability of various regime types, the surveyed private entrepreneurs generally had a highly positive impression of democracy as a regime type and a much more negative impression of military dictatorships (see table 4.12). Furthermore, entrepreneurs who are cadres, members of formal political organizations, and those with state-employment backgrounds view technocracy in a more positive light than respondents without those backgrounds. Finally, the only attribute that yielded statistically significant responses in the evaluation of democracy was that of membership in political organizations: political members rated democracy more positively than nonpolitical members. In other words, entrepreneurs who are already participating in the formal political system view democracy in more positive terms than entrepreneurs who are not politically active.

Additional questions about the nature of democracy underscore the positive attitude that entrepreneurs have toward democracy. Specifically, 56.1 percent of the respondents disagreed with the statement, "Democracy has a detrimental effect on national economic development"; 49 percent of the respondents disagreed with the statement, "Democracies are prone to causing inconsistent opinions or unstable policies"; 55.1 percent of the respondents agreed with the statement, "Democracy may have its problems, but it is still better than other forms of government"; and 47.5 percent of the respondents disagreed with the statement, "Authoritarian political systems are better than democratic ones."[12]

Despite the prodemocratic character of these survey responses, it would not be appropriate to conclude that China's private entrepreneurs therefore hope that China will undergo a democratic transition. At least five factors complicate such an interpretation of the survey results.

First, the response rate for the questions asking respondents to evaluate the above five statements was especially low. On average, 16.3 percent chose to answer "don't know" and 10.2 percent chose the "no comment" option.

---

12. Note that independent samples t-tests showed at the .05 level of significance that respondents without former state employment and those with formal positions in mass associations were more likely to agree with the statement, "Democracy may have its problems, but it is still better than other forms of government." Furthermore, larger enterprises are more likely than individual entrepreneurs to disagree with the statement, "Authoritarian political systems are better than democratic systems," at the .05 level of significance.

Table 4.12. Entrepreneurs' attitudes toward various regime types, 2002

Question: How would you appraise the different types of political systems in the world? [Numbers represent the mean ranking on scale of 1 to 4, with 1 indicating "excellent" and 4 indicating "very bad."]

	Political dictatorship	Technocracy	Military dictatorship	Democracy	N[a]
Full sample	3.28	2.59	3.43	1.50	887
Cadres	3.28	2.39***	3.40	1.47	200
Noncadres	3.29	2.65	3.44	1.50	652
Private entrepreneur	3.33**	2.61	3.43	1.49	606
Individual entrepreneur	3.18	2.55	3.43	1.52	270
State employment	3.28	2.39***	3.40	1.47	200
No state employment	3.29	2.65	3.44	1.50	652
Political members[b]	3.33	2.38***	3.40	1.41*	189
Nonpolitical members	3.27	2.65	3.44	1.53	698

***T-test for equality of means significant at the $p < .001$ level; **significant at the $p < .01$ level; *significant at the $p < .05$ level.

[a] Excludes "don't know" and "no comment" responses.

[b] Includes membership in at least one of the following: National People's Congress, Chinese People's Political Consultative Committee, Chinese Communist Party, People's Government, or village committee.

The finding that 26.5 percent of the respondents did not provide clear answers in this ranking exercise reflects, in part, the political sensitivity of the question.[13] They may have been uncertain about the politically correct answer or were hesitant to express their true opinions in case there was a clearly politically incorrect answer.

Second and relatedly, precisely because of the political sensitivity of the issue, we were not permitted to ask entrepreneurs in the survey about which regime type they believe is most appropriate for China. We were required to phrase the question in general terms: "How would you appraise

13. Indeed, when the World Values Survey was conducted in China in 2000, four of those same five questions were not even asked in 60% of the surveys (the last statement about authoritarian political systems was not on the survey). Out of the other 40% of the questionnaires, an average of 15.8% of the respondents chose "don't know" when asked to evaluate the first four statements about democracy. And out of the remaining valid responses, 72.5% of the general surveyed population in China disagreed that democracy has a negative effect on the economic system, 62.6% disagreed that democracies are indecisive and entail too much squabbling, 77.2% disagreed that democracies are not good at maintaining order, and 80.6% agreed that democracy may have its problems but is better than other types of political systems. Although we cannot compare these responses statistically with those of my survey, they suggest that the general Chinese population has more sympathetic views toward democracy than do private entrepreneurs in particular.

Table 4.13. Correlations among positive evaluations of different political systems

	Political dictatorship is good	Technocracy is good	Military dictatorship is good	Democracy is good
Political dictatorship is good	1.000	.209**	.517**	.030
Technocracy is good	.209**	1.000	.257**	.232**
Military dictatorship is good	.517**	.257**	1.000	.054*
Democracy is good	.030	.232**	.054*	1.000

**Indicates statistical significance at the $p < .01$ level; *indicates statistical significance at the $p < .05$ level.

the following different types of political systems in the world?"[14] Thus, the findings presented in table 4.12 can only be interpreted as indicating an abstract preference for democracy, rather than a specific preference for China to become democratic. Indeed, when another question on the 2002 survey asked how entrepreneurs felt about the pace of China's recent progress in political reform, 51 percent indicated that the pace was neither too fast nor too slow, while 8.5 percent think reforms have gone too fast and 22.6 percent think they have proceeded too slowly.

Third, a positive evaluation of democracy is also correlated with positive evaluations of technocracies and military dictatorship (table 4.13). In other words, entrepreneurs do not necessarily have an exclusive preference for democratic versus nondemocratic political systems—at least when the question is phrased in such general terms.

Fourth, ruling political elites in Beijing have used the term "democracy" in a variety of normatively positive ways. Throughout postimperial Chinese history, "democracy" has appeared repeatedly in official discourse as a politically desirable goal. Yet to say that "democratic centralism," "people's democratic dictatorship," "socialist democracy with Chinese characteristics," or "a harmonious society featuring democracy" is a political objective does not mean that the civil and political liberties intrinsic to liberal democracies will be respected in theory or practice. In contrast, the Leninist concept of

14. In response to that general question, 78.2% of the respondents indicated that as a political system, democracy is "excellent" or "very good." The 2000 World Values Survey asked a similar question in references to how "having a democratic political system" is "as a way of governing this country." When phrased in country-specific terms, 9.6% of the sample of general Chinese citizens responded, "don't know," and 29.4% indicated that democracy was either "very good" or "fairly good." When the "don't know" responses are subtracted from the denominator, 96.3% of the remaining valid responses indicated that democracy was either "very good" or "fairly good."

democratic centralism emphasizes centralized, hierarchical decision making; the Maoist notion of people's democracy referred to mass participation under the leadership of the Communist Party; and in contemporary discussions of socialist democracy with Chinese characteristics and building a harmonious society, former general secretary Jiang Zemin and his successor, Hu Jintao, respectively, have made it clear that political reform must proceed apace with China's social and economic developments—and that current Chinese leaders have no intention of copying Western political systems.

Fifth, in-depth interviews with entrepreneurs and officials reveal that local understandings of "democracy" differ from the broader notion of democracy as a regime type that embodies both procedural respect for electoral democracy and rule of law, as well as substantive protection of individual and minority rights. When asked what democracy means to them, most entrepreneurs cite the example of when they are in a meeting and need to make a decision, participants vote by raising their hands. Very few mentioned having competitive elections at the village level, and none of the entrepreneurs I interviewed associated freedom of speech, press, and assembly with democracy.

Examples of Diversity in Entrepreneurial Views

Those who are outspoken about their democratic views tend to be either red capitalists, meaning entrepreneurs who are local political elites, or business owners who are economic elites and feel that they have been deeply wronged by the present political system. But most other entrepreneurs do not advocate a change of regime type even if they have complaints that could be resolved through democratic channels of political participation.

The red capitalist in Hebei who was discussed in the previous chapter, owner Gong, is a good example of the first type of democratic entrepreneur (Interview 153). As a Communist Party member, a People's Congress deputy, and the vice director of the local chamber of commerce, Gong is clearly politically active in Langfang City. His political status also seems to have imbued him with the confidence to speak openly about problems facing society—including the need to reform tax and credit policy, to combat corruption, to improve the educational, health, and social security systems, and the general need for greater political reform. Owner Gong's belief that democracy is the best regime type had a market-oriented logic. He explained, "Just as it is good to have many different restaurants in town, it is good to have many different political parties. Competition among different parties would make the system run better." He is one of the few entrepreneurs who specified multiparty competition as a procedural component of democracy.

Unlike red capitalists who have a certain degree of political influence within their localities, the other type of entrepreneur who expresses support for democracy tends to be economically successful but is generally not politically active and has had at least one particularly difficult experience in dealing with the legal system. An example of such an entrepreneur is owner Lu who, as of 2002, was running a profitable test tube factory in the suburbs of Wuhan, Hubei Province (Interview 239). Before opening up the current operation, owner Lu had quite a diverse range of employment and entrepreneurial experiences. He had worked for the Agricultural Bank of China, fixed cars for the Agricultural Office, and transported military supplies from Hubei to Shaanxi. In 1990, he started investing in a series of projects with the backing of the local government to develop a tourist hotel, a high-end peach market, and other projects that ultimately enabled him to open his current factory. He was candid in pointing out that his 5 million RMB investment in the business would not have been possible if the local government had not quietly granted him user rights over the building. Owner Lu said quite bluntly, "There is no way that large private entrepreneurs could have built themselves up in a transparent manner."

As suggested already, collaboration between local governments and large private businesses is not unusual and has often proven to be mutually beneficial. But informal partnerships can break down for a variety of reasons. In owner Lu's case, the incident that redefined his political views was a serious car accident in October 1998. A head-on collision completely mangled his Honda Accord, killed his driver, and left owner Lu traumatized. Owner Lu believes that the accident was due to the unmarked lanes and borders on the highway, which encourages chaotic two-way traffic. Hence, he sued the Wuhan City government for using a negligent construction company to build the road. After he filed the suit, the city government issued a fake predated document certifying that the construction company had done a satisfactory job. (He showed us copies of the documents, and, sure enough, the dates were mismatched. It looked like a very sloppy cover-up job.) Lu appealed the case to the Hubei Provincial Higher Court, and the court ruled in favor of the Wuhan City government. As of 2002, he was planning to take the case to Beijing and did not care how much the most expensive Beijing lawyers might cost him.

He no longer blames Hubei Province or even Wuhan City now. He blames "the system," which is based in Beijing. Owner Lu explained, "As a private business owner, I want a real space to talk with government officials. Entrepreneurs need their own organization to express their opinions and protect their interests." As if to clarify his political preferences, he stated, "Democracy is the best form of government." Yet owner Lu also added that China's masses are too ignorant to handle democracy. He

thinks it will take a long time before the country is sufficiently developed
and the masses are sufficiently educated to sustain a democratic political
system.

Even though approximately half of the survey respondents in 2002 had a
positive view of democracy if understood as economic development and political stability, many of the higher-profile entrepreneurs that I interviewed
expressed sentiments that echo familiar arguments about the inappropri-
ateness of democracy for developing countries. Owner Lu's latter comment
about the low "quality" (*suzhi*) of the masses is widely shared not only by entrepreneurs but also by intellectuals and political elites. Indeed, the founding father of modern China, Sun Yat-sen, had said that it would take a long
period of governmental tutelage before the masses would be ready for democracy. Besides the idea that a certain level of education is necessary for democracy to function properly—that is, to maintain political stability—is the
broader notion from modernization theory that a certain level of economic
development is a prerequisite for all the other socioeconomic variables that
support democracy, including a well-educated citizenry and urbanization.
One entrepreneur from Yangzhou sounded like a spokesperson for modernization theory (Interview 245). He said with complete confidence that if
2 percent of Chinese citizens were in the middle class, such that those in
the east earned 10,000 RMB ($1,208) per month and those in central China
earned 5,000 RMB ($604) per month, then the country would be consid-
ered economically developed. Once the economy is developed, then political reform would follow, though "it is obviously too early for China to become
democratic."[15] This view basically implies that it is just a matter of time before China undergoes a democratic transition.

Many other entrepreneurs, however, think that democracy is neither desirable nor probable. Even business owners who complain about governmental
discrimination against the private sector express concern about the viability
of democracy in a country as populous as China. A typical case of this is owner
Zhang, who in 2002 owned a large electronics factory with eight hundred
workers in a rural part of Huiyang City, Guangdong Province (Interview
182). Owner Zhang offered many examples of unfair policies toward private
entrepreneurs. First, the most blatant form of discrimination is in the area
of credit. He complained that state-owned enterprises can get large loans
from state banks and never have to repay them, while private businesses can
only get small loans, if any, and are held completely accountable for them.
Second, foreign investors are charged a lot less for land than private entrepreneurs. He cited a case where a foreign bidder was charged 1 million RMB

15. When I asked the entrepreneur why he thought Singapore remains authoritarian, he
responded that Singapore is too small to be a democracy: "Everyone knows each other. They
practically live in the same building, so what is there to vote on?"

for a certain property, while a local entrepreneur was charged 2 million RMB for the same piece of land. Third, the township government charges private enterprises 25 percent more for the use of electricity than other types of businesses. And finally, even though owner Zhang has made substantial social contributions, the government still does not treat his business fairly. In the last dozen years he has spent approximately one-third of his income on providing various social and public services in town, including building bridges, building schools, paying teachers' wages, helping the elderly (he donates 30 RMB [$3.62] per month in "fruit fees" (*shuiguo fei*) to each of the fifty retirees in town), and he always makes generous contributions during each of the four annual festivals.

Owner Zhang believes that he has a very high economic status in the community given that the registered capitalization of his business is 28.3 million RMB ($3.5 million). Moreover, he also considers himself to have high social status. Besides his charitable giving, he serves as a local moneylender. At the time of our interview, he said that thirty-seven people owed him money and that the sums ranged from tens of thousands to a couple of million RMB. Despite his high profile, owner Zhang believes that the local government continues to discriminate against his business. Given the extent of his grievances, one might expect him to advocate political reforms that offer private entrepreneurs greater input in local politics, if not policy-making at the higher administrative levels. Yet owner Zhang said that the best political system for a country depends on its size: "Small countries can handle democracy, large countries cannot. If India did not have a democratic system, its economy would be a lot more developed. If China were democratic, in two weeks the country would fall apart and it would all be over." In chapter 5 I present additional instances of entrepreneurs such as owner Zhang who are vocal in their complaints but guarded in their advocacy of a democratic prescription for China.

Private Entrepreneurs and the Chinese Communist Party

Ultimately, how entrepreneurs evaluate different regime types is only a theoretical dimension of their political orientation. In contrast, their attitudes toward the Chinese Communist Party provide a more tangible way of assessing the extent to which business owners believe their interests may be adequately protected within the existing political regime, that is, one where political power remains monopolized by the CCP. In examining private entrepreneurs' responses to questions about Jiang Zemin's Theory of the Three Represents and the desirability of entrepreneurs joining the Communist Party, it is apparent that the party that once sharply condemned capitalism has become an acceptable, if not desirable, forum for private entrepreneurs to enhance their political and social status.

As mentioned in chapter 3, Jiang Zemin's 7/1 speech on the CCP's eightieth anniversary in 2001 combined with his Theory of the Three Represents led to the recommendation that private entrepreneurs be admitted to the party. Business owners were then invited to join the party at the Sixteenth Party Congress in late 2002, and the PRC Constitution was amended to protect private property rights in 2004. This general period coincides with the timing of my research. As such, even though the issue of entrepreneurs' party membership may have been subject to debate among central party elites, it was already a salient issue in public discourse. In other words, the various governmental entities that had to approve my survey did not consider it a sensitive issue that had to be excluded from my 2002 survey or that could not be discussed in formal interviews with officials and entrepreneurs.

When asked to evaluate the statement, "Comrade Jiang Zemin's 'Theory of the Three Represents' will improve the policy environment for the private sector," the vast majority of respondents agreed with it: 45.1 percent completely agreed and 43.4 percent basically agreed, while only 3.1 percent basically disagreed, 0.3 percent completely disagreed, and 3.2 percent had no comment.[16] Even though most entrepreneurs expressed confidence in the Three Represents, independent samples t-tests revealed that members of formal political organizations were more likely to agree with the statement than entrepreneurs who do not participate in any formal political activities $(p < .01)$.[17] This is consistent with the reality that all state units, and especially political ones, were required to circulate and study the Three Represents during the 2001 to 2002 period. At least in rhetoric, the central government and party organs widely publicized their recognition of the value of the private sector to China's political economy.

As far as party membership is concerned, previous official national surveys show that nearly 34 percent of private entrepreneurs were already party members by 2003 (see table 3.4 in chapter 3). The results from my 2002 survey are consistent with findings from official surveys, namely, that the majority of entrepreneurs who are now party members were already party members when they became business owners rather than ones who joined after they entered the private sector. Of the 23.5 percent of surveyed entrepreneurs who were party members in 2002, 85.7 percent were

16. Admittedly, the manner in which the question was phrased on the survey was bound to receive high rates of agreement; even then, however, there were statistically significant differences in the extent to which different types of entrepreneurs agreed with the statement.

17. Independent samples t-tests show that former state employees are also more likely to indicate that the Three Represents will improve the policy environment for private entrepreneurs $(p < .01)$.

Table 4.14. Private entrepreneurs' interest in joining various organizations, 2002

Organizations	Yes (%)	No (%)	N/A or missing (%)	Total (%)
Individual Laborers Association	17.9	79.1	3.1	100
Private Entrepreneurs Association	17.3	79.7	3.1	100
Private entrepreneurs networking club	28.1	68.9	3.1	100
Trade association	27.7	69.3	3.0	100
United Front of Industry and Commerce	17.9	79.3	3.0	100
Chinese Communist Party	43.5	30.3	26.2	100
Communist Youth League	0.1	96.5	3.4	100
Democratic parties	26.0	94.2	3.2	100

already party members when they registered their private enterprises; in other words, only 14.3 percent of the entrepreneurs who are party members joined *after* they registered their businesses.[18]

My 2002 survey also asked whether entrepreneurs had any interest in joining various organizations, including the party. Despite popular perceptions that party membership is not as prestigious or advantageous as it once was, of the available choices, a large portion of entrepreneurs, 43.5 percent, indicated that they would be interested in joining the party (table 4.14). Indeed, even after taking into account the high number of missing responses to the question about party membership, a greater portion of entrepreneurs would prefer to join the Communist Party than to join various trade and mass associations that are intended to represent the interests of private entrepreneurs, including the Individual Laborers Association, Private Entrepreneurs Association, official democratic parties, and various nongovernmental trade and networking groups.[19] This suggests that to the extent private entrepreneurs are interested in participating in associational activities, they are more interested in affiliating with the organization that dominates political power than in joining potentially countervailing and less powerful organizations.

When entrepreneurs were then asked why they wanted to join the party out of a list of reasons, 22.4 percent said party membership would enhance

18. Furthermore, former state employees joined the party on average three years earlier (1983–84) than entrepreneurs without state employment experience (1986–87); and former state employees are also more likely to be party members than nonstate workers.

19. The high level (26.2%) of missing responses to the party membership question may be attributed to the respondents' uncertainty about what the politically correct answer would be to the question. Prior to Jiang Zemin's July 1, 2001, speech, expressing interest in joining the party might have seemed inappropriately ambitious. After the 7/1 speech and the campaigns promoting the Theory of the Three Represents, however, some entrepreneurs may have felt pressured to express interest in joining the party.

their political status, 22.8 percent said it would enhance their social status, 27 percent said they were interested due to their individual ideals, 12.2 percent said that it would be for business advantages, 18.9 percent said that it would be an effective way to lead the masses to prosperity, 14.6 percent said it would enhance their political participation, and 4.9 percent said their desire to join the party was influenced by others. A follow-up question concerning what kind of impact capitalists think the policy of allowing entrepreneurs into the party will have shows that most entrepreneurs view it as being favorable to them: 71.1 percent of the respondents agreed that allowing entrepreneurs to join the party would improve their social status; 74.4 percent believe that it would improve their political status; and 45.2 percent believe that it would improve their economic status.

Although most of the entrepreneurs that I interviewed were not interested in joining the party themselves, one business owner was unusually enthusiastic about the prospect of becoming a party member. Owner Xie, the proprietor of the third-largest shoe factory in Huangpu Township, Huidong, Guangdong Province, exclaimed, "I do not care if I cannot get into the party until I am seventy-five years old. I definitely want to join" (Interview 196). Given the size of his factory, owner Xie established a party branch in early 2002, and at the time of our interview several months later he was determined to apply for admission in the spirit of the Three Represents. He even jumped up in the middle of our interview to find a political magazine, from which he quoted a passage from Comrade Jiang Zemin indicating that private entrepreneurs are among the most productive forces and should thus be permitted to join the Communist Party. Owner Xie said that he was extremely grateful to the party for providing a favorable macroeconomic policy environment for private sector development, and added, "As long as we are not called 'capitalists,' things will be fine for us." Apparently, his family had suffered considerable political difficulties during the Mao era. Yet owner Xie seemed genuinely hopeful about the party's new direction.

By way of contrast, owner Zhang, who owns a large electronics factory in rural Huiyang, Guangdong, has many grievances against national policies that discriminate against private entrepreneurs (Interview 182). Yet he has no desire to enter the party. His factory established both a party branch and a labor union in 1994, but Zhang never joined the party. Over the years, local journalists have asked him several times why he has not joined the party, and he would typically respond that he is a member of the exploiting class (*boxue jieji*) and therefore not eligible to join the party. Even though Jiang Zemin's 7/1 speech made it more acceptable for business owners to be party members, owner Zhang still has no interest in participating in it. He explained that managing the business side of the factory already takes up enough of his time, so he would prefer to delegate its political and ideological tasks to those with more experience in such matters.

Although the survey revealed that a higher percentage of entrepreneurs are interested in joining the party than other types of associations, owner Zhang's stated reluctance to pursue party membership was more typical of interviewees than owner Xie's exuberant determination to become a party member. Most of the interviewees who were not already party members said that they were too preoccupied with their businesses to think about participating in politics (*canzheng yizheng*), much less applying for party membership. The apparent discrepancy between the statistical findings and my interviewees can be reconciled if we subtract the "normal" rate of missing responses for the question about joining various organizations (about 3 percent) from the missing response rate of 26.2 percent and assume that about 23 percent of the missing responses would have been negative in the absence of self-censorship. After adding that to the actual negative responses, one could infer that 53 percent of the respondents are not interested in joining the party as compared to 43.5 percent who are interested. In other words, the survey results may underestimate the level of negative interest in party membership, which would explain the generally reserved attitude of interviewees toward the prospect of joining the party.

THE national survey data and field interviews presented in this chapter offer general snapshots of key socioeconomic indicators of private entrepreneurs and their self-reported views of operational challenges and solutions. Although observers have been tempted to make sweeping generalizations about the nature of the private sector, the survey data and case studies provide more evidence of entrepreneurial diversity rather than the emergence of a shared identity and class formation.

First, the demographic and political composition of the private sector has not been stable over the course of the reform era. The earliest group of private traders came from either disadvantaged political and economic backgrounds or had privileged access to state resources by virtue of their political positions. Both street peddlers and red capitalists were part of the "nonstate sector," but their experiences varied considerably. By the time of my research in the early to mid-2000s, it was apparent that entrepreneurs come from all walks of life and that their family and occupational backgrounds fundamentally influence the way that they define their interests. For some entrepreneurs, entering the private sector represents a notable improvement in terms of economic well-being over their previous employment situation; for others, however, running a business is a step down, both materially and socially. These differing experiences translate into differing identities and interests.

Second and relatedly, entrepreneurs lack consensus on the nature of their grievances. Although most entrepreneurs are concerned about basic business issues such as competition, taxes, and access to credit, the relative urgency of these issues varies substantially for different types of entrepreneurs. My survey found that entrepreneurs' policy concerns, public values, and political preferences vary depending on their occupational backgrounds, the scale of their operations, and the nature of their political connections and activities. Given these key differences, at this point in China's transition it would not be appropriate to treat business owners as a distinct social class.

Returning to a broader theme of this book, one might object that the absence of class formation does not indicate the lack of interest in democracy on the part of some segment of the private sector. In the next chapter I explore this issue in greater detail, but the findings presented thus far indicate that even though many entrepreneurs have a favorable impression of "democracy" in the abstract, it would be an unwarranted leap to surmise that they would necessarily support a regime transition to a liberal democratic system in contemporary China. Contrary to structural theories of regime change, which expect the impetus for democratization to come from segments of society excluded from the political system, the entrepreneurs who seem to think the most highly of democracy are those who are already politically active in existing formal institutions. By the same token, membership in the Chinese Communist Party remains an apparently attractive venue for entrepreneurs to enhance their status, even though other associational activities might seem to relate to their business concerns more directly. Especially since 2001, China's leading formal political institution seems to be accommodating private entrepreneurs.

While this chapter focused on the varying backgrounds, attitudes, and perceptions of private entrepreneurs, the next chapter shows that their behavior also differs widely. Not only do business owners lack consensus as to the best means for solving their problems but they also employ a diverse range of coping strategies. Ultimately, only a small fraction of entrepreneurs engage in actions that directly confront the state and could potentially undermine regime durability.

5

Diversity in Private Entrepreneurs' Coping Strategies

> Merchants and traders . . . are cunning and crooked, but not rebellious.
>
> Wang Shituo, *1853–1856 Diary*

> Perhaps the new entrepreneurs . . . are the ones with the real power to change things. . . . Perhaps among them a new force is gathering, an energy that can be directed toward social change. We must not underestimate them.
>
> *River Elegy*, 1988 TV Series

Although the policy environment for the private sector has improved significantly since the late 1970s, business owners nonetheless continue to experience a variety of operational and political challenges. Many industries remain off limits to private investors, domestic equity markets are dominated by state-owned enterprises (SOEs), and the legal system remains biased in favor of governmental entities. On a day-to-day basis, private businesses in China still face numerous obstacles that their counterparts in advanced capitalist economies have generally overcome. Yet many constraints on the private sector have in fact been alleviated since the late 1970s. Examining how private entrepreneurs have dealt with discriminatory policies and handled disputes provides insight into one of the broader questions raised in this book—namely, how can we explain authoritarian durability in light of the various social and political dislocations associated with rapid private sector development?

As mentioned earlier, the answer has two parts. First, China's political institutions have proven to be flexible and responsive to various adaptive informal institutions that business owners have created over the course of the reform era. Second, contrary to the expectations of structural theories of democratization, private entrepreneurs do not constitute a prodemocratic middle class. To illustrate the logic of these two arguments, I propose a working typology of private entrepreneurs' political behavior, which shows that business owners relate to the state in very different ways depending on their backgrounds, their length of experience in the private sector, and their local political and economic status. These attributes, in turn, shape the attitudes of entrepreneurs, as well as the resources available to them when they face various challenges. We will see that most entrepreneurs rely on informal, nonconfrontational means to address their grievances. Ultimately, only a fraction of the current generation of private entrepreneurs has both the ability and desire to confront the state in defense of their interests, and even within this group many use nondemocratic channels for promoting their interests. The ranks of China's capitalists may be growing, but they do not share class-based political preferences, and they are not equally likely to partake in politically noteworthy activities that may contribute to a democratic transition. This does not mean that private entrepreneurs are not politically consequential but, rather, that the nature of their political impact is more diversified, localized, and indirect than observers might expect.

A Typology of Private Entrepreneurs' "Political" Strategies

"Political" is put in quotation marks because the activities that private entrepreneurs engage in have varying levels of direct political impact.[1] Serving in the National People's Congress, the collective lobbying of the Industrial and Commercial Management Bureau, and organizing an autonomous entrepreneurs' association are readily identifiable as political acts; yet the absence of interaction with state agents may also have political implications. Arguably, avoiding the disciplinary and extractive reach of the regulatory state can be subversive (Scott 1985). Therefore, even if entrepreneurs perceive certain activities as being day-to-day survival strategies rather than politically meaningful acts, for heuristic purposes their coping strategies may be classified into four broad categories: *avoidant, assertive, loyally acceptant,* and *grudgingly acceptant.* This categorization roughly mirrors Albert Hirschman's (1970) classic depiction of behavioral "exit," "voice," and "loyalty" in the marketplace. Entrepreneurs may choose the

---

1. Having "political impact" would include outcomes as varied as formal policy changes and issuance of new regulations, changes in the operating procedures of state agents, or calling attention to a particular issue.

exit strategy of avoiding interaction with state agents; they may voice their complaints individually or through organized efforts; or they may exhibit loyalty to the system by complying with official regulations (or enlisting cadre support for special treatment).

This typology goes beyond a simple taxonomy by showing the limits of class formation among private entrepreneurs and, by extension, the absence of axiomatic support for a particular regime type. In order for private sector development to yield democratization according to the expectations of structural arguments, private entrepreneurs must engage in politically *assertive* activities that undermine the existing authoritarian regime and lead to a democratic alternative.[2] This means that business owners must have both the *ability* and the *desire* to confront the state. By "ability," I mean that entrepreneurs possess the social, economic, and political resources to express their concerns to some branch of the state through individual or organized efforts. The "desire" to confront the state refers to the willingness of entrepreneurs to defend their interests in an assertive manner, and a precondition of this is some degree of discontent with their present circumstances.

This can be seen in a two-by-two matrix of private entrepreneurs' political strategies based on these two dimensions (figure 5.1). Assertive entrepreneurs in quadrant I have both the ability and desire to confront the state; avoidant entrepreneurs in quadrant IV have neither the ability nor the desire. Quadrants II and III encompass two subtypes of acceptant entrepreneurs: first, loyally acceptant business owners have the ability to confront the state but choose not to; and second, grudgingly acceptant business owners are not content with their operating conditions but lack the resources to confront the state.

Despite the typology's organization around the intended behavior of entrepreneurs, I am not precluding the possibility that entrepreneurs could have a structural impact on the political system without explicitly intending or acting to do so. It is conceivable that business owners could have a democratizing effect on the regime through nonconsequential causal mechanisms. In this typology I focus on the direct implications of entrepreneurial intentions and capabilities, however, to demonstrate the limits of the popular belief that economic development will lead "a capitalist class" (or even some subset thereof) to push for political democracy. As part of this analytic endeavor, I will elaborate on each of the coping strategies to illustrate how the range of activities in which private entrepreneurs engage has varying levels of direct political impact. Having "direct political impact" refers

2. There are, of course, other potential paths through which private sector development could create the structural conditions for democratization. For example, as discussed in chapter 2, capitalist development could motivate the mobilization of labor for democratic reforms (Rueschemeyer, Stephens, and Stephens 1992). This book only explores the popular expectation that China's capitalists are likely to push for democracy.

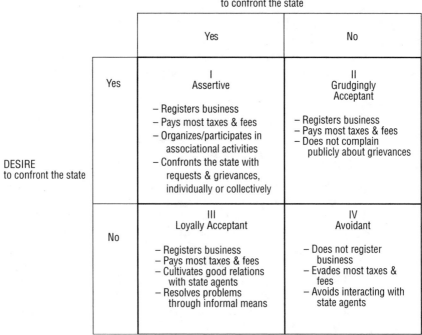

Figure 5.1.   Typology of private entrepreneurs' political orientation and strategies

to behavior that results in any of the following: formal policy changes, is-suance of new regulations, changes in the operating procedures of state agents, or calling the attention of officials or the public, or both, to a par-ticular issue. Although the absence of interaction with state agents also has political implications, avoidant activities do not result directly in program-matic demands for political change; instead, when avoidant coping strate-gies undermine the enforceability of official regulations and become widespread, policy elites may decide to adjust the regulations so that they are better suited to the operating realities of business owners. Assertive and loyally acceptant coping strategies also contribute to the formation of adaptive informal institutions that in turn create pressure on the enforcers and designers of formal institutions to accommodate their existence.

Avoidant Strategies

Entrepreneurs who rely on avoidant strategies of interaction with the state are unlikely to become democrats or to act in ways that give rise to democratic pressures. This pattern of interaction is also the most difficult to measure because private entrepreneurs who rely on avoidant strategies are not registered with the ICMB or PEA, and they often do not conduct business in officially designated market areas (Chan and Unger 1982; Tsai 2002). Based on my own experience in interviewing entrepreneurs and the estimates of a central government official in an unpublished report on the private sector, I estimate that unregistered private businesses account for an average of 15.3 percent of China's private sector.[3] These informal sector entrepreneurs tend to have the following types of backgrounds: (a) state employees who are moonlighting, (b) itinerant peddlers from rural areas, (c) members of the floating population from other provinces (Solinger 1999), and (d) laid-off state workers formally registered as "unemployed" (Li Qiang, personal communication, March 2, 2000).[4] ICMB and local cadres are cognizant of the fact that many private vendors remain unregistered or do not have all the licenses and certificates that businesses are required to display. Such avoidant infractions make it impossible for entrepreneurs to voice complaints or report undisciplined cadres. Only legally registered businesses can credibly report cadre misconduct through formal institutional channels (Solinger 1999).[5]

Some studies of the informal sector (de Soto 1989) have found that bureaucratic complexity poses a disincentive for operators to register themselves. In the case of Chinese street merchants, those that are unregistered also face challenges in keeping a low profile. For example, peddlers from the same suburb may travel into the nearest urban center together and set up their mobile sidewalk stands on the same city block every day. Outside a series of upscale department stores in Beijing, I interviewed a group of peddlers who were selling inexpensive clothes and hair accessories on the sidewalk and out of the back of their bicycle carts (Group interview, September 2, 2001). The street sellers explained that because of their unsophisticated appearance, they probably would not even be permitted to enter the department stores, much less attempt to register for a retail space inside one of them. They estimated that having a permanent counter inside a fancy store would cost them a minimum of 5,000 RMB ($604) per month, which

3. This figure was higher during the earlier years of reform and in remote rural areas where the ICMB infrastructure was less developed. I arrived at the present (conservative) estimate of 15.3% based on an internal government report that estimates that 16.9% of all *getihu* in 2005 were not registered and my own estimate that 3% of *siying qiye* were not registered. (The former figure came from correspondence with Interviewee 148 on October 18, 2006.) The resulting 15.3% estimate is a weighted-average figure based on the relative proportion of registered *getihu* and *siying qiye* at the national level.

4. In his survey of unemployed workers, the sociologist Li Qiang found that some "unemployed" workers spend over forty hours per week peddling.

5. Even then, however, local urban residents may have an advantage over migrants and floaters.

How about some fur from Xinjiang? Migrant peddlers in Wenzhou

is about twice what they earn by camping outside of the department stores during heavily trafficked times. The vendors added that they would also have a difficult time renting a place in state-managed department stores because none of them had urban household registrations.

Depending on the particular locality, the ICMB's policy on regulating "floating street peddlers" is that they should pay a five to ten yuan ($0.60–1.20) Industrial and Commercial Management Bureau fee for each day of operation. Similarly, the Sanitation Bureau also charges the floating peddlers a couple of yuan per day for cluttering up the street. In practice, this means that when ICMB and Sanitation Bureau cadres spot mobile vendors on their daily rounds, they automatically collect their respective fees. Cadres from other local agencies may also collect fees from individual entrepreneurs for various local causes (e.g., road repair, teacher's salaries, community festivals). On occasion, however, the fee collectors may arbitrarily levy exorbitant fines on top of the usual fee, and even confiscate the vendor's goods using coercive tactics. Given these hassles, mobile street vendors usually take turns keeping watch for tax/fee collectors over a two-block radius and give the group advance warning of their imminent arrival so they can gather their merchandise—typically, by rolling up their display cloths into a single bundle—and peddle their bicycle carts into the middle of the street. In many instances, the regulatory sweeping of the streets is a daily cat-and-mouse ritual between unregistered peddlers and various street-level bureaucrats. Why do these types of entrepreneurs put up with such difficult operating conditions? Most respond that their lives as informal vendors may be difficult, but they lack alternative employment options. As one street peddler in Yanting Township told me, "It's too much of a hassle to deal with cadres. There's no point in registering this operation. I need to make a living, but I don't plan to do this forever" (Interview 124).

This situation presents only one particular expression of avoidant behavior, that is, how itinerant entrepreneurs cope with their informality and try to avoid tax and fee collectors. Official reports from the 1990s claim, however, that underreporting income and tax evasion is pervasive among private entrepreneurs in general. As of 1994–95, it was estimated that 80 percent of private businesses paid less tax than legitimately owed (Huang 1996);[6] and the central government collected an estimated 87 percent less in fiscal revenues (worth approximately 267 million RMB) during the period from 1989 to 1998 (Interview 281).[7] Since most vendors tend to underestimate their income, it would not be meaningful to rely solely on the criteria of tax evasion to define avoidant behavior. Instead, the absence of formal registration is a more reliable indicator of entrepreneurial reluctance or inability to operate within state-defined parameters for the private economy.

While mobile vendors are better able to remain unregistered or operate on an informal basis most of the time, private businesses with fixed retail locations are less able to engage in avoidant behavior, mainly because they cannot close up shop and flee from regulators as readily as their itinerant counterparts. This is especially the case in large urban centers where the ICMB is more closely monitored by higher administrative levels and often expected to meet a certain quota of new business registrations and ICMB

6. Note, however, that a common manner of tax collection is preset for a given period (*shuangding*). In that case, if the amount of tax levied is too low, then the tax bureau is also at fault.

7. This estimate is based on the assumption that private enterprises should pay 4 RMB for every 100 RMB in sales. During the 1989–98 period, private enterprises should have paid 305.8 billion RMB in taxes, but they remitted only 38.8 billion RMB (Interview 281). In searching for more recent estimates of tax evasion by private entrepreneurs, I found that official reports in the mid-2000s focused more on the fiscal contribution of the private sector. For example, a 2006 report issued by researchers in the Chinese Academy of Social Sciences found that the tax contribution of private firms increased by 40% between 2000 and 2005, while the growth in fiscal revenue by state businesses increased by only 7% over the same period (*China Daily*, September 22, 2006). Other recent estimates of tax evasion discussed the phenomenon among domestic enterprises of all ownership types: in 2003 and 2004, enterprises paid approximately 32% to 33% of what they legitimately owed (Yang 2006, table 8). Li Jianjun of the Central University of Finance and Economics estimates that private enterprises account for the preponderance of tax evasion in these figures, because it is more difficult for state-owned enterprises to evade taxes (personal correspondence, November 1, 2006).

fees. In rural areas, however, a large portion of agricultural, manufacturing, and wholesale businesses are run directly out of individual residences, which makes their unregistered status somewhat less obvious than retailers operating outdoors in a designated commercial center. Indeed, by the time that economic reform was officially sanctioned, many rural households were already engaged in private farming, animal husbandry, and small-scale commodity production. Yet they were not registered as individual entrepreneurs (*getihu*), and therefore not counted as being part of the private sector. Instead, rural households that specialized in nonagricultural activities were called "specialized households" (*zhuanye hu*), which were considered part of the collective sector (Young 1995, 17–19). But even after regulations on rural individual enterprises were passed in 1984, many rural households remained unregistered.

Consider, for example, the experience of a couple in Hengtang Village, Rui'an County, Zhejiang Province, who run a small knitting factory out of their mud-thatched home (Interview 112). Villager Chen grew up in an impoverished family, so after only three years of elementary school he started working as a farmer and later served as a soldier. During the late 1970s, he traveled through Anhui, Hubei, and Sichuan provinces to peddle small consumer items. After returning to Hengtang Village in 1982, he got married and used his 400 RMB ($212) in savings to purchase two knitting machines to produce socks. Villager Chen and his wife each worked on one machine. By 1988, they were ready to invest 240,000 RMB ($63,661) to build a new home out of concrete and upgrade their machinery. Because they never bothered to register the business, it would have been difficult for them to get a loan from a formal financial institution. Sixty percent of their 1988 investment was brokered through a local moneylender. Villager Chen estimates that their sales volume peaked during 1995–96, when the sock factory was earning 1 million RMB (about $119,760) annually. At that time, his younger brother helped them get a 350,000 RMB ($41,916) loan from the local rural credit cooperative by serving as a guarantor. When I interviewed villager Chen in late 2001, the business consisted of only him, his wife, his son, and two migrant workers; he reported that the factory was going bankrupt due to stiff competition. Although villager Chen believed that he could salvage the business if he had access to larger bank loans, he still had no intention of registering the factory because "it would not be worth the hassle."

In addition to itinerant urban peddlers and rural households engaged in light manufacturing, a third common type of unregistered private business can be found in suburbs that are close to urban centers but still largely rural in topography. In one of the suburban districts of Wuhan City, Hubei Province, for instance, I came across several groups of unregistered mushroom growers from other provinces. A middle-aged couple that I interviewed from Hunan was pretty typical (Interview 243). They left their three children behind with relatives and came to rural Hubei in 1997 because they heard that Wuhan had a lucrative mushroom market. As of 2002, they were renting about eight *mu* of land at 500 RMB ($60) per *mu* annually and a building for 6,000 RMB ($725) per year. Although the scale of their operation looked quite modest, they were earning over 100,000 RMB ($12,077) per year in profits—which is much more than they ever dreamed of earning back home. Moreover, they seemed quite comfortable with their unregistered status, because no one bothers them about it. They just pay their rent and send money home when their children visit during Spring Festival. They also enjoy interacting with the local community of (unregistered) mushroom farmers from Hunan. Despite the positive attitude that the couple has toward their current situation, they do not want their children to become farmers or individual entrepreneurs when they grow up: "As long as they study hard in school, they will have better work opportunities than we had." This sentiment is widely shared by unregistered entrepreneurs.

Given that avoidant entrepreneurs are not formally registered with the ICMB, they have not been included in any of the national surveys of private entrepreneurs, including my own. Statistical data is thus lacking regarding their political opinions. In each of my field sites, however, I made an effort to interview unregistered business owners and ask them the same questions that were on the survey. Based on these interviews, it is apparent that avoidant entrepreneurs have grievances that could be alleviated with changes in national or local policies, but the most they do is to talk about it privately rather than filing formal complaints. In this sense, the avoidant coping strategy reflects not only limited ability to demand official redress for their problems but also distrust of formal authority and formal institutions. None of the unregistered business owners that I interviewed expressed interest in joining the Communist Party or using legal channels to resolve their disputes.[8] Avoidant entrepreneurs do not participate in the types of formal associational activities that are associated with civil society and democratic development. They do, however, use alternative means to deal with the challenges of running an unregistered business. When widely practiced, these alternative means may be considered adaptive informal institutions. The persistent street peddlers discussed above, for example, rely on one another to keep a lookout for various cadres and fee collectors. This common system of mutual assistance in regulatory and tax evasion is an adaptive informal institution. The couple operating the sock factory out of

---

8. Note that some entrepreneurs are "avoidant" by choice. For example, some business owners who are party members, former soldiers, or former state employees share a sense of detachment from official regulations and entities. Such entrepreneurs fall in an intermediate area between the avoidant and loyally acceptant categories in the typology, that is, they may possess the means to confront the state but lack the desire to do so.

Unregistered mushroom growers from Fujian Province in rural district of Wuhan City

their home drew on informal sources of credit and a relative's credit guarantee to expand their business. These types of informal finance are also adaptive informal institutions. And the mushroom growers simply rent land under the table to produce a food product that is in high demand in a neighboring urban center. Granting short-term usufruct rights in exchange for money also constitutes an adaptive informal institution. In each of these instances, the coping strategies used by avoidant entrepreneurs contribute indirectly to changes in the implementation of formal policies, if not formal policies themselves, by virtue of the fact that they are informal and evasive. As a result, over time it has become less cumbersome for entrepreneurs to register their businesses, formal financial institutions are beginning to lend to private entrepreneurs, and it is common practice for landholders to rent out their land.

Acceptant Behavior

Entrepreneurs who exhibit acceptant behavior are unlikely to initiate radical changes, but they are more likely to bandwagon with others if the prevailing rules of the game shift. Acceptant business owners account for the overwhelming majority of business owners, about four out of five.[9] They

9. Acceptant entrepreneurs account for 94.5% of the respondents. If we adjust the denominator of the universe of entrepreneurs to include the 15.3% estimate for avoidant entrepreneurs, then acceptant entrepreneurs account for 80% of all business owners, both registered and unregistered.

comply with most of the official requirements of doing business, meaning that they are registered with the ICMB, display the assorted licenses that may be required for their trade (e.g., restaurants have health and sanitation certificates), and generally pay the fees requested by various agencies. These types of merchants may also observe certain informal norms to improve their interactions with the staff of the state. For example, to foster a sense of goodwill, a barber may not charge an ICMB cadre for a haircut and a restaurant owner might host lavish banquets for cadres on a regular basis. The boundaries separating token gift giving among friends, instrumental cultivation of relationships (*guanxi*), and outright bribery are often ambiguous (Yan 1996; Yang 1994). Giving gifts in exchange for favors or accelerated service is part of the reality of doing business, whether in the private or public sector, and greasing the wheels is certainly not specific to China. However, access to certain types of products and services (such as bank credit) is more likely to entail the use of social networks and gift giving in China than in advanced industrialized countries due to the transitional character of the Chinese economy (cf. Gold, Guthrie, and Wank 2002). All of these practices—gift giving, cultivation of *guanxi*, and bribery—may also be considered adaptive informal institutions because they are an integral part of doing business for most entrepreneurs. In my 2002 survey, on average 40.6 percent of the respondents indicated that they "offer incentives or gifts to enlist the assistance" of various types of professionals and state cadres, including those working for state banks, the ICMB, the tax bureau, law firms, and local NPC or Chinese People's Political Consultative Committee (CPPCC) members.

Although acceptant entrepreneurs comply with most of the official and unofficial requirements for conducting business, my typology takes into account the fact that they may differ in their attitudes about these operational realities (Parris 1999).[10] *Loyally acceptant* entrepreneurs consider that the system generally works for them. They are typically local economic and political elites who believe that reforms have worked in their favor, though individual entrepreneurs with thriving small businesses may also share a similarly positive view of the reform process and of the national government in general. These types of entrepreneurs have the resources to complain to state entities, but they rarely do so because they are generally satisfied with their lot. Overall, loyally acceptant entrepreneurs account for 80.5 percent of the survey sample or, after adjusting for the estimated 15.3 percent of avoidant entrepreneurs, 68.2 percent of the broader universe of business owners.

Unlike red capitalists who are well connected politically and small business owners who are content with the state of China's political economy, *grudgingly acceptant* entrepreneurs comply with the terms of doing business somewhat

10. Five distinct views of citizenship among entrepreneurs are delineated in Parris (1999).

reluctantly. In many cases, entrepreneurs go about their work with an attitude of resignation because other income-generating options may not seem to be available to them. Grudgingly acceptant entrepreneurs usually have assorted grievances but lack the social, political, economic, and perhaps even psychological ability to do anything about it. In response to the survey question, "When you encounter disputes, how do you normally resolve the matter?" grudgingly acceptant entrepreneurs bypass all the standard possibilities for dispute resolution—including the nonconfrontational ones such as asking friends and relatives for assistance—and choose the last option on the questionnaire: "Feel powerless." Taking such responses as a proxy for grudgingly acceptant entrepreneurs, I estimate that they account for 14 percent of the sample—or 11.9 percent of all entrepreneurs, when taking into account the existence of avoidant unregistered ones.[11] Cases of loyally acceptant and grudgingly acceptant entrepreneurs are presented below.

Owner Fang, the proprietor of a real estate development corporation in Huizhou, Guangdong Province, is the prototypical loyally acceptant entrepreneur (Interview 186). He is proud of what he has done with his business and is grateful to the regime for giving him the opportunity to do so. Born in 1962, owner Fang started working as a carpenter's apprentice when he was seventeen years old in 1980. After only six months, he quit the position and started making his own furniture with only 16 RMB ($10.67) in his pocket. In 1988, he entered the real estate business because he noticed a rising demand for houses in rural areas. Owner Fang then opened a lumberyard in 1991 and, two years later, went to the special economic zone of Shenzhen that borders Hong Kong to invest in commercial real estate. As of 2002, his real estate business had twenty-eight hundred employees and the fixed assets of his company were worth over 600 million RMB ($72.5 million). Fang attributes the rapid private sector development in Guangdong Province to national macroeconomic policies, including the opening of Shenzhen to foreign investment—but he made a point of mentioning that he has had to rely on his own hard work, unlike state-owned enterprises that have had their resources budgeted by the government. He believes that these days private entrepreneurs who operate at his scale are now equal in status to state-owned enterprises. As evidence, Fang said that the highest government officials treat him to banquets and credit officers from state commercial banks come over to offer him loans. Furthermore, the local CCP has been encouraging him to join the party since 2000, though he is not interested. Owner Fang's loyally acceptant attitude is best summed up

---

11. The particular situation of grudgingly acceptant entrepreneurs should be distinguished from other entrepreneurs who are economically well off and frustrated with various issues but choose not to pursue active forms of local lobbying or dispute resolution. The two-by-two typology presented in this chapter does not have enough dimensions to capture such business owners in a distinct category.

in his own words: "I have no patience for other private entrepreneurs who complain about being discriminated against. If others look down on you, it's because you haven't done business well. When I run into problems, I just try to come up with compromise solutions (*xietiao jiejue*), which is an inherently Chinese characteristic."

Loyally acceptant entrepreneurs are not limited to those with large, profitable businesses such as owner Fang's real estate company. A number of individual entrepreneurs (*getihu*) are also loyally acceptant (Interview 230). Consider, for instance, the experience of owner Yu who runs a small umbrella store in the old retail district of Hankou in Wuhan, Hubei Province. His family was always involved in small business. Because Yu's father had lung disease, the neighborhood's residential committee allowed him to run a printing business out of his apartment in 1958. This enabled him to buy medicine and raise four children. In 1979, his father opened a formal print shop with a storefront, which was among the first 103 private businesses that opened in the revitalized commercial heart of Hankou during the reform era. Owner Yu opened his umbrella store down the street shortly thereafter and takes pride in his particular trade. He explained, "If I switched from selling one product to another all the time, people would not have confidence in my store. My customers know that if they buy an umbrella from me, next year they can come back and find me if there is a problem." Owner Yu's main government-related complaints concern basic operating conditions; there has been a problem with other vendors selling fake goods, sanitation conditions, and informal sector peddlers operating on the sidewalk in front of his store. Even though owner Yu thinks that other parts of Hubei may be better for business than his current location, he does not intend to move and he does not plan to organize with other retailers on the street to complain to the local ICMB or government about his concerns. He appreciates the opportunities that his family has had to make a living and is confident that the policy environment will continue to improve for the private sector.

In contrast to loyally acceptant entrepreneurs who are essentially satisfied with their lives as business owners—or are relatively successful in using informal means to address their concerns—grudgingly acceptant ones have many grievances and bear them silently. Typically, they complain about being harassed by local government agencies and fee collectors. Unlike the avoidant entrepreneurs, however, grudgingly acceptant ones have a tougher time evading street-level regulators because their businesses are registered, if not fixed in a particular part of town. The owner of a small print and copy shop in the county seat of Hechuan, Chongqing Municipality, for example, feels relatively helpless when it comes to the demands of various local cadres (Interview 263). After graduating from junior high school, owner Yin worked in a collective granary from 1978 to 1997. When she lost her job in 1997, she decided to open a retail copy shop with 5,600 RMB ($676) of her family's savings. During our interview in 2002, she expressed frustration with the City Management Office for fines due to promotional advertisements hanging in the space directly outside of her store. Meanwhile, the City Traffic Office was bothering owner Yin for similar issues, and the Sanitation Office kept blaming her for garbage outside her store even when other businesses or people walking by had left it. When asked if she ever considered asking the local Individual Laborers Association (ILA) for assistance in mediating between her copy shop and local agencies, owner Yin replied that the ILA was not helpful and that there was no point in attempting to contest the fines levied by the various agencies. "Putting up with annoying cadres is just part of what it takes to be an individual entrepreneur. I can't do anything about it," she concluded.

While grudgingly acceptant entrepreneurs tend to express fatalistic attitudes about their difficult lives, they also demonstrate considerable resilience and raw entrepreneurialism. Many business owners in this category seem willing to do whatever it takes to eke out a living and provide for their offspring, even if it means being separated from them for years at a time. In 1996, for example, I interviewed a couple who left their son behind with relatives in Anhui Province and traveled through many different parts of the country over a six-year span before finding an appropriate place to run their restaurant in the southern coastal city of Quanzhou (Tsai 2002, 84). Even then, their son remained in Anhui. Although the couple is part of the so-called floating population of internal migrants, they would not be considered "avoidant" because in each of the cities that they have operated, they attempted to observe local regulations for their form of business. In their hometown, they secured approval from a neighborhood committee to operate in a certain section. In other cities, they received a temporary license from the local ICMB for outdoor food stands. And in Quanzhou they are formally registered with the city's ICMB and subscribe to the ACFIC newsletter, even though they never read it. Given their low literacy level and lack of connections, they do not see the point in complaining publicly. Business owners who fall into this grudgingly acceptant category are generally willing to follow formal and informal norms of operation, but they are not likely to introduce coping strategies that could lead directly to democratizing outcomes.

Assertive Political Strategies

Assertive political behavior is the only category of entrepreneurial coping strategies that holds the direct potential for bringing about democratizing reforms because it includes direct participation in formal political institutions, individual lobbying efforts, associational activities, as well as more contentious forms of collective action in collaboration with other entrepreneurs.

To estimate the percentage of entrepreneurs who rely on assertive political strategies *most of the time*, I added the percentage of respondents who ranked the following means of dispute resolution as their first choices when they encounter problems: "appeal to local government or higher authorities," "appeal through judicial courts," and "attempt to resolve [the problem] by contacting the news media." The total percentage of respondents who privilege such assertive strategies is 5.5 percent, which translates into 4.7 percent of all entrepreneurs if we take the avoidant entrepreneurs into account.[12]

In line with general studies of political participation in China, my survey also considered the frequency with which all types of entrepreneurs express their opinions directly to political leaders; solicit assistance from those who have influence with political leaders; reflect their views through local mass associations; reflect their views through NPC delegates at various levels; express their opinions to members of the CPPCC; communicate their opinions to higher authorities through official business associations (ILA, PEA, UFIC); write letters to the relevant government agency; write letters to the media; write reports to official organizations accepting inquiries or complaints; seek organizations to arbitrate disputes; appeal to the court system; meet with higher authorities for help; and/or refused to give bribes (Shi 1997). The 2002 survey further distinguished among entrepreneurs who engaged in these activities alone, in cooperation with others, or in collaboration with other entrepreneurs. When the survey asked entrepreneurs whether and how often they used these means to deal with various problems, only a very small portion of the respondents said that they frequently use these assertive forms of dispute resolution, and an even smaller percentage pursues these means in collaboration with other entrepreneurs (table 5.1). In other words, these findings show that the vast majority of entrepreneurs do not use assertive means to address their problems on a regular basis, which is consistent with the 5.5 percent estimate of assertive entrepreneurs mentioned above. Furthermore, when business owners do use assertive forms of dispute resolution, they are much more likely to do it alone than to collaborate with others or with other entrepreneurs (see the middle three columns in table 5.1). This provides limited evidence for the extent of class-based collective action among private entrepreneurs.

In addition to the observation that entrepreneurs prefer to resolve their problems on their own rather than to engage in collaborative efforts, the survey results also show that entrepreneurs are more likely to contact individual cadres rather than go through formal institutional channels to

12. This estimate of 5.5% or 4.7% is only meant to capture the slice of the entrepreneurial population that uses directly assertive political strategies on a regular basis. There are many other types of assertive political behavior, and entrepreneurs engage in those activities with varying levels of frequency.

Table 5.1. How private entrepreneurs address their problems, 2002

Means of dispute resolution	Frequently used (%)	Sometimes used (%)	Individual use* (%)	Collaborate with others* (%)	Collaborate with other entrepreneurs* (%)	Give gifts in the process* (%)
Express opinion directly to political leaders	5.0	17.1	76.1	16.8	7.1	46.1
Solicit assistance from those with influence on political leaders	5.1	18.5	70.6	24.5	4.9	55.9
Express opinion through mass associations	2.4	10.5	51.5	33.0	15.5	22.7
Express opinion through people's congress delegates	0.8	4.5	56.9	26.4	16.7	17.7
Express opinion through CPCC members	1.2	5.5	51.2	36.0	12.8	15.3
Express opinion through entrepreneurs associations (ILA, PEA, UFIC)	4.1	12.9	59.2	27.4	13.4	14.7
Write letters to relevant government agencies	0.6	4.7	67.7	22.2	10.1	16.1
Write letters to the media	0.3	2.6	55.3	36.8	7.9	24.0
Report to official organizations accepting inquiries or complaints	0.5	1.8	46.5	32.6	20.9	29.3
Seek organizations to arbitrate the dispute	0.9	4.7	69.6	20.9	9.5	28.1
Appeal to courts	1.0	6.8	81.6	13.1	5.3	35.5
Meet with higher authorities for assistance	0.7	1.1	51.4	31.9	16.7	25.0
Refuse to be bribed	0.9	4.6	43.9	36.0	20.1	30.9

*The percentages in these columns exclude the "no comment," "not applicable," and missing responses.

Table 5.2. Comparison of political assertiveness: Beijing residents, private entrepreneurs, and ordinary citizens (percentage who engage in these activities "frequently, sometimes, or occasionally")

Means of dispute resolution	Beijing residents, 1988 (%)	Beijing residents, 1996 (%)	Private entrepreneurs, 2002 (%)	Ordinary citizens, 2001–2 (%)
Contact deputies to people's congresses	8.6	14.1	10.9	3.2
Write letters to government officials/agencies	12.5	15.3	11.7	3.5
Write letters to editors of newspapers/the media	6.8	8.3	6.2	1.0
Appeal to courts	1.2	4.5	18.6	1.8
N	757	894	1,525	3,183

Sources: Beijing data come from Shi (1997, 94, table 3.1; and 1999, 155, table 7.4). The 2002 data on entrepreneurs come from my own survey. The 2001–2 data on ordinary citizens come from the Asian Barometer Survey.

express their grievances.[13] While 5.1 percent of the respondents said that they frequently solicit assistance from individuals who have access to political leaders, only 1 percent regularly use legal means to settle disputes, and only 0.5 percent frequently report to official organizations that are set up to accept formal inquiries or complaints.

To put these figures in comparative perspective, table 5.2 shows the frequency with which ordinary residents in Beijing versus private entrepreneurs in my sample use assertive political means for solving their problems. In his diachronic study of Beijing residents in 1988 and 1996, Tianjian Shi (1999) found an overall increase in political participation between those years. Although more recent data from his subsequent national survey of the general population was not available at the time of my survey of private entrepreneurs, a comparison with Shi's previously published data shows that when it comes to contacting deputies to people's congresses, writing letters to government officials, and writing letters to the media, surveyed business owners in 2002 were less active than Beijing residents in 1988 and 1996.[14] The only area in which private entrepreneurs in 2002 seemed more assertive was in using the court system to resolve disputes, which is consistent with the

13. This practice of going through individuals rather than institutions appears to be a norm in China, but I would not automatically classify all such practices as adaptive informal institutions, because we cannot assume that *all* instances of relying on personalistic connections are in response to the inaccessibility of formal institutions.

14. A comparison with the 2001–02 ABS survey administered to ordinary citizens throughout China, however, suggests that both Beijingers and private entrepreneurs are much more active than the general population: only 3.2% of the ABS sample (n = 3,183) had contacted deputies to the people's congresses, only 3.5% had written letters to government officials/agencies, only 1% had written letters to newspapers, and only 1.8% had taken a dispute to the courts.

reality that entrepreneurs are at greater risk than the general population for experiencing legal problems. However, we cannot draw any definitive conclusions about the litigious tendencies of entrepreneurs relative to ordinary citizens because the legal system became much more extensive and sophisticated between 1996 and 2002 (Peerenboom 2002).[15] If we bracket the comparative use of the court system, then the basic inference is that private entrepreneurs are probably less likely than the general population in Beijing to rely on formal political institutions for dispute resolution.

In contrast to the relative infrequency with which entrepreneurs work through political leaders and institutions, business owners are more inclined to contact various types of business associations. At one point or another, 34.7 percent of the respondents have expressed their concerns to the official mass associations representing private entrepreneurs (i.e., the ILA, PEA, and UFIC). As will be discussed below, the use of officially sanctioned business associations for expressing discontent and making policy demands reflects the relative success of China's top-down corporatist institutions in recognizing the concerns of private entrepreneurs. At the same time, entrepreneurs also draw on nongovernmental and informal associations. In many areas, larger private entrepreneurs have established autonomous business associations that are registered with the Civil Affairs Bureau as nonprofit societies. These societies are supposed to "assist the poor" and "promote the values of material and spiritual civilization."[16] But most business associations combine welfare or charity activities with more instrumental networking and lobbying functions. The relative popularity of both state-sponsored and informal associations suggests that to the extent that entrepreneurs make policy-oriented or overtly political demands, it is more likely that they would rely on such associations rather than formal political institutions in the process.

There is a diverse range of individual and collective strategies that different types of business owners use. Even though all of these forms of interest articulation and dispute resolution could be regarded as "assertive" strategies, even within this category considerable variation in political impact can still be identified. First we will consider the extent to which private entrepreneurs participate directly in formal political institutions such as the NPC and

15. However, Ethan Michelson's (2006) rural survey in 2002 found that 5.3% of the sample reported having experience with "mobilizing the law" (meaning appearing in court as a plaintiff or seeking the advice of a lawyer for a personal matter or on behalf of a friend or relative), while 9.9% of surveyed entrepreneurs had mobilized the law, and 22% of entrepreneurs with family or household connections to village leaders had mobilized the law. Although these findings are based on a rural sample, they reveal that entrepreneurs are more likely to engage in legal mobilization than nonentrepreneurs. Correspondence with Ethan Michelson, October 31, 2006.

16. On *shetuan* development, see Sun, Wang, and Zhe 1993. For a review in English, see Saich 2000. Cf. Pei 1998.

CPPCC. The second case provides a typical example of how private entrepreneurs may use individual strategies to make policy-related demands. The third set of cases demonstrates the extent to which different types of business associations are effective in recognizing, if not resolving, the concerns of private entrepreneurs. The fourth set of cases presents the far less common instances of spontaneous collective action among business owners—informal networks of entrepreneurs organized by trade, kinship, native place, or former state work unit may provide the basis for collective defense of their interests if the need arises. And, finally, I discuss the most exceptional cases of private entrepreneurs who possess the unusual combination of both substantial resources and discontent with the current regime type.

Entrepreneurs and Formal Political Institutions   As discussed earlier, over one-third of private entrepreneurs are already members of the preeminent formal political institution in China, the Communist Party, but the vast majority of entrepreneurs who are party members joined the party before they became private entrepreneurs. This reflects the fact that members widely ignored the party's earlier prohibition against engaging in capitalist activities. Since Jiang Zemin's 7/1 speech, the party has been more active in recruiting from within the private sector, and as of the time of my 2002 survey, more entrepreneurs reported being interested in joining the party than other types of organizations (see table 4.14). Yet party membership itself does not necessarily translate into political assertiveness. For many members, their level of participation is limited to paying their dues and maybe hanging a plaque on their office wall indicating party membership. As of June 2002, the official occupational breakdown of the CCP was as follows: 45.1 percent were workers in industrial enterprises, laborers in township enterprises, farmers, herders, and fishermen; 21.3 percent were government officials, managing personnel, PLA officers and soldiers, and armed police; 16.4 percent were retirees; 11.6 percent were professionals; and 5.6 percent had "other occupations," which presumably includes private entrepreneurs.[17] In other words, the vast majority of party members are not involved in professions that are overtly political or have any policy relevance. Indeed, many of the business owners I interviewed regarded their party membership as being quite marginal to their daily lives and commercial activities. Besides being a party member, there are three additional political organizations in which entrepreneurs may participate—the NPC and local people's congresses, CPPCC, and the village committee.[18]

17. See http://www.china.org.cn/english/e-16dd/graph/index.htm#.

18. Although party membership does not guarantee active political participation, membership in the NPC and village committee is generally dominated by party members.

The NPC is considered the highest organ of state power and the primary legislative body in the PRC. At the national level, its nearly three thousand deputies meet annually for about two weeks to draft legislation, approve policies (including five-year plans), elect officials, and, if necessary, amend the constitution. The NPC also has branches at the subnational levels, which are called local people's congresses.[19] In theory, deputies to various levels of the people's congresses are elected by deputies at the level directly below it, and deputies at the lowest level are elected directly by the electorate. Since 1953, all citizens have been eligible to vote in local NPC elections, but because the candidates are not subject to popular nomination and the positions are not always contested, the voting process is typically fairly predictable and uncontroversial.[20] Nonetheless, there have been growing instances of NPC members expressing support for accelerated legal reform and investigations into official corruption (Tanner 1999; Xia 2000). When entrepreneurs were asked in 2002 about the nature of their participation in NPC elections, 18.7 percent admitted that they seldom vote in local NPC elections, 11.1 said that they participate whenever they are asked, 2.1 percent delegate the task to others, 13.7 percent said that they participate on occasion, 12.5 percent said that they "sometimes participate earnestly" in elections, and 29.5 said that they "earnestly participate in every election." (It would be reasonable to assume that the latter figure is inflated given that it is the politically correct response to the question.) Overall, this means that 87.7 percent of the respondents report voting in people's congress elections, but if we subtract the percentage of respondents who delegate the task to others (2.1 percent) and seldom vote (18.7 percent), then that leaves a voting rate of 66.7 percent. This rate is lower than the 72.3 percent voter turnout for local deputies in Beijing in the 1988 elections but higher than the voter turnout in 1996, which was almost 10 percent lower than in 1988 (Shi 1997, 93; Shi 1999, 156). Given the difference in timing, the most we can say is that private entrepreneurs in 2002 did not seem to be more active in voting than ordinary citizens in Beijing were several years earlier.

In terms of direct participation in the NPC, in 2002 5.6 percent of the respondents were NPC or local people's congress members, of which 61.6 percent were also party members (table 5.3). While 1.2 percent of my 2002

19. There are local people's congresses at the provincial/autonomous region/municipal, county/city/district, and township/district/neighborhood levels.

20. The election law passed in 1953 granted all citizens, except for the landlord class and counterrevolutionary elements, the right to vote for deputies to the basic-level congresses, meaning township-level congresses in rural areas, district-level congresses in urban areas, and neighborhood-level congresses in special municipalities. However, elections were not held for thirteen years during the Cultural Revolution (1966–79). The 1979 election law then extended direct elections to the local level, i.e., county-, city-, and district-level congresses (Shi 1997, 35). Also see O'Brien 1990.

Table 5.3. Entrepreneurs' participation in formal political institutions, 2002

Political Institution	Percentage who are members (%)	Of which, percentage who are CCP members (%)
National People's Congress or local People's Congress	5.6	61.6
Chinese People's Political Consultative Committee	6.5	32.3
Chinese Communist Party	23.5	100
Village Committee	5.2	53.1

sample were NPC delegates, in the tenth NPC in 2005, 55, or 1.9 percent, of the 2,896 NPC delegates were private entrepreneurs (Interview 281). By 2006, the NPC reported that over 200, or 6.9 percent, of its 2,900 delegates were private entrepreneurs (*China Daily*, October 30, 2006).

While the NPC has formal legislative power, the CPPCC functions more like a consultative body. Established in 1949 as a "people's democratic united front" organization, the CPPCC was intended to bring various groups in society together in a coalition government. Although the Communist Party commands ultimate leadership over the CPPCC, from the very beginning the CPPCC has intentionally included constituents that fall outside the typical scope of the Communist Party, including representatives of Taiwan, Hong Kong, and Macao; ethnic minorities; each of the mass associations representing workers, women, youth, and private entrepreneurs; and members of the eight officially sanctioned democratic parties, that is, the Revolutionary Committee of the Chinese Guomindang, China Democratic League, China Democratic National Construction Association, China Association for Promoting Democracy, Chinese Peasants' and Workers' Democratic Party, China Zhi Gong Party, Jiu San Society, and Taiwan Democratic Self-Government League.[21] The CPPCC actually functioned as the PRC's legislature until the 1956 PRC Constitution transferred that power to the NPC. Since then, the CPPCC has served as an advisory body that discusses various issues but lacks the formal legislative powers to draft, approve, and implement various policies. Like the NPC, the CPPCC also has branches at the subnational level.

In many ways the CPPCC represents a more natural forum than the CCP or NPC for private entrepreneurs to express their concerns. The earliest members of the CPPCC included the national bourgeoisie, reformed

21. The democratic parties differ from those found in liberal democracies in the sense that they are not meant to represent aggregated social interests and compete with one another (much less the ruling CCP) in China's political system. Instead, the democratic parties may be considered an institutionalized form of "loyal opposition." Seymour 1987, 87.

Table 5.4. Overview of China's official democratic parties

Name	Year founded	Primary constituency	Membership (as of 2005)
China Revolutionary Committee of the Kuomingtang (Zhongguo guomindang geming weiyuanhui—mingge)	1948	Former KMT members	60,000
China Democratic League (Zhongguo minzhu tongmeng—minmeng)	1939	Intellectuals	144,000
China Democratic National Construction Association (Zhongguo minzhu jianguohui—minjian)	1945	Business people	78,000
China Association for the Promotion of Democracy (Zhongguo minzhu cujinhui—minjin)	1945	Educators	73,000
Chinese Peasants' and Workers' Democratic Party (Zhongguo nonggong minzhudang—nonggong)	1930	Health professionals	73,000
China Zhi Gong Party or Public Interest Party (Zhongguo zhigong dang)	1925	Returned overseas Chinese	18,000
Jiusan Society or 3rd of September Society (Jiusan xueshe)	1946	Higher intellectuals	78,000
Taiwan Democratic Self-government League (Taiwan minzhu zizhi tongmeng—Taimeng)	1947	Taiwan compatriots	1,800
Total			525,800

Sources: Seymour 1987; Seymour 1991; and General Office, National Committee, Chinese People's Political Consultative Conference official website at http://www.cppcc.gov.cn, accessed March 15, 2005.

elements of the Nationalist Party, and members of the United Front of Industry and Commerce (UFIC). However, a higher percentage of entrepreneurs are Communist Party members than CPPCC members (table 5.3). This is largely due to the sheer size of the CCP; with 70.8 million members as of 2005, it represents the largest political party in the world. In contrast, the membership of the eight official democratic parties in the CPPCC is only 525,800, and none of the parties is nearly as influential or prestigious as the CCP. Indeed, the parties were established to complement the activities of the CCP, not to serve as a source of competition or opposition to the ruling party. (See table 5.4 for a brief summary of the democratic parties.)

Despite the limited autonomy of these parties, in the course of field research I did come across some entrepreneurs who believed that being a member of one of the democratic parties and/or the CPPCC was more meaningful than CCP membership. The owner of a travel agency in Chengdu, Sichuan Province, for instance, identified strongly with the Revolutionary Committee of the Chinese Guomingdang (*minge dang* or Revolutionary Party, for short) (Interview 246). He explained, "The CCP is a party for poor people (*qiongmin dang*) and will never truly respect businesspeople even though Jiang Zemin's 7/1 speech tried to turn it into a party for all the people (*quanmin dang*). But the Revolutionary Party stands for equal opportunity regardless of whether you are rich or poor." When asked if being a member of the Revolutionary Party helps from a business perspective, another entrepreneur from Chengdu said that it definitely does, because being a member of the CPPCC "serves as a form of insurance" from official harassment (Interview 247). It is an honor to be a CPPCC member even if it does not carry as much political clout as being an NPC member or high-ranking CCP official.

Besides joining large-scale political organizations with national representation, entrepreneurs have also started to participate in village-level politics. Since the Organic Law on Village Committees was passed in 1987, village committees have been subject to popular election, though it was not until the 1998 revision of the Organic Law that emphasis was placed on direct voting by villagers. Although there has been substantial variation in the implementation of the Organic Law, by 2005 the vast majority of China's 730,000 villages had had at least one round of village elections. Existing studies have found that a number of business owners, especially Communist Party members, have been candidates in village elections (Diamond and Myers 2001; Dickson 2002, 122–126).[22] My 2002 survey found that 10.3 percent of the respondents had been candidates in village committee elections and 5.2 percent of the sample were village committee members, of which 53.1 percent were party members.

To analyze how members and leaders in formal political institutions differ from nonmembers, I created two variables from the data set, "political member" and "political elite," respectively, to distinguish among respondents who were members of the NPC, CPPCC, CCP, and/or village committee, respondents who held leadership positions in those organizations, and respondents who were not members in any formal political institution. Both political members and political elites are more likely to be older, to have entered the private sector earlier, and to run businesses that are more profitable and larger in terms of number of employees (table 5.5). With respect to capitalization issues, political members and elites are also more likely than other business owners to have access to formal bank loans and private loans, as well as investment by groups of shareholders, the township government, government agencies, and even investors from abroad. On the whole, political members and elites are less likely to encounter disputes with consumers, and

---

22. Dickson's (2002) survey of 524 larger private entrepreneurs found that 15.5% had been candidates for village chief (23). Meanwhile, Tsai's (2007) rural survey, conducted in 2001, found that 3.3% of village officials (including party branch and village committee members) were involved in private business and 15% had run businesses in the past.

Table 5.5. Attributes of members and elites of formal political institutions: t-test comparison of means

General attributes	Nonpolitical members	Political members	Political elites
Birth year	1963	1956**	1956**
Year business started	1995	1992**	1992**
Gross Sales in 2001 (10,000 yuan)	334	1,147,651*	252,045
Net Sales in 2001 (10,000 yuan)	29	183**	195**
Number of employees	44	222**	222**
		Mean of Dummy (0/1) Variables	
Credit and investment conditions			
Use of bank loans	.4514	.6786**	.7095**
Ease of access to bank loans	.1052	.1714**	.1788**
Private loans outstanding	.2795	.4393**	.4358**
Investment by group of shareholders	.0257	.0679**	.1006**
Investment by township government or neighborhood committee	.0024	.0179**	.0168**
Investment by government agency/military/law enforcement	.0032	.0107**	.0112**
Investment from abroad	.0040	.0143**	.0223**
Nature of Disputes Encountered			
With suppliers	.5149	.4893	.4637
With buyers	.6201	.5893	.6089
With employees	.1245	.1179	.1173
With consumers	.4193	.2893**	.3017**
With local government agencies and/or officials	.2169	.2714**	.2682**
With local residents or other local organizations	.1494	.2000**	.2067**
With news media	.0145	.0214	.0223
Policy concerns: Need for improvement			
Property rights	.7068	.7214	.7095
Intellectual property rights	.6410	.7000*	.6983**
Public opinion and propaganda	.6739	.7464**	.7486**
Tax policy	.8386	.8429	.8380
Credit policy	.8345	.8286	.8324
Macroeconomic regulation and policy	.5904	.6357	.6313*
Regulation of business	.7871	.7500	.7430*
Household registration system	.5735	.5714	.5531
Equality of treatment in enterprises	.7695	.8500**	.8436**
Eliminating corruption	.9285	.8857**	.8827**
Reform of the political system	.6803	.7000	.6816
Public utilities	.7582	.7607	.7318
Education system	.8177	.7821**	.7654**
Social security system Forms of dispute resolution used	.8643	.8750	.8715
Negotiate and compromise as much as possible, and then let the issue resolve itself	.8273	.8321	.8380

(*Table 5.5—cont.*)

General attributes	Nonpolitical members	Political members	Political elites
Appeal to local government or higher authorities	.2490	.2786*	.2682
Appeal to court	.2378	.2929**	.2682
Mediation through relatives or friends	.2161	.2161**	.1955
Resolve through society and social relations	.4410	.4357	.4860
Resolve through news media	.0153	.0143	.0168
Feel powerless	.1382	.1536	.1397
Express opinion directly to political leaders	.5165	.7500**	.7318**
Ask for help from those with influence over political leaders	.5454	.5607	.5419
Reflect opinion through mass rally groups	.3470	.4071**	.3911
Reflect opinion through NPC delegates	.1863	.3214**	.2793**
Reflect opinion through CPPCC members	.1904	.3679**	.3184**
Reflect opinion to higher authorities via business associations	.4161	.5357*	.5084
Write letters to the relevant government department	.2129	.2607**	.2514
Write letters to the media	.1703	.1429*	.1173**
Report to organizations accepting inquiries	.1663	.1750	.1508
Look for organizations to arbitrate the dispute	.2120	.2286	.1955
Meet with higher authorities for help	.2546	.3643**	.3017
Refuse to be bribed	.1622	.1500	.1453

**Indicates $p < .01$ level of significance; *indicates $p < .05$ level of significance.

they do not have a higher or lower incidence of disputes with suppliers, buyers, employees, and the news media than other entrepreneurs. But they are more likely than regular entrepreneurs to report that they encounter disputes with local government agencies and residents. Given their membership in formal political institutions, it is not surprising that they are also more likely to express their opinions directly to political leaders, use the court system, and use other formal political institutions to express their views to higher level officials. Yet compared to most entrepreneurs, political members and elites are less likely to be concerned about various policy issues; the main policy areas that they were concerned about were improving protection of intellectual property rights, improving public opinion of private entrepreneurs, and ensuring that different types of enterprises are treated fairly. Meanwhile, nonpolitical members and nonelites are more likely to be concerned about corruption and improving the educational system. In brief, political members and elites may be more active in voicing their complaints to officials and using formal institutional channels for dispute resolution, but as a group their grievances are also relatively limited.

Individual Lobbying and Dispute Resolution Efforts   Most of the entrepreneurs that I surveyed and interviewed prefer to rely on their own efforts to resolve problems. When they experience conflict—with suppliers, consumers, creditors, debtors, employees, partners, cadres—that cannot be resolved through direct negotiation, they typically enlist the assistance of well-placed friends. The latter may include local party/government officials or ordinary citizens such as journalists. Owner Tai, the chief executive officer of a dairy-products factory in Nanjing, Jiangsu Province, used the latter to help her break into a market dominated by SOEs (Interview 166). After selling products ranging from winter coats to lighting fixtures, in 1998 owner Tai opened up her dairy factory with an initial investment of 4.1 million RMB ($495,169). She explained that initially it was difficult to secure her high-end customer base of fancy restaurants because the latter prefer their customers to drink alcohol. Hence, at first she paid restaurants 200,000 RMB ($24,155) each to carry her brand of milk and yogurt. This "entrance fee" turned out to be worth it because she now sells those restaurants 3 million RMB ($361,969) worth of milk annually. Despite the success of her business, owner Tai was quite animated about how unfair the city government had been toward private entrepreneurs. When she first started the factory in 1998, a local state-owned enterprise that sold milk products repeatedly harassed her because her business represented a potential source of competition. Specifically, the SOE repeatedly claimed that her factory failed to meet various standards for producing milk and yogurt. Yet owner Tai's factory was well equipped with the latest machines and coolers, and kept appropriately clean by a large staff of sanitation workers. The unfounded accusations angered owner Tai, so she mobilized her journalist friends to write about the SOE's libelous tactics, which attracted the attention of the local Private Entrepreneurs Association. The latter then went to the Nanjing People's Consultative Committee to complain on her behalf. The SOE eventually stopped giving her a hard time.

Besides being harassed by a competitor in the state sector, owner Tai's other major grievance against the city government concerns the Public Security Bureau. Her delivery workers stole over 1 million RMB ($120,773) worth of dairy products from her. Although she has complained about the theft several times, the local police did not bother to look into it because she believes they do not care about crimes committed against private entrepreneurs. As of our interview in 2002, the issue remained unresolved and owner Tai could not think of anyone who could help her press the case. The city's Public Security Bureau is a more formidable target than a SOE that produces milk.

Even though the PEA proved to be helpful in dealing with the SOE, owner Tai's initial attempt at redressing her problem was to turn to friends who happened to be journalists rather than going through an organization with whom she lacked a preexisting connection. She drew on her social network to complain to political authorities, which is typical of how private entrepreneurs approach their problems. Business owners who are members of trade associations have a more direct forum in which to express their grievances.

The Role of Business Associations   There are two basic types of business associations in contemporary China: top-down mass associations established by the party-state to represent the interests of private entrepreneurs, and relatively autonomous nongovernmental associations organized by business sector, location, or native place.

As mentioned in chapter 3, the first category of associations includes the All-China Federation of Industry and Commerce (ACFIC, *gongshanglian*), which was established in 1953; and the Individual Laborers Association (ILA, *geti laodongzhe xiehui* or *gexie*) and Private Entrepreneurs Association (PEA, *siying qiye xiehui* or *sixie*), which were established during the reform era to represent individual and private entrepreneurs, respectively. The ACFIC is comparable to the All-China Women's Federation and All-China Federation of Trade Unions in that the party-state created all of them shortly after the PRC's founding to represent different sectors in society. Their official tasks include communicating state policy to their members, documenting (and counting) the nature of their constituencies, and advocating favorable policies on behalf of their sector. Although the ACWF and ACFTU have branches going down to the township/neighborhood committee and enterprise level, respectively, the ACFIC has a less extensive network of branches, largely because the legal private sector virtually disappeared during the Mao era and the ACFIC ceased to operate during the Cultural Revolution.[23] Hence, the more recently established ILA and the PEA have more branches than the ACFIC at the local level and also tend to have more activities. Yet the ILA and PEA are also more closely tied to the state agency in charge of regulating the private sector, the Industrial and Commercial Management Bureau (ICMB, *gongshang guanliju* or *gongshangju*) (Young 1995, 123–131). In most localities, when entrepreneurs register their businesses with the ICMB they are automatically members of either the ILA or PEA. Meanwhile, the latter are funded and partially staffed by the ICMB, and adding to their close relationship with the state, the ILA and PEA often have offices directly in the local government compound next to the ICMB. In short, the ILA and PEA are clearly state-related associations, which has led some scholars to refer to them as state corporatist organizations (Nevitt 1996; Unger 1996).

---

23. As of 2002, the ACFIC had 3,059 local branches at or above the county level with a total of 1.64 million members. Official ACFIC site at http://www.acfic.org.cn/gygsl/, accessed March 16, 2005.

Given the close relationship between the ICMB and the ILA/PEA, many of the entrepreneurs I interviewed did not find them particularly helpful and stated quite bluntly, "They are useless." One entrepreneur told me the only reason he joined the ILA was because the county government told the township government to recruit him to bolster local finances (Interview 51).[24] Yet other studies have found that private entrepreneurs find the ILA and PEA to be helpful. For example, Bruce Dickson's study of larger private entrepreneurs with over 1 million RMB in capitalization found that most business owners believe that they represent the interests of their members, most have gone through one of the official associations when they encounter problems, and most would do it again if they encountered another problem (Dickson 2003, 75–79). However, this positive evaluation of state-sponsored associations is positively correlated with the level of local economic development, which suggests that contextual factors such as the overall availability of resources and the structure of the local economy mediate the relative utility of the ACFIC, ILA, and PEA. In chapter 6 I discuss the issue of local variation in greater detail.

Notwithstanding important differences among localities, I found that medium- to larger-scale businesses tended to find the official associations more useful than individual entrepreneurs who, perhaps rightly, view them as being more elite oriented. An example of an official trade association that seems active and relatively successful in addressing its members' grievances is the Wuhan City Federation of Industry and Commerce Watch and Glasses Business Association (*Wuhanshi gongshanglian zhongbiao yanjing tongye shanghui*) (Interviews 231, 232, and 233). The business association was established in December 1990 when Wuhan was still completely dominated by SOEs. At the time, the Wuhan City Department Store monopolized sales of most consumer products, including watches and glasses; all of the business association's early members were thus SOEs. As of 2002, most of its members were private entrepreneurs, and collectively they represented 80 percent of the watch vendors and 70 percent of the glasses vendors in Wuhan. In that year, the six directors of the trade association paid 800 RMB ($97) in dues annually, while regular members paid 500 RMB ($60) annually.[25] The directors are elected through secret ballot for two-year terms, which are renewable three times. Watch and glasses vendors who chose not to join the association include the oldest glasses makers that are well established and independent, especially large vendors with chain stores (e.g., ones with dozens of branches), and very small glasses vendors. The director of the trade association explained that the trade association

24. In that particular locality, ILA members pay 3,000 RMB/year in dues and leaders pay 5,000 RMB/year.

25. The fees for regular members were 50% higher when most of the members were SOEs. They were reduced in 1993 to attract nonstate vendors of watches and glasses.

not only serves to clarify government rules and regulations but works to ensure that its members are treated fairly and have manageable operating conditions. For example, government regulation of watches and glasses has proliferated in recent years due to their increasing popularity among consumers. From the watch and glasses vendors' perspective, the regulations have become excessive. The trade association thus managed to reduce the number of state units and agencies involved in regulating them from seven to five entities. This is an example of how official trade associations can be effective in resolving grievances that private entrepreneurs have against governmental entities.

Meanwhile, an issue that the association was still trying to address in 2002 concerned discrimination against private training centers for laid-off state workers. The state-run training centers charge higher fees and hold sessions for shorter amounts of time than the private ones (six weeks vs. four weeks), and yet laid-off workers are required to attend the state-owned training centers if they wish to learn the watch and glasses trade. In addition to dealing with policy-related issues that affect all of their members, the association also responds to individual requests for mediation. One member, for instance, was fined 16,800 RMB ($2,029) for not having labels on his glasses and accused of selling fake goods; what happened was that the labels fell off, so the trade association went to the relevant city bureau and had the fine lifted. In another case, two members started feuding with each other because they were selling the same brand of glasses at different prices—480 vs. 560 RMB. Because the store with the lower price had a tax-free arrangement, the other store could not compete effectively. The trade association ended up mediating between them. This shows that official business associations can also be effective in defusing conflicts among entrepreneurs themselves, which may reduce the need for sparring business owners to seek redress through political or legal channels.

The second category of business associations consists of relatively autonomous nongovernmental entities that are registered with the Ministry of Civil Affairs as "social organizations" (*shehui tuanti* or *shetuan*) and typically managed by entrepreneurs themselves. These types of business associations are not truly autonomous from the state because all social organizations are subject to a host of regulations that limit the ease of registration, including sponsorship by a state unit (Foster 2002; Pei 1998; Saich 2000). As such, in practice entrepreneurs' business associations range from being closely affiliated to the ICMB, ILA, ACFIC, or PEA to being quite independent from any governmental body and self-sufficient. When asked in the 2002 survey if entrepreneurs need their own trade associations, networking clubs, or related societies, 83.5 percent of the respondents believed there is a need for such associations. However, entrepreneurs view such associations as being helpful for business networking and organizational purposes rather than

Table 5.6. Functions that an autonomous entrepreneurs' association should serve, 2002

Function	Percentage selecting this function (%)
Protect legitimacy of private property rights	36.3
Enhance social status of private entrepreneurs	29.1
Coordinate activities of various enterprises	47.5
Facilitate exchange of information	47.2
Formulate rules and regulations for trading; enable self-regulation	21.1
Provide social contacts for private entrepreneurs	16.4
Be a positive influence within the community	16.4
Reflect opinions and requests to the party and government	17.4
Help private enterprises develop an overseas market	8.6

for explicitly political purposes (table 5.6). Specifically, 47.5 percent of the respondents stated that the purpose of setting up an entrepreneurs' business association would be to coordinate the activities of various enterprises, and 47.2 percent indicated that it should be to facilitate exchange of information, while only 17.4 percent said that it would be to reflect opinions and make requests to the party and government. The cases below offer concrete instances of how entrepreneurs perceive and use their business associations.

Most business associations are organized by sector and set up to address sector-specific concerns. Consider, for example, the footwear industry business association in Huangbu Township, Huidong County, Guangdong Province (Interview 196). The association is registered as a social organization and it has eighty members who pay 1,000 RMB ($121) in annual dues. The director of the association also happens to be the vice director of the local Federation of Industry and Commerce. The director pays 50,000 RMB ($6,039) in annual dues and holds a three-year term, while the vice directors of the footwear association pay 20,000 to 30,000 RMB ($2,415 to $3,623) in annual dues. All the directors and vice directors are elected through a secret ballot. According to the director, the association helps members with external sales and marketing, enables private entrepreneurs to network with one another and exchange information about the footwear industry, and serves as a means for shoe manufacturers to contact the relevant government authorities when necessary. At the time of our interview in 2002, the footwear association had just submitted a proposal to the government of Huidong County requesting permission to hold a "cultural shoe fair" later that year. They planned to charge vendors 10,000 RMB ($1,208) to display their products at a stand and anticipated that at least five thousand people would attend the trade fair. The association had already contacted reporters at Guangdong Television to cover the event. The proposal said that because Huangbu had twenty years of experience in manufacturing shoes, it was about time they held a formal event to share its accomplishments with everyone else. The county government ultimately accepted the proposal, and the shoe manufacturers were pleased with the opportunity to showcase their products.

In addition to networking, public relations, and marketing functions, business associations can also be helpful in persuading the local government to bend rules in a manner that benefits its members. A real estate business association in another part of Guangdong, for example, received complaints from various developers about a regulation that required prospective home buyers to prove that they are in compliance with the one-child policy by producing the requisite forms at the time of purchase (Interview 192). The local real estate developers thought this was a ridiculous requirement that would harm their business. As a result, the real estate association lobbied the local government to be more understanding about their business concerns, and, sure enough, the local government ignored the regulation henceforth. This shows that sector-specific business associations can also be effective in influencing local governmental practices. But note that the relative success of policy advocacy by trade associations is largely contingent on the extent of convergence of the interests between the local government and the particular sector. Of all sectors, real estate development is probably the one where local officials are most likely to benefit directly from its well-being, because fixed-asset investment provides evidence of local economic growth, which is a key performance indicator against which local cadres are evaluated.

Overall, regardless of sector, entrepreneurs who participate in some type of business association, whether government affiliated or nongovernmental, share a number of characteristics that distinguish them from those who are not members of any type of trade association. The 2002 survey found that association members and their leaders, or "association elites," tend to be entrepreneurs who started their businesses earlier, have larger-scale businesses in terms of number of employees, and have a larger sales or profit volume than average entrepreneurs. Members and leaders of business associations are also more likely to be party members than entrepreneurs unaffiliated with associations (table 5.7).

In addition to these economic and political attributes, members of business associations are more likely to have access to bank loans, more likely to have private loans outstanding, and less likely to experience disputes with suppliers, buyers, employees, and consumers. In line with what we would expect of assertive entrepreneurs, they are also more likely than nonmembers to indicate that there is a need for improvement in various types of policies, as well as a need for private entrepreneurs to have their own association. Moreover, association members are more likely than nonmembers to state that the purpose of an autonomous entrepreneurs' association would be to

Table 5.7. Attributes of association members and elites

	Nonmembers	Association members	Association elites
Year business started	1995	1993**	1991**
Gross sales in 2001 (*wan*)	359	539,003	1,237,304**
Net profit in 2001 (*wan*)	41	83*	164**
Number of employees	49	121**	207**
CCP member[a]	.2017	.2884**	.3784**
N	932	593	259

**Indicates $p < .01$ level of significance; *indicates $p < .05$ level of significance.
[a] Number is the average response where 0 indicates nonmember and 1 indicates a CCP member.

formulate rules and regulations for trading (including self-regulation), as well as to express opinions and make requests to the local government. Entrepreneurs with leadership positions in associations share certain attributes with general association members, such as greater access to formal and informal credit, having fewer disputes with consumers, being less likely to resolve disputes by asking friends or relatives to mediate them, agreeing that local authorities appreciate larger businesses, and agreeing that improvements are needed in macroeconomic management and in the protection of intellectual property rights (table 5.8). But note that association elites are more likely to resolve disputes through the court system, less likely to feel powerless when faced with a dispute, and less likely than regular association members to indicate a need for improvement in various policy areas. In short, association members are larger and more politically engaged than nonmembers, but the leaders of business associations seem less concerned with various policy issues, probably due to their somewhat privileged status.

Informal Networks and Spontaneous Collective Action   Although business associations established by entrepreneurs with larger businesses are relatively prominent—and often unabashedly geared toward cultivating good relationships with local officials—entrepreneurs of more modest financial means also participate in associational activities. Discrete groups of microentrepreneurs rarely register themselves as formal associations, but the norms governing their interaction may be equally as strong, if not stronger than those in formal business associations. Many specialized markets are built on native-place networks of migrants (Xiang 1993; Zhang 2001) or former workers of a particular factory. In urban industrial centers with a large concentration of SOEs, for example, there may be entire markets consisting of private entrepreneurs who were all laid off from the same factory. This shared work experience may provide them with an advantage in overcoming collective action dilemmas that otherwise unrelated vendors may face in the event of a shared problem. The case of a traditional Chinese

Table 5.8. Attributes of association members and elites vs. nonmembers: t-test comparison of means

Issue area	Nonmembers	Association members	Association elites
Access to bank loans	.1073	.1332	.1467
Private loans outstanding	.2382	.4199**	.4556**
Disputes with suppliers	.5097	.5110	.4672
Disputes with buyers	.6105	.6206	.6023
Disputes with employees	.1234	.1231	.1236
Disputes with consumers	.4077	.3761	.3166**
Disputes with local government agencies/officials	.2393	.2074	.2355
Disputes with local residents or other local organizations	.1674	.1450	.2008**
Disputes with news media	.0172	.0135	.0193
Resolves disputes by negotiating and compromising as much as possible and then letting the issue resolve itself	.8369	.8145	.7992**
Resolves disputes by appealing to local government or higher authorities	.2586	.2479	.2548
Resolves disputes by appealing to the court system	.2489	.2462	.3050**
Resolves disputes through mediation by friends or relatives	.2307	.1754**	.1583**
Resolves disputes by going through social relations	.4464	.4300	.3707**
Feel powerless when encountering a dispute	.1427	.1383	.1236
Agree that local authorities appreciate larger businesses	.8519	.9123**	.9344**
Need improvement in property rights	.6931	.7352**	.7066
Need improvement in intellectual property rights	.6298	.6863**	.7143**
Need improvement in public opinion and propaganda	.6738	.7083**	.7220**
Need improvement in tax policy	.8262	.8600**	.8263
Need improvement in credit policy	.8155	.8617**	.8610**
Need improvement in macroeconomic management	.5709	.6425**	.6602**
Need improvement in regulation of business	.7833	.7757	.7413**
Need improvement in household registration system	.5590	.5953**	.5830
Need improvement in treatment of private enterprises	.7672	.8111**	.8224*
Need improvement in political system	.6534	.7319**	.7043**
Need improvement in public utilities	.7500	.7723*	.7799*
Need improvement in educational system	.7918	.8415**	.7799
Need improvement in social security system	.8358	.9140**	.9035**
Private entrepreneurs need their own association to enhance their social status	.3101	.2614**	.2703
Private entrepreneurs need their own association to formulate trading rules and regulations, and to engage in self-regulation	.1599	.2917**	.2587**
Private entrepreneurs need their own association to reflect opinions and requests to the government/party	.1502	.2108**	.2046**

**Indicates $p < .01$ level of significance; *indicates $p < .05$ level of significance.

arts-and-crafts market in Zhengzhou, Henan Province, illustrates how former co-workers succeeded in lodging a collective complaint, which is an expression of assertive political activity (see also O'Brien and Li 2006).

After working as a jade sculptor in a state-owned enterprise for thirty years, vendor Hua was forced to retire two years before the official retirement age because the factory went bankrupt (Tsai 2002, 117). Many of her former colleagues set up retail stands near the factory to sell traditional arts and crafts. In early 1996, a seemingly endless string of uniformed officials claiming to be tax collectors started to harass the vendors for numerous taxes and fees, including "20 yuan for sanitation, an environmental fee of 10 yuan, 30 yuan for a license to sell art, a 'city face-lift' fee of 15 yuan, and 50 yuan for the cadres' nicotine habit, and so on." Frustrated by the constant and seemingly arbitrary demand for fees, the two dozen former state workers-turned-storeowners marched to the ICMB office and demanded that only one fee collector be sent to their market each month to collect whatever fees are legally owed to the city government. The ICMB office thought this was a reasonable request and convinced the other local government offices to cooperate with it in simplifying the fee collection process.

Despite the apparent ease with which highly concentrated small-scale vendors may join together for collective action, we should not assume that such situational solidarity portends class formation, because their interests may also conflict with one another. Entrepreneurs who cooperate when faced with a common grievance at one moment may fight among themselves when they no longer share that particular problem. The tenuousness of their connection is apparent in the following instance of situational collective action. In September 2002, the managers of a commercial building in one of the busiest parts of Hankou, Wuhan, decided to expand the space dedicated to retail selling areas (Interview 228). To accommodate the expansion, the building would have to eliminate a substantial shopping area within it during the construction period. Hundreds of storeowners would lose their usual retail space for several months, if not longer. Hence, approximately 250 vendors decided to complain collectively to the building's ILA branch. They reasoned that, after all, the local ILA was supposed to represent their interests. The building's ILA said they could not do anything about it, so the vendors filed a complaint with the building's management office, which also proved to be unresponsive. The vendors then contacted the Qiaokou district government—again to no avail—and finally, went all the way to the Wuhan City government to complain about the disruption of their selling space.[26] The city government told the vendors that they could set up temporary stands on part of the street while the building

26. The vendors reported that they never considered contacting the ICMB or higher levels of the ILA because they had no expectation that either entity would care about their problem.

Chief executive officer of a factory that used to wear a red hat, Nanjing

was being renovated. After spending one month filing complaints with various bureaucratic layers, the retailers were initially grateful for the city's solution. But it quickly became apparent that the allocated area on the street was too small to fit all of them, so the vendors started fighting with one another over the limited selling space. In brief, the individual entrepreneurs were able to come together to defend their livelihoods, but they also came into conflict with one another for essentially the same reasons.

The above examples of membership in formal political institutions, individual lobbying of officials, participation in business associations, and spontaneous collective action are all group-oriented expressions of "assertive political behavior." Yet none of the assertive coping strategies discussed thus far has entailed overt lobbying for political pluralization or representation. Most business owners are finding ways to have their needs met without demanding democratic solutions. Be that as it may, entrepreneurs who are discontented with the current regime and would support a democratic transition are more likely to keep quiet or invest in exit strategies for their families than to advocate political reform in a public manner.

Assertive, Wealthy, and Politically Discontented   Small-scale entrepreneurs who are assertive and have unresolved grievances may pose an inconvenience for the local government, but larger capitalists who are discontented represent a potentially greater threat to the regime, for they possess substantial resources that could be deployed for political purposes. Yet, in the course of my research, I found that even when the wealthiest private entrepreneurs have serious and apparently legitimate grievances against the regime, they rarely engage in activities that would promote a democratic transition. The following two cases offer different instances of how large-scale entrepreneurs have dealt with what they perceive to be grave injustices committed against them and their businesses.

Owner Yi exemplifies the self-made entrepreneur who built up a highly profitable export-oriented manufacturing business through a range of informal arrangements with a variety of governmental entities but later found himself unable to validate the nature of those transactions and subsequently suffered for it (Interview 191). Born in 1952, Yi graduated from junior high in 1966 just as the Cultural Revolution was beginning. After spending over a decade working in the countryside, in 1978 he went to southern Guangdong Province to open a small shop that sold piglets from another part of the province. He explained that because very few people were involved in private trading at the time, he registered the business as a red hat entity with the sponsorship of the local township's communal supply shop. After a few years of peddling grain and piglets, in 1981 owner Yi decided to open a clothing business, and in 1987 he registered it formally as a private enterprise with eighteen employees and a capitalization of 500,000 RMB ($134,409). This was considered a sizable operation for a private business at the time, but owner Yi was not worried because his uncle was an official in the county government and his brother in Hong Kong ensured a steady supply of materials and design templates. Two years later, he wanted to expand the factory and applied for land through the county's work affairs office (*banshichu*) because private individuals were not permitted to request land for commercial use. Owner Yi ended up paying over 1 million RMB ($265,604) and borrowed 2 million RMB ($531,208) from the People's Construction Bank of China (now called the China Construction Bank) to build a garment factory.

Despite the economic downturn after June 4, 1989, owner Yi's plans went forward, and by 1990 he decided to expand the business further by collaborating with the Hunan International Trust and Investment Corporation.[27] HITIC agreed to invest 10 million RMB for a 51 percent share in the venture on paper, but in reality it only supplied 3 million RMB. Owner Yi signed a contract with HITIC for management of the business for fifteen years with a clause built in such that he would pay HITIC 5 million RMB ($1.04 million) upfront and an additional 10 percent of the sales each year. By 1994 the garment business had established a nationally recognized

27. Local investment and trust companies (ITICs) were established in the 1980s to enable provinces to attract foreign investment.

brand name for itself. Owner Yi then hired a team of attorneys to help him figure out how he could get out of the contract with HITIC, and the lawyers found a clause indicating a means for him to buy out HITIC's share of the business. HITIC agreed to sell it to him for 38 million RMB and the Hunan provincial government approved the transaction. The sale was set for completion by the end of 1995, as owner Yi had already paid 28 million RMB and was prepared to pay the remaining 10 million RMB, but then HITIC refused the final payment, claiming that the National State-Owned Enterprise Management Bureau had to approve it first. Owner Yi believes that this last-minute glitch occurred because the business was so successful; he had turned a 3 million RMB investment by the state into an entity worth 50 million RMB. The National SOE Management Bureau claimed that the original contract was void because its office was supposed to approve it and because owner Yi had curtailed the length of the contract by ten years. The transaction remained deadlocked.

As owner Yi was on his way to Hong Kong to visit his brother in 1997, the Shenzhen Customs Agency detained him and then sent him to Hunan. The provincial Investigation Bureau put him under house arrest (*jianshi juzhu*) in a random farmer's home for 108 days without notifying his family or employees. The Investigation Bureau claimed that he had bribed Hunan officials with 500,000 RMB in salaries to serve on the board of directors of his company. Although owner Yi denies ever having paid that money, he signed a confession (*tiaojie shu*) because he thought that was the only way that he would ever be freed. When he finally returned to Guangdong, he sued HITIC at a city-level court and won.[28] But then the Arbitration Committee (*zhongcaiwei*) said it needed to be approved at the provincial level. Finally, in 1999, the sale price was increased to 45 million RMB, and in mid-2000 owner Yi paid the remaining amount to own the factory.

His protracted negotiations with various governmental entities, and his experience of having been arbitrarily placed under house arrest led owner Yi to believe, as he said during our interview in 2002, that the rule of law needed to be strengthened at every administrative level, starting with regulations passed in the NPC. Moreover, he contended, private entrepreneurs need to have a better understanding of their rights and of the legal system. Owner Yi also had strong opinions about different regime types: "Poor countries should be run by military dictatorships because people are too poor to understand laws. Developed countries should be run by rule of law and democracy. Developing countries [such as China] need to develop rule of law." When asked whether he thought there was a difference between rule of law and democracy, he replied that they are the same. Despite his

---

28. In an unrelated case, the former head of HITIC was sentenced to death in 1998 for accepting a $250,000 bribe.

preference for a democratic political system, owner Yi did not think that there was much he could do to promote a regime transition in China— either directly or indirectly. He is extremely active in business-related groups such as the FIC and numerous trade associations, but owner Yi did not think that such associational activity could contribute to political liberalization even in an incremental manner. Besides, he had no interest in joining the CCP or participating in overtly political activities. Merely expanding his business has been sufficiently political for owner Yi.

Like Yi, many entrepreneurs in the wealthiest tier of China's capitalists have opted to avoid political commitments because owning a large private business already presents its share of challenges. Several of my interviewees said that they would never want their businesses to be so large that they attracted media attention at the national level; and they would certainly not want to land on the annual *Forbes* magazine list of individuals with the highest net worth, for the list is viewed as a convenient reference for the Chinese government to use in accusing private entrepreneurs of corruption. Meanwhile, most of the interviewees with large businesses had already established exit options for their immediate family members because they believe that it is safer for them to be wealthy abroad rather than within China. Indeed, many entrepreneurs have been forced to flee the country. The experience of Yang Rong of Brilliance China Automotive provides another instance of how initial success in collaborating with local governmental entities may backfire later on. Unlike owner Yi's situation, however, the case of the disputed assets of Brilliance China ended up in litigation in the District Court in the District of Columbia because Yang's wife was already a permanent resident of the United States when the dispute occurred. Based on existing news accounts, legal documents, and an interview with him and his relatives in 2004, his story is as follows (Interviews 278, 280).[29]

Yang Rong is the former chairperson, president, and chief executive officer of a holding company that has a majority interest in China's largest minivan producer. In 2001, *Forbes* ranked him as the third wealthiest businessperson in China ($840 million net worth). Like many others on the *Forbes* list, he came from an impoverished background, for his father was labeled a rightist during the Anti-Rightist campaign in 1957 and a counterrevolutionary during the Cultural Revolution. Despite his family's politically disadvantaged background, by the time he was thirty-two years old, in 1990, Yang had earned a doctorate in economics from the Southwest Finance and Economics University, taught at the China Finance College in Beijing, served as the general manager of a finance company in Hong Kong, and accumulated sufficient

---

29. This is one of the few instances in this book in which the entrepreneur's real name is used in the text because it is a high-profile case. When I interviewed him in February 2004, however, Yang Rong was operating under a pseudonym to avoid attracting the attention of PRC authorities.

capital to invest in a state-owned auto factory, Golden Cup Automotive, in the provincial capital of Liaoning in northeastern China.[30]

Yang's 39.45 percent stake in Golden Cup was arranged through innovatively indirect means.[31] First, in 1991 he established Broadsino Finance Company in Hong Kong with a partner. Yang invested a 70 percent equity stake in Broadsino Finance and became its president and chairman. Later in the year, Broadsino collaborated with Golden Cup Automotive and Hainen Huayin International Trust Investment Company to incorporate the Shen Yang Golden Cup Passenger Vehicle Manufacturing Company (hereafter, Shen Yang Automotive) as a joint venture to manufacture minivans in China. In early 1992, Broadsino, acting on behalf of Yang, invested $7.5 million in Shen Yang Automotive and then purchased Hainen Huayin ITIC's 15 percent share in Shen Yang Automotive, which gave Broadsino a 40 percent interest in the company (*Yang Rong v. Liaoning Province Government* 2003, 19).[32] The next step in May 1992 further obscured his investment: in collaboration with Brilliance, the China Finance Institute, Huayin Trust, and the People's Bank of China Education Office, Broadsino established a social organization, the China Finance Educational Development Foundation. The foundation was entrusted to the People's Bank of China Education Office and served as a vehicle to hold Yang's shares, which were invested in the name of Broadsino Finance. In June 1992, the foundation registered China Brilliance Automotive Holdings Limited (CBA) in Bermuda to serve as a financing vehicle. Two months later, CBA became the first Chinese company to list on the New York Stock Exchange. One of the Western investment bankers involved in the transaction recalls that the listing essentially occurred in an institutional void, that is, in the absence of formal PRC securities regulations or a securities commission. As he explained, "It was an under the table deal at a time there was no table."[33]

The Liaoning provincial government was initially grateful for Yang's leadership and management in generating local employment and taxes, because as a Mao-era heavy industrial center, Liaoning's Stalinist-scale economic base required heavy subsidization. But one decade later, the institutional creativity employed in structuring Yang's stake in CBA backfired. In March 2002, the Liaoning provincial government established a working committee to take control of the educational foundation and acquire the shares in Brilliance

30. Mark O'Neil and Winston Yau, "Brilliance Shrouded," *South China Morning Post,* June 22, 2002.

31. The most comprehensive discussion of the transaction is "Huachen caiji" (Brilliance's Financing Technique), *Sohu.com,* April 11, 2002, available online in Chinese at: http://business.sohu.com/06/98/article200489806.shtml.

32. *Yang Rong v. Liaoning Province Government,* No. 1:03-CV-1687 (D.C. filed August 7, 2003).

33. Carl Walter quoted in Studwell 2002, 77–78. CBA went on to issue shares on both the Hong Kong Stock Exchange and Shanghai Stock Exchange in October 1999.

that it held in trust for Broadsino. They claimed that Yang was holding state assets, but he disagreed and refused to transfer his equity interest in the foundation to Liaoning. Under political pressure, Brilliance's board of directors dismissed Yang as chairman, president, and chief executive officer in June 2002. In September, Broadsino filed a complaint against the foundation in Beijing's Municipal High Court to clarify the nature of Broadsino's interest in the Brilliance shares held by the foundation. The following month, the Liaoning provincial government issued a warrant for Yang's arrest and accused him of committing "economic crimes." To avoid arrest, he fled to the United States where his wife and three sons were already living. The CBA's board then ousted him as chair and sold his shares in the educational foundation at a 96 percent discount. The fire sale effectively gave Liaoning Province control over Brilliance China. According to Yang, his conflict with Liaoning emerged when he wanted to undertake a joint venture with the British car company MG Rover in Ningbo, in the coastal southern province of Zhejiang.[34] As of 2004, Yang was living in exile and working with a major Washington, D.C., law firm to sue the Liaoning provincial government for the 39.45 percent stake of $690 million that he claims was arbitrarily confiscated from him, as well as the associated litigation fees.[35]

Yang's predicament is not exceptional. Other Chinese capitalists on the *Forbes* list have been accused of economic crimes, and countless others with lower net worth, such as owner Yi, have experienced similar conflicts with various government entities. To date, a large assortment of ambiguous ownership structures and investment vehicles coexist, and it would be premature to expect greater transparency in corporate governance and protection of private property rights at this point. The logic of other cases presented in this book, however, indicates that the accumulation of disputes between entrepreneurs and the state may at least create pressure on policy elites to reform increasingly anachronistic formal institutions— and create ones required for new types of economic activities. Meanwhile, even though Yang hopes that China will become a multiparty democracy that respects the rule of law, he has no plans to return to China and prefers to help his native country through charitable donations in rural education. He is not interested in forming an alternative political party or organizing with other *Forbes*-ranked entrepreneurs to defend their interests.

34. Richard McGregor, "Exiled Chinese Tycoon Fights to Regain Stake in Carmaker," *Financial Times*, July 22, 2003.

35. Richard McGregor, "Exiled Chinese Magnate Sues for $690m," *Financial Times*, August 14, 2003; Eugene Tang, "Made and Confiscated in China," Bloomberg News, *International Herald Tribune*, April 14, 2003.

Analysis of Private Entrepreneurs' Political Strategies

As explained earlier, both the structural and voluntarist causal pathways linking private sector development and democratization require a certain degree of common identity among business owners in order for them to act collectively in a politically relevant manner. The typology of private entrepreneurs' coping strategies shows that even if one interprets certain trends from the survey data as indicating capitalist class formation—for example, the broadly shared concern over credit and tax policies—the apparent "class of itself" is fragmented in political orientation and behavior. Furthermore, the variation among China's entrepreneurs is not random or sui generis. The typology identifies four attitudinal and behavioral patterns based on the ability and desire of entrepreneurs to confront the state—avoidant, grudgingly acceptant, loyally acceptant, and assertive. And the above cases show that different types of private entrepreneurs vary in their interactions with local state actors and vary in the ways that they satisfy their individual interests.

The social and political background of private entrepreneurs, combined with their length of experience in the private sector and local political and economic status, shapes their ability and desire to confront the state (summarized in figure 5.2). Note that while economic indicators such as size and profitability of business affect the resources that entrepreneurs have for engaging governmental entities, these material conditions alone do not tell us much about whether they are likely to use those resources in a confrontational manner. The "desire" to confront the state is also contingent on their particular business experiences. Some business elites have excellent working relations with local officials and have no reason or "desire" to confront the state. Others suffer from negative official attention precisely because the large scale of their businesses makes them convenient targets for charges of economic crimes, whether warranted or not.

Given the dynamic quality of China's private sector, a key issue concerns the extent to which entrepreneurs may shift from one pattern to another. Based on the logic of structural theories that expect economic development to generate a prodemocratic capitalist class, if a critical mass of business owners became and remained assertive, then in aggregate their parochial demands could have wider impact. Returning to the two-by-two matrix of entrepreneurs' political strategies (see figure 5.3), this would be the case if those in quadrants II, III, and IV all moved into I (assertive). I hypothesize, however, that such a convergence is unlikely to be a stable equilibrium for the following reasons.

First, avoidant entrepreneurs are unlikely to shift directly to becoming assertive. Business owners who rely primarily on avoidant strategies tend to lack the relevant social networks, economic resources, and confidence to make

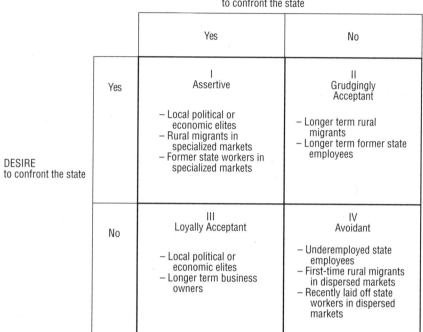

Figure 5.2.   Relationship between private entrepreneurs' background and political strategies

claims on the state by virtue of their recent entry into the private sector and the disempowering circumstances under which they were forced to turn to petty entrepreneurship for economic survival. The backgrounds of avoidant entrepreneurs include underemployed state employees who are moonlighting, recently laid-off state workers in dispersed markets, and first-time rural migrants in dispersed markets (figure 5.2). These types of merchants generally do not identify themselves as "private entrepreneurs"—they tend to view working in the private sector as a short-term coping strategy. Therefore, to the extent that avoidant entrepreneurs end up complying with the minimum official requirements for conducting business, it is more likely that they would become grudgingly acceptant first, and then acquire the means to act more assertively. Indeed, many grudgingly acceptant entrepreneurs start out as avoidant vendors who are then persuaded to register their businesses—either due to official pressure or out of a desire to scale up and operate in a more legitimate manner. The itinerant couple from Anhui, for example, probably started out serving homemade noodles out of the back of a bicycle cart and were later convinced that it would be easier to get a temporary license for a food cart rather than to operate in constant

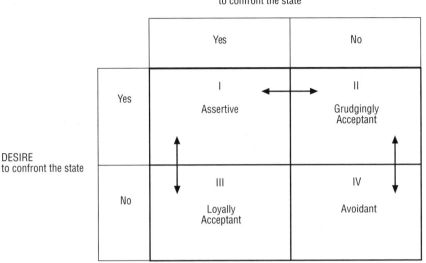

Note: Arrows indicate the direction that entrepreneurs are likely to shift from one category to another.

Figure 5.3.   Changes in private entrepreneurs' political orientation and strategies

fear of street regulators. Meanwhile, as the Wuhan City district expands its borders into the adjacent suburbs, it would not be surprising if the migrant mushroom farmers came under regulation of the city's ICMB. In the particular case discussed above, the farmers might go from being avoidant to loyally acceptant if registering their business and paying taxes proved to be a relatively smooth process.

Second, if grudgingly acceptant entrepreneurs developed the ability to complain to the state and became assertive, their concerns still might be resolved through either informal or existing state channels, thereby shifting them toward being loyally acceptant. A number of entrepreneurs who experienced difficulties in the initial years of their operations have found that being more established has alleviated many of the problems they encountered earlier on. Better access to land, skilled labor, and preferential policy treatment is correlated with the length of time in which a private business has been operating, as well as the scale of the business. In addition, as discussed in the next chapter, local operating conditions also play an important role in mediating the extent to which entrepreneurs are avoidant, grudgingly or loyally acceptant, or assertive. Especially in the first two decades of reform, localities varied substantially in their relative support of private sector development. And in many areas, the local government's stance toward private entrepreneurs has shifted substantially over time.

The third reason that most entrepreneurs are unlikely to converge on assertive coping strategies for an extended period is entrepreneurs who pursue loyally acceptant or assertive modes of operation have better developed ties with one another and with the staff of the state. In turn, these stronger networks enable entrepreneurs to resolve many of their problems without resorting to official channels for lodging complaints or staging protests. The main difference between those in the assertive versus loyally acceptant categories is that the latter benefit from maintaining good relations with various state cadres and agencies and seek to promote their interests by striking private bargains with them rather than by confronting them through autonomous organization. The assertive fraction of entrepreneurs may also have hospitable working relations with certain local officials, but when their grievances cannot be redressed through informal personalistic means, these types of entrepreneurs are able to draw on their preexisting social networks—forged through factory employment or native-place loyalty—to engage in collective action. This type of solidarity is narrower and more exclusive than structural notions of class formation would expect because this group lobbies for particularistic rather than collective benefits on behalf of the broader "class." Furthermore, recall that when local governmental entities are able to meet these particularistic demands, previously assertive entrepreneurs may return to being loyally acceptant.

In sum, it is certainly reasonable to expect that business owners might shift from one category to another as their circumstances change over time. However, there is little evidence to suggest that assertive entrepreneurs would advocate a transition to democracy as the most desirable means for satisfying their interests. Instead, China's private entrepreneurs are having an effect on both the nature and implementation of policies through either formal associational channels or, more typically, informal networks and practices.

RESULTS from my national survey support a proposed typology that links the value orientations of entrepreneurs with their coping strategies, and classifies the latter into four categories: avoidant, grudgingly acceptant, loyally acceptant, and assertive. Avoidant, grudgingly acceptant, and loyally acceptant entrepreneurs all use coping strategies that have an impact on the policy environment through indirect, informal means. But only those in the assertive category hold the potential for making direct demands for democracy—and even then, assertive coping strategies may be further subdivided into more finely differentiated types of activities that have varying degrees of political impact. First, entrepreneurs who serve in formal political institutions such as the NPC and local people's congresses, CPPCC, and village committees are more likely to express their opinions to officials through existing institutional channels when it comes to dispute resolution, but they also have fewer grievances than most entrepreneurs. Second, the majority of business owners rely on individual rather than group-oriented strategies to make policy-related demands. Third, entrepreneurs who are members of either governmental or nongovernmental business associations share certain characteristics with members of formal political organizations, such as having greater access to credit and experiencing fewer disputes. Unlike members and leaders of formal political institutions, however, association members see a need for improvement in many policy areas and are more likely to believe that entrepreneurs need autonomous organizations to deal with trading regulations and to express their opinions to the government. At the same time, many associations already appear to be effective in addressing the concerns of private entrepreneurs. The fourth type of assertive political behavior is spontaneous collective action among business owners, which happens infrequently and appears to be based on situational concerns rather than ongoing shared concerns. And, finally, the fifth type of assertive entrepreneur includes economic elites who also have significant political grievances. Despite their discontent with the current regime type and desire to see contemporary China governed by the rule of law, they are active neither in lobbying for democracy nor in defending the rights of private entrepreneurs. They are more likely to invest in exit strategies for their families than to advocate political reform. And, ultimately, entrepreneurs who use assertive coping strategies are more interested in defending particularistic material interests than in changing the regime.

6

Local Variation in Private Sector Conditions

The central government has no overarching strategy for private sector development. If you really want to understand China's private economy, you need to look at the differences in local conditions. For example, the northeast is dominated by state-owned enterprises, so private enterprises come and go; they don't get big like the ones in Zhejiang. . . . Shanghai is like the United States was in the 1920s and 1930s—the government picks certain firms and gives them all the privileges.

> Chief executive officer of a software company, Beijing, 2005

The local government has gone from favoring the state sector to favoring the foreign sector. Even though I had enough cash to buy a controlling stake in state-owned enterprises that were being restructured, the local government wouldn't allow me to buy even one share because they wanted to attract outside capital. No one [in the local government] values local capital.

> Owner of a pharmaceutical chain, rural Chongqing, 2002

The rapidity of China's private sector growth in the last few decades suggests that the national policy environment has provided a permissive, if not hospitable, environment for business owners. Yet the actual experience of operating a private firm varies throughout the country. The local political economy mediates the relative availability and accessibility of capital, land, workers, distribution networks, and markets to nonstate entities. At the broadest level, this variation is reflected in regional differences in the volume and scale of private businesses. As of 2003, 69.3 percent of registered private enterprises (*siying qiye*) were concentrated in eastern China, while 17.1 percent were in central provinces, and 13.5 percent were in the west. Meanwhile, 48.3 percent of the total registered individual entrepreneurs (*getihu*) were in the east, 31 percent were in central China, and 20.7 percent were in the west (UFIC 2005, 69, 71). These official statistics reveal that larger private enterprises are concentrated in the east, the result of the sequence of market-oriented reforms that privileged the coastal south, while central provinces with industrial state sectors undertook restructuring later in the reform era. The mountainous western provinces have always been less developed relative to the rest of the country.[1]

Yet it would be overly simplistic to surmise that the concerns of business owners vary primarily along these broad regional lines. Instead, substantial intraregional differences in conditions for private sector development are apparent.[2] Private entrepreneurs operate in structural contexts that differ spatially. There are several reasons for this spatial variation. First, Mao-era developmental legacies have conditioned the relative ease and desirability of private sector development and privatization in various localities (Oi 1999; Tsai 2002; Whiting 2001). Less-developed rural localities, for example, have had a greater incentive to develop the local private economy than areas with larger state sectors on the eve of reform.

Second, due to differing resource and geographical endowments, certain localities are better positioned to attract foreign investment than others (e.g., Wang and Chiu 2000). In many cases, the center's reform policies have reinforced these developmental differences as seen in the fact that special economic zones for foreign investment and export processing were first introduced in the coastal south.

Third, as numerous studies have shown, the multiple tiers of local government and bureaucratic administration adapt national policies to local conditions in the process of policy implementation.[3] Decisions made in Beijing often look very different in scope and substance by the time they reach particular localities. Taken together, this means that numerous opportunities exist for both entrepreneurs and local officials to shape the contours of various rules and regulations. With repetition these practices may become adaptive informal institutions, which reflect the practical outcomes of local negotiations and bear the potential to influence national reformers.

1. Official statistics have classified provincial units into three regions since the Seventh Five-Year Plan (1986–90). The east includes Liaoning, Hebei, Beijing, Tianjin, Shandong, Jiangsu, Shanghai, Zhejiang, Fujian, Guangdong, Guangxi, and Hainan; central China includes Jilin, Heilongjiang, Inner Mongolia, Shanxi, Henan, Hubei, Anhui, Hunan, and Jiangxi; and the west includes Ningxia, Gansu, Shaanxi, Sichuan (and Chongqing since 1997), Guizhou, Qinghai, Yunan, Xinjiang, and Tibet. A review of China's changing regional policy is Li 2000.

2. On subregional differences in economic conditions before the Chinese Revolution, see Skinner 1977 and cf. 1964–65.

3. For example, see Alfred Chan 2001; Lampton 1987; Manion 1991; O'Brien and Li 1999; Zhang 2003; and Zweig 1985. Cf. Remick 2004.

This raises the question of what types of adaptive informal institutions originate in different types of localities. To demonstrate the spatial variation in adaptive informal institutions, in this chapter I examine the trajectory of private sector development in five local patterns of political economy. The combination of survey data and field interviews shows that private entrepreneurs face greater operational difficulties in areas dominated by the state, collective, and foreign-invested sectors, as well as in areas that are relatively rural and underdeveloped. To overcome the discrimination against private enterprises, adaptive informal institutions in these areas generally involve practices that require collaboration with representatives of the state on the local level and present direct personal benefits to local cadres. Entrepreneurs in localities with a legacy of large collective sectors and ongoing lower levels of economic development are also more likely to use assertive political means to resolve their disputes. In contrast, entrepreneurs in localities with larger private sectors tend to have fewer government-related grievances. In these areas, business owners have devised creative means to evade state regulations on private financing—typically with the discrete, informal collaboration of local officials—and are much less likely than entrepreneurs in other types of localities to use formal political institutions for dispute resolution. These findings provide additional evidence for the internal division of private entrepreneurs rather than class formation and a consequent low degree of potential for unified collective action. Furthermore, the reality of local differences in adaptive informal institutions adds another dimension of complexity to the present analysis: not only are adaptive informal institutions more likely to emerge in certain localities than others but the relative potential of adaptive informal institutions to influence policy elites also varies, depending on the politics of how receptive the central government is to developmental challenges in those localities.

Local "Models" of Development

Although it is beyond the scope of this chapter to provide a comprehensive overview of all the local models of political economy that have been identified in China, a number of regional developmental models have acquired particular salience among Chinese scholars, journalists, and policymakers during the reform era.[4] These include the Wenzhou model, which is known for its early start on private sector development; the Sunan model, which achieved

4. A critical overview is Zhang 2002. Also, note that the use of the term "developmental model" in this chapter is not meant to imply that the developmental characteristics associated with each one are worth copying or adapting. Instead, the term is used to denote particular configurations of developmental traits and patterns. This argument is further developed in Tsai 2006.

rural industrialization based on collectively owned township and village enterprises; and the south China or Zhujiang (Pearl River Delta) model, which relies on foreign direct investment (FDI), especially from overseas Chinese. In addition to these well-known regional types, I would include two other patterns of political economy: first, what is best described as the "state-dominated model" refers to localities that had large state sectors on the eve of reform; second, the pattern of "limited development" refers to less-developed rural areas that typify much of western and southwestern China, but can also be found in the more remote and peripheral areas of eastern and central provinces. Due to a combination of differential national policies and local responses to those policies, the legitimacy and viability of the private sector varies substantially in these five developmental patterns.[5] These various dimensions of diversity are mirrored in the self-perception of private entrepreneurs, as well as in the manner in which they relate to the local state and society.

Wenzhou Model

Wenzhou is a rural mountainous municipality with a population of seven million people in the southeastern province of Zhejiang. It was especially impoverished during the Mao era (1949–76) for both demographic and political reasons. Wenzhou has limited arable land as it consists primarily of mountains and river tributaries, yet it also has a relatively concentrated population, which meant that even subsistence agriculture posed a challenge for its inhabitants. Exacerbating the disadvantages of having limited arable land and a large population were national policies that intentionally deprived the southern coastal provinces of Zhejiang, Fujian, and Guangdong of capital investment due to their propinquity to Taiwan and, thus, to their geostrategic sensitivity. The center concentrated its industrial belt inland so that it would be better protected in the event of a Chinese Nationalist and/or U.S. invasion from the southeastern coast (Naughton 1988). Hence, on the eve of reform in the late 1970s, Wenzhou's rural per capita GDP of 114 RMB ($68) per year was 15 percent lower than the national average. One decade later, however, Wenzhou was nationally known as a prosperous locality with a vibrant private sector based on household factories, specialized wholesale markets, informal financial intermediaries, and a steady supply of merchants who were willing to travel and live all over the country to market their products. In a series of reports and monographs in 1985, Chinese economists and policymakers began to refer to the rise of the

5. These five developmental patterns are neither exhaustive nor mutually exclusive categories of political–economic conditions in China. Some localities may exhibit hybrid characteristics of different developmental patterns. For example, in recent years local governments in state-dominated localities have endeavored to attract more FDI in the hopes of achieving the prosperity associated with the south China model.

"Wenzhou model."[6] Officials and prominent scholars even made the relatively arduous trip from Beijing to witness the model in action and to conduct field surveys.[7]

The original accounts of Wenzhou's economic success in the mid-to-late 1980s described the emerging model as having the following characteristics: (1) the private rural household as the primary productive unit; (2) production of low-end consumer items employing simple, labor-intensive technology; (3) horizontal division of labor among households as seen in the development of specialized commodity markets; and (4) extensive sales, purchasing, and marketing networks throughout the country.[8] These are the most frequently cited ingredients underlying its particular pattern of political economy during the reform era, though a fifth component—reliance on informal sources of finance—is also a fundamental part of the model (Wang, Tsai, and Li 2004; Zhang and Mao 1993). Taken together, the five elements have been associated with impressive economic performance, which in Wenzhou's case is defined as rural industrialization led by the private sector. Between 1978 and 2002, Wenzhou's GDP increased at an annual average of 18.6 percent, and the share of the state sector in industrial output shrank from 35.7 percent to 2.5 percent (Wenzhou Municipal Statistics Bureau 2003). By 2002, the private economy accounted for over 97 percent of the locality's industrial output, of which 93.5 percent was generated by small and medium enterprises.

What set Wenzhou apart from other localities in the first decade of reform was not only its growth in standard economic indicators but also that this growth was driven by private businesses and private finance during a period when the political status of the nonstate sector was still highly controversial. Throughout the 1980s, there were several phases during which national political campaigns were highly critical of what was labeled "bourgeois liberalization," "spiritual pollution," and corruption—all undesirable symptoms associated with the spread of market forces. As such, during those periods it also became politically sensitive to imply that Wenzhou's petty capitalism might serve as a model worthy of replicating in other parts of the country. In fact, the emulatory connotations of the word "model" (*moshi*) became so politically charged in the 1980s that less controversial terms such as "style/pattern" (*geju*) and "emblematic case" (*dianxing*) came to replace "model" in official discussions of Wenzhou.

6. The phrase "Wenzhou model" first appeared in the Shanghai newspaper *Jiefang ribao* (Liberation Daily) on May 12, 1985 (Xie and Ren 2000, 37–38). See also Yuan 1987. Articles written in 1986 by members of the Economic Research Institute of the Chinese Academy of Social Sciences are translated into English and compiled in Nolan and Dong 1989. For early journalistic discussions, see *Jingji ribao* (Economic Daily), July 1986. In addition, newspaper articles from 1988 are collected in Yu 1989.

7. Due to infrastructural neglect, it was quite difficult to reach Wenzhou from elsewhere during the 1980s. Its airport did not open until 1990.

8. See references in note 4 and Forster 1990–91.

Despite these political complications, between 1978 and 1986 the number of registered individual businesses (*getihu*) in Wenzhou went from 2,800 to 140,600, and by the end of 1986 small private businesses accounted for 35 percent of the locality's industrial output, 40 percent of retail sales, 50 percent of local transportation services, and 65 percent of the total volume of shipping services (Xie and Ren 2000, 18). Meanwhile, due to restrictions on businesses with more than eight employees, these figures underestimated the true scale of the private sector. By 1986 it was estimated that 89 percent of all collective enterprises in Wenzhou were wearing red hats; that is, they were really private businesses registered as collective ones. And during the 1983 to 1985 period, local economists estimated that up to 95 percent of all financial flows in the locality were occurring outside of the state banking system (Liu 1992, 298). Wenzhou's reform-era development thus came to be associated with not only success in rural industrialization but also a high degree of local initiative and even disregard for national regulations that stood in the way of its entrepreneurs (Parris 1993).

Indeed, local political support influenced the State Council's decision to designate Wenzhou as an experimental reform zone in a variety of areas, including rural reforms, ownership reform, and interest-rate reform. The prefectural party secretary Yuan Fanglie (1981–85) was active in promoting the private sector, which helped Wenzhou become better known in Beijing. The vice premier at the time, Wan Li, visited a market town in Cangnan County in 1983, and then Premier Zhao Ziyang visited various parts of Wenzhou in 1985. Apparently, both officials were impressed by the dynamism of Wenzhou's entrepreneurs, and Zhao Ziyang recommended that Wenzhou be treated as a pilot locality for reform (Parris 1993, 253–256). In 1986 the center announced the establishment of experimental reform zones, after which both the Wenzhou Industrial and Commercial Management Bureau and the Zhejiang party committee and government proposed various measures to the Central Committee and State Council to make Wenzhou such a zone (Qian 1996; Whiting 2001, 135). Wenzhou received this formal status only in September 1987, which gave it permission to experiment more deeply with interest-rate reforms. But this formal permission was post hoc and reactive on the part of the center. In the course of my research, I found that local rural credit cooperatives were floating their interest rates as early as 1979 and 1980 (Wang, Tsai, and Li 2004). Furthermore, the Wenzhou Agricultural Bank of China had already initiated interest-rate reform in mid-1985 by allowing 387 rural credit cooperatives (which accounted for 78.8 percent of the cooperatives at the time) to float their interest rates (Huang 1993, 87). Meanwhile, in the early 1980s private money houses, moneylenders, pawnshops, and rotating credit associations were also charging market-determined interest rates that were two to three times higher than the rates in state banks (Tsai 2002, 143). In short, local entrepreneurs were already engaging in a variety of innovative financing practices well before Wenzhou became an experimental reform zone.

Sunan Model

The Sunan region refers to the part of Jiangsu Province south of the Changjiang (Yangzi River) and includes the cities of Wuxi, Suzhou, and Changzhou. Flanked by Nanjing to the west and Shanghai to the east, Sunan had a population of over fourteen million in the mid-2000s and is known as being one of the most densely populated and commercially vibrant parts of the country. By the late nineteenth century, it had become one of China's main industrial bases, supported by a well-developed transportation network. During the Mao era, local officials established a range of commune and brigade-level enterprises that branched out beyond agricultural-related products and were intended to create linkages between rural industry and the urban state sector (Whiting 2001, 53–62). This strategy expanded into (revitalized) labor-intensive production of the area's traditional industries, including textiles, machinery, chemicals, and electronics; and during the 1980s, the so-called Sunan model became associated with rapid rural industrialization based on the collective sector (Fei 1986; Mo 1987; Wu and Ju 1991; Zhu and Sun 1994; Wu 2001).[9] By 1985, for example, collectively owned township village enterprises or TVEs were generating 96 percent of local industrial output in Wuxi (Huang 2003, 15). Meanwhile, private industry remained negligible in the Sunan area because it was "severely hampered by administrative restrictions" (Byrd and Lin 1990, 25).[10] Even as late as 1990, the private sector accounted for only 8 percent of industrial enterprises in Wuxi (Whiting 2001, 142–143).

In contrast to Wenzhou's reform-era rural development, which grew out of self-reliant strategies on the part of private entrepreneurs, various scholars attribute the early success of Sunan's township and village enterprises to the leading role of local governments in providing land, credit, managerial guidance, and other types of favorable treatment to collective firms (Byrd and Gelb 1990; Kung 1999). Jean Oi (1992) dubbed this pattern of rural industrialization "local state corporatism" because the local governments acted as if they were boards of directors committed to promoting local industrial growth. She explains, "Relying heavily on the existence of a collectively owned economic base and administrative power, local governments treated the enterprises within their administrative purview as components of a

9. The sociologist Fei Xiaotong first coined the phrase "Sunan model" in 1984.
10. Note that Hangzhou, the provincial capital in northern Zhejiang, is more similar developmentally to the Sunan model than the Wenzhou model. For example, in 1994 collective TVEs accounted for over 96% of the gross industrial output in Xihu, a district of Hangzhou. *Xihuqu jingji tongji nianjian* 1994 (Hangzhou: Hangzhou shi Xihuqi tongji ju, 1995), cited in Sargeson and Zhang 1999, 83.

larger corporate whole (1999, 97).[11] According to this account, what motivated this local developmentalism was the combination of decollectivization and decentralizing fiscal reforms. Decollectivization produced a vast reserve of agricultural surplus labor available for reemployment. It also had the fiscal effect of diverting agricultural income from township and village governments—formerly communes and brigades—to individual rural households. Meanwhile, fiscal reforms in the 1980s gave local governments an incentive to maximize the economic performance of their TVEs, because they were effectively granted property rights over residual revenues, that is, above the negotiated tax quotas. These macrolevel policies inspired rural industrialization in areas beyond Sunan.[12] Indeed, between 1978 and 1987, national rural industrial output increased by an estimated 26 percent annually; the fixed assets of collectively owned TVEs increased at over 20 percent annually; and bank loans to collective TVEs grew by 44 percent (Byrd and Gelb 2001, 173). But overall, the growth of rural industrial enterprises was concentrated on the east coast. For example, Jiangsu, Zhejiang, and Shangdong accounted for 43 percent of China's rural industry in 1988, but only 17 percent of the population (Naughton 1996, 154).

Despite the initial widespread success of the Sunan model in fostering rural industrialization, over the course of the 1990s collectively owned TVEs became less profitable. At the same time, the central government identified shareholding cooperatives (*gufenzhi hezuo qiye*) as one of the preferred models for reforming collective enterprises and small SOEs. As a result, mass conversion/privatization of collectively owned TVEs into shareholding cooperatives, joint-stock companies (*hezuo gufen gongsi*), and private enterprises (*siying qiye*) occurred.

Various reasons have been identified for the declining profitability of collective enterprises and the subsequent denouement of the Sunan model in practice. First, the monitoring costs incurred by local officials in overseeing enterprise managers grew over time (Kung 1999; Walder 1995). As the number of collective enterprises increased, it became increasingly difficult for local cadres to remain involved in everyday managerial decisions, which enabled enterprise managers to enhance their own nonmonetary benefits rather than enterprise profits. This, in turn, led local officials to focus their energies on maintaining larger TVEs and soliciting joint ventures with foreign investors, while giving up their claim to residual profits in smaller TVEs.

11. Note that Oi does not claim that the phenomenon of local state corporatism is specific to Sunan; in fact, she conducted most of her interviews in Shandong, which is north of Jiangsu, and views Fujian and Wenzhou as exceptions to the pattern.

12. In the prototypical Sunan areas such as Wuxi, this process of rural industrialization was accompanied by significant growth in the industrial labor force and decline in agricultural labor. Between 1978 and 1985, the industrial labor force increased by 19% annually and the agricultural labor force declined by 13% annually. Byrd and Gelb 2001, 173.

Second, the production linkages between collective TVEs and SOEs led to a decline in marginal returns over time. In the early reform years, collective enterprises were able to flourish by supplying SOEs with various inputs and processing components, but the profit margins associated with such subcontracting arrangements became thinner with the rise of competition from other firms (Naughton 1992, 1996).

Third and relatedly, the growth in private firms in Zhejiang and other southern coastal localities also presented collective TVEs with greater market pressure. The differential performance between collective and private enterprises has been attributed to the fact that most private firms lacked access to formal sources of credit and therefore faced hard budget constraints, while collective TVEs received loans guaranteed by local governments and other types of preferential treatment (Park and Shen 2003).

Fourth, reform of the cadre management system in 1993 changed the incentives of local officials in their choice of developmental strategy (Wu 1998, 166). Increased rotation of township-level cadres shortened their time horizons for pursuing rural industrialization. Hence, rather than encouraging local investment in enhancing indigenous industrial capacity, newly assigned cadres were more likely to engage in predatory behavior.[13] Indeed, scholars have found that some TVE managers "chose to lose" by underestimating the profitability of their enterprises, which enabled both managers and local officials to acquire collective assets at a substantial discount (Sargeson and Zhang 1999; Wu 1998, 167).

For all these reasons, by the mid-1990s local officials who had previously privileged the collective sector shifted toward promoting privatization of TVEs, larger private businesses, and foreign-invested enterprises (Huang 2003; Oi 1999). Yet, this reorientation in developmental strategy does not mean that conditions for private entrepreneurs in former Sunan model areas have converged with that of the Wenzhou model. Moreover, within the "private sector," indigenous private businesses—meaning those founded and operated by private individuals—have very different experiences from recently privatized firms, which are typically run by former managers of state-owned enterprises.

South China Model

The south China or Zhujiang (Pearl River Delta) model of development originated in Guangdong Province by the Pearl River Delta, but it extends to

---

13. Some TVEs declined in profitability because local governments levied excessive fees on them to provide local public goods, but there were also reports of township cadres embezzling the assets of TVEs by holding lavish banquets and building large houses for themselves. Dong 2004.

areas in south China that have also attracted high levels of foreign direct investment, especially from overseas Chinese.[14] The developmental literature on China's reform-era political economy also refers to the "Jinjiang model," "Quanzhou model," and "Xiamen model" in southern Fujian (e.g., Fang 2004), but for illustrative purposes this section is limited to the specific experience of Guangdong. Broadly speaking, the Zhujiang model combines elements of both the Wenzhou and Sunan models with an earlier orientation toward external trade and foreign capital (Deng 2003). Given its proximity to Hong Kong, Guangdong received little capital investment during the Mao era; like its neighbors along the coastal south, Guangdong was also quite impoverished on the eve of reform. As in Sunan, much of rural industrialization in Guangdong grew out of the communal and brigade institutions and started during the late 1970s and early 1980s in the form of collectively owned TVEs, that is, before the central government formally encouraged them as a strategy for rural development (Vogel 1989).[15] Yet, as in the Wenzhou model, private entrepreneurs in certain localities were able to pool their capital to establish small factories in light-industrial sectors such as textiles, shoes, and construction materials (Unger 2002). What distinguishes the Zhujiang model from the others, however, is Guangdong's propinquity to Hong Kong and the center's resulting policy decision in 1979 to establish three of the first four special economic zones (SEZs) in Guangdong. The resulting transformation of Zhuhai, Shantou, and especially Shenzhen from rural counties into modernized investment zones was relatively swift and paved the way for the opening of an additional fourteen coastal cities to foreign investment in 1984.[16] By 1988 Guangdong's entire coast was open to foreign capital and offered investors a variety of preferential tax policies to encourage export-oriented ventures. The economist Guo Zhiyi has declared, "The most successful model of China's 'reform and opening' policy is the 'Zhujiang model,' which is best demonstrated by the establishment of the Shenzhen Special Economic Zone and its sudden economic rise" (Guo 2003).

As with the other models, the success of the Zhujiang model is subject to debate and relative to normative definitions of success. If one of the main

14. The PRC definition of FDI includes the following three types of legal foreign-invested enterprises: wholly foreign-owned enterprises, Sino-foreign joint ventures, and Sino-foreign cooperative ventures. "Foreign investors" refers to any foreign individual or foreign-registered entity, including those in Taiwan, Hong Kong, and Macao. Foreign-invested enterprises' reinvestment of profits earned in the PRC and foreign debt incurred for the purpose of PRC projects also constitutes FDI.

15. Overall, however, the Zhujiang region was much more rural and less developed than Sunan. For example, in 1978 agriculture accounted for 44.5% of Xizhu's economy, while it only accounted for 28.1% in Suzhou. Moreover, the collective sector never generated more than 40% of industrial output during the 1960–89 period. Wu 1998, 170, 176.

16. Vogel (1989) shows that developing the SEZs in Guangdong was by no means a linear or uncontested process. Cf. Ge 1999; Pak 1997; and Pearson 1991.

This real estate developer in Guangdong is happy in China but keeps his family in Canada

objectives of establishing the SEZs in the coastal south was to provide a favorable policy and spatial environment to attract foreign capital, then the
model has been effective. By the 1990s, China had become the second
largest recipient of FDI in the world. Although this did not increase the
economy's overall rate of investment (due to capital outflows and increases
in foreign exchange reserves), international financial institutions such as
the World Bank attributed the country's rapid growth to the influx of foreign capital (Lardy 2002, 120; World Bank 1997). Among the cited developmental benefits of FDI include the generation of foreign exchange
reserves through export-led growth, urbanization, enhanced opportunities
for technology transfer, and even diffusion of corporate managerial practices and respect for rule of law (Guthrie 1999). Yasheng Huang (2003),
however, argues that China's reliance on FDI has reinforced inefficiencies
in the state sector and effectively penalized the most efficient part of the
economy, the private sector. Rather than indicating economic health,
Huang contends that the high levels of FDI are actually symptoms of institutional weaknesses:

> [FDI] has come to play a substantial role in the Chinese economy because of sys-
> temic and pervasive discrimination against efficient and entrepreneurial domes-
> tic firms. This discrimination was not purposely instituted to benefit foreign
> firms. . . . It was instituted mainly to benefit the inefficient SOEs. As such China's

large absorption of FDI is not necessarily a sign of the strengths of its economy. Instead it may be a sign of some rather substantial distortions. (Huang 2003, 4)

These distortions include subsidization of the state sector at the expense of the private sector, lack of protection of private property rights, and economic fragmentation, which inhibits cross-regional capital mobility.

Be that as it may, the reason that the so-called Zhujiang model is considered a regional developmental model is because its dynamics were initially concentrated in south China. In 1993, for example, cities in Guangdong accounted for 32 percent of the top twenty cities receiving FDI, and the eastern seaboard overall accounted for 86.8 percent of urban FDI (*China Urban Statistical Yearbook, 1994*, cited in Yeh 2000, 48–49). Meanwhile, 49.9 percent of the country's FDI in the same year came from Hong Kong and Macau, and 8.1 percent came from Taiwan (ibid., 42).[17] These patterns reflect in large part the combination of Guangdong and Fujian's regional proximity, as well as their linguistic and cultural similarities with Hong Kong and Taiwan, respectively (Hsing 1998; Johnson 1994; Lever-Tracy, Ip, and Tracy 1996; and Zweig 1995).[18]

Despite the Pearl River Delta and southern Fujian's earlier start in attracting FDI, by the early 1990s southern Jiangsu was not far behind. Following Deng's 1992 "southern tour," which signaled the regime's willingness to continue market-oriented reforms after the crisis of 1989, local governments in Sunan began appropriating farmland for industrial parks devoted to joint ventures and offered foreign investors a variety of concessionary policies (Wu 1998). The Sunan model of rural industrialization shifted into an all-out drive toward what David Zweig (2002) has called "rural internationalization." By 1993, joint ventures accounted for one-third of all TVEs in Suzhou, and neighboring counties were busy striking deals with foreign investors (Zweig 2002, 153). Since then, Jiangsu has consistently outpaced Fujian in attracting FDI and ranked second after Guangdong in provincial rankings of FDI receipts.[19]

State-Dominated Model

Although the Wenzhou, Sunan, and Zhujiang models dominate the literature on China's regional developmental models (e.g., Zhang 2002), they

---

17. Note that official statistics understate the amount of investment from Taiwan because much of it is funneled through Hong Kong. For example, see Ash and Kueh 1993.

18. This has led some scholars to speculate about the possibility of a free-trade bloc comprising China, Hong Kong, and Taiwan. Ng and Tuan 1996.

19. Over the 1992 to 2002 decade, Guangdong received 25.5% of the country's total FDI inflows, Jiangsu received 13.1%, and Fujian received 8.9%. *China Statistical Yearbook 2001*, 605, and *2003*, 675, cited in Tao 2005, table 7.4.

may also be contrasted with an additional pattern of political economy that I call the "state-dominated model." Rather than being concentrated in a particular province or region, the state-dominated model can be found in the major industrial centers of the Mao era, including many of the central and northeastern provincial capitals.[20] Examples include Shanghai, Tianjin, Zhengzhou (Henan), Luoyang (Henan), Taiyuan (Shanxi), Wuhan (Hubei), Shenyang (Liaoning), and Changchun (Jilin).[21] In contrast to the three regional patterns discussed above, localities that I have classified as following the state-dominated model of political economy were more urbanized and had more developed industrial economies on the eve of reform. During the Mao era these localities received a higher level of capital investment from the center. Furthermore, their state-employed urban residents generally enjoyed a higher standard of living than their rural counterparts, who were limited by the household registration system from migrating to cities (Cheng and Selden 1997; Wang 2005; cf. Solinger 1999).

These developmental advantages, however, waned and even became relative liabilities during the reform era. As mentioned earlier, the center granted the southern coastal provinces (especially Fujian and Guangdong) various fiscal and policy incentives to attract foreign capital, while cities with large preexisting state sectors were not formally "opened" for foreign investment until several years later. Relatedly, the southern coastal provinces were also granted more generous fiscal contracting arrangements with the center. The 1980 fiscal reforms allowed Fujian and Guangdong to retain 100 percent of their above-quota revenues; in contrast, Beijing, Shanghai, and Tianjin were not permitted to retain any of their above-quota revenues. As Shanghai mayor Wang Daohan explained to Susan Shirk in 1984, "Of course we're behind Guangdong on reform. If the center gave us the same financial deal they gave Guangdong, we would be moving faster on reform" (Shirk 1993, 141 n11).

In addition to these policy disadvantages, local governments became responsible for bearing the fiscal costs of maintaining SOEs. During the PRC's first three decades, SOEs were subsidized by the central government budget. Starting in the 1980s, however, SOEs had to rely on loans from state banks to finance their operations (Lardy 1998). This reliance on bank loans has not only posed a serious burden on China's financial system but also limited the availability of credit to the private sector. At the same time, localities in the state-dominated model have experienced significant

20. By way of contrast, Hurst (2004) delineates three regional categories in China's political economy: the "Stalinist Rustbelt" in the northeast, the "Tentative Transitional" in the upper Changjiang and north-central China, and the "Booming Market" along China's central coast.

21. Beijing municipality could also be considered an example of the state-dominated model; however, I will not include it in the present discussion due to its special position as the political capital of the country.

political and social pressures to minimize urban unemployment, compensate laid-off state workers, and meet the pension requirements of retirees. In 1995 the central government announced deeper state sector reforms—called the "retaining the large and releasing the small" (*zhuada fangxiao*) policy—whereby all but the five hundred to one thousand largest SOEs would be sold, restructured, or privatized (Garnaut et al. 2005, 3). Since then, the vast majority of small and medium SOEs have been restructured and tens of millions of workers have been laid off. Between 1995 and 2003, the number of SOEs declined by 52.7 percent (from 2.22 to 1.05 million firms) and the number of workers employed by SOEs dropped from 112.6 million to 68.8 million (SAIC 2005). As a result, labor unrest has increased substantially in urban industrial centers. In 1998, for example, there were 247 workers' protests in Henan (Hurst and O'Brien 2002, 345). And in the spring of 2002, protracted labor unrest in the three northeastern cities of Liaoyang (Liaoning), Daqing (Heilongjiang), and Fushun (Liaoning) involved a range of five thousand to fifty thousand workers at a time (Human Rights Watch 2002). Local governments in these areas thus face difficult developmental dilemmas. On the one hand, they have fewer resources to devote to promoting the nonstate sector due to the financial burdens associated with maintaining and/or reforming local SOEs. On the other hand, private sector development represents a potentially fruitful strategy for reemployment of laid-off workers and local job creation (cf. Solinger 2001).

As in the other developmental models, the local policies toward the private sector have shifted over time in localities with initially large state sectors. Up through the early 1990s governments in state sector–dominated localities generally prioritized their state sectors and discriminated against private entrepreneurs. Starting in the mid-to-late 1990s, many of the state-dominated localities then deepened their efforts to link state sector reform with private sector development. In practice this pattern has had varying developmental results, depending on the locality's particular policies and preexisting resources (natural endowments, transportation infrastructure, local human capital, marketing networks, availability of capital, and so forth). Consider, for example, the contrasting experiences of Shanghai and Zhengzhou, two densely populated cities that became Maoist bases for heavy industry.

Because of Shanghai's historical links with international capital, during the 1950s the central government made special efforts to restructure its economy by nationalizing its private sector, closing it off from external trade, and establishing large SOEs in heavy industry (Howe 1981). Over the course of the Mao era, Shanghai's SOEs remained tightly controlled by central planners and became a major revenue source for the center. As a result, Beijing was not inclined to allow experimental reforms in Shanghai during the early reform years. Meanwhile, local officials were not inclined to circumvent national regulations to push for private sector development. The municipal government restricted land use and the scale of buildings for private factories, and its neighboring counties refused to grant business licenses to entrepreneurs who wished to operate in industries dominated by collective enterprises (Whiting 2001, 143–144). Even in the mid-1980s, when the proportion of the state sector generating industrial output in Jiangsu and Zhejiang had declined to less than half, SOEs continued to produce over 80 percent of industrial output in Shanghai (White 1998, vol. 1, 125). (Indeed, many observers date the beginning of economic reform in Shanghai as late as 1992 when the Pudong New Zone was established.) Although Shanghai has regained its position as China's financial center since then, according to Adam Segal the "Shanghai government continues to reproduce a development strategy centered on large enterprises, horizontal coordination, and state intervention" (Segal 2003, 89).

Zhengzhou, the provincial capital of Henan in central China, also represented a major industrial base during the Mao era. In 1978, its large-scale SOEs accounted for 87.5 percent of industrial output. As in Shanghai, albeit for different reasons, Zhengzhou's leaders were also especially attuned to the center's demands and policy shifts (Domenach 1995; Yang 1996). Yet Zhengzhou embraced the opportunity to develop its nonstate sector once it was politically acceptable to do so. For example, it established a branch of the Industrial and Commercial Management Bureau in 1979 and the Individual Laborers Association in 1984, earlier than in many southern coastal localities (Tsai 2002). And Zhengzhou promoted collective sector development with even greater zeal. As Wu Jieh-min has observed, in the very same year that Beijing issued "Number 4 Document of 1984" authorizing the status of TVEs, "village and household units" suddenly made up 17 percent of industrial output (Wu 2000, 314). In other words, in addition to maintaining its state sector, the Zhengzhou government pursued a highly interventionist "drive for rapid industrialization" by appropriating farmland from rural households to establish collective TVEs in various "model villages" (Wu 1998, chap. 5). By 1984, SOEs were producing only 67 percent of industrial output, and the figure had declined to 26.4 percent in 1995, while village enterprises and joint ventures constituted 57 percent of industrial output and urban collectives and township enterprises accounted for the remaining 16.5 percent (ibid.). In contrast, even though present-day Shanghai is much more prosperous than Zhengzhou, as of 2005 nonstate businesses accounted for only 13.5 percent of Shanghai's GDP (*China Daily*, May 19, 2005).[22] A related consequence of the significant downsizing of Zhengzhou's

22. As of 2003, Shanghai's per capita GDP of 45,586 RMB ($5,620) ranked 13 out of 659 cities, while Zhengzhou's per capita GDP of 16,028 ($1,940) ranked 117.

state sector is that it has experienced much more labor unrest in recent years than Shanghai (*China Labor Bulletin*, various issues). Although official reports and news articles frequently tout the private sector's contribution to alleviating unemployment, in reality private businesses generally employ fewer workers than SOEs, and "reemployment" in the private sector often means barely surviving on the fringes of the informal economy rather than earning a living wage or becoming a big capitalist boss (Solinger 2002; Kanamori and Zhao 2004, 28).

Pattern of Limited Development

Three of the four patterns of political economy discussed above developed in areas that were relatively neglected and impoverished during the Mao era. However, vast stretches of rural areas in China's western interior have remained underdeveloped even during the reform era. Broadly speaking, this characterizes the developmental situation of rural Gansu, Guizhou, Ningxia, Sichuan, Tibet, Qinghai, Xinjiang, and Yunan.[23] To alleviate the gap between the eastern and western provinces, in 2000 the central government launched a developmental drive called the "Opening Up the West" or "Go West" (*xibu da kaifa*) campaign. Between 2000 and 2005, the center invested about $48 billion, mainly in infrastructure, energy, and natural resource extraction projects. This state investment drive was intended to stimulate local economic development and make western China more attractive to foreign investors.[24] Although scholars have disputed the relative success of the Go West policy in general, my own research can only affirm that the operating conditions for private businesses remain poor—even in county seats that have paved roads, renovated government buildings, and established a commercial district.

An example of such a locality is Hechuan, a county-level city that lies in a mountainous area north of Chongqing. With a total population of 1.5 million (including 291,500 people in the county seat), Hechuan is considered a small- to medium-sized city. Furthermore, its urban per capita GDP of 7,213 RMB ($871) in 2004 was 23.4 percent below the national average, but its rural per capita GDP of 3,150 RMB ($380) was 7.3 percent above the

23. Note that the pattern of "limited development" can also be found in most of the provinces that have the better-known models of political economy. For example, western Fujian, rural Henan, and northern Jiangsu all have impoverished counties where no formal "model" of political economy has been identified—largely because reform-era development in such areas has been limited. Bernstein and Lü (2000) call these types of rural localities "agricultural China," in contrast to "industrial China," which has benefited from the development of TVEs. But those terms are meant to denote general categories rather than developmental models per se.

24. For more detail on the Go West campaign see the special issue of *China Quarterly* (July 2004) and the *Journal of Contemporary China* (November 2004).

national average (All China Data Center, China Data Online website 2006; Hechuan City Government website 2006). What official government statistics do not highlight, however, is that three hundred thousand Hechuan people are working outside of the county, especially in Chongqing where there are more employment and business opportunities (Interview 249). Until a highway was built connecting Chongqing and Hechuan in 2002, the latter was isolated due to its mountainous terrain and thus, when locals left town, they would do so for most of the year, if not permanently. In short, even though Hechuan is not impoverished by national standards, its economy has lagged behind that of other cities during the reform era and remains on the periphery of major economic and industrial developments.

To the extent that the private economy exists in areas such as Hechuan, it mainly consists of smaller-scale individual entrepreneurs and rural households that operate at a near-subsistence level and have little to offer predatory cadres (see also Sun 2004, chap. 4). Meanwhile, larger businesses in the limited-development localities are often expected to contribute substantial funds to local coffers. As a result, business owners in these localities have many complaints, and tend to idealize the economic conditions for private firms in other places. Even local officials seem to envy the locational advantages of other areas, bemoan the paucity of interest by foreign investors in their own locality, and believe that truly successful private entrepreneurs will all move elsewhere once they have the resources to do so.

Variation in Local Realities, Coping Strategies, and Adaptive Informal Institutions

Given the wide variation in local models of political economy, what generalizations can be drawn about the implications of these spatial and structural differences for private entrepreneurs? To what extent do the coping strategies of entrepreneurs vary by locality? Answers to these questions provide additional insight into the broader analytical concern in this book about the emergence of adaptive informal institutions, which at times may become sufficiently widespread to influence formal institutions. As suggested already, the causal mechanisms underlying this influence are generally an indirect outgrowth of day-to-day interactions among business owners and local bureaucrats. In this sense, private sector development has had a structural impact on the national policies that affect the political and economic welfare of business. To clarify the origins of this causal influence, we turn now to the local contexts framing entrepreneurs' concerns.

One of the recurring themes in interviewing business owners is that they regard many of their operational challenges as locally contingent. Itinerant entrepreneurs and those who travel extensively for business purposes share this view. It was also interesting to learn about the preconceived notions that entrepreneurs have about how business conditions in their particular locality compare with those in other areas. In an open-ended question on the 2002 survey, respondents stated that the best localities for private business were Zhejiang (15.2 percent), Wenzhou (in Zhejiang, 10.1 percent), Shanghai (7.6 percent), Guangdong (9 percent), Guangzhou (in Guangdong, 6.4 percent), Shenzhen (4.9 percent), and Beijing (4 percent). At first glance, these responses correspond roughly with the conventional wisdom implied by the above models of political economy. Given the temporal differences in private sector development, for example, it makes sense that Zhejiang, including Wenzhou, received the highest proportion of favorable ratings. Similarly, Guangdong, Guangzhou, and Shenzhen were also listed by a fair number of respondents. Indeed, these particular survey responses correspond with the scope and scale of the private sector in those provinces. Guangdong and Zhejiang have the largest total number of private firms; private businesses in those provinces also have the largest number of employees and high levels of registered capital (table 6.1).

Yet the responses diverge notably from the rankings of these provincial-level statistics in the cases of Jiangsu, Shandong, Shanghai, and Beijing. Starting in 2001, Jiangsu surpassed Guangdong in terms of the total number of registered private enterprises (*siying qiye*) yet very few entrepreneurs indicated that Jiangsu provided the best environment for conducting private business ventures. Along similar lines, Shandong ranks above Jiangsu in terms of the total number of private businesses (*siying* and *geti*), number of workers employed in the private sector, and the average registered capitalization of private firms—but few respondents selected Shandong as having a hospitable environment for the private sector. Meanwhile, the surveyed entrepreneurs have a positive impression of the private business environment in Shanghai and Beijing, even though both municipalities had a later start on private sector development relative to many other localities.

Differences in population size explain in part these apparent discrepancies between surveyed perceptions and official statistics. For example, in 2003 Zhejiang Province had 44.5 million people, while Shandong and Jiangsu had populations of 91.1 and 74.1 million people, respectively (*China Statistical Yearbook* 2004). Hence, on a per capita basis, the private sector involves a much larger proportion of the population in Zhejiang than in the other two provinces. But this does not explain why other provinces with a large number of private businesses relative to population (such as Liaoning) do not have better reputations. Probably the main reason for the disjuncture between perceptions and aggregate statistics is that the latter do not distinguish between businesses that are established based on the entrepreneurial initiative of private individuals versus recently privatized enterprises that may still have close links with public sector entities. Even though most

Table 6.1. Provincial rankings of the private sector, 2003

Province	Registered Siying qiye	Registered Getihu	Private Firms	Siying Employees	Getihu Employees	Total Employees	Reg. Cap. of Siying	Reg. Cap. of Getihu [in 10,000 RMB]	Total Registered Capitalization
Guangdong	323,077	1,855,085	2,178,162	2,849,621	3,899,487	6,749,108	45,227,995	3,979,705	49,207,700
Zhejiang	302,136	1,585,223	1,887,359	4,143,100	2,983,394	7,126,494	29,240,602	4,293,418	33,534,020
Shandong	228,554	1,586,406	1,814,960	3,063,831	3,470,498	6,534,329	45,227,995	2,671,077	47,899,072
Jiangsu	343,680	1,401,196	1,744,876	3,865,466	2,062,081	5,927,547	36,326,092	3,233,757	39,559,849
Sichuan	110,359	1,433,517	1,543,876	1,214,519	2,244,639	3,459,158	10,419,164	1,452,880	11,872,044
Liaoning	114,415	1,409,250	1,523,665	1,823,366	3,067,398	4,890,764	12,589,057	3,499,385	16,088,442
Henan	81,300	1,211,930	1,293,230	613,854	2,581,536	3,195,390	7,129,470	1,232,932	8,362,402
Anhui	74,815	1,200,804	1,275,619	999,721	2,863,314	3,863,035	6,622,927	1,237,872	7,860,799
Hubei	86,155	1,049,386	1,135,541	847,710	2,486,919	3,334,629	10,720,929	1,761,131	12,482,060
Hebei	86,031	1,036,036	1,122,067	1,603,665	2,566,313	4,169,978	8,064,158	2,274,527	10,338,685
Guangxi	34,860	990,286	1,025,146	1,096,587	1,490,508	2,587,095	3,666,096	1,017,607	4,683,703
Hunan	56,534	940,403	996,937	802,108	1,978,624	2,780,732	6,953,687	1,952,391	8,906,078
Heilongjiang	51,402	942,370	993,772	627,766	2,054,563	2,682,329	5,116,508	1,838,005	6,954,513
Shaanxi	80,761	765,077	845,838	1,096,587	1,583,137	2,679,724	8,992,104	837,366	9,829,470
Yunnan	43,734	728,130	771,864	445,471	1,236,848	1,682,319	5,958,603	1,102,529	7,061,132
Jiangxi	48,995	593,816	642,811	820,232	1,429,264	2,249,496	5,283,665	951,925	6,235,590
Beijing	186,805	446,851	633,656	2,191,735	588,340	2,780,075	23,395,283	516,219	23,911,502
Nei Menggu	35,114	555,513	590,627	410,971	1,083,796	1,494,767	3,869,079	833,066	4,702,145
Shanghai	291,711	267,751	559,462	2,557,064	314,278	2,871,342	41,737,629	297,988	42,035,617
Fujian	87,510	463,866	551,376	868,470	923,974	1,792,444	13,175,161	2,081,047	15,256,208
Chongqing	54,922	476,904	531,826	710,253	1,008,248	1,718,501	6,982,525	604,638	7,587,163
Xinjiang	36,617	449,911	486,528	378,658	706,556	1,085,214	4,970,091	798,906	5,768,997
Shanxi	42,874	406,038	448,912	997,990	759,210	1,757,200	6,422,399	636,083	7,058,482
Guizhou	28,100	415,492	443,592	222,723	616,493	839,216	2,989,748	593,479	3,583,227
Jilin	38,135	404,764	442,899	327,151	744,900	1,072,051	4,705,131	696,669	5,401,800
Gansu	26,462	332,327	358,789	294,498	616,920	911,418	2,718,529	455,367	3,173,896
Tianjin	59,076	188,735	247,811	515,004	259,145	774,149	9,198,800	495,700	9,694,500
Hainan	26,161	130,772	156,933	213,817	260,483	474,300	5,955,985	151,330	6,107,315
Qinghai	8,815	123,243	132,058	182,147	244,021	426,168	1,122,996	199,626	1,322,622
Ningxia	14,591	88,374	102,965	145,106	154,888	299,994	1,388,823	142,321	1,531,144
Xizang	1,823	52,401	54,224	28,493	85,643	114,136	380,404	63,952	444,356
Total	3,005,524	23,531,857	26,537,381	35,957,684	46,365,418	82,323,102	376,551,635	41,902,898	418,454,533

Source: SAIC, *Zhongguo siying jingji nianjian, 2002–2004* (China private economy yearbook, 2002–2004), 73–74.

Table 6.2. Developmental patterns and entrepreneurs' political backgrounds, 2002 survey

Developmental pattern*	Previously employed by the state (%)	Worked as a cadre (%)	CCP member (%)	Member of formal political organization (%)
Wenzhou model	9.0	1.8	22.2	6.6
Sunan model	27.0	20.8	24.3	14.0
South China model	6.7	13.9	12.2	12.8
State-dominated model	38.7	31.4	26.5	28.0
Limited-development pattern	20.3	8.9	21.0	6.5
Sample average	27.8	21.6	23.5	18.4

*Each of the sampled counties and cities was classified into one of these developmental patterns. See appendix A for more detail.

localities now recognize the value of the private economy—at least in rhetoric if not in practice—the legacies of different developmental models still have bearing on the types of adaptive strategies private entrepreneurs and local officials formulate in the course of their daily interactions and negotiations.

At the most basic level, these developmental differences can be seen in the demographic composition of the private sector. In particular, my 2002 survey found that the employment and political background of entrepreneurs varies by developmental pattern. Entrepreneurs in the Wenzhou model are the least likely to have state employment backgrounds and are also among the least likely to be cadres or members of formal political organizations (table 6.2). Business owners operating in localities characterized by the south China model and limited development are also less likely than those in the Sunan and state-dominated models to have public sector and political experience. These findings reflect the overall reform-era trend of private sector development: the earliest cohort of private business owners tended to come from agricultural backgrounds, while more recent participants in the private sector are more likely to have worked as state employees and to have better political networks. Yet these apparent advantages in employment and political background do not translate neatly into better experiences as private entrepreneurs.[25]

Instead, my survey results show that entrepreneurs in provinces with a legacy of larger collective and state sectors (the Sunan and state-dominated models, respectively) faced more difficulty than those in provinces with more developed private economies. Respondents in the Wenzhou model

25. As noted in the previous chapter, this finding is at odds with Wank's (2002) contention that entrepreneurs with state employment backgrounds and cadres are able to convert their social capital into operating advantages in the private sector. The main reason for our divergent findings is that my larger and more recent sample includes laid-off state workers.

Table 6.3. Breakdown of perceived problems by developmental pattern, 2002 survey

Developmental pattern	Wenzhou model	Sunan model	South China model	State-dominated model	Limited-development pattern	Sample average
Have disputes with local government (%)	14.4	24.1	10.8	27.9	16.1	22.7
Have serious capital constraints (%)	28.4	71.8	62.3	78.8	73.2	69.6
Problems with land for production site (%)	13.8	27.5	39.9	43.8	32.3	34.4
Problems with utilities (%)	3.0	8.0	35.1	19.6	25.8	19.3
Problems with taxes (%)	8.4	32.2	59.5	45.0	34.7	37.8
Problems with fees (%)	11.4	44.1	59.5	58.4	39.5	47.7
Problems with government services (%)	3.6	34.9	45.6	48.1	47.6	39.0
Ranking of developmental type by level of complaints*	5	4	2	1	3	n.a.

*Number 1 indicates that the respondents in that developmental type have the highest overall level of complaints, while 5 indicates the lowest overall level of complaints.

consistently report having fewer disputes with the local government and are less likely than entrepreneurs in other areas to report serious capital constraints for expansion or problems with land use, utilities, taxes, fees, and government services (table 6.3). In direct contrast, business owners report the most serious operational challenges in the state-dominated model, that is, areas with large Mao-era state sectors. The finding that entrepreneurs in the south China model also report having many difficulties may seem counterintuitive given that those localities have exhibited robust economic performance during the reform era, but the complaints stem from the fact that foreign-invested enterprises enjoy privileged treatment relative to private firms.

Although adherents of the most basic version of modernization theory might expect that capitalists in provinces with better developed private sectors would be more politically assertive than those with a less developed private economy, my survey found evidence for the opposite conclusion. Out of the five developmental patterns, respondents in the Wenzhou model are the least likely to use assertive political strategies such as conveying their opinions through formal political institutions, writing letters to governmental and media outlets, and using the judicial system. For example, on average 6 percent of all the surveyed entrepreneurs have contacted delegates of the National People's Congress, local people's congresses, and Chinese People's Political Consultative Conference, but only 0.6 percent of those from the Wenzhou model have gone through similar channels (table 6.4).

Table 6.4. Means of addressing problems by developmental pattern, 2002 (Percentage of respondents who indicated they use these means either "sometimes" or "frequently")

Developmental pattern	Wenzhou model	Sunan model	South China model	State-dominated model	Limited-development pattern	Sample average
Express opinion directly to political leaders	4.8	25.3	16.4	27.3	16.9	22.4
Solicit assistance from those with influence on political leaders	11.4	27.3	12.1	30.4	6.5	23.8
Express opinion through mass organizations	24.7	7.9	6.4	15.5	10.5	13.0
Express opinion through NPC delegates	0.6	7.0	2.9	5.9	5.6	5.4
Express opinion through CPPCC members	0.6	5.9	5.7	9.5	4.8	6.7
Express opinion through entrepreneurs associations (ILA, PEA, UFIC)	27.7	17.8	7.8	17.3	10.5	17.2
Write letters to relevant government agencies	0.6	5.4	5.0	5.8	9.7	5.4
Report to official organizations accepting inquiries or complaints	0.6	5.2	5.0	2.0	0.8	3.0
Seek organizations to arbitrate the dispute	0	3.4	1.4	2.7	0.8	2.3
Appeal to courts	1.2	9.7	3.5	9.4	6.5	7.8
Percentage of assertive entrepreneurs*	0.6	9.0	4.8	4.8	8.8	5.5

*The survey asked respondents, "When you encounter disputes, how do you normally resolve the matter? (Please rank the following eight choices.)" Those who selected "appeal to government or higher authorities," "appeal to courts," or "resolve through news media" as their typical first course of action constitute "assertive entrepreneurs" in my typology of entrepreneurs' coping strategies. Note that these percentages are calculated directly from the survey and do not take into account the estimated 15.3 percent of unregistered entrepreneurs. When the latter are taken into account the raw percentages from the survey are reduced by 15.3 percent.

To the extent that Wenzhou model entrepreneurs express their opinions to political entities, they are more inclined to contact governmental leaders directly or go through contacts with political influence—but they perform these acts far less frequently than do entrepreneurs in other localities. At the same time, compared with respondents from other types of localities, those in the Wenzhou model are among the most likely to express their concerns through mass organizations and business associations that are intended to serve the private sector. Overall, these findings confirm that local officials in Zhejiang are generally more supportive of the nonstate sector or, at a minimum, less likely to give private entrepreneurs a hard time than officials in other provinces. These relatively favorable conditions, in turn, explain why entrepreneurs in the Wenzhou model are more focused on the commercial aspects of their businesses, have fewer disputes with local governmental entities, and, compared to business owners in other types of localities, are more likely to be loyally acceptant.

At the other extreme, private entrepreneurs in the state-dominated model are nearly twice as likely as those in the Wenzhou model to report having disputes with local government agencies and officials. While 27.9 percent of state-dominated model respondents indicated that they frequently have problems with governmental entities, only 14.4 percent of those in the Wenzhou model had similar complaints (table 6.3). This contrast is mirrored in the higher incidence of political assertiveness by registered business owners in state-dominated localities. Of the state-dominated model respondents, 27.3 percent said they had expressed their views directly to political leaders, and a higher-than-average percentage of the respondents had gone through formal political institutions to resolve their disputes. However, when we calculate the percentage of respondents who use assertive means (appeal to governmental authorities, judicial courts, or news media) to resolve their problems as their *first* course of action, only 4.8 percent of the respondents regularly resort to assertive coping strategies. Recall that the unadjusted sample average of entrepreneurs using assertive strategies is 5.5 percent. In other words, although entrepreneurs in the state-dominated model have more grievances and may have more cumulative experience in political assertiveness, they are somewhat less likely to be assertive repeatedly than the sample average. Due to the often disempowering effects of being laid off from state-owned enterprises, there are also somewhat larger proportions of grudgingly acceptant business owners (16.2 percent) in the state-sector dominated localities, as compared to the sample average (14 percent).

Respondents in the south China model do not use assertive means for dispute resolution as frequently as respondents in the Wenzhou or the state-dominated model. With the exception of "reporting to official organizations accepting inquiries or complaints," where respondents in the south China model matched the level of their Sunan model counterparts at 5 percent, entrepreneurs in the south China model are less likely to contact mass organizations, NPC delegates, CPPCC members, entrepreneurs' associations, and arbitration organizations than are entrepreneurs in most of the other developmental patterns. Overall, 4.8 percent of the south China model respondents regularly turn to assertive means for dispute resolution, which is slightly below the sample average.

Respondents in the Sunan model have many complaints and they are much more assertive than their counterparts in the Wenzhou, south China, and state-dominated models. Sunan respondents are more likely to express their opinions to political leaders and NPC delegates, report to official organizations accepting complaints, and appeal to courts. Moreover, when asked about their first choice for dispute resolution, 9 percent of the Sunan respondents choose assertive means before considering less contentious strategies. Out of all the respondents in the five developmental patterns, Sunan model entrepreneurs are the most assertive. They operate in a context where the local economy has been transformed from being dominated by the collective sector to a pattern of political economy that emphasizes larger privatized enterprises and foreign-invested operations. Under these conditions, many private entrepreneurs are former managers of collective enterprises who were accustomed to policy advantages before the spread of privatization and now have little tolerance for perceived discriminatory treatment in their new capacity as business owners. At the other end of the economic, social, and political spectrum, however, are petty entrepreneurs who also have many complaints but limited resources for articulating their concerns, because they may be laid-off workers from collective enterprises or rural migrants in search of better business conditions within the Sunan model areas. Because of this, Sunan model localities also have the highest levels of grudgingly acceptant entrepreneurs at 17.6 percent of the respondents.

Finally, business owners in areas with limited development have more complaints about utilities and government services than respondents in the other models of political economy, and they are more active in writing letters to relevant government agencies. When asked about their primary means of dispute resolution, limited-development respondents appear to be as assertive as their Sunan counterparts: 8.8 percent use assertive forms of dispute resolution before trying other channels.[26] Note, however, that the total number of private entrepreneurs per capita in the limited-development localities is much lower than in the Sunan model areas. Thus, even though a comparable percentage of business owners in both localities use assertive political strategies on a regular basis, the overall number of assertive entrepreneurs is much higher in the Sunan model than in areas with limited development.

The composition of business owners in each of the developmental patterns can be broken down according to the typology of entrepreneurs' coping strategies delineated in the previous chapter (table 6.5).

Beyond these descriptive statistical findings from the survey, ultimately the orientation of the local government toward the private sector also plays a key role in explaining the perceived variation in business conditions for entrepreneurs and, by extension, the extent to which entrepreneurs use assertive political means to resolve their problems. These differences in local

26. More specifically, 5.6% of the respondents in the limited-development model indicated that they "appeal to the local government or higher authorities," and 3.2% of the respondents "appeal to the court system" as their first course of action to resolve a dispute.

Table 6.5. Summary of entrepreneurs' coping strategies by developmental pattern

Developmental pattern	Assertive	Grudgingly acceptant	Loyally acceptant	Avoidant*
Wenzhou model	0.6	6.0	93.4	n.a.
	0.5	5.1	78.7	14.7
Sunan model	9.0	17.6	73.4	n.a.
	7.7	15.0	62.4	15.0
South China model	4.8	9.5	85.7	n.a.
	4.1	8.0	72.2	14.7
State-dominated model	4.8	16.2	79.0	n.a.
	4.0	13.6	66.5	15.8
Limited-development pattern	8.8	7.2	84.0	n.a.
	7.4	6.1	71.0	15.5
Sample average	5.5	14.0	80.5	n.a.
	4.7	11.9	68.2	15.3

Note: In each row, the top number represents the percentage of survey respondents, while the lower number represents the proportion of entrepreneurs using that particular strategy after accounting for the percentage of unregistered entrepreneurs.

*The percentage of unregistered business owners was estimated for each of the developmental patterns by calculating the average relative proportion of *getihu* and *siying qiye* in each province within the developmental pattern, and then multiplying the proportion of *getihu* by 16.9 percent (the national estimate of unregistered *getihu*) and the proportion of *siying qiye* by 3 percent (the national estimate of unregistered *siying qiye*) and adding the two numbers together to arrive at a weighted average estimate of unregistered business owners.

governmental treatment of the private economy are highlighted below in the context of the specific models of political economy and the resulting adaptive informal institutions that have emerged.

Informal Financial Institutions in Wenzhou

Wenzhou's cadres and entrepreneurs are both quick to point out—with a sense of self-made pride—that the Wenzhou model in Zhejiang was forged out of local economic desperation and despite initial political opposition from above. The corollary to this popular explanation attributes Wenzhou's economic success to the flexibility of its local officials and diligence of its entrepreneurs. One local cadre put it bluntly, "Of course the local government has supported the private economy. Wenzhou people have had no choice but to make something out of nothing" (Interview 65). Indeed, most observers agree that what facilitated private petty commodity production in Wenzhou was a host of innovative practices that entailed the quiet complicity of local state entities. The resulting adaptive informal institutions included red hat enterprises and a motley range of private financial intermediaries such as large-scale rotating credit associations, underground moneylenders, and private banks disguised as other types of entities. The following cases of a small factory operator, a part-time moneylender, and a daring financial entrepreneur illustrate the importance of these informal practices to Wenzhou's private economy.

The manner in which owner Peng pieced together investment and working capital to operate a hydraulic valve factory out of his home is typical of Wenzhou's entrepreneurs (Interview 50). After decollectivization, owner Peng had nothing to do, so he started out by processing individual parts of hydraulic valves. To purchase equipment, in 1982 he borrowed 150,000 RMB ($79,365) from his friends and family and 5,000 RMB ($2,646) from a loan shark at 20 percent annual interest. When he needed additional working capital in 1996, he started borrowing in 10,000 RMB increments (at 21 percent annual interest) from a rural cooperative foundation. Owner Peng explained that rural cooperative foundations were really run by private individuals and that he could never get a bank loan without connections (*guanxi*). "Besides," he added, "it would take too long to borrow from a bank because they want to investigate everything."

Interviews with moneylenders in Wenzhou revealed that they take pride in providing their clients with efficient services, which generally entail brokering between savers who seek higher returns on their savings and entrepreneurs who need credit. Manager Lao in Clear River Village, for example, has a small clothing factory, but about half of his income derives from his other position as a manager of the village's old folks association (OFA, *laoren xiehui*) (Interview 57). Many villages have OFAs that provide a space for retired villagers, and especially widows without relatives, to socialize with one another. Villagers usually make modest contributions so their elderly neighbors can enjoy nicer meals on holidays and other special occasions. In various parts of rural Wenzhou, however, the OFAs also offer larger-scale financial services. Manager Lao explained that OFAs involved in curb market finance come in two forms. First, some OFAs consist of retired villagers who wish to earn higher rates of interest than that offered by state banks; hence, they pool their money and lend it out to local enterprises. The second type of OFA is simply a low-profile disguise for younger moneylenders who operate private banks using the OFA name as a cover. Manager Lao considered his financial activities as falling into the intermediate category, because he manages the finances of a real OFA but also brokers the members' savings to entrepreneurs in need of loans. His OFA has over one hundred members who have entrusted him with about 400,000 RMB ($48,309) of their savings. Lao then extends loans of 3,000 to 50,000 RMB to small private businesses, most of which are within the village.

While most curb market operators prefer to broker funds by either providing financial services out of their homes or registering the business in a disguised form, a small but influential number of Wenzhou's entrepreneurs take the bolder path of simply conducting their financial businesses in a transparent manner. Owner Chan of Jinxiang Township, for example, is outspoken and unapologetic about what he has had to do to succeed in his various ventures (Interview 121). As mentioned in chapter 3, owner Chan had already started peddling coal shovel handles when he was a sent-down youth in Heilongjiang during the Cultural Revolution. When he decided to open an aluminum factory in his hometown of Jinxiang in 1980, owner Chan raised 8,500 RMB ($5,667) in capital by enlisting sixteen other shareholders. Because he also needed land for his production site, he dug up abandoned family tombs on the side of a mountain where villagers had been burying their ancestors for centuries.[27] For building materials, he stripped the bamboo off old ships.

By the end of 1985, owner Chan was ready for a major expansion. Despite the absence of domestic stock markets at the time, he ended up raising 15 million RMB ($5.1 million) by selling shares of his company to the public. He had received approval from the Wenzhou branch of the People's Bank of China, which then secured approval from the Zhejiang-level branch of the People's Bank. The application process took over one year, but he was finally able to issue printed stock certificates in 1987. People came directly to the factory to buy them at 100 RMB ($27).[28] Inspired by the experience of being, so he claimed, the first entrepreneur in post-1949 China to issue private stocks, owner Chan decided to enter the financing business. In early 1988 he established a private bank by registering it as part of his factory, and by the end of the year the Cangnan County People's Bank gave him permission to establish the Jinxiang Financial Service Society (*Jinxiang jinrong fuwushe*) with a registered capitalization of 500,000 RMB ($132,625). The "financial service society" was basically a private commercial bank. After 1989, owner Chan sold it to a group of shareholders, and it was eventually converted into an urban credit cooperative.

Local economists estimated in 2000 that the scale of informal finance in Wenzhou was at least 100 billion RMB ($12.1 billion), which exceeded the volume of savings deposits in local state banks (approximately 60 billion RMB or $7.2 billion) (Interview 62).[29] Even state banking officials in Wenzhou readily admit that, despite their illegality, institutionalized forms of informal finance have played an important part in the local economy and can often be quite efficient (Interview 63). One state bank manager explained it almost as a matter of unofficial policy: "We are not opposed to our clients borrowing from

27. Apparently no one noticed at the time because the land is not arable given the mountainous terrain and the graves had been neglected for decades.

28. At the time of our interview in late 2001, he estimated that they were worth between 6,000 and 7,000 RMB ($732 to $854).

29. As of year-end 2003, out of 134.3 billion RMB in loans, 96.4 billion were informal. In other words, 71.8 percent of total lending in Wenzhou in 2003 was informal. "Informal Money Lending Is Still Hot in Wenzhou," *Nanfang shibao*, January 18, 2005.

Urban credit cooperative in Wenzhou: "Open 365 days a year and all night long"

informal sources while borrowing from us as well" (Interview 53). These are the type of observations that give Wenzhou its reputation for having a particularly permissive environment for private sector development, and for inspiring "reform from below" (Liu 1992; Parris 1993).

Wenzhou's financial innovations provide the most powerful illustrations of my argument about the causal power of adaptive financial institutions. After all, formal national approval of larger private enterprises, floating interest rates, and investment companies occurred after the practices had been well established in Wenzhou. Yet the diffusion of adaptive informal institutions from Wenzhou to Beijing has not been seamless or comprehensive. The reasons that informal finance remains pervasive in Wenzhou include that the state banking sector is still not operating in a commercially viable manner and that significant restrictions remain on private sector finance. The conversion of urban credit cooperatives into urban commercial banks (UCBs) in 1997 was intended to increase the availability of credit to private businesses and reduce the popular reliance on illegal financing mechanisms.[30] But Wenzhou's businesses owners, especially the proprietors of small and medium enterprises, continue to complain about their exclusion from formal sources of capital. And national banking regulators continue to fight a losing battle with informal financiers. As the director of Wenzhou's Bank Business Association put it, "Every time the People's Bank closes down one illegal financial institution, five more will spring up" (Interview 62).

In this sense, Wenzhou's informal financial institutions also represent an example of adaptive institutional failure. Even though the central government has sanctioned a number of creative financing mechanisms popularized by Wenzhou's entrepreneurs, as of 2005 privately owned banks are still illegal.[31] This is not to say that the ban on private money houses (or banks) will remain indefinitely. Instead, the point is that private finance is one issue area in which the emergence of adaptive informal institutions has yet to inspire deeper reform of formal institutions.[32] As such, in Wenzhou and other localities where the local government is especially supportive of the private sector, entrepreneurs draw on many different forms of curb market finance. In the absence of local governmental complicity in sanctioning or ignoring violations of national banking regulations, it would be much more difficult for informal finance to thrive and service private sector clients (Tsai 2002).

Private Sector Challenges in Sunan

Although Jiangsu Province now boasts the largest number of private enterprises (*siying qiye*) in the country, private sector development has emerged

30. Given the difficulties of managing urban credit cooperatives (UCCs) and the inability of existing banking institutions to meet the demand for private sector finance, in 1995 the central bank started to reform UCCs by forcing them to merge with one another and converting them into urban commercial banks. Unlike UCCs, which were collectively owned nonbanking financial institutions, urban commercial banks are considered joint-stock commercial banks. The former shareholders of UCCs would be allowed a 50% to 60% share of the UCBs, while the local government would hold 30% of the shares, and individuals and state units could invest in the remaining 10% to 20% of the shares. The conversion of UCCs into UCBs was first carried out on a pilot basis in the five cities of Beijing, Shanghai, Shenzhen, Shijiazhuang, and Tianjin, and then it was extended to Wenzhou's UCCs starting in 1997.

31. The only legal private bank in China is Minsheng Bank, which was established in January 1996 as a national joint-stock commercial bank. Many observers question the extent to which it may be considered a truly "private" bank, however.

32. There are, of course, broader macroeconomic reasons why Beijing has not liberalized the financial system in a manner that would legitimize the informal financing practices of private entrepreneurs. Ultimately, having a competitive and commercially viable banking system will require more complex restructuring of the preexisting bad loans in state banks.

primarily as an outgrowth of its former collective enterprises. Moreover, private business owners have faced greater challenges than their counterparts in Zhejiang. Up through the mid-1990s private enterprises faced stringent licensing procedures and experienced greater difficulty in hiring skilled workers due to regulations limiting the availability of labor to the private sector. They also faced greater capital constraints than entrepreneurs in Zhejiang. While loans extended to private entities by state banks accounted for 8 percent of total lending in Zhejiang during the 1990 to 1995 period, only 4.3 percent of bank loans went to private businesses in Jiangsu during the same time frame (Huang 2004, 17). Exacerbating this structural disadvantage in the supply of bank credit is the paucity of curb market finance in Jiangsu as compared to Zhejiang. To the limited extent that local governments in Jiangsu (and especially Sunan) have allowed unconventional financing activities, it has been to support collective enterprises rather than private businesses.

Local officials readily admit that private enterprises have operated at a distinct disadvantage relative to state and collective ones. It was not until the Fifteenth Party Congress in late 1997—followed by the widespread publicity of Jiang Zemin's Theory of the Three Represents and, especially, his 7/1 speech—that local governments in Sunan began taking the politically elevated status of the private economy more seriously.[33] The director of the Nanjing United Front for Industry and Commerce, for example, said that UFIC did not even keep statistics on the private economy until after the Fifteenth Party Congress. He further noted that shortly after the July 1 speech, Nanjing organized three conferences on private entrepreneurs, which resulted in the publication of a book presenting the profiles of successful business owners (Interview 161). During my visit in October 2002, UFIC was also eager to share with me a colorful poster documenting the swift expansion of Nanjing's private economy between 1997 and 2001 with the politically compliant purpose of "celebrating the spirit of the Three Represents and the July 1 speech."[34] For a city where the public sector accounts for 71 percent of the local GDP, UFIC believed that such a display of private sector dynamism was noteworthy.

33. In 1999 a new provincial party secretary, Hui Liangyu, was appointed in Jiangsu, and he started to pay more attention to the private sector. He even went to Wenzhou in 1999 to learn more about its private economy. Li Yuanchao, a native of Jiangsu, replaced Hui as provincial party secretary in 2002.

34. The poster showed that between 1997 and 2001 the number of registered individual and private enterprises had increased from 98,010 to 134,883 businesses, their total registered capitalization had increased from 7.3 billion to 22.5 billion RMB, the number of employees in the private sector had increased from 274,132 to 629,000, the total production value of private sector businesses had increased from 2.3 billion to 8.7 billion RMB, the total sales had increased from 17.4 billion to 39.3 billion RMB, total consumer retail sales had increased from 7.8 billion to 23 billion RMB, and total taxes paid by the private sector had increased from 203 million to 1.4 billion RMB.

Jiangsu's, and especially Sunan's, later start on private sector development is reflected in the demographic composition of its entrepreneurs. In my 2002 survey only 9 percent of entrepreneurs in the Wenzhou model had previously been employed by the state as compared to 27 percent of the respondents in the Sunan model (table 6.2). Relatedly, the surveyed business owners in Sunan model localities also have more extensive ties with the staff of the state and are much better educated than their Wenzhou model counterparts.[35]

For an example of how some of Jiangsu's larger-scale entrepreneurs have been able to leverage their state employment backgrounds to run private businesses, however, consider the case of He Chaobing, the chief executive officer of Dahe International Advertising Group (Interview 164).[36]

Born in 1962, he spent three years, from 1977 to 1980, in the countryside as a sent-down educated youth during the Cultural Revolution. When he returned to Nanjing City at age eighteen he started working at a state-owned textile factory that employed one thousand people. In 1989, he decided to complete his education while working and attended the Nanjing Arts College where he learned key skills for his advertising business. Bored and restless at the SOE, in 1991 he announced that he wanted to "jump into the sea" of the private economy (*xiahai*). The SOE did not want him to quit, however, so they tried to retain him by granting him his long-standing desire to enter the party. Although he joined the CCP, the following year owner He paid the factory 5,000 RMB ($905) in order to leave his position and start his own textile business. He named it the Art Design Research Institute (*yishu sheji yanjiusuo*) because it sounded less commercially oriented. The resulting entity was a variant of a red hat business known in China as a "hang-on enterprise" (*guahu qiye*) because it used the SOE's resources (and sold its inventory), but the Art Design Research Institute was really a privately owned, for-profit business.

In 1994, owner He decided to take off the red hat and established a private advertising business with 30,000 RMB ($3,480) that he had earned from the textile factory. "Things were really tough for private businesses back then," owner He recalled. "We didn't receive any support from the government, and no one respected private entrepreneurs." It was not until 1997 that he was able to get a loan from the Agricultural Bank of China using a 4 million RMB ($482,509) digital printing machine as collateral. Even though he had access to bank credit at the time of our interview in 2002,

35. In the 2002 survey, 47.5% of respondents from Jiangsu had postsecondary education versus only 13.2% in Zhejiang.

36. This is another case where real names are used because the chief executive officer's biographical details have been documented in the firm's promotional materials and in Chinese newspapers. Additional information about the business is available at http://www.dahe-ad.com.

owner He was planning to take his company public on the Hong Kong Stock Exchange the following year. He added that it was ridiculous that Jiangsu did not have any publicly traded companies even though it has the largest number of private enterprises in the country. Given the complexity of preparing for an initial public offering (IPO), owner He hired the vice director of the Industrial and Commercial Bank of China to serve as Dahe's vice president. To make it worth his while, owner He offered the former state banker an annual salary of 200,000 RMB ($24,155) plus an upfront retirement bonus in cash. The arrangement worked: on November 11, 2003, the Jiangsu Dahe International Advertising Group Company Ltd. went public on the Hong Kong Stock Exchange.

Although the case of Dahe International Advertising is somewhat unusual, as Jiangsu's first private enterprise to have an IPO, owner He's success depended in large part on his connections with state entities. He sold cloth from his former SOE employer, he registered his first business with his SOE's sponsorship, and he recruited expertise from a state bank to tap international equity markets. In contrast to the theme of self-reliance running through the business histories of Wenzhou's entrepreneurs, most of the larger private enterprises in Sunan started out wearing red hats. And while Wenzhou's proprietors have relied heavily on informal finance, business owners in Jiangsu do not admit to drawing on informal sources of credit because, as a number of them explained, "it's illegal."[37]

Foreign-Invested Enterprises in the South China Model

Although Guangdong has the largest private sector in the country, its reform-era economy has been oriented toward FDI, especially from Hong Kong. A comparable situation is apparent in the role of Taiwanese investment in southern Fujian (*min'nan*) and, since the 1990s, general FDI in Jiangsu. Local officials in these coastal southern provinces tend to measure local economic success in terms of FDI. The mayor of Xiamen, one of the original SEZs in Fujian, revealed the local prioritization of FDI quite pointedly. In 2005 he publicly announced, "We need to take care of FDI the way that we care for our eyes" (Interview 302). Pride in the role of FDI in Xiamen's economy is captured in a local numerical saying, "3, 4, 5, 6, 7, 8," meaning that in 2005 FDI accounted for 30 percent of fixed asset investment

---

37. Part of the reluctance of interviewees in Jiangsu to acknowledge the existence of informal finance may be because Wuxi gained national notoriety when Deng Bin, the general manager of the Wuxi Xinxing Industrial Corporation, and other officials were convicted of running a pyramid scheme that raised 3.2 billion RMB ($380 million) from individuals and investors from over three hundred government bureaus and state-owned firms in several provinces from 1989 to 1994. This was considered the PRC's largest financial scandal at the time. United Press International, July 29, 1995.

in Xiamen, 40 percent of its tax revenues, 50 percent of its labor force, 60–70 percent of its exports, and over 80 percent of its industrial output.[38] In a somewhat irreverent indicator of how much the Xiamen government values FDI, locals have even rephrased part of the Theory of Three Represents. Instead of repeating Jiang Zemin's overpublicized slogan that the CCP represents the most advanced productive forces, in Xiamen foreign capital has replaced the party: "Foreign enterprises represent the most advanced productive forces," one of my interviewees recited with a mischievous grin (Interview 307).

This sense that FDI levels trump other descriptive and developmental indicators has had mixed implications for private entrepreneurs in the south China model localities. On the one hand, local officials are eager to help certain entrepreneurs attract foreign capital and engage in export-processing industries. On the other hand, private businesses that lack connections to overseas Chinese or other international ties are relatively disadvantaged. As a result, private enterprises face incentives to register themselves falsely as foreign-invested enterprises to overcome local policy biases, much as private enterprises in the early reform years wore red hats. These issues are illustrated by the cases below.

In the absence of sufficient investment resources from higher governmental levels, village leaders in coastal China are often quite entrepreneurial in finding ways to attract foreign capital in the form of joint ventures or FDI. Owner Zhang, discussed in chapter 4, believes that he could not have raised sufficient capital to run larger-scale businesses without the assistance of the village party branch in his hometown of Bailin Village, Huiyang City, Guangdong (Interview 182). After working on construction sites in Shenzhen for five years, in 1984 Zhang decided that he was ready to open his own construction company in Huiyang. He registered it as a private enterprise with 18,000 RMB ($7,725) in savings and donations from his in-laws. One year later the party branch in his village introduced him to a Hong Kong investor who was interested in investing 300,000 RMB ($102,041) to set up a paper factory in Guangdong. In 1989, the village committee introduced him to yet another Hong Kong investor who contributed 3 million RMB ($795,756) toward owner Zhang's "five metals" (*wujin*: gold, sliver, copper, iron, and tin) factory.

Why were village leaders so willing to help owner Zhang? Later in the interview we learned that his family is politically well connected. His father served as the leader of the production brigade during the 1960s (though

---

38. In 1983, foreign-invested enterprises accounted for only 1.2% of industrial output in Xiamen; by 1990, they accounted for 59.8% of industrial output; and since 1998, foreign-invested enterprises have accounted for over 80% of Xiamen's industrial output. *Xiamen Statistical Yearbook*, various years.

he had trouble as a target of struggle sessions during the Cultural Revolution). After the production brigade was converted into Bailin Village, his brother became the village party secretary and the chair of the village committee. Even though he is not a party member and does not hold any political positions, owner Zhang is now considered a local boss as well. Villagers borrow money from him and consult him for commercial advice. Despite his success in collaborating with Hong Kong investors, owner Zhang is very critical of the discriminatory nature of government policies toward private entrepreneurs: "It is completely unfair that foreign-invested enterprises and SOEs enjoy cheaper access to credit, land, and electricity." If owner Zhang had been able to raise investment capital from domestic commercial banks, he would not have relied so heavily on financing from Hong Kong.

Compared with most entrepreneurs, however, Zhang was lucky to have local governmental support and foreign capital for his various ventures. In an environment in which so many businesses have ties with overseas investors, the absence of such ties can be a liability. For instance, owner Kong in Hualong Township, Huizhou City, Guangdong is a school teacher-turned-entrepreneur who believes that he will always have difficulty keeping up with the foreign-invested enterprises (Interview 188). Although he now owns an air-conditioning store with forty employees, it took him the entire decade of 1983 to 1993 to save up enough money to register the business. After early retirement from teaching in 1982, he fixed consumer electronics for a local vendor and spent a number of years in Shenzhen selling color TVs. When he first established the air-conditioning company in 1993, Huizhou was going through a major real estate development boom. Owner Kong said that since 1998, however, the competition has gotten too intense because so many foreign-invested businesses have entered the refrigeration and air-conditioning industry. Meanwhile, he would like to expand his business but has had difficulty getting loans from state banks. Part of the problem is that his profit margin has declined substantially. In the mid-1990s he was able to earn 1,000 RMB on each air conditioner sold, but as of 2002 owner Kong was simply trying to dump his inventory.[39] When asked about what types of government policies would help him—besides enhancing the private sector's access to credit—he leaned forward and responded, "You know, I don't really want to cheat on taxes, but the tax system simply isn't fair. It would be different if this were a foreign company."

Foreign-invested enterprises (FIEs) indeed enjoy many policy advantages, including tax breaks and preferential access to land. Domestic

39. To save on electricity expenses, he wasn't even using his own products at the time of our interview. Owner Kong's business office was disconcertingly hot and humid for an operation that sells air conditioners.

firms, for example, are subject to a tax rate of 33 percent, but FIEs enjoy a concessionary rate of 15 percent for their first three years, followed by a two-year tax holiday after they report profits. Having an international or overseas Chinese connection also enables firms to convey a sense of financial security, cultural prestige, and technological sophistication, however far from reality that may be in practice.[40] For these reasons, many private entrepreneurs seek to present their businesses as foreign-invested companies or Sino-foreign joint ventures.[41] The resulting entities are considered fake foreign enterprises—or literally, in Chinese, "fake foreign devils" (*jia yangguizi*). For a firm to qualify legally as a "foreign-invested enterprise" in the PRC, the foreign equity stake must be at least 25 percent. The most common strategies for creating this impression among the proprietors of fake foreign enterprises include "round tripping" capital from China, which may entail registering a firm abroad or convincing a foreigner (or foreign entity) to use their name for such purposes. Each strategy is discussed below.

First, round-trip capital can refer to any money that leaves and reenters a particular country, but for the present purposes it refers to the practice of exporting money abroad for the purpose of reimporting it into China in the guise of real FDI. Most of the round-trip FDI goes through Hong Kong, though the British Virgin Islands, the Cayman Islands, and Samoa are also popular stops for RMB in transit. Estimates of round-trip FDI as a percentage of China's total FDI vary widely. On the high end, an economist at the Asian Development Bank Institute estimates that round-trip FDI accounts for 40 percent of total FDI with a range of 29.2 to 50.2 percent (Xiao 2004, 23). At the low end, researchers at the International Monetary Fund estimated it to be 7 percent in 1997 (Tseng and Zebregs 2002, in Huang 2003, 38). And most discussions of round-trip FDI estimate it to be between 25 to 30 percent based on studies from the mid-1990s (Lardy 1995, 1067; World Bank 1996, 41).

The most typical manner in which a domestic enterprise engages in round tripping FDI is to establish an offshore entity in Hong Kong or some other tax haven. Then the domestic firm transfers money directly to the offshore entity's bank account. In the final leg of the trip, the offshore entity (re-)invests in the domestic firm, which enables it to qualify as a foreign-invested enterprise. This practice is so common that it was not difficult for me to identify and interview fake FIEs. Officials in the local Foreign Investment Bureaus are well aware of which FIEs are genuinely foreign-invested

40. Factories run by overseas Chinese investors are known for having poor working conditions, including widespread safety violations, use of child labor, and excessive working hours. See Anita Chan 2001.

41. For an analysis of why state sector entities engage in outward FDI, see Ding 2000.

versus private enterprises that are merely disguised as FIEs. By the same token, owners of fake FIEs, especially the better established ones, proved to be quite open about their deceptive registration status. As the owner of a major exporter of holiday decorations explained:

> When I first registered my business as a private enterprise, local governmental agencies hassled me all the time and it was difficult to get things done. But it wasn't personal; the local government simply does not respect private enterprises. Things have completely turned around ever since I registered my business in Hong Kong and hung a large sign outside of the factory that has 'Hong Kong' in the name. Now everyone treats me like a foreign merchant (*waishang*)—that is, with respect. I'm even a high-ranking officer in the business association for foreign investors (*waishang touzi shanghui*). It doesn't matter that my business is a fake foreign-invested enterprise—the money is still coming in from abroad. (Interview 307)

Besides registering in Hong Kong, another popular way to round trip capital is "transfer pricing," whereby the domestic firm overvalues its exports and undervalues its imports. This is accomplished by overinvoicing exports and underinvoicing imports so that there is a net transfer of funds from abroad. According to Mei Xinyu of the Chinese Academy of International Trade and Economic Cooperation, a sophisticated network of informal financiers are accustomed to arranging these offshore payments: "There are professional money brokers, underground cashiers, and so-called cell phone banks that will respond promptly to requests for cash with just a phone call" (*China Daily*, June 22, 2004).

The third major expression of round-trip capital is less common than transfer pricing, but much larger in scale—namely, the creation of offshore shell companies to facilitate IPOs of mainland companies on international stock exchanges. Given that SOEs dominate the domestic stock markets, private enterprises that wish to raise equity are inclined to look abroad. For example, the chief executive officer of the Guangdong-based Qiaoxing Enterprise Group explained that on February 17, 1999, Qiaoxing became the first mainland Chinese company to list on NASDAQ by creating a shell company in Hong Kong and then setting up a bank account in Bermuda (Interview 190). This mirrored Yang Rong's experience in having Brilliance China Automotive listed on the New York Stock Exchange in 1992 (discussed in chapter 5). Increasingly, however, domestic enterprises choose to go public as "red chip" companies in Hong Kong. The share of red-chip offerings as a total of mainland IPOs grew from 30 percent in 1991 to 84 percent in 2002 (Xiao 2004, 20). Meanwhile, between 1992 and 2002 the share of mainland IPOs in Hong Kong's market capitalization grew from 4.8 to 26.3 percent (ibid.). The practice of round tripping from red-chip companies can also be seen in the growing portion of Hong Kong's outward FDI toward China: 41.1 percent in 1998, 52.3 percent in 1999, 78.1 percent in 2000, 79.4 percent in 2001, and 91.3 percent in 2002 (ibid., 18).[42]

Finally, a more basic way of establishing a fake FIE is to persuade a foreign individual or entity to invest a nominal amount in a domestic enterprise to give the appearance that it meets the 25 percent equity stake required to qualify as a FIE. While conducting research in Fujian, various local governmental entities asked whether I would be willing to invest in a local enterprise for a nominal sum. My first response was that I was only an academic researcher on a modest budget. But apparently they were less interested in the potential scale of investment than the use of my name as a non-PRC citizen. When I explained that it would be a conflict of interest for a researcher to engage in such an activity, they asked whether my parents would be interested in collaborating with Chinese compatriots.[43]

All of the above practices represent popular ways in which entrepreneurs and, in many cases, SOE managers and political cadres gain access to the concessionary terms in the foreign-invested sector. They may also be considered adaptive informal institutions because they are inspired by a formal policy environment that favors FIEs and discriminates against private entrepreneurs. As with the other forms of informal finance discussed in the context of the Wenzhou model, fake FIEs and round-trip FDI could also be considered instances of adaptive struggle—or at least sluggishness—on the part of formal institutions. The central government has been well aware that such illicit practices are prevalent, but it was not until 2007 that the formal policy environment started to shift in a manner that would reduce the material incentives for private enterprises to disguise themselves as foreign-related ones. In March 2007, the fifth session of the Tenth NPC passed an Enterprise Income Tax Law that mandates a unified income tax rate of 25 percent for both domestic and foreign-funded enterprises.

Meanwhile, the local coping strategies associated with the south China model have had the structural effect of liberalizing, and perhaps undermining, China's FDI regulations. As David Zweig explains, "These [developmental] communities did not collectively press Beijing to liberalize its foreign trade and foreign investment rules. Instead, as each county or township pursued its own global linkages, this unorganized collective action undermined the central state's regulatory regime" (Zweig 2002, 159–160).

42. Of course not all of Hong Kong's outward FDI to China is round tripping. See Huang 2003, 37–41.

43. A particularly persistent investment solicitation came from a local branch of the Women's Federation. Even after I had left that research site, the women cadres traveled eight hours by car to solicit me again. They reasoned that even if I could not contribute capital or my own name to engage in a joint venture (for what purpose was never clarified), then perhaps I could convince my former employer, an international NGO, to do so.

Hong Kong tycoon Li Kaishing's Oriental Plaza displaced the world's largest McDonald's and sits atop a twenty-thousand-year-old Paleolithic settlement in the Wangfujing shopping district, Beijing

Zweig's observation is made in the context of local governments granting foreign partners (illegal) access to the domestic market instead of complying with the requirement that they export 70 percent of production for tax privileges.[44] Nonetheless, the logic can be extended to the types of adaptive informal institutions that private entrepreneurs have adopted in response to a policy environment that favors FIEs. The cumulative effect of these "fake foreigner" adaptive informal institutions has arguably compromised central state capacity when it comes to tax collection and targeted credit policy, which is why the center has recently reformed the formal incentives for such deviance. Indeed, in his explanation to NPC deputies for the rationale behind the 2007 Enterprise Income Tax Law, Finance Minister Jin Renqing referred to (the adaptive informal institutions of) fake FIEs and round-trip FDI as one of the reasons why it was

44. Zweig points out that the center's initial motive in liberalizing FDI and foreign trade was to protect TVEs from competing with SOEs in the domestic market. TVEs were encouraged to engage in export-led growth in collaboration with foreign capital. In a competitive desire to attract FDI, however, local governments ended up granting foreign investors preferential access to the domestic market in a manner unintended by the central government. See Zweig 2002, chap. 3. For our purposes, note that this dynamic further enhances the discrimination against private businesses producing for the domestic market, thereby reinforcing preexisting incentives for pretending to be a FIE.

necessary to unify the tax treatment of domestic and foreign firms (*Xinhua*, March 8, 2007).

Selling versus Stealing State Assets

As discussed earlier, local governments in the state-dominated model have pursued a diversity of developmental strategies. Some have taken an active role in promoting the collective sector, some have focused on promoting the foreign-invested sector, and others have endeavored to support larger private enterprises. Most localities with large state sectors have pursued some combination of these strategies, and all of them have had to deal with restructuring the state sector in the process. Given that state sector reform is a developmental task that unifies the wide range of localities in this model, the adaptive informal institutions discussed in this section focus on patterns of state sector restructuring. Although restructuring in some cases entails the transfer of public assets to private ownership—which economists call "privatization"—as of 2006 the term privatization remained politically sensitive. Hence, official statements do not refer to the restructuring or selling of state assets as "privatization" (*siyouhua*) but, rather, use "restructuring" (*gaizhi*) and "corporatization" (*gufenhua*). The significance of this linguistic distinction lies in the resulting ambiguity in the property rights structure of reformed SOEs. Restructured SOEs are not necessarily privatized ones, which obfuscates the targets of blame when SOE reform is associated with high social costs. Although this ambiguity has proven to be politically useful, it has also facilitated rent-seeking behavior, sometimes to the detriment of preexisting private business. A brief overview of how the restructuring program has evolved over time will show the incentives underlying these effects, and the resulting types of adaptive informal institutions that have emerged in the course of state sector reform.

Shortly after the PRC Company Law went into effect in 1994, the center recommended the "corporatization" of one hundred large- and medium-sized SOEs firms as part of a new strategy to create a "modern enterprise system" and enhance the profitability of China's industrial sector. The SOEs would be converted into either limited-liability companies (LLCs), in which each shareholder would assume liability in proportion to his/her capital contribution, or shareholding enterprises (SHEs), in which the shares have equal value and the liability of shareholders would be proportional to their shareholdings (Ma 1998, 381). The main difference between LLCs and SHEs in this reform program was that LLCs had to have between two and fifty shareholders and could essentially remain state-owned, whereas the state needs to hold only 35 percent of the shares in an SHE so that the remaining shares could be held by the general public, including private individuals not previously affiliated with the SOE. Most large SOEs were converted into LLCs during the 1994 to 1997 period, and their ownership structure remained essentially the same. Moreover, LLCs did not perform any more profitably than SOEs—presumably because LLCs still did not face hard budget constraints.

Next, the 1995 launching of the "retaining the large and releasing the small" policy encouraged the conversion of small and medium SOEs into more diverse organizational forms, including employee shareholding cooperatives and private enterprises. This policy was reinforced and deepened at the Fifteenth Party Congress in 1997, such that small SOEs would be subject to more radical reform measures, including mergers, leases, outright sales, and bankruptcy. SOE restructuring accelerated. By 1998 nearly 48 percent of the industrial SOEs had initiated the restructuring process.[45] And by 2003 approximately 85 percent of China's small and medium SOEs had been restructured (*Renmin ribao*, September 29, 2004).[46] Meanwhile, the pace of restructuring large and medium SOEs also picked up: between 1997 and 2002, the number of large and medium SOEs declined by 41.4 percent (from 14,811 to 8,675 firms) and the number of large and medium SHEs more than tripled from 1,801 to 5,659 firms (Jefferson and Su 2005, 8). As with everything else in China, however, there has been a wide range of variation in the modalities and consequences of SOE restructuring. Based on existing studies of SOE reform, the following observations can be made.

First, despite the apparent rapidity of SOE restructuring, various studies have found that the state has continued to maintain a dominant ownership stake in the majority of larger restructured enterprises (Lin and Zhu 2001; Ma 1998; Oi 2005). In other words, in most cases restructured enterprises have not been privatized in the technical sense of the word. As Jiang Zemin explained at the Fifteenth Party Congress, "We cannot say in general terms that the shareholding system is public or private. The key lies in who holds the controlling share" (Ma 1998, 395). One reason the state retains the majority of shares is that, in the case of large SOEs, workers and managers may not be able to afford the SOEs' assets (Oi 2005, 121).

Second, based on 1995 to 2001 data, the more prosperous eastern and southern coastal provinces have been more likely to undertake SOE restructuring than those in other regions (Jefferson and Su 2005, 20).

---

45. This is based on a survey conducted by the National Bureau of Statistics in mid-1998. The sample size of 40,238 represented 62% of the industrial SOEs operating at the time. See Lin and Zhu 2001.

46. Given that municipal governments own most of the smaller SOEs, some local officials were highly motivated to restructure their smaller SOEs because the process presented them with revenue-raising opportunities. In other cases, however, local governments were less enthusiastic about restructuring their small and medium SOEs because the latter's poor performance meant that local governments would have to put money into the process to compensate workers for severing ties with these SOEs. I thank Jin Zeng for this last observation.

Furthermore, as of mid-1998, restructured firms in coastal areas were more likely to have LLCs, SHEs, and other shareholding structures, while those in inland areas had higher levels of insider-held equity shares (Lin and Zhu 2001). These regional findings are correlated with the observation that SOEs with higher levels of surplus labor and debt have been slower in undertaking restructuring (Garnaut et al. 2005, 79; Lin and Zhu 2001, 318; Oi 2005, 121).

Third, many cases of "spontaneous insider privatization" have been documented (Ding 1999, 2000). Parallel to the instances of corruption when some TVEs are converted into shareholding cooperatives, SOE officials and managers may intentionally undervalue firm assets in order to purchase large quantities of shares and resell them at a profit after the restructuring has occurred. As a scholar of corruption has delineated:

> Common schemes include siphoning off assets to private savings and profiteering; concealing the real size of a firm's resources, revenues and credits; inflating firm expenditures and debt burdens to depress the price of a buyout; and excluding land and other elusive assets from appraisal. To ensure that cronies become new owners at below-market prices, some executives set price ceilings for buyouts, discount asset values, limit open bids, collude with appraisers, or falsify data. (Sun 2004, 93–94)

Although these illicit practices clearly violate the spirit of SOE restructuring, they nonetheless constitute a type of informal privatization in the sense that state assets are transferred to private hands. Besides the accounting strategies associated with the specific process of SOE restructuring, informal privatization also occurs on a more routine basis when state employees strip the assets of SOEs. The form of illicit asset stripping most akin to "privatization" is the strategy of "one manager, two businesses" in which state managers establish private enterprises registered under someone else's name and then divert SOE resources to supporting the private firm (Ding 2000; He 1998).

What implications do these state-sector trends have for indigenous private entrepreneurs? At the broadest level, even if Beijing does not refer to SOE restructuring as privatization, the fact that private individuals are eligible to purchase shares of SHEs blurs the distinction between strictly public versus nonpublic enterprises, which may enhance the legitimacy of the private sector in general. Indeed, as beneficiaries of the restructuring program, proprietors of former SOEs may have a more positive view of their social standing as private entrepreneurs. My 2002 survey found that respondents who owned restructured SOEs were more likely than those running regular private businesses to have a higher self-perception of their social status. While 90 percent of the respondents running privatized SOEs viewed themselves as having middle to upper-middle levels of social status, only 68.7 percent of indigenous business owners ranked their social status in the middle to upper-middle range. This difference may be attributed in part to the fact that the sample only included proprietors of registered "private enterprises"; hence, it is certainly possible that the owners of restructured SOEs that are not formally counted as part of the private sector have a less favorable view of the social status of private entrepreneurs. Nonetheless, the point remains that the introduction of restructured SOEs into the private sector has helped to alleviate some of the earlier ideological stigma associated with being a private entrepreneur.

Relatedly, I have found that most of the larger private enterprises in the state-dominated model have evolved out of ambiguous relationships with collective and state-owned enterprises, and relied on state assets to achieve economies of scale. This pattern differs significantly from the south China model where FDI has played a significant role in private sector development. It also differs from the Wenzhou model, which relied on indigenously generated informal finance. Local officials and entrepreneurs in the state-dominated model readily acknowledge that the most impressive private businesses in their localities could not have developed to that point without some form of public-private collaboration. They also concur that the central government's support for creating SHEs since 1997 has in theory enabled private entrepreneurs to build on state assets in a more transparent manner.

In other ways, however, the SOE restructuring process has not been as beneficial to indigenous entrepreneurs. First, as suggested above, most studies have found that even though private individuals are permitted to purchase shares of SHEs, in practice local governments prefer that SOE managers and workers become the dominant shareholders. This is not merely a function of the potential rent-seeking opportunities associated with insider privatization, as an official at the Shanghai State Assets Management Bureau explained: "Outsiders may lay off workers after a year or two of operation and will bring us lots of social problems. But the original managers will be less likely to do the same due to their long-term relationship with the workers at the SOE" (Zeng 2007). As shown in one of the cases below, this is not always the case if the local government has its way.

Second, even though privatized SOEs and regular private businesses are supposed to face equal treatment in taxation, land use, and access to credit, actual practices reveal a host of complexities (Interviews 310, 312, 313, 314). For example, some local governments grant recently privatized SOEs a two-year tax exemption as a subsidy for development. But there have been instances in which the newly converted shareholding enterprise remains classified as an SOE and subject to a higher rate of taxation. In the case of land use, when an SOE is undergoing restructuring it is common practice to undervalue the price of its land. By way of contrast, private entrepreneurs frequently complain about having to pay higher market-level prices for land, or about not having the opportunity to acquire land for expansion. And in terms of credit policy, in state-dominated localities private entrepreneurs have more difficulty accessing official sources of credit. Recall that the creation of urban commercial banks was supposed to enhance the availability of credit to the private sector. In state-dominated localities such as Wuhan, however, even large-scale entrepreneurs do not bother applying for loans because the urban commercial banks lend primarily to SOEs (Interview 238).

Third, private enterprises in state-dominated localities often experience political pressure to cooperate with restructured SOEs in exchange for land and capital. Private sector cooperation may take the form of hiring laid-off state workers, purchasing unwanted portions of an SOE, and making contributions to lessen the social impact of SOE restructuring. In the Wuchang District of Wuhan, for example, I interviewed a the owners of a private auto repair shop that took on substantial liabilities from a bankrupt SOE because the city's Economic System Reform Committee persuaded the shop to do so (Interviews 119 and 220). Vice General Manager Shou explained that the bankrupt SOE called itself a research center, but it also produced tools and industrial gadgets that were sometimes used in repairing automobiles. Given that the private auto shop needed land to expand its operations, its owners decided to merge with the SOE, which pleased the local government. The problem with this arrangement was that the private repair shop inherited 130 employees, 58 retirees, and over 3 million RMB (over $362,319) in debt, unpaid wages, and pensions. Even though all the workers were technically laid off after the SOE declared bankruptcy, the city required that the repair shop keep 20 percent of the workers and pay off the SOE's debts. In addition to these financial liabilities, the repair shop agreed to collaborate with the local labor office to establish an auto repair training school. The latter would be salvaged from the vocational television college (*dianshi daxue*) run by the original SOE. As of 2002, they were planning to train two hundred people at a time for three-month-long sessions, run three sessions annually, and charge 500 RMB ($60) in tuition. The whole point of the school is to retrain laid-off state workers. When asked if embarking on these various activities was worth the land and financial contributions from local governmental entities, manager Shou replied, "We have spent a lot of time negotiating with various agencies. I am not sure we had much of a choice here."

The adaptive informal institutions that have emerged out of the state-dominated model center around the political dilemmas generated by state sector reform. Insider privatization enables state workers and especially state managers to profit from the restructuring process. At the same time, it also alleviates local governmental concern about the prospect of mass unemployment. Yet the above cases show that instances of "forced privatization" or restructuring may also accomplish similar goals. Such occurrences have the greatest impact on larger-scale private entrepreneurs, for they are the ones most likely to seek access to inputs effectively monopolized by the local state. Meanwhile, owners of smaller-scale businesses in state-dominated localities also lack capital and land, but they have less to offer in terms of reemployment opportunities. As a result, entrepreneurs in the state-dominated model in general are much more likely than those in the Wenzhou model of political economy to seek assertive political solutions to ameliorate these discriminatory conditions, but there is also a higher-than-average proportion of grudgingly acceptant entrepreneurs who lack the resources to confront the state.

Limited Development: Leave It or Live with It

The business environment for private entrepreneurs in limited-development localities is characterized by restricted market opportunities, fiscal predation, and other bureaucratic inconveniences. Given such circumstances, business owners in these areas are more likely than those in other types of localities to express a preference for political change, and they are also more likely than entrepreneurs in other places to use assertive means to address their problems. In other words, contrary to the expectations of modernization theory, private entrepreneurs in areas with the lowest level of economic development are the most likely to express political discontent. However, disgruntled businesspeople from such localities also are more likely to leave their hometowns in search of better operating conditions for their businesses. To stem the outflow of entrepreneurial talent, some local governments have endeavored to support the private sector, albeit not always with success.

Hechuan in rural Chongqing is an example of such a locality. In 2002 the Hechuan city government established the Bureau for the Development of the Nonpublic Economy (*fei gongyou fazhan ju*, or *feifaju* for short), which has branches called Economic Development Offices (*jingji fazhan bangongshi*) in all thirty-one rural townships of Hechuan. The purpose of the bureau and local offices is to serve "people-run enterprises" (*minying qiye*), a euphemistic term for private enterprises. The bureau's intended services include supporting thirty large enterprises, especially when they experience disputes with one another or with other governmental entities, while keeping an eye on an additional twenty smaller enterprises that may have potential to scale up. Although the stated objectives of the bureau might sound progressive vis-à-vis private sector development, the fact that it has "nonpublic economy" in its official title, rather than the more direct term "private economy," reveals lingering bureaucratic biases against capitalist activity. Indeed, the director of the bureau told us in 2002 that most of the larger private operations were still wearing red hats because collective enterprises still enjoyed more favorable terms in taxation, use of land, and access to official credit; moreover, registering as a private enterprise (*siying qiye*) remained more complicated than registering falsely as a collective enterprise or simply registering as an individual business (*getihu*) (Interview 250). As owner Yi, a former soldier who now runs one of the largest private retail chains in Hechuan, explained: "My business employs over 230 people, but yes, I am still registered as a *getihu*. If a business gets too big, then it might get inconvenient. Various agencies will show up looking for trouble, so I don't dare to convert my operation into a private enterprise" (Interview 258).

When I asked whether the *getihu* registration status really protected him from predation, given that the number of people working in his business obviously exceeded eight employees, owner Yi elaborated:

> As long as I'm registered as a *getihu* the governmental bureaucracies governing *siying qiye* will leave me alone. But you shouldn't think that it's easy being a *getihu* either. State-owned enterprises can get away with not paying taxes, but private business owners always have to pay up. *Getihu* have to pay a fixed tax, but it's really unfair because if I don't make as much as they estimated, then I don't get a refund. But if I make more than the estimated level of sales—and the tax collector doesn't like me—then I get fined anywhere from one to ten times the amount of the tax. This is called rent-seeking behavior (*xunzu xingwei*). (Interview 258)

In addition to the Bureau for the Development of the Nonpublic Economy, Hechuan has a number of government-sponsored business associations, which are also geared toward serving larger private businesses. Interviews with various business owners who are active in these associations echoed many of the retail chain owner's complaints. For one, business owners have to put up with demands from too many different agencies, for example, the Sanitation Bureau, central Tax Bureau, local Tax Bureau, Public Security Bureau, Industrial and Commercial Management Bureau, City Quality Inspection Bureau, City Technical Management Bureau, and so forth. Many of these bureaus have overlapping functions, so *getihu* dread having to deal with all of them.

But what, exactly, makes it so challenging to interact with different bureaucratic entities? My interviewees in Hechuan were eager to answer this question. One shoe-store owner lamented, "Local cadres abuse their power" (Interview 255). In 1999, a Sanitation Bureau cadre came into his store and insisted on receiving a large discount on a pair of shoes; when the owner

Private pharmacy in rural Chongqing

refused, the cadre summoned an obscure regulation from the 1970s and accused the store owner of not having a health certificate. The owner of a computer store said he suffered from many instances of arbitrary legal enforcement (*luan zhifa*) (Interview 256). For example, once the owner set up a pair of tables that occupied four square meters outside his storefront for advertising purposes. The City Management Office came by, confiscated the computers, and forced him to sign a form indicating that the space occupied twelve square meters. The computer store owner did not realize that the fines were based on space, so he was fined over twice what was legitimately owed. When he went to the City Management Office to complain, they detained him for four hours and tried to make him sign another document verifying his infraction. One business association director concluded, "Government agencies act as if they are still running a planned economy. The cadres all have a 'planned economy attitude.' Everything involves a tremendous amount of paperwork and time" (Interview 251).

The other major burden is arbitrary and excessive taxation. This is due in part to malfeasance on the part of tax collectors who extend tax breaks to their friends and collect too much from others, as recounted by owner Yi and many other interviewees. But there is also an economic reason for the problem: localities with limited development—and, indeed, the majority of rural counties and townships in general—face fiscal deficits. According to a rural sociologist at the Chinese Academy of Social Sciences, 70 percent of rural counties in China are in the red and 90 percent of the townships are bankrupt (Interview 148). Hechuan's fiscal deficit is an ongoing difficulty for its officials. In 2004, for instance, local governmental expenditures were 744 million RMB, while its revenues were only 377 million RMB (Hechuan city government 2006). In an effort to make up the difference, every October the local government dispatches teams of cadres to collect taxes from private businesses. But it is never enough, and local entrepreneurs resent the annual predatory ritual.

While the survey showed that respondents in the state-dominated and south China models were more likely to complain about taxes and fees than their counterparts in the limited-development localities (see table 6.3), the latter rely on assertive means of dispute resolution—especially appealing to the local government or higher authorities—as their first course of action more frequently than respondents in the state-dominated, south China, and Wenzhou models. Furthermore, politically assertive interviewees in the limited-development localities also expressed opinions that suggest they would be more likely than entrepreneurs in other localities to support reforms that liberalize the political system. One of the local red capitalists, for instance, believed that there is a need for greater transparency in Chinese politics: "Everyone in America knows about the errors of its president, but here we don't even know when the local leaders are going to change. The only clue we get is that when fresh flowers are placed along the roads, then we know that a new leader is coming to town" (Interview 258). Another assertive entrepreneur attributed the problems of bureaucratic complexity and corruption to deficiencies in the political system: "You see, we don't vote for our leaders; they are appointed from above. It is a problem with the system (*tizhi*)" (Interview 251). Finally, some of the bigger entrepreneurs did flat out say that democracy is a desirable form of government and that private entrepreneurs should participate in politics (Interviews 254, 255, 256, and 258).

In sum, even though the majority of business owners in limited-development localities are neither politically active nor interested in supporting political change, such localities also seem to have a higher percentage of politically opinionated and assertive entrepreneurs than one might expect judging solely by level of economic development. Indeed, as discussed earlier, in my survey the proportion (though not the absolute number) of assertive respondents in the limited-development localities was equivalent to that of assertive respondents in the Sunan model.

As discussed in the previous two chapters, private entrepreneurs differ widely in terms of their employment background, policy concerns, political attitudes, resources, values, and coping strategies. In addition to the variation in these qualities, private entrepreneurs face very different operating environments depending on the nature of the local political economy. These contextual differences, in turn, affect the types of adaptive informal institutions that business owners rely on, as well as the extent to which central policymakers are likely to be responsive to such local practices. Highlights from this chapter's consideration of five patterns of local political economy include the following:

First, entrepreneurs in localities with a supportive attitude toward private sector development (the Wenzhou model) have fewer disputes with local governmental entities and are better able to devise informal financing mechanisms to meet their credit needs. Due to the relative convergence in interests between local officials and entrepreneurs, the adaptive informal institutions that have developed in the Wenzhou model have proven to be particularly resilient and persistent. Indeed, Beijing's banking regulators have opted to regulate and learn from Wenzhou's financial innovations rather than wage a fruitless battle against curb market operators. In this sense, the Wenzhou model provides the most direct illustration of my argument about the role of adaptive informal institutions in affecting changes in formal institutions.

Second, private business owners in areas formerly dominated by the collective sector (the Sunan model) experience various operating difficulties, especially if they are running smaller operations or firms without significant ties to cadres and former public enterprise mangers. Out of all the developmental patterns, Sunan model entrepreneurs are the most likely to use assertive means of dispute resolution that directly engage local governmental entities. Conversely, but relatedly, Sunan model entrepreneurs are among the least likely to devise adaptive informal institutions, and Sunan model localities also have the highest proportion of grudgingly acceptant entrepreneurs. Hence, in contrast to the Wenzhou model localities, the political economy of private sector development in the Sunan model has produced a polarized combination of, on the one hand, politically assertive entrepreneurs and, on the other hand, discontented entrepreneurs who are not particularly proactive in pursuing informal means to address their grievances.

Third, in areas with high levels of foreign direct investment (the south China model), private businesses operate at a marked disadvantage relative to foreign-invested ones, especially when it comes to taxes and fees. Rather than turning to assertive means of dispute resolution with greater frequency, however, private entrepreneurs in the south China model are more likely to disguise their operations as foreign-invested ones. Fake foreign-invested enterprises have thus become adaptive informal institutions in south China localities, and the popularity of this informal coping strategy has more recently influenced at least central, if not local authorities to extend the favorable treatment accorded to foreign enterprises to domestic businesses.[47]

Fourth, in areas with large state sectors (the state-dominated model), the local government views the private economy as a potential solution for absorbing laid-off state workers, but it remains difficult for smaller businesses to scale up without substantial government support. Out of the five developmental patterns, private entrepreneurs in the state-dominated localities report the highest level of operating difficulties. Their complaints range from having disputes with the local government to experiencing extreme credit constraints, difficulties with access to land, excessive taxes and fees, and problems with government services. Despite these complaints, business owners in the state-dominated model are not more assertive than average. Instead, they are much more likely to be avoidant or grudgingly acceptant than their counterparts in other areas.

Fifth, in areas with limited development, private entrepreneurs express high levels of dissatisfaction with local business conditions. They are also more likely to be avoidant or use assertive political channels to express this discontent. However, areas with limited development also have smaller absolute numbers of private business owners. As such, the potential direct political impact of a vocal minority in the more remote areas of China should not be overestimated.

Although these five developmental patterns provide an overview of some of the key developmental differences among localities in contemporary China, they are by no means representative of the full range of political economic realities that private entrepreneurs face. Furthermore, over the course of the reform era, all of the developmental "models" have evolved into hybrid versions of their original form, which means that entrepreneurs themselves have also experienced these changes, for better or worse. On the one hand, most local governments now welcome private sector development and partial privatization of their public enterprises. On the other hand, the drive to attract foreign investment has extended well beyond south China. The transformation of the 1980s Sunan model encompasses both these trends: privatization of collective enterprises has enhanced the legitimacy of the private economy, but at the same time Jiangsu's economy has become much more reliant on FDI financing.[48] Meanwhile, even the original Wenzhou model has evolved over time. While the local government maintained

47. The passage of the Enterprise Income Tax Law by the fifth session of the Tenth NPC in March 2007 was intended to eliminate differential tax treatment of domestic and foreign-funded firms, but it remains to be seen how effectively the law will be enforced in practice.

48. The potential relationship between private sector growth and reliance on FDI financing in Jiangsu remains subject to debate. In a comparative analysis of Jiangsu and Zhejiang, Yasheng Huang (2004) argues that biases against the private sector contribute to greater dependency on FDI.

a relatively hands-off approach toward the private economy during the 1980s, by the mid-1990s county governments began to play a more interventionary role by prioritizing larger-scale enterprises in a local developmental program called the Second Pioneering Initiative (*dierci chuangye*). The initiative entailed directing credit to larger enterprises in priority industries, which is one of the reasons why policy measures to enhance the private sector's access to formal sources of credit has not curbed the scale of informal finance in Wenzhou (Wang, Tsai, and Li 2004). Wenzhou's traditional household factories still face capital constraints.

Ultimately, the dynamic character of these developmental models suggests that private entrepreneurs will continue to formulate adaptive strategies that violate the spirit of certain national regulations but make operational sense given local political and economic realities. In some cases, the resulting adaptive informal institutions have already had a structural impact on broader national policies. Yet the fact that informal finance, fake foreign-invested enterprises, and insider privatization thrives in various parts of the country demonstrates that deeper reforms are needed to level the playing field for China's private economy. But few entrepreneurs and other members of society believe that these reforms require a regime transition to a liberal democracy.

7

Changing China: Adaptive Informal Institutions

> China's democracy is a people's democracy under the leadership of the Chinese Communist Party. Without the Communist Party there would be no New China. Nor would there be people's democracy. This is a fact that has been borne out by history.
>
> PRC State Council White Paper,
> "Building Political Democracy in China,"
> October 19, 2005

Calls for "democracy" in China date back to Sun Yat-sen's Three Principles of the People (1905), which aimed to create a prosperous, powerful, and democratic nation. Arguably, the People's Republic of China has achieved two of those three goals under the leadership of the Chinese Communist Party. China has one of the largest economies in the world.[1] Other countries fret about its military capabilities and intentions. But will the world's most populous country become democratic? Efforts to address this big question are muddled by the fact that the Chinese government is committed to developing "political democracy with Chinese characteristics." Although no blueprint exists for what that will look like, Beijing's leaders insist that China's political democracy will never mimic "Western-style democracy." The official reason for this contention is presented in general terms: "Because situations differ from one country to another, the paths the people of different countries take to win and develop democracy are different" (PRC State Council 2005, 1).

---

1. As of 2005, China's GDP ranked fourth in the world, behind the United States, Japan, and Germany.

China's conditions indeed differ from those of early industrializing countries whose experiences form the basis for the popular association between capitalism and democracy. China's conditions also differ from those of developing and former socialist countries that underwent democratic transitions at the end of the twentieth century. I have focused on one of those apparent differences: the political diversity and quiescence of China's private entrepreneurs. Contrary to the expectations of modernization and structural theorists, economic growth has not created a prodemocratic capitalist class. Only a handful of intellectuals, dissidents, and foreigners have openly called for political reforms that would result in multiparty competition, competitive, direct elections at the national and local levels, and guarantees for political and civil liberties. An even smaller number of private entrepreneurs support political liberalization. Overall, China's business owners are either tolerating the existing political system or leaving the country rather than demanding democratizing changes domestically. Within a span of three decades, China has developed an increasingly market-oriented economy in which the private sector accounts for nearly half of GDP, yet private entrepreneurs remain politically passive and the PRC remains authoritarian. We have, in short, a case of (emerging) capitalism without democracy.

Although policy analysts in Beijing might view these trends as constituting special "Chinese characteristics," there is nothing culturally predetermined or comparatively different in logic about the political coping strategies of private entrepreneurs in contemporary China. As discussed in the first two chapters of this book, we should not assume that capitalists must demand democracy in a teleological manner. Indeed, historically this pattern of democratic development has been the exception rather than the prevailing pattern of authoritarian breakdown. Except for the cases of Great Britain, the United States, and possibly France, business owners have not played a direct role in initiating democratic transitions.

With this in mind, at the macrolevel the limited assertiveness of business owners in China can be explained by several intuitive reasons. First, fear of political persecution. During the Communist revolution, landlords and capitalists suffered the brunt of political violence, and even during the first decades of reform private entrepreneurs remained highly cautious about the security of their political status and material assets. A second reason, accepted among nonentrepreneurs in China, is that business owners have little to complain about. Despite episodes of political tightening, the policy environment for private enterprise has improved over the course of the reform era. A related third reason that private entrepreneurs are not demanding democracy is they are now permitted to join the Communist Party, China's most influential political organization. Capitalists have never had better access to the political system in PRC history.

Although reasonable, these explanations are ultimately superficial. The concern about provoking repressive government treatment is realistic and widely shared, but it does not explain why members of other social groups, namely intellectuals, have undertaken politically inflammatory activities, such as criticizing the regime through both official and unofficial channels (Goldman 2005; cf. Fewsmith 2001a). Meanwhile, the argument that the party-state's stance toward the private economy has improved and become more inclusive merely describes the results of deeper processes that have been at work. The fact that 10.3 million members of the Chinese Communist Party identified themselves as private entrepreneurs in 2005 only indicates how dramatically China's most powerful political institution has changed (Interview 293); it does not tell us anything about the causal mechanisms underlying institutional change. Moreover, the sheer range of institutional reforms associated with private sector development raises the deeper issue of how to account for the coexistence of institutional change without regime change.

Two paradoxes thus present themselves: China's private sector has become politically consequential even though capitalists have not asserted themselves as a class to attain such influence. At the same time, China's key governing institutions have undergone remarkable transformations, while avoiding authoritarian collapse. How can these apparently disparate observations be explained?

Contrary to conventional modes of examining high politics and political participation, in this book I have traced a variety of macrolevel outcomes back to everyday interactions between economic and political actors at the grassroots level. Even though these interactions are typically informal, they may be highly institutionalized and carry more relevance than the formal rules that are supposed to govern the political economy. By emphasizing this microlevel relational approach, I am not disputing the importance of ruling elites, formal institutions, and organized political efforts. Instead, my research demonstrates that grassroots interactions are an equally central, and easily overlooked, component of the causal processes underlying formal institutional change and durability. The reality is that millions of larger private enterprises registered and therefore disguised themselves as individual entrepreneurs (*getihu*) or collective enterprises before 1988; millions of party members were involved in the private economy before 2001; and the continuing reality is that the vast majority of business owners rely on curb market financing, even though most types of private financial institutions remain illegal. These common, taken-for-granted infractions, which I call adaptive informal institutions, have directly and indirectly influenced the course of national reforms. They have contributed to changing formal institutions in a manner that obviates the need and desire of private entrepreneurs to pursue more radical and risky coping strategies, such as contesting the CCP's monopoly on political power. Private entrepreneurs have had a structural impact on Chinese politics through the spread of adaptive informal institutions.

The argument that apparently localized informal institutions affect changes in national politics and formal institutions can help us understand similar processes in contexts beyond China. Given that most scholars focus on the formal attributes of political institutions, the analytic value of this contention is that it draws our attention to the informal causal dynamics of institutional flexibility regardless of regime type. When major political changes occur due to crises such as wars, revolutions, and foreign occupation, political scientists and historians can point to relatively discrete episodes of institutional destruction and reconstruction.[2] But in the absence of obvious external or internal shocks, it becomes more challenging to provide an endogenous explanation for what are apparently incremental, yet in aggregate quite extensive, institutional changes. Part of the solution lies in recognizing that adaptive informal institutions have the potential to link ordinary practices with larger institutional reforms. With one key caveat: adaptive informal institutions are more than intervening variables in a linear chain of efficient causality. Ultimately, the processes of institutional emergence, subversion, and conversion evolve in a manner that eludes strict definition of variables, tidy hypotheses, and bold predictions.

Political Change without Regime Change

The fact that China remains authoritarian does not mean that the country's political institutions have remained static. Despite the absence of liberal democracy, the political process has become much more inclusive and—in a 180-degree reversal of the PRC's founding ideology—accessible to private entrepreneurs. Existing scholarship on Chinese politics offers a number of compelling reasons for why the center has become more attentive to the private sector, but these studies provide only partial insight into the puzzle of how the PRC party-state has managed to implement radical institutional self-transformation without self-destruction. What accounts for the coexistence of political change without regime change?

First, top-down or elite-oriented approaches to Chinese politics view the regime's dramatic ideological and institutional reorientation as an effort to preempt political opposition by an emerging capitalist class. From this vantage point, the Communist Party decided to admit private entrepreneurs as a means to ensure organizational survival. As Bruce Dickson (2003) explains, "The co-optation of new elites is a classic strategy of adaptation for Leninist parties and for organizations in general" (115).[3] CCP leaders and

---

2. A notable exception is McAdam, Tarrow, and Tilly 2001.
3. Dickson (2003) also cautions that this is a "risky strategy."

theoreticians are well aware of the practices and fate of other Communist parties. In defense of expanding the party's membership base, for example, the vice president of the Central Party School, Li Junru, wrote, "One lesson of political parties that have lost their ruling positions in the late 20th and early 21st centuries is that they have lost the support of youthful entrepreneurs and young intellectuals" (*Lilun dongtai*, July 20, 2001, cited in Fewsmith 2002, 4). Thus, despite virulent opposition by party leftists, the Three Represents became incorporated into the party's constitution, and party branches have since been encouraged to recruit new members from among the "most advanced productive forces," meaning successful business owners. Political elites were simply being strategic and pragmatic.

I do not contest this realistic assessment of why Beijing's leaders have taken such sharp political turns in favor of market forces and actors. To understand the underlying reasons for why party-state elites viewed this as a necessary strategy for regime survival, however, requires looking beyond major speeches, party documents, and other official expressions of support for or condemnation of the private economy. The CCP's sense of political pressure and resulting decision to revise its ideological stance did not spontaneously materialize behind closed doors during a brainstorming session of the Standing Committee of the Politburo. Major political transformations do not occur in a societal void. Not even in dictatorships.

A potential response to this critique is adopting a societal perspective to understand improvements in the policy environment for private enterprise. Although analysts of authoritarian regimes do not typically invoke the discourse of pluralism or interest-group politics, various studies have found that some business associations in China are useful for both articulating the members' concerns and effecting changes in regulations and policies (Dickson 2003; Kennedy 2005; Nevitt 1996; Unger 1996). The value of focusing on social forces to explain political change is that it acknowledges the capacity of nonstate actors to mobilize and convey their concerns to apparently rigid bureaucratic entities. It takes the agency of ordinary business owners seriously.

However, the limitation of the society-centric approach is that it runs the risk of overstating the aggregate influence of business associations—or, as Thomas Heberer puts it, the rise of Chinese business owners as a "strategic [interest] group" (Heberer 2003). Various scholars have engaged the speculative issue of whether these types of associations can be considered evidence of a burgeoning civil society—and often by extension, the foundation for democratization (e.g., Gilley 2004; He 1996; Ogden 2002; White, Howell, and Shang 1996; cf. Skilling 1966). Anecdotal cases of business associations that are especially autonomous and assertive seem to corroborate the expectations of modernization theory and structural theories of democratic development. A frequently cited example is how indigenously organized chambers of commerce in Wenzhou succeeded in affecting local regulations on industry standards, sending representatives to the CPPCC to advocate for infrastructural improvements, and even defending local industry from the European Union's attempt to impose trade barriers on Wenzhou's products (e.g., Fewsmith 2005; Ma 2005). Casual readers of such examples might surmise that business groups have played a pivotal role in making China's political institutions more inclusive. Perhaps marketization does foment capitalist demands for political pluralization, if not democratization.

Broader comparative studies, however, have found considerable sectoral variation in the extent and effectiveness of lobbying efforts by business groups (Kennedy 2005). And as discussed in chapter 5, my own research has found significant variation among different types of entrepreneurs in their use of trade associations to represent their interests. Private businesses that are older, larger in scale, more profitable, and have principals that are party members are more likely to participate in associations and have favorable impressions about their utility. They are also more politically engaged in general. But most of the surveyed business owners are not active in such organizations—and the vast majority of my respondents do not believe that (autonomous) trade groups should be used for expressing opinions and making requests to party-state organs. In short, the handful of vocal and effective business associations hardly warrants the conclusion that organized lobbying by capitalists has steered the direction of major political changes.[4] Local corporate victories, such as reducing local fees and clarifying local industry regulations, are a far cry from requesting political representation in the CCP, ideological acceptance of capitalists, or constitutional protection of private property rights. Notwithstanding the rare cases of individual activist entrepreneurs, business owners have not used organized means to make national-level political demands.[5]

An alternative way of characterizing the relationship between the party-state and the private sector provides a middle-ground way of explaining institutional changes amid regime continuity. Specifically, rather than emphasizing either the machinations of inner-court politics in Beijing or the

4. As Kennedy (2005) has pointed out, firms may lobby individually or loosely together on economic issues at the national level, but they do not lobby for public policy or regime-oriented concerns.

5. Two exceptions come to mind. First, the constitutional scholar Cao Siyuan is literally an intellectual entrepreneur; he earns a living selling his own prodemocratic books and providing consulting services. He also gets detained from time to time. Second, Hebei farmer Sun Dawu opened a private rural credit cooperative and was imprisoned for several months in 2003 when he started calling for democracy.

rising influence of civic associations, a number of China scholars have used the concept of corporatism to convey the continuing dominance of state entities despite economic decentralization and pluralization of societal interests.[6] In these analyses, descriptions of state corporatist arrangements between local state entities and entrepreneurs generally trump predictions of democracy (e.g., Dickson 2003; Nee 1992; Parris 1995–96; Pearson 1994; Unger and Chan 1995). Vivienne Shue (1994) observes:

> Most of these associations are by no means entirely self-constituted, nor do most of them apparently seek or enjoy much relative autonomy from the state. Some are more autonomous, and others are less so. All, however, are enveloped in a rhetoric of corporatist interpenetration and encapsulated in a self-conception that stresses corporatist consultation, cooperation, and harmony in action with the party-state and its aims. (83)

Even scholars who do not invoke the corporatist framework have taken this "middle-ground" perspective on state-society relations in China by emphasizing the mutual dependence between state and private economic actors (Foster 2002; Wank 1995). In so doing, these studies provide familiar reasons for why China's capitalists—especially the larger ones—are not politically assertive. For one, the party-state already offers business owners channels for expressing their concerns. For another, local governments have political and fiscal incentives to keep their primary revenue producers satisfied (Oi 1999; Whiting 2001). At the same time, to the extent that entrepreneurs attempt to organize relatively autonomous activities and associations, they are typically co-opted by official entities. In this interpretation of China's political economy, cadres and capitalists generally have convergent interests.

How should we assess the analytic value of the middle-ground approach? Joel Migdal's (2001) expression of disappointment from another context comes to mind: "We are left in the end with individuals who are either relentlessly rational or maddeningly passive" (147). What happens when the interests of capitalists and cadres diverge? And, more to the point, how do institutions change in this apparently harmonious pact?

To be fair, the studies cited above all recognize the potential for local state and economic actors to stretch the rules and functions of existing institutions

6. Philippe Schmitter (1974) defines corporatism as "a system of interest representation in which the constituent units are organized into a limited number of singular, compulsory, non-competitive, hierarchically ordered and functionally differentiated categories, recognized or licensed (if not created) by the state and granted a deliberate representational monopoly within their respective categories in exchange for observing certain controls on their selection of leaders and articulation of demands and supports" (93–94). Despite its association with fascism in the 1930s, corporatism is not necessarily associated with a particular regime type. Authoritarian regimes may have state corporatism while democracies may have liberal or societal corporatist arrangements.

and even stimulate the creation of new ones. Some scholars who have drawn on the corporatist framework can envision a gradual movement from state to societal corporatism in China—albeit not in the immediate future (Unger and Chan 1995; Wank 1995). Dickson (2003), however, clearly questions the sustainability of this incremental view of reform: "The depiction of a gradual and incremental evolution from state to societal corporatism is not consistent with the wider literature. . . . We should not expect that the transition from state to societal corporatism will occur amidst regime continuity" (67). Yet writing over a decade earlier, Shue (1994) questions this direction of potential political change and anticipates, instead, the gradual revitalization of state capacities.

These studies are all grounded in careful empirical research and analysis, and should not be discounted. However, none of them specify the process through which remarkable institutional changes have already occurred in reform-era China. Evidence from the previous chapters shows that various parts of the party-state have indeed proven to be attentive to the private sector, but not as a result of collective action by business owners. Instead, many of the institutional transformations that have occurred may be traced to informal interactions, which affect the efficacy of formal institutions. A number of scholars have argued that interpersonal relationships (*guanxi*)—and, in particular, its instrumental expression as clientelism—distorts the implementation of official policies in China's political economy.[7] In countless instances, state and economic actors rely more on informal social networks than formal rules and regulations. I expand on this widely accepted observation by contending that a diverse range of informal coping strategies, not just *guanxi*, has the potential to generate macrolevel changes in political institutions.

Adaptive Informal Institutions

Institutional Emergence

Even though my research found limited evidence of class formation and collective action on the part of business owners, private entrepreneurs are nonetheless active in pursuing and defending their interests. They are, after all, *entrepreneurs*. Individuals who assume the responsibility, risk, and rewards of running commercial ventures (in a transitional economy, no less)

---

7. See Gold, Guthrie, and Wank 2002 for an overview of this vast literature. Of direct relevance to the private sector, Pearson (1997) contends, "Instead of civil society, the dominant pattern [of state-society relations] consists of a combination of socialist corporatism and clientelism" (141). According to Pearson, this is one of the key reasons why China's business elites have not translated their economic status into political power.

are self-motivated. They work for themselves and their families.[8] To establish and maintain a business, they also have to be resourceful in navigating bureaucracies and markets—and when neither exists for the purposes at hand, entrepreneurs participate in creating them. This is a pretty standard, albeit abbreviated, depiction of entrepreneurs as agents and innovators.

Without denying the consequentialist character of entrepreneurial agency, I suggest that the coping strategies of everyday actors, including private entrepreneurs, may have unintended transformative effects on formal institutions. Most people do not run their businesses or live their lives with the intention of changing national political institutions. Yet their quotidian interactions with one another and with local bureaucrats can nonetheless have major political impact. I propose that two intermediate processes render institutional change more likely: institutional subversion and institutional conversion. When these processes become widespread against the backdrop of particular institutional constraints or opportunities, such regularized practices constitute adaptive informal institutions—which coexist, rather awkwardly, with increasingly dysfunctional formal ones.

My argument is premised on the assumption that the legitimacy and efficacy of institutions, whether formal or informal, depends on their reproduction by social, economic, and political actors (cf. Bourdieu and Wacquant 1992; Powell and DiMaggio 1991). This sociological view of institutions is agnostic about the comparative relevance of formal versus informal institutions. What matters is how people interact in either reproducing or undermining various institutions. By the same token, institutions become irrelevant, even noninstitutions, when they consistently fail to have any impact on the attitudes and behavior of the people they are intended to govern.

With this in mind, *institutional subversion* occurs when people ignore formal institutions. This may occur out of ignorance ("I didn't realize there was a law prohibiting X"), inconvenience ("Who has time to apply for all those different licenses?"), or incongruities in official rules ("If I comply with Regulation A, then it will violate Regulation B, so there's no way to comply with both"). Although people with criminal intent also typically bypass certain institutions, the legitimacy of institutions suffers more damage when everyday people violate them. Criminals and corrupt politicians are expected, by nomenclature, to breach formal institutions. Others are not. But irrespective of the underlying motivation for institutional subversion, the point is that repeated infractions weaken formal institutions, both symbolically and practically.

---

8. To be sure, sometimes entrepreneurs also work on behalf of their communities and for noneconomic rewards. See Schumpeter (1976 [1942]), Dahl 1961, and for a more contemporary review of the literature, Sheingate 2003.

Quick cash from a pawnshop in rural Chongqing

I have documented the near ubiquity of institutional subversion in the process of private sector development in China: the early reemergence of petty entrepreneurship; the rise of red capitalists; the private moneylenders' interest rates; the displacement of communal farmland by sweatshops; the red-chip IPOs in Hong Kong. These commonly accepted dimensions of China's private economy all entail practices that compromised the integrity of various formal institutions. The practices evolved into adaptive informal institutions that, in some cases, became more popular than the formal ones.

The second process associated with the rise of adaptive informal institutions is *institutional conversion*, which occurs when actors appropriate formal institutions to serve their own ends (Thelen 2004). Although institutional subversion does not necessarily involve the complicity of state actors, institutional conversion usually requires some form of collaboration with bureaucrats—or at least those with access to enforcers of formal institutions. Given that formal institutions have, by definition, official legal status, they provide a legitimating cover for people to engage in activities that may not be officially sanctioned. Examples of institutional conversion from

China's private sector include registering private firms as collective enterprises and running profit-oriented businesses out of government offices.[9]

Institutional subversion and conversion are different expressions of processes that give rise to adaptive informal institutions. They do not have to occur sequentially, even though institutional conversion certainly conveys a degree of institutional subversion. But both processes are more likely to occur in certain institutional environments. As discussed in chapter 2, complex multilayered institutional settings provide more opportunities for actors to maneuver around institutions that may be anachronistic or work at cross-purposes. Although the literature on endogenous institutional change and institutional development draws primarily from advanced industrial democracies, the dynamics of institutional layering and friction among multiple political orders can also be observed in less developed, nondemocratic countries. And, indeed, one might expect formal structures in reforming socialist systems to exhibit especially perplexing combinations of Communist, market-oriented, and even prerevolutionary-era institutions.

It is precisely such contexts of institutional bricolage rather than institutional precision that facilitate the emergence of adaptive informal institutions. This is where entrepreneurial agency can make a big difference. Leaving aside the lone operator or criminal who exploits a loophole and makes headlines (if not "history"), I am interested in the hundreds of thousands, even millions, of business owners and bureaucrats who have disregarded or distorted certain rules in strikingly consistent ways. Their resourceful use of adaptive informal institutions has not only contributed to private sector development but also, unwittingly, to formal institutional development.

Emergent Causation

By the time that repeated acts of institutional subversion and institutional conversion become routinized coping strategies—adaptive informal institutions—we know that at least lower-level bureaucrats are well aware of these infractions. The latter may also face a host of economic and professional incentives to conceal their participation in adaptive informal institutions. But cadres rotate, leaks occur, journalists write revealing stories, and in most cases higher-level elites eventually learn about informal practices that are not quite legal and particularly widespread. This raises the issue of what happens after those with the authority and ability to reform formal institutions become aware that adaptive informal institutions are challenging

9. Although some might protest that using party-state assets to generate private ones simply constitutes theft and misappropriation of public resources, I am also referring to situations where the use of those resources for alternative sources of income does not necessarily dissipate them. Consider, for instance, the entrepreneurial ventures run by commerce and real estate departments (Duckett 1998).

the integrity of official rules and regulations. Under what circumstances do elites decide to change or create formal institutions in response to adaptive informal institutions? Can we anticipate when these changes will occur?

These are reasonable questions, which could be addressed by delineating a nomothetic set of testable and falsifiable hypotheses. Rather than proposing said hypotheses, however, I will point out that based on positivist criteria for evaluating social science explanations, the concept of adaptive informal institutions has two main explanatory limits.

First, there is uncertainty about timing. We do not know when formal institutions will react to informal ones. Some informal institutions may coexist with formal institutions for a long time without effecting official reforms. This book does not supply an elegant deterministic model specifying that formal institutions will change (the dependent variable) when policy elites decide that it is "practically important" (one independent variable) and "politically feasible" (another independent variable) to initiate changes, ceteris paribus. There is no point in clothing a political truism in the form of a formal prediction.

Second, adaptive informal institutions are not always relevant in explaining formal institutional change. Sometimes institutional reforms are motivated solely by elite politics, external intervention, or natural disasters. I do not contend that a potent adaptive informal institution lurks behind every institutional transformation. My argument does suggest, however, that even in instances in which institutions are clearly associated with innovative political leaders and exogenous shocks, we should expect informal practices to deviate from and shape the new institutions. To what end is not necessarily predictable. But analyzing politics with the expectation that informal adaptations will arise expands the empirical scope of where to look for transformative phenomena and otherwise inconspicuous agents of change.

In short, I do not believe that the processes discussed here can be reduced to discrete causal claims. William Connolly's (2004) notion of emergent causality best captures this epistemological position:

> Emergent causality, when it occurs, is causal (rather than simply definitional) in that a movement at the immanent level has effects at another level. But it is emergent in that, first, the character of the immanent activity is not knowable in precise detail prior to effects that emerge at the second level, second, the new effects become infused into the very being or organization of the second level in such a way that the cause cannot be said to be fully different from the effect engendered, and third, a series of loops and feedback loops operate between first and second levels to generate the stabilized result. (Connolly 2004, 342)

In spatial terms, adaptive informal institutions lie between informal practices and formal institutions (see figure 2.1). Adaptive informal institutions are both an effect of innovative coping strategies by everyday actors and an emergent cause of changes in formal institutions. They are intermediate, Janus-faced institutions that simultaneously embody local repertoires of informal practices and bear weight on the efficacy and relevance of formal institutions. By the same token, formal institutions are an emergent cause of adaptive informal practices. The constraints, the conflicts, and the silences left by formal institutions make this possible. To be sure, some local actors may attempt to reform formal institutions in a consequential manner (through contentious forms of political participation such as lobbying or staging protests). But my argument proposes that the repetition and diffusion of nonconsequentialist practices may have an equally powerful effect on the landscape of formal institutions.

Analytic Value

In a field beset by conceptual stretching (Collier and Levitsky 1997) and elusive jargon, one might question the value of introducing yet another term: adaptive informal institutions. The analytic rationale for calling these routinized coping strategies "adaptive informal institutions"—not just informal practices or culturally familiar ways of getting things done—lies in its conceptual specificity. Unlike informal institutions writ large, *adaptive* informal institutions refer to regularized patterns of interaction that emerge in reaction to constraints and opportunities in the formal institutional environment. Adaptive responses should not be lumped with customs, norms, values, traditions, and rules of the game that constitute common definitions of informal institutions or "cultural constraints" (e.g., North 1990). Differentiating between long-standing informal practices and those that appear in the context of new opportunities enables us to focus on a subset of informal coping strategies that derive from shorter-term considerations of convenience, efficiency, and possibility. In this sense, the concept of adaptive informal institutions privileges the agency of ordinary actors in identifying, devising, and reproducing informal practices that are either unsanctioned or unregulated by formal institutions. Adaptive informal institutions result from calculated acts. By way of contrast, cultural conventions, or what Pierre Bourdieu (1990) refers to as *habitus*, are deeply internalized and therefore reproduced in a less conscious manner.[10]

Therein lies an apparent paradox: adaptive informal institutions emerge from consequentialist actions, but they may have broader nonconsequentialist

10. I do not want to overstate the dichotomy between informal institutions that are adaptive versus reflexive because adaptive informal institutions may also acquire the taken-for-granted quality of other types of informal or cultural practices. By the same token, fulfilling the obligations associated with primordial ties and loyalties may entail a high degree of self-consciously consequentialist behavior.

effects. Yet this analytic asymmetry is what endows adaptive informal institutions with explanatory potential. First, adaptive informal institutions serve as a barometer for the sources of compliance and noncompliance with formal institutions. Adaptive informal institutions reflect the local logics that inform the practices of everyday actors. As a result, examining the etiology of adaptive informal institutions can help to explain why certain formal institutions lack efficacy or deviate from their intended mandates. Relatedly, the concept also demonstrates how formal institutions may inspire the sources of their own reform. Existing accounts of endogenous institutional change acknowledge the role of political and economic elites in appropriating or redefining the boundaries of formal institutions, but they fail to recognize that formal institutions can also elicit imaginative adaptations on the part of regular actors. As I have attempted to show, even in authoritarian regimes where the most important political decisions are made in a centralized manner, adaptive informal institutions can influence institutional reforms. We should not assume the deafness of dictatorships.

This is not to say that authoritarian regimes in general or China's party-state in particular lack the coercive capacity to deny, disregard, or obfuscate the interests and desires embodied in adaptive informal institutions. Rather, the point is that even in countries where the threat of sudden and arbitrary use of force to curb behavioral transgressions is a daily possibility, both state and nonstate actors can engage in informal interactions that become officially sanctioned. State power is mediated by social forces (Migdal, Kohli, and Shue 1994). While "social forces" such as village clans, overtaxed farmers, underemployed workers, criminal gangs, and greedy officials are more readily identified as potential threats to formal state institutions, the adaptive informal institutions that they quietly create (and rely on) express the practical manifestations of dysfunctional formal institutions. The actions that constitute adaptive informal institutions speak for themselves. In response, the enforcers of formal institutions could attempt to ban certain informal practices and punish subsequent violators. I present another possibility: the designers of formal institutions might learn about the rationale for the popularity of adaptive informal institutions and decide to formalize them instead.

As indicated above, however, the dynamics of emergent causation preclude meaningful specification *ex ante* of how long it will take for adaptive informal institutions to capture the attention of political elites (if at all), and whether the latter will then amend formal institutions to acknowledge, accommodate, or appropriate the coping strategies embodied in adaptive informal institutions. These key issues are contextually contingent and should be explored through empirical study of both the high politics *and* the apparently apolitical low politics of grassroots adaptations to formal institutions. Considering the following questions can help to determine whether adaptive informal institutions have potential political consequences in particular contexts: How effective are formal institutions in structuring political and economic interactions? How united are political elites in their assessment of the country's political institutions? What types of adaptive informal practices are especially popular? Are various types of adaptive informal institutions concentrated spatially or are they relatively evenly distributed? Are certain segments of society more likely to participate in informal coping strategies than others? To what extent are local and higher-level state bureaucrats cognizant of or participants in these practices? How do political leaders and their advisers view various grassroots adaptations?

Taken together, the answers to these types of questions present a portrait of politics in practice that bears only a passing resemblance to conventional political descriptors. Instead of focusing on the concept of regime type—which connotes the normative and analytically circumscribed modes of political participation associated with democratic versus authoritarian regimes—this approach interrogates a broader spectrum of channels for political influence, whether formal or informal, and, indeed, whether intended or unintended. Paying attention to adaptive practices that deviate from the intentions of formal institutions can reveal endogenous sources of change that might not be apparent if we only looked at policy pronouncements, judicial codes, legislative processes, organized interests, sectoral or class-based cleavages, and other textbook indicators of normal politics. Irrespective of regime type, adaptive informal institutions may represent dialectical seeds of change that are simultaneously inconspicuous yet pervasive, commonly accepted yet unapologetically illegal.

Indeed, my emphasis on adaptive informal institutions is meant to contribute to existing theories of endogenous institutional change, which are mostly based on studies of advanced industrial economies but also cast in general terms (Streek and Thelen 2005). Thus far, political scientists who analyze institutional change in the absence of exogenous shocks have either introduced terms that describe the particular effects of institutional change, such as institutional "layering" (Schickler 2001; Thelen 2004), institutional "conversion" (Thelen 2004), institutional "drift" (Hacker 2004), and institutional "self-undermining" (Greif and Laitin 2004), or emphasized familiar concepts in novel ways, such as the role of ideas (Blyth 2002; Hay 1999) or political entrepreneurship (Sheingate 2003). Although none of these scholars explicitly addresses how informal institutions may affect formal ones, a review of the causal sequence in their arguments reveals that attending to adaptive informal practices (if not "institutions") could complement many of these accounts of endogenous institutional change.

First, as suggested earlier, the notions of institutional layering and conversion both involve informal opportunities for actors to work around the limitations of existing formal institutions in creative ways. In layering, new institutions are established alongside old ones, which dilutes the relevance of the old institutions. This enables the creators of new institutions to avoid direct efforts at reforming politically entrenched institutions. As such, layering can be seen as an informal strategy for generating changes in the topography and aggregate effects of formal institutions. Meanwhile, institutional conversion is even more likely than layering to entail informal adaptive responses that exploit internal ambiguities in certain institutions or simply reinterpret the spirit of preexisting institutions. In conversion, actors adapt old institutions for new ends.

Second, the processes of institutional drift and institutional breakdown may also involve informal responses—or intentional lack of response—to changing environmental conditions. What Jacob Hacker (2004) calls "drift" refers to changes in the effects of certain policies even though the policies have not been changed substantively: "Drift may be inadvertent. Or it may be the result of active attempts to block adaptation of institutions to changing circumstances" (248). While policy drift stems from institutional neglect, institutional breakdown results from self-undermining, as opposed to self-reinforcing, processes generated by earlier institutional dynamics. Over time, institutions may generate marginal changes in contextual conditions, or what Greif and Laitin (2004) call "quasi-parameters." In turn, these ecological changes could facilitate either self-reinforcing or self-undermining processes in the institutions. As they explain, "Institutional change will endogenously occur only when the self-undermining processes reaches a critical level such that past patterns of behavior are no longer self-enforcing." In other words, institutions might gradually "cultivate the seeds of their own demise" (634).[11] As in my notion of adaptive informal institutions, the causal logic in Greif and Laitin's account is that any given set of institutions may result in contextual changes that generate endogenous adaptive responses. In turn, the adaptive responses may either be self-reinforcing or self-undermining vis-à-vis the original institutions.[12]

Third, while the above theories trace the logic of change to the internal dynamics of institutions or broader configurations of institutions, explanations for institutional change that highlight the role of entrepreneurship

11. Streek and Thelen (2005) call this mode of institutional change "institutional exhaustion."

12. Greif and Laitin (2004) illustrate the difference between self-reinforcing and self-undermining institutions by tracing how similar political regimes in medieval Venice and Genoa generated differences in "quasi-parameters"; in Venice, this facilitated political adjustments to changes in economic conditions, but in Genoa, the shifts in quasi-parameters strengthened clan structures and undermined political order, which furthered its economic decline. Arguably, the endogenously inspired response in Genoa of continuing interclan rivalry and competition could be seen as an adaptive informal institution that ultimately undermined the original political regime.

and ideas, respectively, emphasize how moments of uncertainty provide special opportunities for endogenous institutional transformation. Sheingate (2003) contends that "entrepreneurs exploit uncertainty to engage in speculative acts of creativity" (187), while Blyth (2002) finds that "ideas allow agents to reduce uncertainty, propose a particular solution to a moment of crisis, and empower agents to resolve that crisis by constructing new institutions" (11). Although neither Sheingate nor Blyth explicitly examines informal responses, their shared focus on the role of entrepreneurs and agents during uncertain times provides complementary insight to my argument about the possibilities for institutional innovation from below. The key contribution of my account, however, is the accent placed on the impact of adaptive informal institutions on formal ones.

Having said that, I would like to caution against overdiagnosing the causal potential of informal institutions. In a researcher's version of medical student syndrome, all deviations from formal institutions could take on unwarranted significance. Ultimately, the substantive political impact of everyday practices ranges from trivial to revolutionary (Scott 1985). To reiterate a methodological theme in this book, distinguishing between novel curiosities of habit and adaptations with broader structural effects requires careful and creative empirical investigation. It also requires an agnostic stance toward the apparent functionality of adaptive informal institutions. As discussed in the previous chapter, instances of adaptive institutional failure abound.

Comparative Relevance

Given that this argument is derived from observations about the politics of private sector development in China, the comparative question arises of whether adaptive informal institutions may have transformative influence on formal institutions in other countries. Is the analytic argument limited to reform-era China, or can comparable dynamics of endogenous institutional change be observed in other nondemocratic transitional contexts or even democratic settings? A sampling of secondary literature suggests that adaptive informal institutions indeed arise in vastly different political and economic contexts. For illustrative purposes, I briefly consider such examples from two contrasting settings. First, a situation that would be the "most similar" to China concerns the role of informal vs. formal institutions in shaping the political economy of transitional and post-Communist societies. The second set of examples represent "least likely" comparisons from liberal democratic contexts where formal institutions seem more enduring and efficacious: the development of banking regulations in the United States and legislative changes in the European Union.

First, even though we might expect the logic of adaptive informal institutions to be most prevalent in transitional contexts where formal institutions are less likely to be well consolidated and may simply be up for grabs, few studies of transitional economies in eastern Europe and the former Soviet Union have focused on the emergence of *adaptive* informal institutions in response to the constraints of formal ones—or the reform of formal institutions in response to widespread consistent departures from them. Instead, the more familiar refrain is that Communist-era informal institutions are more relevant than formal institutions in shaping economic and political outcomes. For example, the Communist legacy of noncompliance has not only endured but flourished in the form of a reinvigorated second economy in Russia, Belarus, and Ukraine following the collapse of Communism (Feige 1997; Humphrey 2002; Smallbone and Welter 2003). In those cases, entrenched informal institutions both subvert and circumvent formal institutions (cf. Böröcz 2000). By contrast, extant informal institutions have also shaped the formal design of institutional reforms in transitional economies, as seen in the widely varying modes of privatization in the Czech Republic, Poland, and Hungary (Raiser 2001).[13] Meanwhile, the collapse of collective farming in Vietnam (Kerkvliet 2005), "spontaneous privatization" in Hungary (Frydman, Murphy, and Rapaczyinski 1998), and legalization of private security services in Russia (Volkov 2002) have also been traced to informal everyday practices that became widespread and commanded the attention of national authorities. And in the political realm, informal institutions have reinforced formal institutions such as political parties by offering decision rules for the formation of formal coalitions and other power-sharing arrangements (Grzymala-Busse 2004).

These studies hint at a feedback effect between informal and formal institutions, which resonates with my observations about China's reform process. But more targeted research could be conducted to distinguish between deeply entrenched informal institutions from the socialist era versus more recent strategic adaptations.[14] Arguably, evasive practices now associated with the socialist "legacy of noncompliance" were adaptive informal institutions that originally emerged in response to the formal institutions of socialism; the observation that they have persisted and even extended their reach with the introduction of postsocialist institutions thus presents a host of research opportunities for studying the evolution of informal institutions.

---

13. In particular, Raiser (2001) suggests that "the existence of implicit property rights in state-owned enterprises may influence what privatization method is politically acceptable and hence feasible" (3).

14. I suspect that one of the main reasons for this apparent difference between China and its formerly socialist counterparts is related to the speed and overarching commitment on the part of political elites in the latter cases to a dual-track transition process. Arguably, China's more gradualistic and experimental approach to reform has created more space for the emergence of adaptive informal institutions.

While we might expect the institutional environment in transitional contexts to be syncretic, formal institutions in liberal democratic settings convey a greater degree of stability, authority, and efficacy. Moreover, from a functionalist perspective, there would seem to be less need for informal adaptations to formal institutions that are in theory meant to be responsive. After all, liberal democracies offer multiple channels for political expression and participation. Yet even in the formal legalistic context of the United States, examples of the formal-informal-formal iterative dynamic may be identified. In his analysis of the U.S. banking system, for example, Edward Kane (1981, 1988) observes a "regulatory dialectic," whereby official regulations motivate economic actors to engage in "loophole mining" to evade existing regulations. The resulting innovations are adaptive informal institutions—they emerge in reaction to the restrictions or opportunities of formal institutions and become widely practiced by various economic and political actors. The extensive use of adaptive financial innovations then stimulates another round of financial regulations, thereby fueling another cycle of regulation and innovation. In short, despite major differences in regime type and economic development, the process of regulatory development in the United States arguably exhibits dynamics similar to that observed in reform-era China.

Finally, this dynamic is not limited to the economic realm where we would most expect actors to act opportunistically. The European Union represents a political example of how formal institutions in a democratic context may give rise to informal institutions, which then affect formal institutional design at a later point. As Henry Farrell and Adrienne Héritier (2002) have argued, "Under certain circumstances, one can identify a *recursive relationship* between formal and informal institutions. When informal institutions come into being, they represent a new status quo, which affects subsequent Treaty negotiations." By informal institutions, these authors mean modes of decision making that override formal rules and change the interaction between the European Parliament and European Council, thereby affecting the legislative process. Lest readers object that ongoing renegotiation of formal rules typifies youthful organizations such as the European Union, scholars of American political development have observed comparable dynamics in the longer-established legislative bodies. Gregory Wawro and Eric Schickler (2006), for instance, have demonstrated that for much of its history the U.S. Senate effectively relied on informal "relational legislating" in the absence of formal rules of debate. But when growth in the size and workload of the Senate expanded substantially in the early twentieth century, repeated obstruction of important legislation prompted formal regulation of debate. In sum, adaptive informal institutions can also contribute to changing the formal economic and political rules of the game in democratic settings.

Informal Sources of Democratization?

A final twist: If informal practices can elicit formal institutional reforms, then, theoretically, adaptive informal institutions should have the potential to precipitate democratic transitions in autocratic regimes. Indeed, my analytic argument does not preclude the possibility that China might democratize through endogenous processes. In a manner evocative of Western parliamentary development, democratic norms and institutions could arise as a product of ongoing interactions between informal practices and formal responses. Popular elections could be extended from villages to higher (official) levels of government.[15] The Communist Party could splinter into different factions that turn into competing political parties.[16] Regardless of such possibilities, however, my empirical research shows that these possibilities are unlikely to grow out of either direct demands from private entrepreneurs or their informal coping strategies.[17]

Moreover, in a broader sense, the claims made in this book point to the limits of analyzing Chinese politics through concepts and causal models ahistorically transplanted from other contexts. In his reflections on African studies, Mahmood Mamdani (1996) critically dubs this practice "history by analogy":

> The Africanist is akin to those learning a foreign language who must translate every new word back into their mother tongue, in the process missing precisely what is new in a new experience. From such a standpoint, the most intense controversies dwell on what is indeed the most appropriate translation, the most adequate fit, the most appropriate analogy that will capture the meaning of the phenomenon under observation. Africanist debates tend to focus on whether contemporary African reality most closely resembles the transition to capitalism under seventeenth-century European absolutism or that under other Third World experiences, or whether the postcolonial state in Africa should be labeled Bonapartist or absolutist. (12)

Both popular and scholarly debates about the political implications of China's economic reforms echo this tendency to translate distinctive phenomena into

---

15. This has occurred only on a pilot basis in select townships. See the Carter Center's webpage on Chinese elections and governance at http://www.chinaelections.org/.

16. The admission of capitalists into the CCP could, for example, be viewed as an initial step in increasing the pluralization, and by extension, political polarization of the CCP.

17. As discussed in the previous chapters, the most disgruntled business owners (in the state-dominated model) are no more assertive than the sample average, and the most assertive entrepreneurs in the Sunan and limited development patterns either are incorporated by existing political institutions already or are intent on migrating to areas with better business conditions. To the extent that a slice of the entrepreneurial population could spark a significant political incident or collaborate with other segments of society, it would be the assertive and grudgingly acceptant entrepreneurs with state employment backgrounds, for they have the highest levels of discontent and a sense of entitlement from the party-state.

more common terms. In so doing, translation becomes anticipation. The mere mention of civil society, middle class, and capitalism foreshadows some discussion of democracy. In contrast, while Chinese leaders and intellectuals also use these prefabricated terms, they are framed with an exceptionalist clause—"with Chinese characteristics." Chinese modifiers confound otherwise familiar ideas. Yet the official slogans "market socialism with Chinese characteristics" and "political democracy with Chinese characteristics" are not intended to mock conventional notions of the market, socialism, or democracy. Instead, they represent self-conscious efforts to distinguish China's economic and political development from preexisting developmental paths.[18]

In this book I have endeavored to strike a balance between the extremes of Chinese exceptionalism and universal theory. On the one hand, the empirical findings demonstrate that China's private entrepreneurs show no evidence of reenacting the prodemocratic roles of their eighteenth- and nineteenth-century counterparts in Britain and the United States. There is no capitalist class, and there is certainly no democracy in contemporary China. In addition, even if China eventually were to develop a capitalist class (a class for itself), there is no reason to expect that it would lead or ally with other classes in pushing for political change. Beyond these negative conclusions—that is, determining what is not going on in China—the foregoing chapters have also detailed the day-to-day dynamics of what it takes to run, regulate, and even ruin a private business. The field interviews and statistical findings show that for better or worse informal interactions between state and economic actors have created a variety of adaptive informal institutions, some of which have had a transformative impact on formal institutions. The resulting institutional patchwork of formal intentions, informal adaptations, and formal reactions is distinctively Chinese in its descriptive and political details.

On the other hand, there is comparative analytic value in viewing adaptive informal institutions as vehicles for change in formal institutions. Despite the indeterminacy of when and whether adaptive informal institutions will have such catalytic effects, attending to the rise of informal adaptive responses expands the scope of what we typically deem to be relevant in political analysis. Local innovations, evasive tactics, and other extralegal practices often seem distant from political elites and their associated formal political institutions. The concept of adaptive informal institutions brings them a little closer. Sporadic acts of noncompliance or random criminality are not of concern. But strategic responses that are repeated, widespread, systematically reproduced, and, therefore, "institutionalized" through informal praxis

---

18. In this respect, the Confucian connotations implied by the more recent political slogan of "building a harmonious society" represents a more distinctively Chinese turn in official discourse.

generally elicit official attention in some form or another. This claim is intended to travel beyond the case of private sector development in China.

Finally, by suggesting that the transformative potential of adaptive informal institutions occurs in a variety of regimes, I am not denying the coercive essence of authoritarianism, romanticizing the possibilities of informality, or discounting the desirability of liberal democracy. The point is that political and institutional change occurs through multiple processes, including informal ones. That is why we can have capitalism without democracy, political change without regime change, and, indeed, capitalists in a communist party.

Appendix A

Research Methodology

In order to derive meaningful insights about differences among entrepreneurs, this book presents data based on national surveys of business owners. Most of the previous studies of private entrepreneurs rely on data from particular localities and, therefore, reach conclusions that may not travel beyond their respective research sites. For example, Doug Guthrie's study (1999) of joint ventures in Shanghai finds that foreign-invested enterprises use more rationalized rather than personalistic modes of operation, while David Wank's study (1999) of private entrepreneurs in Xiamen finds that local officials and entrepreneurs are mutually dependent. Meanwhile, various studies of Wenzhou have found the locality's business owners to be particularly autonomous and self-reliant (Parris 1993). Taken together, these in-depth analyses provide valuable observations about the potential nature of regional variation in private sector development, an issue addressed in chapter 6. However, with few exceptions, most of the area-specific accounts of business owners do not even discuss the variation among private entrepreneurs in terms of their social, economic, and political characteristics within a particular locality.[1] Most studies focus on either small-scale entrepreneurs or red capitalists, either disenfranchised peddlers or privileged elites. This research project was thus designed with the intention of capturing the full range of business owners in a nationally representative sample of localities, which was supplemented by in-depth interviews.

The data presented in chapters 3, 4, 5, and 6 come from both preexisting national surveys and an original national survey of private entrepreneurs.

1. David Goodman (1999) and Ole Odgaard (1992) are key exceptions.

The official surveys were conducted by the All-China Federation of Industry and Commerce (ACFIC), in collaboration with the Institute of Sociology of the Chinese Academy of Social Sciences (CASS). The data from those surveys is available from China Economic System Reform Committee and State Administration for Industry and Commerce (1991), Chinese University of Hong Kong (1993), and the *China Private Economy Yearbook* (1994, 1996, 2000, 2005), issued by the State Administration for Industry and Commerce. The annual *Blue Book of Private Enterprises: A Report on the Development of China's Private Enterprises*, edited by Zhang Houyi, Ming Lizhi, and Liang Zhuanyun at CASS, also presents selected data from the official ACFIC and CASS surveys. Note that the official surveys focused on different strata of the private economy over time: 86 percent of those surveyed in 1991 were individual entrepreneurs, while the 1993, 1995, 1997–98, 2000, and 2004 surveys focused on larger private enterprises.

Original National Survey

My survey was funded by an International Research Fellowship Program grant from the National Science Foundation (INT-0107326) and conducted in collaboration with the Private Economy Research Center of CASS over the course of 2002 and 2003. My collaborators assumed responsibility for securing the requisite official clearances for the project. The survey was drafted and tested twice in both rural and urban Hebei Province during the summer of 2002. (Copies of the final survey instrument are available on my website in both Chinese and English at: https://jshare.johnshopkins.edu/ktsai1/web/.) The sampling frame was a stratified multistage area probability sample. In the first stage, the primary sampling units (PSUs) were provinces stratified by region according to the relative development of the private sector. Of the ten provincial-level units sampled, five were in the east (Hebei, Shandong, Jiangsu, Zhejiang, and Fujian), three were in central China (Henan, Jiangxi, and Hubei), and two were in the west (Chongqing and Shaanxi). Within each of the provinces, the secondary sampling units (SSUs) were two cities and two counties,[2] and at the third stage two districts or townships were randomly selected within each city or county, respectively. At the district and township level, registration lists from the Industrial and Commercial Management Bureau (ICMB) were used to select businesses according to probability proportional to size (PPS) measures, using a random-start fixed-interval system.

2. In three of the more rural provinces, only one city and two counties were sampled rather than a total of two cities and two counties. This means that a total of thirty-seven cities and counties were sampled at the second stage. As a condition of my collaboration with local researchers, I agreed not to reveal the identity of the SSUs.

In October 2002, we held a training-of-trainers workshop in Nanjing for the lead interviewers from each of the ten provinces. Because the workshop was held at a university, a select number of graduate students were also permitted to observe the training session. The workshop reinforced the importance of maintaining the integrity of our sampling frame, clarified the content and objective of the survey instrument, and discussed means to ensure proper implementation of the survey. In turn, the lead interviewers returned to their provincial bases to recruit and train local undergraduate and graduate students to serve as interviewers. The interviewers were instructed to ensure that the respondent was indeed the primary proprietor of the business, to guarantee the anonymity of the respondent, to offer the respondent the opportunity to decline participation in the survey, to ask all the questions on the survey verbally, and to record the responses themselves on the questionnaire. Due to low rates of literacy among certain types of business owners, in our experience administering such surveys orally increases the response rate, reduces the level of missing data, and increases the reliability of completed responses. The lead interviewers were responsible for monitoring the actual interviewers, and lead interviewers were informed that principal members of our research team would make unannounced visits to various sampling sites to ensure compliance with the survey procedures.

The actual administration of the surveys lasted from November 2002 to August 2003 (with a brief SARS-related interruption during the spring of 2003). A total of 1,800 surveys were administered and 1,525 were completed, yielding a response rate of 84.7 percent. Unfortunately, not all of the interviewers recorded the reasons for the nonresponses. Hence, we do not have a complete breakdown of what percentage of the nonresponses was due to refusals on the part of prospective respondents, incorrect contact information from the ICMB registration lists, or the unavailability of intended respondent (i.e., the primary owner of the business). Based on partial and anecdotal reporting, it appears that most of the nonresponses were due to errors from the registration lists.

Field Interviews

In addition to the national survey, I conducted 317 in-depth interviews with a range of researchers, government officials, rank-and-file bureaucrats, bankers, and private entrepreneurs (including unregistered business owners) over the course of 2001 to 2005. As shown in appendix B, with the exception of five interviews conducted in Hong Kong and fourteen interviews conducted in the United States, the remaining were conducted in China. Most of the interviews with government employees residing in China were organized by official hosts at the local level, though in several cases I was able to interview local officials and bureaucrats through less formal means. Interviews with private entrepreneurs were arranged through a combination of local government hosts, academic contacts, and my own (private and informal) solicitations. The interviews lasted an average of two hours, though some were as brief as one hour and some extended beyond six hours and were capped off with a banquet. All informants were guaranteed anonymity, and I have intentionally altered identifying details in a few cases as an extra precaution. Only four cases in the book use real names: the interviewees gave me permission to use their names and their situations have been documented in both the Chinese and foreign media.

Potential Biases in the Data

The survey is biased toward registered entrepreneurs because we used the registration lists of the ICMB as our sampling frame. This means that de facto private enterprises registered as collective ones (aka "red hat enterprises") and unregistered businesses were not captured by the survey. Note, however, that the survey included several questions that enabled me to identify enterprises that may not have presented themselves as private businesses in earlier years. Specifically, question 8a. asked the respondent owner to specify the year in which he or she started running the business and how it was registered (i.e., as a state-owned enterprise, urban collective, rural collective, joint-household enterprise, shareholding enterprise, foreign-invested joint venture, private enterprise, individual business, partnership, or other). Follow-up questions on the survey also asked why the owner decided to convert the business from a collective into a private one, as well as how the business was converted from a state or collective enterprise into a private one (i.e., stock share conversion, auction, ownership transfer, or other). Therefore, even though the survey was only administered to registered private businesses, it was able to identify some of the reasons that business owners did not register their operations as private enterprises in the initial stages. The survey was also supplemented with in-depth interviews of unregistered businesses. Not surprisingly, a number of the unregistered proprietors were reluctant to let me fill out an informal survey or speak with me, but overall most of the unregistered owners that I approached were willing to share their experiences—especially when I agreed not to take notes during the interview. On those occasions, I would document the interviews in my field notes as soon as it was logistically possible.

The other source of bias in the sample concerns the relative distribution of localities across the developmental patterns delineated in chapter 6.

Each of the thirty-seven sampled counties and cities was classified into one of the five developmental patterns based on the relative size of the private, collective, and state sectors, as well as the overall level of industrial and agricultural output as of 1997, on the eve of large-scale restructuring of the state sector. In most cases, it was not difficult to classify the county- and city-level units using the 40 percent decision rule, whereby whatever sector accounted for over 40 percent of the local GDP would determine its classification. For example, according to official statistics, in 1997 95.4 percent of industrial output in County X came from the non-state sector, and 63.9 percent was generated by the private enterprises, which puts County X clearly in the Wenzhou model. In contrast, during the same year foreign-invested enterprises accounted for 74.8 percent of industrial output in City Y, which placed City Y in the south China model; and state-owned enterprises accounted for 56.9 percent of industrial output in City Z, which placed City Z in the state-dominated model. In a handful of counties or cities where no one sector dominated industrial output (e.g., where it was roughly evenly divided among the private, state, and collective sectors), we referred to local statistics in 1990 and 1995 to identify a dominant trend during the reform era. The rationale for choosing economic indicators from both 1990 and 1995 is that 1990 represented a downturn in private sector growth, but after Deng's 1992 southern tour both the private and foreign-invested sectors saw accelerated growth in certain areas. Localities classified in the limited-development pattern were those where the level of gross value of industrial and agricultural output was at the 40th percentile of the national level or lower in 1997.

Based on these definitions, the resulting distribution of the survey sample can be seen across the five developmental patterns (table A.1). Although we did not classify all the counties and cities in the country within one of these five developmental patterns, based on our understanding of China's economic geography it is apparent that the state-dominated model is overrepresented in the sample and limited-development localities are

Table A.1. Distribution of sample across developmental patterns

Developmental pattern	N	Percentage (%)
Wenzhou model	167	11.0
Sunan model	444	29.1
South China model	148	9.7
State-dominated model	642	42.1
Limited-development model	124	8.1
Total	1,525	100

clearly underrepresented. Furthermore, as mentioned in chapter 6, these developmental patterns are neither monolithic nor static. Since the late 1990s the Sunan model has become more similar to the south China model, and the state-dominated model also presents hybrid qualities of the Sunan, south China, and limited-development patterns. In light of these imbalances in the sample, I make no claims about the distributional representation of the developmental patterns in China as a whole. Instead, the discussion in chapter 6 focuses on explaining the political-economic dynamics of private sector development within each developmental pattern.

Finally, one could object that the 40 percent decision rule (and indeed, the 40th percentile cutoff for limited development localities) based primarily on 1997 data is arbitrary and too rough for characterizing the political economy of counties and cities. Be that as it may, the empirical definitions were only meant to facilitate classification of the subprovincial localities in my particular sample and not intended to denote absolute indicators of local development. Thus, the bulk of the book's discussion on local variation relied on qualitative observations gleaned in the process of field visits and interviews. Ultimately, the quantitative figures in chapter 6 are only meant to be suggestive, which is why tests of statistical significance were not conducted on the survey data relating to the five developmental patterns.

Appendix B

List of Interviews: 2001–2005

No.	Date	County	Locality/Level	Position	Institutional type
1	1/11/2001	Beijing	City	Researcher	Research
2	1/12/2001	Beijing	City	Researcher	Research
3	1/15/2001	Wenzhou	City	Vice Director	Government
4	1/16/2001	Wenzhou	City	Vice Chair	Research
5	1/16/2001	Wenzhou	City	Staff	Government
6	1/16/2001	Wenzhou	City	Director	Government
7	1/17/2001	Ou Hai	Yongzhong Township	Owner	Private Enterprise
8	1/17/2001	Ou Hai	Yongzhong Township	Owner	Private Enterprise
9	1/17/2001	Ou Hai	Yongzhong Township	Owner	Private Enterprise
10	8/4/2001	Hong Kong	N.T.	Professor	Research
11	8/4/2001	Hong Kong	N.T.	Professor	Research
12	8/4/2001	Hong Kong	N.T.	Researcher	Research
13	8/6/2001	Hong Kong	N.T.	Professor	Research
14	8/6/2001	Hong Kong	N.T.	Researcher	Research
15	8/11/2001	Beijing	City	Researcher	Research
16	8/11/2001	Beijing	City	Researcher	Research
17	8/15/2001	Beijing	City	Researcher	Research
18	8/31/2001	Beijing	City	Director	Int'l Organization
19	9/3/2001	Beijing	City	Director	Research
20	9/5/2001	Beijing	City	Chairperson	Private Enterprise
21	9/5/2001	Beijing	City	Researcher	Research
22	9/5/2001	Beijing	City	Professor	Research
23	9/5/2001	Beijing	City	Professor	Research
24	9/6/2001	Beijing	City	Director	Research
25	9/6/2001	Beijing	City	Researcher	Research
26	9/6/2001	Beijing	City	CEO	Private Enterprise
27	9/12/2001	U.S.	Cambridge, MA	Researcher	Research
28	9/12/2001	U.S.	Cambridge, MA	Researcher	Research
29	9/26/2001	U.S.	telephone call	Researcher	Research

No.	Date	County	Locality/Level	Position	Institutional type
30	9/26/2001	U.S.	Baltimore, MD	Assoc. Professor	Research
31	9/26/2001	U.S.	Baltimore, MD	Government	Research
32	10/26/2001	Beijing	City	Government	Research
33	10/29/2001	Beijing	City	Managing Director	Foreign Business
34	10/29/2001	Beijing	City	CEO	Consulting Firm
35	10/30/2001	Beijing	City	Professor	Research
36	10/30/2001	Beijing	City	Researcher	Research
37	10/31/2001	Beijing	City	Researcher	Research
38	11/1/2001	Beijing	City	Vice Secretary	Government
39	11/1/2001	Beijing	City	Country Rep	Int'l Organization
40	11/3/2001	Beijing	City	China Strategist	Foreign Business
41	11/4/2001	Beijing	City	CEO	Private Enterprise
42	11/4/2001	Beijing	City	CEO	Int'l Bank
43	11/5/2001	Beijing	City	Journalist	Media
44	11/5/2001	Beijing	City	CEO	Private Enterprise
45	11/6/2001	Beijing	City	Economist	Int'l Bank
46	11/8/2001	Yongjia	Ou Bei Township	Director	Government
47	11/8/2001	Yongjia	Ou Bei Township	Owner	Private Enterprise
48	11/8/2001	Yongjia	Ou Bei Township	Owner	Private Enterprise
49	11/9/2001	Yongjia	Ou Bei Township	Owner	Private Enterprise
50	11/9/2001	Yongjia	Ou Bei Township	Owner	Private Enterprise
51	11/9/2001	Yongjia	Ou Bei Township	Owner	Private Enterprise
52	11/9/2001	Yongjia	Ou Bei Township	Owner	Private Enterprise
53	11/10/2001	Yongjia	Ou Bei Township	Credit Officer	Bank - ABOC
54	11/10/2001	Yongjia	Ou Bei Township	Owner	Getihu
55	11/10/2001	Yongjia	Ou Bei, Zhu Au Village	Owner	Getihu
56	11/10/2001	Yongjia	Ou Bei, Zhu Au Village	Owner	Getihu
57	11/10/2001	Yongjia	Ou Bei, Bai Shui Village	Owner	Private Enterprise
58	11/11/2001	Wenzhou	City	Academic	Research
59	11/11/2001	Wenzhou	City	Vice Editor	Research
60	11/11/2001	Wenzhou	City	Academic	Research
61	11/11/2001	Wenzhou	City	Vice Director	Research
62	11/12/2001	Wenzhou	City	Secretary Gen'l	Business Association
63	11/12/2001	Wenzhou	City	Director	Bank - PBOC
64	11/12/2001	Wenzhou	City	Director	Government
65	11/13/2001	Yongjia	Township	Vice Director	Government
66	11/14/2001	Wenzhou	City	Vice Director	Government
67	11/14/2001	Rui'an	County	Division Chief	Government
68	11/14/2001	Rui'an	County	Vice Director	Government
69	11/15/2001	Rui'an	County	Staff	Government
70	11/15/2001	Rui'an	Tangxia, Qingtou Village	Owner	Private Enterprise
71	11/15/2001	Rui'an	Tangxia Township	Vice Director	Government
72	11/15/2001	Rui'an	Tangxia Township	Owner	Private Enterprise
73	11/15/2001	Rui'an	Tangxia Township	Owner	Private Enterprise
74	11/15/2001	Rui'an	Tangxia Township	Owner	Private Enterprise
75	11/15/2001	Rui'an	Tangxia Township	Owner	Private Enterprise
76	11/15/2001	Rui'an	Tangxia Township	Owner	Private Enterprise
77	11/15/2001	Rui'an	Tangxia Township	Owner	Private Enterprise

No.	Date	County	Locality/Level	Position	Institutional type
78	11/15/2001	Rui'an	Tangxia Township	Owner	Private Enterprise
79	11/15/2001	Rui'an	Tangxia Township	Owner	Private Enterprise
80	11/15/2001	Rui'an	Tangxia Township	Owner	Private Enterprise
81	11/15/2001	Rui'an	Tangxia Township	Owner	Private Enterprise
82	11/15/2001	Rui'an	Tangxia Township	Owner	Private Enterprise
83	11/15/2001	Rui'an	Tangxia Township	Owner	Private Enterprise
84	11/15/2001	Rui'an	Tangxia Township	Owner	Private Enterprise
85	11/15/2001	Rui'an	Tangxia Township	Owner	Private Enterprise
86	11/15/2001	Rui'an	Tangxia Township	Owner	Private Enterprise
87	11/15/2001	Rui'an	Tangxia Township	Owner	Private Enterprise
88	11/15/2001	Rui'an	Tangxia Township	Owner	Private Enterprise
89	11/15/2001	Rui'an	Tangxia Township	Owner	Private Enterprise
90	11/15/2001	Rui'an	Tangxia Township	Owner	Private Enterprise
91	11/15/2001	Rui'an	Tangxia Township	Owner	Private Enterprise
92	11/15/2001	Rui'an	Tangxia Township	Owner	Private Enterprise
93	11/15/2001	Rui'an	Tangxia Township	Owner	Private Enterprise
94	11/15/2001	Rui'an	Tangxia Township	Owner	Private Enterprise
95	11/15/2001	Rui'an	Tangxia Township	Owner	Private Enterprise
96	11/15/2001	Rui'an	Tangxia Township	Owner	Private Enterprise
97	11/15/2001	Rui'an	County	Vice Mayor	Government
98	11/16/2001	Rui'an	Tangxia Township	Owner	Private Enterprise
99	11/16/2001	Rui'an	Tangxia Township	Owner	Private Enterprise
100	11/16/2001	Rui'an	Tangxia, Nanhe Village	Owner	Getihu
101	11/16/2001	Rui'an	Tangxia, Nanhe Village	Village Chief	Government
102	11/16/2001	Rui'an	Tangxia, Nanhe Village	Village Secretary	Government
103	11/16/2001	Rui'an	Tangxia Township	Staff	Government
104	11/16/2001	Rui'an	Tangxia Township	Staff	Government
105	11/17/2001	Rui'an	Tangxia, Hou Zhu Village	Owner	Getihu
106	11/17/2001	Rui'an	Tangxia, Hou Zhu Village	Owner	Private Enterprise
107	11/17/2001	Rui'an	Tangxia, Hou Zhu Village	Owner	Getihu
108	11/17/2001	Rui'an	Tangxia, Hou Zhu Village	Organizer	Hui
109	11/17/2001	Rui'an	Tangxia, Hou Zhu Village	Director	Association
110	11/19/2001	Rui'an	Bishan Township	Director	Government
111	11/19/2001	Rui'an	Bishan, Huajin Village	Owner	Private Enterprise
112	11/19/2001	Rui'an	Bishan, Hengtang Village	Owner	Getihu
113	11/19/2001	Rui'an	Bishan, Hengtang Village	Owner	Getihu
114	11/20/2001	Rui'an	County	Director	Government
115	11/20/2001	Rui'an	County	Staff	Government
116	11/20/2001	Rui'an	County	Staff	Government
117	11/20/2001	Rui'an	County	Owner	Private Enterprise
118	11/20/2001	Rui'an	County	Staff	Government
119	11/22/2001	Cangnan	Jinxiang Township	Owner	Getihu
120	11/22/2001	Cangnan	Jinxiang Township	Owner	Getihu
121	11/22/2001	Cangnan	Jinxiang Township	Owner	Private Enterprise
122	11/23/2001	Cangnan	Yanting Township	Director	RCC
123	11/23/2001	Cangnan	Yanting Township	Village Chief	Government
124	11/23/2001	Cangnan	Yanting Township	Owner	Private Enterprise

No.	Date	County	Locality/Level	Position	Institutional type
125	11/23/2001	Cangnan	Yanting Township	Owner	Private Enterprise
126	11/23/2001	Cangnan	Yanting Township	Director	Government
127	11/23/2001	Cangnan	Yanting Township	Staff	Government
128	11/23/2001	Cangnan	County	Vice Director	Government
129	11/23/2001	Cangnan	County	Director	Government
130	11/24/2001	Cangnan	Wangli Township	Vice Director	Government
131	11/24/2001	Cangnan	Wangli Township	Owner	Private Enterprise
132	11/24/2001	Cangnan	Qianku Township	Division Chief	Government
133	11/24/2001	Cangnan	Qianku Township	Gen'l Secretary	Government
134	11/26/2001	Wenzhou	City	Researcher	Government
135	11/26/2001	Wenzhou	City	Gen'l Manager	Fin'l Institution
136	11/26/2001	Wenzhou	City	Operating Mgr	Fin'l Institution
137	11/29/2001	Beijing	City	Researcher	Research
138	11/29/2001	Beijing	City	Researcher	Journalist
139	11/30/2001	Beijing	City	COO	Int'l Bank
140	11/30/2001	Beijing	City	Analyst	Int'l Bank
141	11/30/2001	Beijing	City	Analyst	Int'l Bank
142	11/30/2001	Beijing	City	Analyst	Int'l Bank
143	11/30/2001	Beijing	City	Country Director	Int'l Organization
144	12/3/2001	Washington	D.C.	Vice President	Research
145	12/3/2001	Washington	D.C.	Vice Chair	Research
146	12/3/2001	Washington	D.C.	Researcher	Research
147	8/12/2002	Beijing	City	Researcher	Research
148	8/13/2002	Beijing	City	Researcher	Research
148	8/13/2002	Beijing	City	Researcher	Research
149	8/20/2002	Langfang	Guangyang District	Vice Gen'l Sec	Government
150	8/20/2002	Langfang	Guangyang District	Director	Government
151	8/20/2002	Langfang	Guangyang District	Vice Gen'l Sec	Government
152	8/20/2002	Langfang	Guangyang District	Vice Director	Government
153	8/20/2002	Langfang	Guangyang District	Owner	Private Enterprise
154	8/20/2002	Langfang	Guangyang District	Owner	Private Enterprise
155	8/21/2002	Langfang	Guangyang District	Owner	Private Enterprise
156	8/21/2002	Langfang	Guangyang District	Owner	Getihu
157	8/22/2002	Langfang	Guangyang District	Director	Government
158	8/24/2002	Beijing	City	Journalist	Media
159	8/25/2002	Beijing	City	Journalist	Media
160	10/8/2002	Beijing	City	Researcher	Research
161	10/9/2002	Nanjing	City	Director	Government
162	10/9/2002	Nanjing	City	Manager	Government
163	10/9/2002	Jiangsu	Province	Director	Government
164	10/10/2002	Nanjing	City	President	Private Enterprise
165	10/10/2002	Nanjing	City	Gen'l Manager	Private Enterprise
166	10/10/2002	Nanjing	City	Gen'l Manager	Private Enterprise
167	10/11/2002	Nanjing	City	President	Private Enterprise
168	10/11/2002	Nanjing	City	Manager	Private Enterprise
169	10/11/2002	Nanjing	City	Staff	Research
170	10/11/2002	Nanjing	City	Professor	Research
171	10/11/2002	Chongqing	Municipality	Director	Government
172	10/12/2002	Shaanxi	Province	Director	Government

No.	Date	County	Locality/Level	Position	Institutional type
173	10/12/2002	Shangdong	Province	Researcher	Research
174	10/12/2002	Shishi	City	Researcher	Research
175	10/12/2002	Nanyang	City	Researcher	Research
176	10/12/2002	Hebei	Province	Researcher	Research
177	10/12/2002	Jiangsu	Province	Director	Government
178	10/13/2002	Huizhou	City	Vice Director	Government
179	10/13/2002	Huizhou	City	Manager	Government
180	10/13/2002	Huizhou	City	Manager	Government
181	10/14/2002	Huizhou	City	Gen'l Secretary	Government
182	10/14/2002	Bailin	Village	Gen'l Manager	Private Enterprise
183	10/14/2002	Huizhou	City	Staff	Government
184	10/14/2002	Huizhou	City	Staff	Government
185	10/14/2002	Huizhou	City	Gen'l Manager	Private Enterprise
186	10/15/2002	Huizhou	City	President	Private Enterprise
187	10/15/2002	Huizhou	City	Manager	Private Enterprise
188	10/15/2002	Huizhou	City	Gen'l Manager	Private Enterprise
189	10/15/2002	Tangquan	Township	Manager	Private Enterprise
190	10/15/2002	Tangquan	Township	Chairperson	Private Enterprise
191	10/16/2002	Huizhou	City	Gen'l Manager	Private Enterprise
192	10/16/2002	Huizhou	City	President	Private Enterprise
193	10/16/2002	Huizhou	City	Vice Secretary	Government
194	10/17/2002	Huidong	County	Director	Government
195	10/17/2002	Huangbu	Township	Director	Government
196	10/17/2002	Huangbu	Township	Director	Private Enterprise
197	10/17/2002	Jilong	Township	Vice Director	Government
198	10/17/2002	Jilong	Township	Director	Government
199	10/17/2002	Jilong	Township	Gen'l Manager	Private Enterprise
200	10/18/2002	Boluo	County	Vice Director	Government
201	10/18/2002	Longxi	Township	Staff	Government
202	10/18/2002	Longxi	Township	Vice President	Private Enterprise
203	10/18/2002	Futian	Township	President	Private Enterprise
204	10/18/2002	Futian	Township	Manager	Private Enterprise
205	10/18/2002	Futian	Township	Manager	Government
206	10/19/2002	Hubei	Province	Researcher	Research
207	10/19/2002	Hubei	Province	Staff	Research
208	10/19/2002	Hubei	Province	Researcher	Research
209	10/20/2002	Wuhan	City	Researcher	Research
210	10/20/2002	HK	SAR	Researcher	Research
211	10/21/2002	Hubei	Province	Vice Director	Government
212	10/21/2002	Wuhan	City	Vice Director	Government
213	10/21/2002	Qiaokou	District	Director	Government
214	10/21/2002	Qiaokou	District	Vice Director	Government
215	10/21/2002	Qiaokou	District	Vice Secretary	Association
216	10/21/2002	Qiaokou	District	Owner	Getihu
217	10/21/2002	Qiaokou	District	Owner	Private Enterprise
218	10/21/2002	Qiaokou	District	Staff	Association
219	10/22/2002	Wuchang	District	Secretary Gen'l	Government
220	10/22/2002	Wuchang	District	Vice President	Private Enterprise
221	10/22/2002	Wuchang	District	President	Private Enterprise

No.	Date	County	Locality/Level	Position	Institutional type
222	10/22/2002	Hankou	District	Manager	Private Enterprise
223	10/22/2002	HK	SAR	Professor	Research
224	10/23/2002	Qiaokou	District	Director	Government
225	10/23/2002	Qiaokou	District	Staff	Government
226	10/23/2002	Qiaokou	District	Owner	Getihu
227	10/23/2002	Qiaokou	District	Owner	Getihu
228	10/23/2002	Qiaokou	District	Staff	Getihu
229	10/23/2002	Qiaokou	District	Owner	Getihu
230	10/23/2002	Qiaokou	District	Owner	Getihu
231	10/24/2002	Hankou	District	Secretary Gen'l	Association
232	10/24/2002	Hankou	District	Director	Association
233	10/24/2002	Hankou	District	Director	Association
234	10/24/2002	Hankou	District	Manager	Private Enterprise
235	10/24/2002	Hankou	District	Vice Director	Government
236	10/24/2002	Hankou	District	Vice Director	Government
237	10/25/2002	Hebei	Province	Director	Association
238	10/25/2002	Hanyang	District	Owner	Private Enterprise
239	10/25/2002	Hanyang	District	Owner	Private Enterprise
240	10/25/2002	Hanyang	District	Office Manager	Private Enterprise
241	10/25/2002	Hanyang	District	Staff	Private Enterprise
242	10/26/2002	Suburb	District	Owner	Getihu
243	10/26/2002	Suburb	District	Owner	Getihu
244	10/26/2002	Suburb	District	Owner	Getihu
245	10/27/2002	Yangzhou	City	Owner	Private Enterprise
246	10/27/2002	Chengdu	City	Owner	Private Enterprise
247	10/27/2002	Chengdu	City	Owner	Private Enterprise
248	10/27/2002	Chengdu	City	Owner	Private Enterprise
249	10/29/2002	Hechuan	County	Director	Government
250	10/29/2002	Hechuan	County	Director	Government
251	10/29/2002	Hechuan	County	Vice Director	Government
252	10/29/2002	Hechuan	County	Director	Association
253	10/29/2002	Hechuan	County	Director	Association
254	10/29/2002	Hechuan	County	Owner	Private Enterprise
255	10/30/2002	Hechuan	County	Owner	Private Enterprise
256	10/30/2002	Hechuan	County	Owner	Private Enterprise
257	10/30/2002	Hechuan	County	Owner	Private Enterprise
258	10/31/2002	Hechuan	County	Owner	Getihu
259	10/31/2002	Hechuan	County	Gen'l Secretary	Association
260	10/31/2002	Hechuan	County	Director	Association
261	10/31/2002	Hechuan	County	Owner	Getihu
262	11/1/2002	Hechuan	County	Owner	Getihu
263	11/1/2002	Hechuan	County	Owner	Getihu
264	11/1/2002	Hechuan	County	Director	Government
265	11/1/2002	Hechuan	County	Director	Government
266	11/1/2002	Hechuan	County	Owner	Private Enterprise
267	11/10/2002	Shanghai	Municipality	Owner	Getihu
268	11/11/2002	Shanghai	Municipality	Journalist	Media
269	11/11/2002	Shanghai	Municipality	Manager	Private Enterprise

No.	Date	County	Locality/Level	Position	Institutional type
270	11/11/2002	Shanghai	Municipality	Staff	Foreign Business
271	11/12/2002	Shanghai	Municipality	Researcher	Research
272	11/12/2002	Shanghai	Municipality	Researcher	Research
273	11/12/2002	Shanghai	Municipality	Researcher	Research
274	11/13/2002	Shanghai	Municipality	Staff	Private Enterprise
275	11/13/2002	Shanghai	Qibao Town, Jiuxing cun	Gen'l Manager	Private Enterprise
276	11/14/2002	Shanghai	Municipality	President	Private Enterprise
277	11/14/2002	Shanghai	Municipality	Vice Gen'l Manager	Private Enterprise
278	2/6/2004	Washington	D.C.	Chairperson	Private Enterprise
279	2/11/2004	Washington	D.C.	Chairperson	Private Enterprise
280	10/9/2004	Washington	D.C.	Researcher	Government
281	10/25/2004	Washington	D.C.	Director	Government
282	11/24/2004	Washington	D.C.	Former Director	Government
283	11/24/2004	Washington	D.C.	Director	State Bank
284	10/16/2005	Beijing	Municipality	Owner	Getihu
285	10/16/2005	Beijing	Municipality	Owner	Getihu
286	10/16/2005	Beijing	Municipality	Owner	Getihu
287	10/16/2005	Beijing	Municipality	Owner	Getihu
288	10/16/2005	Beijing	Municipality	Owner	Getihu
289	10/16/2005	Beijing	Municipality	Owner	Getihu
290	10/16/2005	Beijing	Municipality	Owner	Getihu
291	10/16/2005	Beijing	Municipality	Owner	Getihu
292	10/16/2005	Beijing	Municipality	Program Officer	Int'l Organization
293	10/16/2005	Beijing	Municipality	Researcher	Research
294	10/16/2005	Beijing	Municipality	Researcher	Research
295	10/17/2005	Beijing	Municipality	Researcher	Int'l Organization
296	10/17/2005	Beijing	Municipality	Researcher	Research
297	10/18/2005	Beijing	Municipality	President	Fin'l Institution
298	10/18/2005	Beijing	Municipality	Chairperson	Private Enterprise
299	10/19/2005	Beijing	Municipality	Bureau chief	Government
300	10/20/2005	Beijing	Municipality	Director	Int'l Organization
301	10/20/2005	Beijing	Municipality	Chairperson	Private Enterprise
302	10/21/2005	Xiamen	SEZ	Vice Director	Government
303	10/21/2005	Xiamen	SEZ	Gen'l Manager	Foreign Enterprise
304	10/21/2005	Xiamen	SEZ	Managing Director	Foreign Enterprise
305	10/21/2005	Xiamen	SEZ	Manager	Foreign Enterprise
306	10/21/2005	Haicang	District	Vice Director	Government
307	10/21/2005	Xiamen	SEZ	President	Fake FIE
308	10/22/2005	Xiamen	SEZ	Policeman	Government
309	10/22/2005	Xiamen	SEZ	Director	Government
310	10/24/2005	Shanghai	Municipality	Director	SHC
311	10/25/2005	Shanghai	Municipality	Vice Director	Association
312	10/25/2005	Pudong	Municipality	Manager	Government
313	10/25/2005	Pudong	Municipality	Manager	Government
314	10/25/2005	Pudong	Municipality	Vice Manager	Government
315	10/25/2005	Shanghai	Municipality	Manager	Joint Venture
316	10/25/2005	Shanghai	Municipality	Gen'l Manager	Private Enterprise
317	10/26/2005	Shanghai	Municipality	Owner	Private Enterprise

Glossary of Chinese Terms

Pinyin	Chinese	English
banshichu	办事处	work affairs office
boxue jieji	剥削阶级	exploiting class
canzheng yizheng	参政议政	participate in politics
chengshi shangye yinhang	城市商业银行	urban commercial bank
chunhunxie	春昏鞋	morning to evening shoes
dai hong maozi	戴红帽子	wearing a red hat
dianshi daxue	电视大学	television college
dianxing	典型	model or emblematic
dier ci chuangye	第二次创业	Second Pioneering Initiative
dixia qianzhuang	地下钱庄	underground money house
fei gongyou fazhan ju	非公有发展局	Bureau for the Development of the Nonpublic Economy
gaizhi	改制	restructuring (of public enterprises)
geju	格局	style or pattern
getihu	个体户	individual entrepreneur
geti laodongzhe xiehui	个体劳动者协会	Individual Laborers Association
geweihui	革委会	Revolutionary Committee
gongshang guanliju	工商管理局	Industrial and Commercial Management Bureau

guahu qiye	挂户企业	hang-on enterprise
guanxi	关系	relationship
gufenhua	股份化	corporatization
jia yangguizi	假洋鬼子	fake foreign devils (fake foreign enterprises)
jianshi juzhu	监视居住	house arrest
jingji fazhan bangongshi	经济发展办公室	Economic Development Office
Jinxiang jinrong fuwushe	金乡金融服务社	Jinxiang Financial Service Society
Jiusan xueshe	九三学社	Jiu San Society or 3rd of September Society
laoren xiehui	老人协会	old folks association
lizhi	离职	leave work temporarily
luan zhifa	乱执法	arbitrary legal enforcement
min'nan	闽南	southern Fujian
minying qiye	民营企业	civilian-run enterprise
minzhu dangpai	民主党派	democratic party group
moshi	模式	model
qiongmin dang	穷民党	a (political) party for poor people
quanguo gongshang lian	全国工商联	All-China Federation of Industry and Commerce
quanmin dang	全民党	a (political) party for all the people
quanqian jiaoyi	权钱交易	power-money exchanges
renqing feiyong	人情费用	cost of friendship
san luan	三乱	Three Chaoses (arbitrary extraction)
shehui tuanti	社会团体	social organization
shuiguo fei	水果费	fruit fees (donations)
siying qiye	私营企业	private enterprise
siying qiyejia xiehui	私营企业家协会	Private Entrepreneurs Association
siyouhua	私有化	privatization
Sunan	苏南	southern Jiangsu
Taiwan minzhu zizhi tongmeng (Taimeng)	台湾民主自治同盟	Taiwan Democratic Self-Government League
tiaojie shu	调解书	written confession
tingxin liuzhi	停薪留职	retain one's position with one's salary suspended
tizhi	体制	system (as in political system)

Wuhanshi gongshanglian zhongbiao yanjing tongye shanghui	武汉市工商联钟表 眼镜 同业商会	Wuhan City Federation of Industry and Commerce Watch and Glasses Business Association
wujin	五金	five metals (gold, sliver, copper, iron, tin)
xiahai	下海	jump into the sea (of the private sector)
xietiao jiejue	协调解决	compromise solutions
xunzu xingwei	寻租行为	rent-seeking behavior
yishu sheji yanjiusuo	艺术设计研究所	Art Design Research Institute
zhongcaiwei	仲裁委	arbitration committee
Zhongguo guomindang geming weiyuanhui (mingge)	中国国民党革命委员会	China Revolutionary Committee of the Guomingdang
Zhongguo minzhu cujinhui (minjin)	中国民主促进会	China Association for Promoting Democracy
Zhongguo minzhu jianguohui (minjian)	中国民主建国会	China Democratic National Construction Association
Zhongguo minzhu tongmeng (minmeng)	中国民主同盟	China Democratic League
Zhongguo nonggong minzhudang (nonggong)	中国农工民主党	Chinese Peasants and Workers Democratic Party
Zhongguo zhigong dang	中国致公党	China Zhi Gong Party or Public Interest Party
zhuada fangxiao	抓大放小	retaining the large, releasing the small
zhuanye hu	专业户	specialized household
Zhujiang	珠江	Pearl River Delta in Guangdong

References

Abercrombie, Nicolas, and John Urry. 1983. *Capital, Labour and the Middle Classes.* London: George Allen and Unwin.

Adelman, Jonathan. 2001. "Why We Should Be Pleased China Landed the Olympics." *Rocky Mountain News,* July 19, 41A.

Almond, Gabriel, and Sidney Verba. 1963. *The Civic Culture.* Princeton: Princeton University Press.

American Society for Competitiveness. 2002. "The Middle Class Bridge: Determinate of Business and Societal Success or Failure." *Global Competitiveness* 10, no. 2: S173.

Amsden, Alice. 1992. *Asia's Next Giant: South Korea and Late Industrialization.* New York: Oxford University Press.

Anderson, Lisa, ed. 1999. *Transitions to Democracy.* New York: Columbia University Press.

Arthur, Brian. 1994. *Increasing Returns and Path Dependence in the Economy.* Ann Arbor: University of Michigan Press.

Ash, Robert F., and Y. Y. Kueh. 1993. "Economic Integration within Greater China: Trade and Investment Flows between China, Hong Kong, and Taiwan." *China Quarterly* 136: 711–745.

Barnett, A. Doak. 1964. *Communist China: The Early Years, 1949–1955.* New York: Praeger.

Barr, Michael D. 2000. *Lee Kuan Yew: The Beliefs behind the Man.* Washington, D.C.: Georgetown University Press.

Barthes, Roland. 1972. *Mythologies.* Trans. by Annette Lavers. New York: Hill and Wang.

Bates, Robert. 1988. "Contra Contractarianism: Some Reflections on New Institutionalism." *Politics and Society* 16, nos. 2–3: 387–401.

Baum, Richard. 1994. *Burying Mao: Chinese Politics in the Age of Deng Xiaoping.* Princeton: Princeton University Press.

Baum, Richard, and Alexei Shevchenko. 1999. "The 'State of the State.'" In *The Paradox of Post-Mao Reforms,* edited by Merle Goldman and Roderick MacFarquhar, 333–360. Cambridge: Harvard University Press, Contemporary China Series.

Beblawi, Hazem, and Giacomo Luciano, eds. 1987. *The Rentier State.* London: Croom Helm.

Bellin, Eva. 2000. "Contingent Democrats: Industrialists, Labor, and Democratization in Late-Developing Countries." *World Politics* 52, no. 2: 175–205.

———. 2002. *Stalled Democracy: Capital, Labor, and the Paradox of State-Sponsored Development.* Ithaca: Cornell University Press.

———. 2004. "The Robustness of Authoritarianism in the Middle East: Exceptionalism in Comparative Perspective." *Comparative Politics* 36, no. 2: 139–157.

Berman, Sheri. 2001. "Ideas, Norms, and Culture in Political Analysis (Review Article)." *Comparative Politics* 33, no. 2: 231–250.

Bernstein, Thomas P., and Xiaobo Lü. 2003. *Taxation without Representation in Rural China.* New York: Cambridge University Press.

Bianco, Lucien. 2001. *Peasants without the Party: Grass-roots Movements in Twentieth-Century China.* Armonk, N.Y.: M. E. Sharpe.

Blackbourn, David, and Geoff Eley. 1984. *The Peculiarities of German History: Bourgeois Society and Politics in Nineteenth-Century Germany.* Oxford: Oxford University Press.

Blecher, Marc. 1991. "Developmental State, Entrepreneurial State: The Political Economy of Socialist Reform in Xinji Municipality and Guanghan County." In *The Chinese State in the Era of Economic Reform: The Road to Crisis,* edited by Gordon White, 265–291. Armonk, N.Y.: M. E. Sharpe.

Blecher, Marc, and Vivienne Shue. 2001. "Into Leather: State-Led Development and the Private Sector in Xinji." *China Quarterly* 166: 368–393.

Blyth, Mark. 2002. *Great Transformations: Economic Ideas and Institutional Change in the Twentieth Century.* New York: Cambridge University Press.

Bonnell, Victoria E., and Thomas B. Gold, eds. 2002. *The New Entrepreneurs of Europe and Asia: Patterns of Business Development in Russia, Eastern Europe, and China.* Armonk, N.Y.: M. E. Sharpe.

Böröcz, József. 2000. "Informality Rules." *East European Politics and Societies* 14, no. 2: 348–380.

Bourdieu, Pierre. 1985. "Social Space and the Genesis of Groups." *Theory and Society* 14, no. 6: 723–744.

———. 1990. *The Logic of Practice.* Stanford: Stanford University Press.

Bourdieu, Pierre, and Loïc J. D. Wacquant. 1992. *An Invitation to Reflexive Sociology.* Chicago: University of Chicago Press.

Bratton, Michael, and Nicolas van de Walle, eds. 1997. *Democratic Experiments in Africa: Regime Transitions in Comparative Perspective.* New York: Cambridge University Press.

Brenner, Robert. 1993. *Merchants and Revolution: Commercial Change, Political Conflict, and London's Overseas Traders, 1550–1653.* New York: Cambridge University Press.

Brownlee, Jason. 2002. ". . . And Yet They Persist: Explaining Survival and Transition in Neopatrimonial Regimes." *Studies in Comparative International Development* 37, no. 3: 35–63.

Bruun, Ole. 1988. *Business and Bureaucracy in a Chinese City: The Ethnography of Individual Business Households in Contemporary China.* Berkeley: University of California, Institute of East Asian Studies.

Bueno de Mesquita, Bruce, and George W. Downs. 2005. "Development and Democracy." *Foreign Affairs* 84, no. 5: 77–86.

Bunce, Valerie. 2000. "Comparative Democratization: Big and Bounded Generalizations." *Comparative Political Studies* 33, nos. 6–7: 699–702.

———. 2003. "Rethinking Recent Democratization: Lessons from the Postcommunist Experience." *World Politics* 55, no. 2: 167–192.

Byrd, William A., and Alan Gelb. 1990. "Why Industrialize? The Incentives for Rural

Community Governments." In *China's Rural Industry: Structure, Development, and Reform,* edited by William Byrd and Lin Qingsong, 358–388. New York: Oxford University Press.

——. 2001. "Township, Village and Private Industry in China's Economic Reform." In *Growth without Miracles: Readings on the Chinese Economy in the Era of Reform,* edited by Ross Garnaut and Yiping Huang, 170–188. New York: Oxford University Press.

Byrd, William, and Qingsong Lin. 1990. "Research Design, Methodology, and Data." In *China's Rural Industry: Structure, Development, and Reform,* edited by William Byrd and Lin Qingsong, 19–40. New York: Oxford University Press.

Campbell, John L. 2004. *Institutional Change and Globalization.* Princeton: Princeton University Press.

Chan, Alfred L. 2001. *Mao's Crusade: Politics and Policy Implementation in the Great Leap Forward.* Oxford: Oxford University Press.

Chan, Anita. 2001. *China's Workers under Assault: The Exploitation of Labor in a Globalizing Economy.* Armonk, N.Y.: M. E. Sharpe.

Chan, Anita, and Jonathan Unger. 1982. "Grey and Black: The Hidden Economy of Rural China." *Pacific Affairs* 55, no. 3: 452–471.

Chaudhry, Kiren. 1994. "Economic Liberalization and the Lineages of the Rentier State." *Comparative Politics* 27, no. 1: 1–25.

Chehabi, H. E., and Juan J. Linz, eds. 1998. *Sultanistic Regimes.* Baltimore: Johns Hopkins University Press.

Chen, An. 2002. "Capitalist Development, Entrepreneurial Class, and Democratization in China." *Political Science Quarterly* 117, no. 3: 401–422.

Cheng, Tiejun, and Mark Selden. 1997. "The Construction of Spatial Hierarchies: China's *Hukou* and *Danwei* Systems." In *New Perspectives on State Socialism in China,* edited by Timothy Cheek and Tony Saich, 23–50. Armonk, N.Y.: M. E. Sharpe.

Chow, Ching-wen. 1960. *Ten Years of Storm: The True Story of the Communist Regime in China.* Westport, Conn.: Greenwood Press.

Collier, David, and Ruth Berins Collier. 1991. *Shaping the Political Arena: Critical Junctures, the Labor Movement, and Regime Dynamics in Latin America.* Princeton: Princeton University Press.

Collier, David, and Steven Levitsky. 1997. "Democracy with Adjectives: Conceptual Innovation in Comparative Research." *World Politics* 49, no. 3: 430–452.

Collier, Ruth Berins. 1999. *Paths toward Democracy: The Working Class and Elites in Western Europe and South America.* New York: Cambridge University Press.

Colomer, Josep. 2000. *Strategic Transitions: Game Theory and Democratization.* Baltimore: Johns Hopkins University Press.

Connolly, William E. 2004. "Method, Problem, Faith." In *Problems and Methods in the Study of Politics,* edited by Ian Shapiro, Rogers M. Smith, and Tarek E. Masoud, 332–349. New York: Cambridge University Press.

Dahl, Robert A. 1961. *Who Governs? Democracy and Power in an American City.* New Haven: Yale University Press.

David, Paul. 1985. "Clio and the Economics of QWERTY." *American Economic Review* 75: 332–337.

de Bary, Wm. Theodore, and Weiming Tu, eds. 1998. *Confucianism and Human Rights.* New York: Columbia University Press.

Deng, Yuwen. 2003. "San da moshi: shutu er tonggui" [Three big models: Reaching the same goal by different routes]. *Zhongguo jingji kuaisu zhoukan* [Quick weekly news on the Chinese economy], 39.

de Soto, Hernando. 1989. *The Other Path: The Invisible Revolution in the Third World.* New York: Harper and Row.

Diamond, Larry. 1999. *Developing Democracy: Toward Consolidation.* Baltimore: Johns Hopkins University Press.

——. 2002. "Elections without Democracy: Thinking about Hybrid Regimes." *Journal of Democracy* 13, no. 2: 21–35.

Diamond, Larry, and Raymond H. Myers, eds. 2001. *Elections and Democracy in Greater China.* New York: Oxford University Press.

Diamond, Larry, and Marc F. Plattner, eds. 1996. *The Global Resurgence of Democracy.* Baltimore: Johns Hopkins University Press.

——. 1998. *Democracy in East Asia.* Baltimore: Johns Hopkins University Press.

Dickson, Bruce J. 2000. "Co-optation and Corporatism in China: The Logic of Party Adaptation." *Political Science Quarterly* 115, no. 4: 517–540.

——. 2002. "Do Good Businessmen Make Good Citizens? An Emerging Collective Identity among China's Private Entrepreneurs." In *Changing Meanings of Citizenship in Modern China,* edited by Elizabeth J. Perry and Merle Goldman, 255–287. Cambridge: Harvard University Press.

——. 2003. *Red Capitalists in China: The Party, Private Entrepreneurs, and the Prospects for Political Change.* New York: Cambridge University Press.

Ding, X. L. 1994. "Institutional Amphibiousness and the Transition from Communism: The Case of China." *British Journal of Political Science* 24, no. 3: 293–318.

——. 1999. "Who Gets What, How? When Chinese State-Owned Enterprises Become Shareholding Companies." *Problems of Post-Communism* 46, no. 3: 32–41.

——. 2000. "Informal Privatization through Internationalization: The Rise of Nomenklatura Capitalism in China's Offshore Businesses." *British Journal of Political Science* 30: 121–146.

——. 2001. "The Illicit Asset Stripping of Chinese State Firms." *China Journal* 43: 1–28.

Di Palma, Giuseppe. 1990. *To Craft Democracies: An Essay on Democratic Transitions.* Berkeley: University of California Press.

Domenach, Jean-Luc. 1995. *The Origins of the Great Leap Forward: The Case of One Chinese Province.* Translated by A.M. Berrett. Boulder: Westview Press.

Dong, Furen. 2004. "Sunan moshi de zhongjiezhe" [Termination of the Sunan model]. *Economic Information Daily,* April 23.

Duckett, Jane. 1998. *The Entrepreneurial State in China: Real Estate and Commerce Departments in Reform Era Tianjin.* London: Routledge.

Easton, David. 1965. *A Systems Analysis of Political Life.* New York: Wiley.

Eckert, Carter J. 1993. "The South Korean Bourgeoisie: A Class in Search of Hegemony." In *State and Society in Contemporary Korea,* edited by Hagen Koo, 95–130. Ithaca: Cornell University Press.

Esherick, Joseph W., and Jeffrey N. Wasserstrom. 1994. "Acting Out Democracy: Political Theater in Modern China." In *Popular Protest and Political Culture in Modern China,* edited by Jeffrey N. Wasserstrom and Elizabeth J. Perry, 28–66. Boulder: Westview Press.

Evans, Peter. 1995. *Embedded Autonomy: States and Industrial Transformation.* Princeton: Princeton University Press.

Fang, Chixiong. 2004. "'Quanzhou moshi,' ni neng zou duoyuan?" ["Quanzhou model," how far can you go?]. *Jingji xinxi* [Economic information], August 13.

Farrell, Henry, and Adrienne Héritier. 2002. "Formal and Informal Institutions under Codecision: Continuous Constitution Building in Europe." *European Integration online Papers (EIoP)* 6, no. 3 at http://eiop.or.at/eiop/texte/2002-003a.htm.

Fei, Xiaotong. 1986. *Small Towns in China: Functions, Problems, and Prospects.* Beijing: New World Press.

Feige, Edgar L. 1997. "Underground Activity and Institutional Change: Productive, Protective, and Predatory Behavior in Transition Economies." In *Transforming Post-Communist Political Economies*, edited by Joan M. Nelson, Charles Tilly, and Lee Walker, 21–34. Washington, D.C.: National Academy Press.

Fewsmith, Joseph. 1994. *Dilemmas of Reform in China: Political Conflict and Economic Debate.* Armonk, N.Y.: M. E. Sharpe.

——. 2001a. *China since Tiananmen: Politics of Transition.* New York: Cambridge University Press.

——. 2001b. *Elite Politics in Contemporary China.* Armonk, N.Y.: M. E. Sharpe.

——. 2002. "Rethinking the Role of the CCP: Explicating Jiang Zemin's Party Anniversary Speech." *China Leadership Monitor* 1, pt. 2: 1–11.

——. 2005. "Chambers of Commerce in Wenzhou and the Potential Limits of 'Civil Society' in China." *China Leadership Monitor* 16: 1–9.

Forster, Keith. 1990–91. "The Wenzhou Model for Economic Development: Impressions." *China Information* 5, no. 3: 53–62.

Foster, Kenneth W. 2002. "Embedded within the Bureaucracy: Business Associations in Yantai." *China Journal* 47: 41–65.

Frydman, Roman, Kenneth Murphy, and Andrzej Rapaczyinski. 1998. *Capitalism with a Comrade's Face.* Budapest: Central European University Press.

Frye, Timothy. 2002. "The Perils of Polarization: Economic Performance in the Postcommunist World." *World Politics* 54, no. 3: 308–337.

Fukuyama, Francis. 1992. *The End of History and the Last Man.* New York: Free Press.

Garnaut, Ross, Ligang Song, Stoyan Tenev, and Yang Yao. 2005. *China's Ownership Transformation: Process, Outcomes, Prospects.* Washington, D.C.: International Finance Corporation and the International Bank for Reconstruction and Development (World Bank).

Ge, Wei. 1999. *Special Economic Zones and the Economic Transition in China.* River Edge, N.J.: World Scientific Press.

Geertz, Clifford. 1973. *The Interpretation of Cultures.* New York: Basic Books.

Giddens, Anthony. 1976. *New Rules of Sociological Method: A Positive Critique of Interpretive Sociologies.* New York: Basic Books.

——. 1986. *The Constitution of Society: Outline of a Theory of Structuration.* Berkeley: University of California Press.

Giles, John, Albert Park, and Fang Cai. 2006. "How Has Economic Restructuring Affected China's Workers?" *China Quarterly* 185: 61–95.

Gilley, Bruce. 2004. *China's Democratic Future: How It Will Happen and Where It Will Lead.* New York: Columbia University Press.

Glassman, Ronald M. 1991. *China in Transition: Communism, Capitalism, and Democracy.* New York: Praeger.

Gold, Thomas B. 1989. "Urban Private Business in China." *Studies in Comparative Communism* 22: 187–201.

——. 1990. "Urban Private Business and Social Change." In *Chinese Society on the Eve of Tiananmen: The Impact of Reform*, edited by Deborah Davis and Ezra F. Vogel, 155–178. Cambridge: Harvard University Press.

Gold, Thomas B., Doug Guthrie, and David Wank, eds. 2002. *Social Connections in China: Institutions, Culture, and the Changing Nature of Guanxi.* New York: Cambridge University Press.

Goldman, Merle. 2005. *From Comrade to Citizen: The Struggle for Political Rights in China.* Cambridge: Harvard University Press.

Goldman, Merle, and Roderick MacFarquhar, eds. 1999. *The Paradox of Post-Mao Reforms.* Cambridge: Harvard University Press, Harvard Contemporary China Series.

Gong, Shiqi. 1988. "Economic Features of the Primary Stage of Socialism." *Beijing Review* (February 15–28): 18–21.

Gong, Xiaoxia, and Andrew J. Walder. 1993. "Workers in the Tiananmen Protests: The Politics of the Beijing Workers' Autonomous Federation." *Australian Journal of China Affairs* 29: 1–30.

Goodman, David S. G. 1995. "Collectives and Connectives, Capitalism and Corporatism: Structural Change in China." *Journal of Communist and Transition Studies* 11, no. 1: 12–32.

———. 1996. "The People's Republic of China: The Party-State, Capitalist Revolution and New Entrepreneurs." In *The New Rich in Asia: Mobile Phones, McDonald's and Middle-Class Revolution,* edited by Richard Robison and David S. G. Goodman, 225–242. New York: Routledge.

———. 1999. "The New Middle Class." In *The Paradox of China's Post-Mao Reforms,* edited by Merle Goldman and Roderick MacFarquhar, 241–261. Cambridge: Harvard University Press, Harvard Contemporary China Series.

Goodman, David S. G., and Richard Robison, eds. 1996. *The New Rich in Asia: Mobile Phones, McDonald's and the Middle-Class Revolution.* London: Routledge.

Gourevitch, Peter. 1986. *Politics in Hard Times.* Ithaca: Cornell University Press.

Greif, Avner, and David Laitin. 2004. "A Theory of Endogenous Institutional Change." *American Political Science Review* 98, no. 4: 633–652.

Gries, Peter Hays, and Stanley Rosen, eds. 2004. *State and Society in 21st Century China: Crisis, Contention, and Legitimation.* New York: Routledge.

Grusky, David B., and Kim A. Weeden. 2001. "Decomposition without Death: A Research Agenda for a New Class Analysis." *Acta Sociologica* 44: 203–218.

Grzymala-Busse, Anna. 2004. *Redeeming the Communist Past: The Regeneration of the Communist Successor Parties in East Central Europe.* Cambridge: Cambridge University Press.

Guo, Xiaolin. 1999. "The Role of Local Government in Creating Property Rights: A Comparison of Two Townships in Northwest Yunnan." In *Property Rights and Economic Reform in China,* edited by Jean C. Oi and Andrew Walder, 71–94. Stanford: Stanford University Press.

Guo, Xiaoqin. 2003. *State and Society in China's Democratic Transition: Confucianism, Leninism, and Economic Development.* New York: Routledge.

Guo, Zhiyi. 2003. "Wo guo gongyehua, xiandaihua de moshi bijiao" [A comparison of our country's industrialization and modernization models]. *Zhongguo jingji shibao* [China economic times], January 7.

Guthrie, Doug. 1999. *Dragon in a Three-Piece Suit: The Emergence of Capitalism in China.* Princeton: Princeton University Press.

Hacker, Jacob S. 2004. "Privatizing Risk without Privatizing the Welfare State: The Hidden Politics of Social Policy Retrenchment in the United States." *American Political Science Review* 98, no. 2: 243–260.

Haggard, Stephan, and Robert Kaufman. 1995. *The Political Economy of Democratic Transitions.* Princeton: Princeton University Press.

Hagopian, Frances. 1990. "Democracy by Undemocratic Means? Elites, Political Pacts, and Regime Transition in Brazil." *Comparative Political Studies* 23, no. 2: 147–170.

———. 1993. "After Regime Change: Authoritarian Legacies, Political Representation, and the Democratic Future of South America." *World Politics* 45, no. 3: 464–500.

Harrison, Lawrence E., and Samuel P. Huntington, eds. 2000. *Culture Matters: How Values Shape Human Progress.* New York: Basic Books.

Hay, Colin. 1999. "Crisis and the Structural Transformation of the State: Interrogating Processes of Change." *British Journal of Politics and International Relations* I, no. 3: 317–344.

He, Baogang. 1996. *The Democratization of China.* New York: Routledge.

He, Qinglian. 1998. *Xiandaihua de xianjing* [Pitfalls of modernization]. Beijing: Jinri zhongguo chubanshe.

Heberer, Thomas. 2003. *Private Entrepreneurs in China and Vietnam: Social and Political Functioning of Strategic Groups.* Leiden: Brill.

Helmke, Gretchen, and Steven Levitsky. 2004. "Informal Institutions and Comparative Politics: A Research Agenda." *Perspectives on Politics* 2, no. 4: 725–740.

——, eds. 2006. *Informal Institutions and Democracy: Lessons from Latin America.* Baltimore: Johns Hopkins University Press.

Hershkovitz, Linda. 1985. "The Fruits of Ambivalence: China's Urban Individual Economy." *Pacific Affairs* 58, no. 3: 427–450.

Heydemann, Steven. 1999. *Authoritarianism in Syria: Institutions and Social Conflict, 1946–1970.* Ithaca: Cornell University Press.

Hinnebusch, Raymond. 2004. "The Viability of Authoritarian Rule in the Middle East: An Overview and Critique of Theory." *Mafhoum Press and Studies Review,* January 14. Available from http://www.mafhoum.com.

Hirschman, Albert O. 1970. *Exit, Voice, and Loyalty.* Cambridge: Harvard University Press.

Hong, Zhaohui. 2004. "Mapping the Evolution and Transformation of the New Private Entrepreneurs in China." *Journal of Chinese Political Science* 9, no. 1: 23–42.

Howe, Carolyn. 1992. *Political Ideology and Class Formation: A Study of the Middle Class.* New York: Praeger.

Howe, Christopher, ed. 1981. *Shanghai: Revolution and Development in an Asian Metropolis.* New York: Cambridge University Press.

Hsing, You-tien. 1998. *Making Capitalism in China: The Taiwan Connection.* New York: Oxford University Press.

Hu, Shaohua. 2000. *Explaining Chinese Democratization.* Westport, Conn.: Praeger.

Huang, Chonghu, ed. 1993. *Wenzhou huojiang jinrong lunwen huicui* [Compilation of essays on Wenzhou's financial riches]. Zhejiang: Zhejiang daxue chubanshe.

Huang, Weiting. 1996. "Getisiying jingji he yinxing jingji" [Privately owned economy and the hidden economy]. In *Zhongguo de yinxing jingji* [China's hidden economy], 89–120. Beijing: Zhongguo shangye chubanshe.

Huang, Yasheng. 2003. *Selling China: Foreign Direct Investment during the Reform Era.* New York: Cambridge University Press.

——. 2004. "Ownership Biases and FDI in China: Evidence from Two Provinces." Unpublished paper. September. Sloan School of Management, MIT.

——. 2005. "Government and Economy: Economic Policymaking in China during the Reform Era." Unpublished paper. Sloan School of Management, MIT.

Human Rights Watch. 2002. *Paying the Price: Worker Unrest in Northeast China.* Vol. 14, no. 6. New York: Human Rights Watch.

Humphrey, Caroline. 2002. *The Unmaking of Soviet Life: Everyday Economies after Socialism.* Ithaca: Cornell University Press.

Huntington, Samuel P. 1968. *Political Order in Changing Societies.* New Haven: Yale University Press.

——. 1991. *The Third Wave: Democratization in the Late Twentieth Century*. Norman: University of Oklahoma Press.

Hurst, William. 2004. "Understanding Contentious Collective Action by Chinese Laid-Off Workers: The Importance of Regional Political Economy." *Studies in Comparative International Development* 39, no. 2: 94–120.

Hurst, William, and Kevin J. O'Brien. 2002. "China's Contentious Pensioners." *China Quarterly* 170: 345–360.

Information Office of the State Council. 2004. "China's Employment Situation and Policies." White Paper, April 26.

Jeans, Roger B., ed. 1992. *Roads Not Taken: The Struggle of Opposition Parties in Twentieth-Century China*. Boulder: Westview.

Jefferson, Gary H., and Su Jian. 2005. "Privatization and Restructuring in China: Evidence from Shareholding Ownership, 1995–2001." Unpublished paper, January 25. Brandeis University and Peking University.

Jessop, Bob. 2001. "Institutional (Re)Turns and the Strategic-Relational Approach." *Environment and Planning* 33, no. 7: 1213–1235.

Johnson, Chalmers. 1982. *MITI and the Japanese Miracle*. Stanford: Stanford University Press.

Johnson, Graham E. 1994. "Open for Business, Open to the World: Consequences of Global Incorporation in Guangdong and the Pearl River Delta." In *The Economic Transformation of South China*, edited by Thomas P. Lyons and Victor Nee, 55–88. Ithaca: Cornell East Asia Program.

Kanamori, Toshiki, and Zhijun Zhao. 2004. *Private Sector Development in the People's Republic of China*. Manila: Asian Development Bank Institute.

Kane, Edward J. 1981. "Impact of Regulation on Economic Behavior: Accelerating Inflation, Technological Innovation, and the Decreasing Effectiveness of Banking Regulation." *Journal of Finance* 36, no. 2: 355–371.

——. 1988. "Interaction of Financial and Regulatory Innovation." *American Economic Review* 78: 328–334.

Katzenstein, Peter J. 1985. *Small States in World Markets: Industrial Policy in Europe*. Ithaca: Cornell University Press.

Katznelson, Ira. 1986. "Working-Class Formation: Constructing Cases and Comparisons." In *Working-Class Formation*, edited by Ira Katznelson and Aristide Zolberg, 3–41. Princeton: Princeton University Press.

Kedourie, Elie. 1994. *Democracy and Arab Political Culture*. London: Frank Cass.

Keller, William W., and Richard J. Samuels, eds. 2003. *Crisis and Innovation in Asian Technology*. Ithaca: Cornell University Press.

Kelliher, Daniel. 1993. *Peasant Power: The Era of Rural Reform, 1979–1999*. New Haven: Yale University Press.

Kennedy, Scott. 2005. *The Business of Lobbying in China*. Cambridge: Harvard University Press.

Kerkvliet, Benedict J. Tria. 2005. *The Power of Everyday Politics: How Vietnamese Peasants Transformed National Policy*. Ithaca: Cornell University Press.

Kim, Sunhyuk. 2000. *The Politics of Democratization in Korea: The Role of Civil Society*. Pittsburgh: University of Pittsburgh Press.

King, Charles. 2000. "Post-Postcommunism: Transition, Comparison, and the End of 'Eastern Europe.'" *World Politics* 53, no. 1: 143–172.

Kirchheimer, Otto. 1988 [1941]. "Changes in the Structure of Political Compromise." In *The Essential Frankfurt School Reader*, edited by Andrew Arato and Eike Gebhardt, 49–70. New York: Continuum.

Kitschelt, Herbert. 1993. "Comparative Historical Research and Rational Choice Theory: The Case of Transitions to Democracy." *Theory and Society* 22, no. 3: 413–427.

Koo, Hagen. 1991. "Middle Classes, Democratization, and Class Formation." *Theory and Society* 20: 485–509.

———. 2001. *Korean Workers: The Culture and Politics of Class Formation.* Ithaca: Cornell University Press.

Krasner, Stephen D. 1984. "Approaches to the State: Alternative Conceptions and Historical Dynamics." *Comparative Politics* 16, no. 2: 223–246.

Kraus, Richard Curt. 1977. "Class Conflict and the Vocabulary of Social Analysis in China." *China Quarterly* 69: 54–74.

Kraus, Willy. 1991. *Private Business in China: Revival between Ideology and Pragmatism.* Translated by Erich Holz. Honolulu: University of Hawaii Press.

Krug, Barbara, ed. 2004. *China's Rational Entrepreneurs: The Development of the New Private Business Sector.* New York: RoutledgeCurzon.

Kung, James Kai-sing. 1999. "The Evolution of Property Rights in Village Enterprises: The Case of Wuxi County." In *Property Rights and Economic Reform in China*, edited by Jean C. Oi and Andrew G. Walder, 95–120. Stanford: Stanford University Press.

Lakoff, George, and Mark Johnson. 2003. *Metaphors We Live By.* 2nd ed. Chicago: University of Chicago Press.

Lam, Ricky, and Leonard Wantchekon. 2003. "Political Dutch Disease." Unpublished manuscript. April 10. Northwestern University and New York University.

Lampton, David M., ed. 1987. *Policy Implementation in Post-Mao China.* Berkeley: University of California Press.

Lardy, Nicholas R. 1995. "The Role of Foreign Trade and Investment in China's Economic Transformation." *China Quarterly* 144: 1065–1082.

———. 1998. *China's Unfinished Economic Revolution.* Washington, D.C.: Brookings Institution.

———. 2002. *Integrating China into the Global Economy.* Washington, D.C.: Brookings Institution.

Lauth, Hans-Joachim. 2000. "Informal Institutions and Democracy." *Democratization* 7, no. 4: 21–50.

Lever-Tracy, Constance, David Ip, and Noel Tracy. 1996. *The Chinese Diaspora and Mainland China.* New York: Macmillan.

Levi, Margaret. 1990. "A Logic of Institutional Change." In *The Limits of Rationality*, edited by K. S. Cook and M. Levi, 402–418. Chicago: University of Chicago Press.

Li, Cheng. 2001. *China's Leaders: The New Generation.* Lanham, Md.: Rowman and Littlefield.

Li, Chengrui. 1997. "Dangqian jingji chengfenlei he suoyouzhi goucheng de tongji wenti" [Current statistical issues for economic sector classification and ownership composition]. *Jingji yanjiu* [Economic research] 7: 63–67.

Li, Ding, and Baoshan Ye. 1993. *Record of Major Events in the China National United Front Chamber of Commerce.* Beijing: Zhongguo gongshang lianhe chubanshe.

Li, Lianjiang. 2004. "Political Trust in Rural China." *Modern China* 30, no. 2: 228–258.

Li, Si-ming. 2000. "China's Changing Spatial Disparities: A Review of Empirical Evidence." In *China's Regions, Polity, and Economy: A Study of Spatial Transformation in the Post-Reform Era*, edited by Si-ming Li and Wing-shing Tang, 155–185. Hong Kong: Chinese University Press.

Li, Yan. 2005. "Qieshi jiaqiang fei gongyouzhi jingji zhuzhi dangjian gongzuo buduan guangda dang de gongzuo de fugai mian [Work practically to expand continuously and build Party branches in non-public economic organizations]." In Zhonghua renmin gongheguo guojia gongshang xingzheng guanli zongju [SAIC], *Zhongguo siying jingji nianjian 2002–2004* [China private economy yearbook]. Beijing: Zhonghua gongshang lianhe chubanshe.

Li, Yun, et al. 1989. *Diankuang de she nian zhixia* [The tumultuous summer of the year of the snake]. Beijing: Guofang keji daxue chubanshe.

Lieberman, Robert C. 2002. "Ideas, Institutions, and Political Order: Explaining Political Change." *American Political Science Review* 96, no. 4: 697–712.

Lieberthal, Kenneth G., and David M. Lampton, eds. 1992. *Bureaucracy, Politics, and Decision-Making in Post-Mao China.* Berkeley: University of California Press.

Lieberthal, Kenneth G., and Michael Oksenberg. 1988. *Policy Making in China: Leaders, Structures, and Processes.* Princeton: Princeton University Press.

Liebowitz, S. J., and Stephen E. Margolis. 1990. "The Fable of the Keys." *Journal of Law and Economics* 33: 1–25.

Lin, Nan. 1995. "Local Market Socialism: Local Corporatism in Action in Rural China" *Theory and Society* 24: 301–354.

Lin, Yi-min, and Tian Zhu. 2001. "Ownership Restructuring in Chinese State Industry: An Analysis of Evidence on Initial Organizational Change." *China Quarterly* 166: 305–341.

Lindblom, Charles. 1977. *Politics and Markets: The World's Political-Economic Systems.* New York: Basic Books.

Lingle, Christopher. 1996. *Singapore's Authoritarian Capitalism: Asian Values, Free Market Illusions, and Political Dependency.* Fairfax, Va.: Locke Institute.

Lipset, Seymour Martin. 1959. "Some Social Requisites of Democracy: Economic Development and Political Legitimacy." *American Political Science Review* 53, no. 1: 69–105.

Lipset, Seymour Martin, and Stein Rokkan. 1967. *Party Systems and Voter Alignments: Cross-National Perspectives.* New York: Free Press.

Liu, Ya-Ling. 1992. "Reform from Below: The Private Economy and Local Politics in the Rural Industrialization of Wenzhou." *China Quarterly* 130: 293–316.

Lollar, Xia Li. 1997. *China's Transition: Toward a Market Economy, Civil Society and Democracy.* Bristol: Wyndham Hall Press.

Lü, Xiaobo. 2000. "Booty Socialism, Bureau-preneurs, and the State in Transition: Organizational Corruption in China." *Comparative Politics* 32, no. 3: 273–294.

Lu, Xueyi, ed. 2002. *Dangdai Zhongguo shehui jieceng yanjiu baogao* [Research report on social stratification in contemporary China]. Beijing: Shehui kexue wenxian chubanshe.

Ma, Qiusha. 2005. *Nongovernmental Organisations in Contemporary China: Paving the Way to Civil Society?* London: RoutledgeCurzon.

Ma, Shu Y. 1998. "The Chinese Route to Privatization: The Evolution of the Shareholding System Option." *Asian Survey* 38, no. 4: 379–397.

Mahoney, James. 2000. "Path Dependence in Historical Sociology." *Theory and Society* 29, no. 4: 507–548.

——. 2001. "Path-Dependent Explanations of Regime Change: Central America in Comparative Perspective." *Studies in Comparative International Development* 36, no. 1: 111–141.

Maitland, F. W. 1997 [1909]. *The Forms of Action at Common Law,* edited by A. H. Chaytor and W. J. Whittaker. New York: Cambridge University Press.

Mak, Lau-Fong. 1999. "The Middle Classes and the Government: Reciprocal or Interdependent?" In *East Asian Middle Classes in Comparative Perspective,* edited by Hsin-Huang Michael Hsiao, 257–289. Taipei: Institute of Ethnology, Academia Sinica.

Malik, Rashid. 1997. *Chinese Entrepreneurs in the Economic Development of China*. Westport, Conn.: Praeger.

Mamdani, Mahmood. 1996. *Citizen and Subject: Contemporary Africa and the Legacy of Late Colonialism*. Princeton: Princeton University Press.

Manion, Melanie. 1991. "Policy Implementation in the People's Republic of China: Authoritative Decisions versus Individual Interests." *Journal of Asian Studies* 50, no. 2: 253–279.

——. 1996. "Corruption by Design: Bribery in Chinese Enterprise Licensing." *Journal of Law, Economics, and Organization* 12: 167–195.

Mao, Zedong. 1967. *Selected Works of Mao Tse-Tung*. Vol. 4. Beijing: Foreign Languages Press.

Marx, Karl. 1926 [1852]. *The Eighteenth Brumaire of Louis Bonaparte*. Translated by P. Eden. London: George Allen and Unwin.

——. 1959 [1867]. *Das Kapital*. Edited by F. Engels and condensed by S. Levitsky. Chicago: H. Regnery.

McAdam, Doug, Sidney Tarrow, and Charles Tilly. 2001. *Dynamics of Contention*. New York: Cambridge University Press.

McFaul, Michael. 2002. "The Fourth Wave of Democracy *and* Dictatorship: Noncooperative Transitions in the Postcommunist World." *World Politics* 54, no. 2: 212–244.

McMillan, John, and Barry Naughton. 1992. "How to Reform a Planned Economy: Lessons from China." *Oxford Review of Economic Policy* 8, no. 1: 130–143.

Meisner, Maurice. 1986. *Mao's China and After: A History of the People's Republic*. New York: Free Press.

Michelson, Ethan. 2006. "Opening a Chinese Black Box: How and Why Do Political Connections Matter in Rural China?" Unpublished paper, June. University of Indiana—Bloomington.

Migdal, Joel S. 2001. *State in Society: Studying How States and Societies Transform and Constitute One Another*. New York: Cambridge University Press.

Migdal, Joel S., Atul Kohli, and Vivienne Shue, eds. 1994. *State Power and Social Forces: Domination and Transformation in the Third World*. New York: Cambridge University Press.

Mills, C. Wright. 1951. *White Collar: The American Middle Class*. New York: Oxford University Press.

Mo, Yuanren. 1987. *Jiangsu xiangzhen gongye fazhanshi* [History of township and village industrial enterprises in Jiangsu]. Nanjing: Gongxueyuan chubanshe.

Moore, Barrington, Jr. 1966. *Social Origins of Dictatorship and Democracy: Lord and Peasant in the Making of the Modern World*. Boston: Beacon Press.

Muller, Edward M., Thomas O. Jukam, and Mitchell A. Seligson. 1982. "Diffuse Political Support and Antisystem Political Behavior. *American Journal of Political Science* 26, no. 2: 240–264.

Munck, Gerardo. 1994. "Democratic Transitions in Comparative Perspective." *Comparative Politics* 26, no. 4: 355–375.

Nathan, Andrew J. 1985. *Chinese Democracy*. Berkeley: University of California Press.

——. 1990. *China's Crisis: Dilemmas of Reform and Prospects for Democracy*. New York: Columbia University Press.

——. 2003. "Authoritarian Resilience." *Journal of Democracy* 14, no. 1: 6–17.

Nathan, Andrew J., and Bruce Gilley. 2003. *China's New Rulers: The Secret Files*. 2nd ed. New York: New York Review of Books.

Nathan, Andrew J., and Tianjin Shi. 1993. "Cultural Requisites for Democracy in China." *Daedalus* 122: 95–124.

Naughton, Barry. 1988. "The Third Front: Defense Industrialization in the Chinese Interior." *China Quarterly* 115: 351–386.

——. 1992. "Implications of State Monopoly over Industry and Its Relaxation." *Modern China* 18, no. 1: 14–41.

——. 1994. "Chinese Institutional Innovation and Privatization from Below." *American Economic Review, Papers and Proceedings* 84, no. 2: 266–270.

——. 1996. *Growing Out of the Plan: Chinese Economic Reform, 1978–1993.* New York: Cambridge University Press.

Nee, Victor. 1989. "Peasant Entrepreneurship and the Politics of Regulation in China." In *Remaking the Economic Institutions of Socialism: China and Eastern Europe,* edited by Victor Nee and David Stark, 169–207. Stanford: Stanford University Press.

——. 1991. "Social Inequalities in Reforming State Socialism: Between Redistribution and Markets in China." *American Sociological Review* 56, no. 3: 267–282.

——. 1992. "Organizational Dynamics of Market Transition: Hybrid Forms, Property Rights, and Mixed Economy in China." *Administrative Science Quarterly* 37, no. 1: 1–27.

Nevitt, Christopher Earle. 1996. "Private Business Associations in China: Evidence of Civil Society or Local State Power?" *China Journal* 36: 25–43.

Ng, Linda Fung-Yee, and Chyau Tuan. 1996. *Three Chinese Economies: China, Hong Kong, and Taiwan; Challenges and Opportunities.* Shatin, N.T., Hong Kong: Chinese University Press.

Nolan, Peter, and Dong Fureng, eds. 1989. *Market Forces in China: Competition and Small Business—The Wenzhou Debate.* London: Zed Books.

North, Douglass C. 1990. *Institutions, Institutional Change, and Economic Performance.* Cambridge: Cambridge University Press.

O'Brien, Kevin J. 1990. *Reform without Liberalization: China's National People's Congress and the Politics of Institutional Change.* New York: Cambridge University Press.

——. 1994. "Chinese People's Congresses and Legislative Embeddedness: Understanding Early Organizational Development." *Comparative Political Studies* 27, no. 1: 80–109.

O'Brien, Kevin J., and Li Lianjiang. 1999. "Selective Policy Implementation in Rural China." *Comparative Politics* 31, no. 2: 167–186.

——. 2006. *Rightful Resistance in Rural China.* New York: Cambridge University Press.

Odgaard, Ole. 1992. "Entrepreneurs and Elite Formation in Rural China." *Australian Journal of Chinese Affairs* 28: 89–108.

O'Donnell, Guillermo. 1973. *Modernization and Bureaucratic Authoritarianism: Studies in South American Politics.* Berkeley: Institute of International Studies.

——. 1992. "Substantive or Procedural Consensus? Notes on the Latin American Bourgeoisie." In *The Right and Democracy in Latin America,* edited by Douglas A. Chalmers, Maria do Carmo Campello de Souza, and Atilo A. Borón, 43–47. New York: Praeger.

——. 1997. "Illusions about Consolidation." In *Consolidating the Third World Democracies,* edited by Larry Diamond, Marc F. Plattner, Yun-han Chu, and Hung-mao Tien, 40–57. Baltimore: Johns Hopkins University Press.

O'Donnell, Guillermo, and Philippe Schmitter. 1986. *Transitions from Authoritarian Rule: Tentative Conclusions about Uncertain Democracies.* Baltimore: Johns Hopkins University Press.

O'Donnell, Guillermo, Philippe Schmitter, and Laurence Whitehead, eds. 1986. *Transitions from Authoritarian Rule: Prospects for Democracy.* Baltimore: Johns Hopkins University Press.

Ogden, Suzanne. 2002. *Inklings of Democracy in China.* Cambridge: Harvard University Press, Harvard University Asia Center.

Oi, Jean C. 1985. "Communism and Clientelism: Rural Politics in China." *World Politics* 37, no. 2: 238–266.

——. 1992. "Fiscal Reform and the Economic Foundations of Local State Corporatism in China." *World Politics* 45: 99–126.

——. 1999. *Rural China Takes Off: Institutional Foundations of Economic Reform.* Berkeley: University of California Press.

——. 2005. "Patterns of Corporate Restructuring in China: Political Constraints on Privatization." *China Journal* 53: 115–136.

Oi, Jean, and Andrew G. Walder, eds. 1999. *Property Rights and Economic Reform in China.* Stanford: Stanford University Press.

Orren, Karen, and Stephen Skowronek. 1994. "Beyond the Iconography of Order: Notes for a 'New Institutionalism.' " In *The Dynamics of American Politics: Approaches and Interpretations*, edited by L. C. Dodd and C. Jillson, 311–330. Boulder: Westview.

Paige, Jeffery M. 1971. "Political Orientation and Riot Participation." *American Sociological Review* 36, no. 5: 810–820.

Pak, Jung-Dong. 1997. *The Special Economic Zones of China and Their Impact on Its Economic Development.* Westport, Conn.: Praeger.

Park, Albert, and Minggao Shen. 2003. "Joint Liability Lending and the Rise and Fall of China's Township and Village Enterprises." *Journal of Development Economics* 71: 497–531.

Parris, Kristen. 1993. "Local Initiative and National Reform: The Wenzhou Model of Development." *China Quarterly* 134: 242–263.

——. 1995–96. "Private Entrepreneurs as Citizens: From Leninism to Corporatism." *China Information* 10, nos. 3–4: 1–28.

——. 1999. "Entrepreneurs and Citizenship in China." *Problems of Post-Communism* 46, no. 1: 43–61.

Payne, Leigh A. 1994. *Brazilian Industrialists and Democratic Change.* Baltimore: Johns Hopkins University Press.

Pearson, Margaret M. 1991. *Joint Ventures in the People's Republic of China: The Control of Foreign Direct Investment under Socialism.* Princeton: Princeton University Press.

——. 1994. "The Janus Face of Business Associations in China: Socialist Corporatism in Foreign Enterprises." *Australian Journal of Chinese Affairs* 31: 24–46.

——. 1997. *China's New Business Elite: The Political Consequences of Economic Reform.* Berkeley: University of California Press.

——. 2002. "Entrepreneurs and Democratization in China's Foreign Sector." In *The New Entrepreneurs of Europe and Asia: Patterns of Business Development in Russia, Eastern Europe, and China*, edited by Victoria E. Bonnell and Thomas B. Gold, 130–155. Armonk, N.Y.: M. E. Sharpe.

Peerenboom, Randall. 2002. *China's Long March toward Rule of Law.* New York: Cambridge University Press.

Pei, Minxin. 1998. "Chinese Civic Associations: An Empirical Analysis." *Modern China* 24, no. 3: 285–318.

——. 2006. *China's Trapped Transition: The Limits of Developmental Autocracy.* Cambridge: Harvard University Press.

Pei, Shuping, Sheng Liren, and Chen Naixing. 1993. *Sunan gongyehua daolu yanjiu* [Research on industrialization in the Sunan area]. Beijing: Jingji guanli chubanshe.

Pempel, T. J. 1998. *Regime Shift: Comparative Dynamics of the Japanese Political Economy.* Ithaca: Cornell University Press.

Peng, Yali. 1996. "The Politics of Tobacco: Relations between Farmers and Local Governments in China's Southwest." *China Journal* 36: 67–82.

People's Republic of China State Council. 2005. "White Paper on Political Democracy." Beijing: PRC State Council.

Perry, Elizabeth J., and Mark Selden, eds. 2003. *Chinese Society: Change, Conflict, and Resistance*. 2nd ed. New York: Routledge.

Pierson, Paul. 2000a. "Increasing Returns, Path Dependence, and the Study of Politics," *American Political Science Review* 94, no. 2: 251–267.

——. 2000b. "Not Just What, But *When*: Timing and Sequence in Political Processes." *Studies in American Political Development* 14, no. 1: 79–92.

——. 2004. *Politics in Time: History, Institutions, and Social Analysis*. Princeton: Princeton University Press.

Posusney, Marsha Pripstein. 2004. "Enduring Authoritarianism: Middle East Lessons for Comparative Theory." *Comparative Politics* 36, no. 2: 127–138.

Poulantzas, Nicos. 1975. *Classes in Contemporary Capitalism*. London: New Left Books.

Powell, Walter W., and Paul J. DiMaggio, eds. 1991. *The New Institutionalism in Organizational Analysis*. Chicago: University of Chicago Press.

Przeworski, Adam. 1991. *Democracy and the Market: Political and Economic Reforms in Eastern Europe and Latin America*. New York: Cambridge University Press.

——. 1995. *The Sustainability of Democracy*. New York: Cambridge University Press.

Przeworski, Adam, Michael E. Alvarez, José Antonio Cheibub, and Fernando Limongi. 2000. *Democracy and Development: Political Institutions and Well-Being in the World, 1950–1990*. New York: Cambridge University Press.

Pye, Lucian. 1985. *Asian Power and Politics*. New York: Cambridge University Press.

——. 1990. "Political Science and the Crisis of Authoritarianism." *American Political Science Review* 84, no. 1: 3–19.

Qian, Xingzhong, ed. 1996. *Wenzhou shichang: Gaige kaifang de shuoguo* [Wenzhou's market: Great achievements of reform and opening]. Beijing: Zhonggong dangshi chubanshe.

Raiser, Martin. 2001. "Informal Institutions, Social Capital and Economic Transition: Reflections on a Neglected Dimension." In *Transitions and Institutions: The Experience of Gradual and Late Reformers*, edited by Giovanni Andrea Cornia and Vladimir Popov. London: Oxford University Press.

Rawski, Thomas G. 2000. "The Political Economy of China's Declining Growth." In *China in the World Economy*, edited by Peter Lloyd and Xiaoguang Zhang, 28–42. Aldershot, England: Edward Elgar.

Remick, Elizabeth J. 2004. *Building Local States: China during the Republican and Post-Mao Eras*. Cambridge: Harvard University Press, Harvard East Asian Monographs.

Remmer, Karen. 1991. "New Wine or Old Bottlenecks? The Study of Latin American Democracy." *Comparative Politics* 23, no. 4: 479–495.

Richman, Barry M. 1969. *Industrial Society in Communist China*. New York: Random House.

Rosen, Daniel H. 1999. *Behind the Open Door: Foreign Enterprises in the Chinese Marketplace*. Washington, D.C.: Institute for International Economics.

Ross, Michael. 2001. "Does Oil Hinder Democracy?" *World Politics* 53, no. 3: 325–361.

Rowen, Henry S. 1996. "The Short March: China's Road to Democracy." *National Interest* 45: 61–70.

Rueschemeyer, Dietrich, Evelyn Huber Stephens, and John D. Stephens. 1992. *Capitalist Development and Democracy*. Chicago: University of Chicago Press.

Rustow, Dankwart. A. 1970. "Transitions to Democracy: Toward a Dynamic Model." *Comparative Politics* 2, no. 2: 337–363.

Sadowski, Yahya. 1993. "The New Orientalism and the Democracy Debate." *Middle East Report* 183: 14–21.

Saich, Tony. 2000. "Negotiating the State: The Development of Social Organizations in China." *China Quarterly* 161: 124–141.

Santoro, Michael A. 2000. *Profits and Principles: Global Capitalism and Human Rights in China*. Ithaca: Cornell University Press.

Sargeson, Sally, and Jian Zhang. 1999. "Reassessing the Role of the Local State: A Case Study of Local Government Interventions in Property Rights Reform in a Hangzhou District." *China Journal* 42: 77–99.

Sautman, Barry. "Sirens of the Strongman: Neo-authoritarianism in Recent Chinese Political Theory." *China Quarterly* 129: 72–102.

Saxer, Carl J. 2002. *From Transition to Power Alternation: Democracy in South Korea, 1987–1997*. New York: Routledge.

Schickler, Eric. 2001. *Disjointed Pluralism: Institutional Innovation and the Development of the U.S. Congress*. Princeton: Princeton University Press.

Schmitter, Philippe C. 1974. "Still the Century of Corporatism?" In *The New Corporatism*, edited by Frederick B. Pike and Thomas Stritch, 85–131. Notre Dame: University of Notre Dame Press.

Schumpeter, Joseph. 1976 [1942]. *Capitalism, Socialism, and Democracy*. New York: George Allen and Unwin.

Scott, James C. 1985. *Weapons of the Weak: Everyday Forms of Resistance*. New Haven: Yale University Press.

Segal, Adam. 2003. *Digital Dragon: High-Technology Enterprises in China*. Ithaca: Cornell University Press.

Selznick, Philip. 1949. *TVA and the Grassroots: A Study in the Sociology of Formal Organization*. Berkeley: University of California Press.

Sewell, William H., Jr. 1992. "A Theory of Structure: Duality, Agency, and Transformation." *American Journal of Sociology* 98, no. 1: 1–29.

Seymour, James D. 1987. *China's Satellite Parties*. Armonk, N.Y.: M. E. Sharpe.

——. 1992. "A Half Century Later." In *Roads Not Taken: The Struggle of Opposition Parties in Twentieth-Century China*, edited by Roger B. Jeans. Boulder: Westview.

Sharabi, Hishan. 1988. *Neopatriarchy: A Theory of Distorted Change in Arab Society*. New York: Oxford University Press.

Sheingate, Adam D. 2003. "Political Entrepreneurship, Institutional Change, and American Political Development." *Studies in American Political Development* 17: 185–203.

Shi, Tianjian. 1997. *Political Participation in Beijing*. Cambridge: Harvard University Press.

——. 1999. "Mass Political Behavior in Beijing." In *The Paradox of China's Post-Mao Reforms*, edited by Merle Goldman and Roderick MacFarquhar, 145–169. Cambridge: Harvard University Press, Harvard Contemporary China Series.

——. 2001. "Cultural Values and Political Trust: A Comparison of Mainland China and Taiwan." *Comparative Politics* 33, no. 4: 401–420.

Shirk, Susan. 1993. *The Political Logic of Economic Reform in China*. Berkeley: University of California Press.

Shue, Vivienne. 1994. "State Power and Social Organization in China." In *State Power and Social Forces: Domination and Transformation in the Third World*, edited by Joel S. Migdal, Atul Kohli, and Vivienne Shue, 65–88. New York: Cambridge University Press.

Skilling, H. Gordon. 1966. "Interest Groups and Communist Politics." *World Politics* 18, no. 3: 435–451.

Skinner, G. William. 1964–65. "Marketing and Social Structure in Rural China, Parts I–III." *Journal of Asian Studies* 24, nos. 1–2 (November, February, May): 3–43, 195–228, 363–399.

——. 1977. "Regional Urbanization in Nineteenth-Century China." In *The City in Late Imperial China*, edited by G. William Skinner, 212–249. Stanford: Stanford University Press.

Smallbone, David, and Friederike Welter. 2003. "Institutional Development and Entrepreneurship in Transition Economies." Paper presented at 48th World Conference of the International Council for Small Business, "Advancing Entrepreneurship and Small Business," Belfast.

Smart, Alan. 2000. "The Emergence of Local Capitalisms in China: Overseas Chinese Investment and Patterns of Development." In *China's Regions, Polity, and Economy: A Study of Spatial Transformation in the Post-Reform Era*, edited by Si-ming Li and Wing-shing Tang, 63–95. Hong Kong: Chinese University Press.

Smith, Benjamin. 2004. "Oil Wealth and Regime Survival in the Developing World, 1960–1999." *American Journal of Political Science* 48, no. 2: 232–246.

Smith, William C. 1989. *Authoritarianism and the Crisis of the Argentine Political Economy.* Stanford: Stanford University Press.

Solinger, Dorothy J. 1984. *Chinese Business under Socialism: The Politics of Domestic Commerce in Contemporary China.* Berkeley: University of California Press.

——. 1992. "Urban Entrepreneurs and the State: The Merger of State and Society." In *State and Society in China: The Consequences of Reform*, edited by Arthur Lewis Rosenbaum, 121–141. Boulder: Westview.

——. 1999. *Contesting Citizenship in Urban China: Peasant Migrants, the State, and the Logic of the Market.* Berkeley: University of California Press.

——. 2001. "Research Note: Why We Cannot Count the 'Unemployed.'" *China Quarterly* 167: 671–688.

——. 2002. "Labor Market Reform and the Plight of the Laid-off Proletariat." *China Quarterly* 170: 304–326.

Solnick, Steven. 1996. "The Breakdown of Hierarchies in the Soviet Union and China: A Neo-institutional Perspective." *World Politics* 48, no. 2: 209–238.

Stepan, Alfred C. 2000. "Religion, Democracy, and the 'Twin Tolerations.'" *Journal of Democracy* 11, no. 4: 37–57.

Stephens, John D. 1989. "Democratic Transition and Breakdown in Western Europe, 1870–1939: A Test of the Moore Thesis." *American Journal of Sociology* 94, no. 5: 1019–1077.

Streek, Wolfgang, and Kathleen Thelen. 2005. *Beyond Continuity: Institutional Change in Advanced Political Economies.* New York: Oxford University Press.

Studwell, Joe. 2002. *The China Dream: The Quest for the Last Great Untapped Market on Earth.* New York: Grove Press.

Sun, Bingyao, Wang Ying, and Zhe Xiaoye. 1993. *Shehui zhongjian ceng: Gaige yu Zhongguo de shetuan zuzhi* [The intermediary level of society: Reform and China's social organizations]. Beijing: Zhongguo fazhan chubanshe.

Sun, Yan. 2004. *Corruption and Market in Contemporary China.* Ithaca: Cornell University Press.

Tam, Waikeung, and Dali Yang. 2005. "Food Safety and the Development of Regulatory Institutions in China." *Asian Perspective* 29, no. 4: 5–36.

Tanner, Murray Scot. 1999. *The Politics of Lawmaking in Post-Mao China: Institutions, Processes, and Democratic Prospects.* New York: Oxford University Press.

Tao, Yi-feng. 2005. "A Catch-up Strategy? China's Policy towards Foreign Direct Investment." In *Japan and China in the World Political Economy*, edited by Saadia M. Pekkanen and Kellee S. Tsai, 130–150. London: Routledge.

Thelen, Kathleen. 2000. "Timing and Temporality in the Analysis of Institutional Evolution and Change." *Studies in American Political Development* 14, no. 1: 101–108.

———. 2002. "How Institutions Evolve: Insights from Comparative-Historical Analysis." In *Comparative Historical Analysis in the Social Sciences*, edited by James Mahoney and Dietrich Rueschemeyer, 208–240. New York: Cambridge University Press.

———. 2004. *How Institutions Evolve: The Political Economy of Skills in Germany, Britain, the United States, and Japan*. New York: Cambridge University Press.

Thompson, E. P. 1966. *The Making of the English Working Class*. New York: Vintage Books.

———. 1995. "The Making of Class" and "Class and Class Struggle." In *Class*, edited by Patrick Joyce, 131–142. Oxford: Oxford University Press.

Tilly, Charles. 1998. "Micro, Macro, or Megrim?" In *Mikrogeschichte—Makrogeschichte: Komplementär oder incommensurable*, edited by Jürgen Schlumbohm. Göttingen: Wallstein Verlag, Göttinger Gespräch zur Geschichtswissenschaft.

Tsai, Kellee S. 2002. *Back-Alley Banking: Private Entrepreneurs in China*. Ithaca: Cornell University Press.

———. 2003. "Locating the Local State in Reform-Era China." *Politologiske Studier* 6, no. 2: 71–82.

———. 2006. "Debating Decentralized Development: A Reconsideration of the Wenzhou and Kerala Models." Special issue on India and China, *Indian Journal of Economics and Business*, 47–67.

Tsai, Kellee S., and Sarah Cook. 2005. "China's Developmental Dilemmas: Socialist Transition and Late Liberalization." In *Japan and China in the World Political Economy*, edited by Saadia M. Pekkanen and Kellee S. Tsai, 45–66. London: Routledge.

Tsai, Lily L. 2007. *Accountability without Democracy: Solidary Groups and Public Goods Provision in Rural China*. New York: Cambridge University Press.

Tsebelis, George. 1990. *Nested Games: Rational Choice in Comparative Politics*. Berkeley: University of California Press.

Tseng, Wanda, and Harm Zebregs. 2002. "Foreign Direct Investment in China: Some Lessons for Other Countries." *IMF Discussion Paper* (February).

Unger, Jonathan. 1996. "Bridges: Private Business, the Chinese Government, and the Rise of New Associations." *China Quarterly* 147: 795–819.

———. 2002. *The Transformation of Rural China*. Armonk, N.Y.: M. E. Sharpe.

Unger, Jonathan, ed. 2002. *The Nature of Chinese Politics: From Mao to Jiang*. Armonk, N.Y.: M. E. Sharpe.

Unger, Jonathan, and Anita Chan. 1995. "China, Corporatism, and the East Asian Model." *Australian Journal of Chinese Affairs* 33: 29–53.

Vanhanen, Tatu. 2003. *Democratization: A Comparative Analysis of 170 Countries*. New York: Routledge.

Vogel, Ezra F. 1989. *One Step Ahead in China: Guangdong under Reform*. Cambridge: Harvard University Press.

Volkov, Vadim. 2002. *Violent Entrepreneurs: The Use of Force in the Making of Russian Capitalism*. Ithaca: Cornell University Press.

Wade, Robert. 1990. *Governing the Market: Economic Theory and the Role of Government in East Asian Industrialization*. Princeton: Princeton University Press.

Walder, Andrew G. 1986. *Communist Neo-traditionalism: Work and Authority in Chinese Industry*. Berkeley: University of California Press.

———. 1994. "The Decline of Communist Power: Elements of a Theory of Institutional Change." *Theory and Society* 23: 297–323.

———. 1995. "Local Governments as Industrial Firms: An Organizational Analysis of China's Transitional Economy." *American Journal of Sociology* 101, no. 2: 263–301.

Waldner, David. 2004. "Democracy and Dictatorship in the Post-Colonial World." Unpublished paper, January. University of Virginia.

Walkowitz, Daniel J. 1999. *Working with Class: Social Workers and the Politics of Middle-Class Identity.* Chapel Hill: University of North Carolina Press.

Wang, Fei-ling. 2005. *Organizing through Division and Exclusion: China's Hukou System.* Stanford: Stanford University Press.

Wang, Sze-yueh, and Lee-in Chen Chiu. 2000. "The Impact of Mainland China's Open-Door Policy on Regional Industrial Development." In *China's Regions, Polity, and Economy: A Study of Spatial Transformation in the Post-Reform Era,* edited by Si-ming Li and Wing-shing Tang, 133–152. Hong Kong: Chinese University Press.

Wang, Xiaoyi, Kellee Tsai, and Li Renqing. 2004. *Nongyehua yu minjian jinrong: Wenzhou de jingyan* [Rural industrialization and informal finance: Wenzhou's experience]. Taiyuan: Shanxi jingji chubanshe.

Wank, David L. 1995. "Civil Society in Communist China? Private Business and Political Alliance." In *Civil Society: Theory, History, Comparison,* edited by John A. Hall. Cambridge: Polity Press.

——. 1999. *Commodifying Communism: Business, Trust, and Politics in a Chinese City.* New York: Cambridge University Press.

——. 2002. "The Making of China's Rentier Entrepreneur Élite: State, Clientelism, and Power Conversion." In *Politics in China: Moving Frontiers,* edited by Francoise Mengin and Jean-Louis Rocca, 118–139. New York: Palgrave Macmillan.

Watson, Andrew. 1983. "Agriculture Looks for 'Shoes That Fit': The Production Responsibility System and Its Implications." *World Development* 11, no. 8: 705–730.

Wawro, Gregory J., and Eric Schickler. 2006. *Filibuster: Obstruction and Law Making in the U.S. Senate.* Princeton: Princeton University Press.

Weber, Max. 1946. "Class, Status, and Party." In *From Max Weber: Essays in Sociology,* translated and edited by H. H. Gerth and C. Wright Mills, 180–195. New York: Oxford University Press.

Wedeman, Andrew. 1997. "Stealing from the Farmers: Institutional Corruption and the 1992 IOU Crisis." *China Quarterly* 152: 81–107.

Wendt, Alexander. 1999. *The Social Theory of International Politics.* Cambridge: Cambridge University Press.

Wenzhoushi tongji ju [Wenzhou municipality statistics bureau]. 2003. *Wenzhou tongji nianjian 2003* [Wenzhou statistical yearbook]. Beijing: Zhongguo tongji chubanshe.

White, Gordon. 1994. "Democratization and Economic Reform in China." *Australian Journal of Chinese Affairs* 31: 73–92.

White, Gordon, Jude A. Howell, and Shang Xiaoyuan. 1996. *In Search of Civil Society: Market Reform and Social Change in Contemporary China.* New York: Oxford University Press.

White, Lynn T. 1998. *Unstately Power: Local Causes of China's Economic Reforms.* 2 vols. Armonk, N.Y.: M. E. Sharpe.

Whiting, Susan H. 2001. *Power and Wealth in Rural China.* New York: Cambridge University Press.

"Will China Democratize?" Special issue, *Journal of Democracy* 9, no. 1: 3–64.

Woo, Jung-en. 1991. *Race to the Swift: State and Finance in Korean Industrialization.* New York: Columbia University Press.

Woo, Wing Thye. 1999. "The Real Reasons for China's Growth." *China Journal* 41: 115–137.

Woo-Cumings, Meredith, ed. 1999. *The Developmental State.* Ithaca: Cornell University Press.

World Bank. 1996. *Managing Capital Flows in East Asia.* Washington, D.C.: World Bank.

——. 1997. *China Engaged: Integration with the Global Economy.* Washington, D.C.: World Bank.

Wright, Erik Olin. 1985. *Class, Crisis and the State.* London: New Left Books.

——. 2000. *Class Counts.* New York: Cambridge University Press.

Wu, Dasheng, and Ju Futian. 1991. *Sunan moshi* [Sunan model]. Nanjing: Jiangsu renmin chubanshe.

Wu, Jieh-min. 1998. "Local Property Rights Regime in Socialist Transition: A Case Study of China's Informal Privatization." PhD diss., Columbia University.

——. 2000. "Launching Satellites: Predatory Land Policy and Forged Industrialization in Interior China." In *China's Regions, Polity, and Economy: A Study of Spatial Transformation in the Post-Reform Era,* edited by Si-ming Li and Wing-shing Tang, 309–349. Hong Kong: Chinese University Press.

Wu, Junxiang. 2001. "Sunan moshi de lishi gongji jiqi zhongjie" [Historical merits of the Sunan model and its end]. *Jingji guanli wenzhai* [Digest of economics and management], 17.

Wu, Yongping. 2005. *A Political Explanation of Economic Growth: State Survival, Bureaucratic Politics, and Private Enterprises in the Making of Taiwan's Economy, 1950–1985.* Cambridge: Harvard University Press.

Xia, Ming. 2000. "Political Contestation and the Emergence of the Provincial People's Congresses as Power Players in Chinese Politics: A Network Explanation." *Journal of Contemporary China* 9, no. 24: 185–214.

Xiamenshi tongji ju [Xiamen statistical bureau], ed. Various years. *Xiamen tongji nianjian* [Xiamen statistical yearbook]. Beijing: Zhongguo tongji chubanshe.

Xiang, Biao. 1993. "Beijing youge 'Zhejiangcun'" [Beijing has a 'Zhejiang village']. *Shehuixue yu shehui diaocha* [Sociology and social investigation] 3: 36–39.

Xiao, Geng. 2004. *People's Republic of China: Round-Tripping FDI; Scale, Causes, and Implications.* ADB Institute Discussion Paper No. 7. Manila: Asian Development Bank Institute.

Xie, Jian, and Ren Baiqiang. 2000. *Wenzhou minying jingji yanjiu: Touguo minying jingji kan wenzhou moshi* [Research on Wenzhou's private economy: A penetrating private sector look at the Wenzhou model]. Beijing: Zhonghua gongshanglian chubanshe.

Yan, Yunxiang. 1996. *The Flow of Gifts: Reciprocity and Social Networks in a Chinese Village.* Stanford: Stanford University Press.

Yang, Dali L. 1996. *Calamity and Reform in China: State, Rural Society, and Institutional Change since the Great Leap Famine.* Stanford: Stanford University Press.

——. 2004. *Remaking the Chinese Leviathan: Market Transition and the Politics of Governance in China.* Stanford: Stanford University Press.

Yang, Liensheng. 1970. "Chuantong zhongguo zhengfu dui chengshi shangren zhi tongzhi" [Government control of urban merchants in traditional China]. *Qinghua xuebao chouyin ben* [Qinghua journal of Chinese studies] (August).

Yang, Mayfair M. 1994. *Gifts, Favors, and Banquets: The Art of Social Relationships in China.* Ithaca: Cornell University Press.

Yang Rong v. Liaoning Province Government. No. 1:03-CV-1687 (D.C. filed August 7, 2003).

Yang, Shaoyuan. 2006. "Wo guo shuishou liushi guimo de cesuan" [Estimate of the scale of tax evasion in our country]. *Jilin caishui gaodeng zhuanke xuexiao bao* [Report of the Jilin academy of finance and taxation] 79: 1–5.

Yeh, Anthony Gar-on. 2000. "Foreign Investment and Urban Development in China." In *China's Regions, Polity, and Economy: A Study of Spatial Transformation in the Post-Reform Era,* edited by Si-ming Li and Wing-shing Tang, 35–64. Hong Kong: Chinese University Press.

Young, Susan. 1989. "Policy, Practice, and the Private Sector in China." *Australian Journal of Chinese Affairs* 21: 57–80.

———. 1995. *Private Business and Economic Reform in China*. Armonk, N.Y.: M. E. Sharpe.

Yu, Shizhang, ed. 1989. *Wenzhou gaige moshi yanxin yinxiang* [New reflections on Wenzhou's reform model]. Wenzhou: Zhonggong Wenzhoushi weixuanchuanbu.

Yuan, Enzhen. 1987. *Wenzhou moshi yu fuyu zhilu* [The Wenzhou model and the road toward affluence]. Shanghai: Shanghai shehui kexueyuan chubanshe.

Yudkin, Marcia. 1986. *Making Good—Private Business in Socialist China*. Beijing: Foreign Languages Press.

Zakaria, Fareed. 1997. "The Rise of Illiberal Democracy." *Foreign Affairs* 76: 22–43.

Zeng, Jin. 2007. "Let the Small Go: The Privatization of Small and Medium Public Enterprises in China." PhD diss., Johns Hopkins University.

Zhang, Dunfu. 2002. *Qucheng fazhan moshi de shehuixue fenxi* [A sociological analysis of regional development models]. Tianjin: Tianjin renmin chubanshe.

Zhang, Houyi, and Ming Lizhi, eds. 1999. *Zhongguo siying qiye fazhan baogao* [Report on the development of China's private enterprises]. Beijing: Shehui kexue wenxian chubanshe.

Zhang, Houyi, Ming Lizhi, and Liang Zhuanyun, eds. 2002. *Siying qiye lanpi shu: Zhongguo siying qiye fazhan baogao, no. 3 (2001)* [Blue book of private enterprises: A report on the development of China's private enterprises]. Beijing: Shehui kexue wenxian chubanshe.

———. 2003. *Siying qiye lanpi shu: Zhongguo siying qiye fazhan baogao, no. 4 (2002)* [Blue book of private enterprises: A report on the development of China's private enterprises]. Beijing: Shehui kexue wenxian chubanshe.

———. 2004. *Siying qiye lanpi shu: Zhongguo siying qiye fazhan baogao, no. 5 (2003)* [Blue book of private enterprises: A report on the development of China's private enterprises]. Beijing: Shehui kexue wenxian chubanshe.

Zhang, Li. 2001. *Strangers in the City: Space, Power, and Identity in China's Floating Population*. Berkeley: University of California Press.

Zhang, Yang. 2003. *Local Government and Politics in China: Challenges from Below*. Armonk, N.Y.: M. E. Sharpe.

Zhang, Zhenning, and Mao Chunhua. 1993. *Wenzhou jinrong xianxiang toushi* [Perspectives on the phenomenon of finance in Wenzhou]. Hangzhou: Zhejiang daxue chubanshe.

Zhao, Suisheng, ed. 2000. *China and Democracy: Reconsidering the Prospects for a Democratic China*. New York: Routledge.

Zheng, Yongnian. 2004. *Will China Become Democratic? Elite, Class and Regime Transition*. Singapore: Eastern Universities Press.

Zhongguo renmin yinhang diaocha tongji si [Research and statistics department of the People's Bank of China], ed. 1992. *Zhongguo jinrong tongji, 1952–1991* [China financial statistics, 1952–1991]. Beijing: Zhongguo jinrong chubanshe.

Zhongguo renmin yinhang diaocha tongji si [Research and statistics department of the People's Bank of China], ed. 1992. *Zhongguo jinrong nianjian 1986* [China financial yearbook 1986]. Beijing: Zhongguo jinrong nianjian bianji bu.

Zhonghua quanguo gongshangye lianhe hui (UFIC) and Zhongguo min(si)ying jingji yanjiu hui [China United Front for Industry and Commerce and China Private Economy Research Association]. 2005. "Zhongguo siying jingji nianjian, 2002 nian–2004 nian 6 yue" [China private economy yearbook, 2002–June 2004]. Beijing: Zhongguo zhigong chubanshe.

Zhonghua renmin gongheguo guojia gongshang xingzheng guanli zongju [China State Administration for Industry and Commerce, SAIC]. 1994. *Zhongguo siying jingji nianjian, 1978–1993* [China private economy yearbook]. Hong Kong: Xianggang jingji daobaoshe.

———. 1996. *Zhongguo siying jingji nianjian, 1996* [China private economy yearbook]. Beijing: Zhonghua gongshang lianhe chubanshe.

———. 2000. *Zhongguo siying jingji nianjian, 1997–1999* [China private economy yearbook]. Beijing: Huawen chubanshe.

———. 2005. *Zhongguo siying jingji nianjian, 2002–2004* [China private economy yearbook]. Beijing: Beijing zhigong chubanshe.

Zhonghua renmin gongheguo guojia tongji ju [PRC National Bureau of Statistics]. Various years. *Zhongguo tongji nianjian* [China statistical yearbook]. Beijing: Zhongguo tongji chubanshe.

Zhou, Kate Xiao. 1996. *How the Farmers Changed China.* Boulder: Westview.

Zhou, Xuegang, Qiang Li, Wei Zhao, and He Cai. 2003. "Embeddedness and Contractual Relationships in China's Transitional Economy." *American Sociological Review* 68, no. 1 (February): 75–102.

Zhu, Tonghua, and Sun Bin. 1994. *Sunan moshi fazhan yanjiu* [Research on development of the Sunan model]. Nanjing: Nanjing daxue chubanshe.

Zuckoff, Mitchell. 2005. *Ponzi's Scheme: The True Story of a Financial Legend.* New York: Random House.

Zweig, David. 1983. "Opposition to Change in Rural China: The System of Responsibility and Rural Communes." *Asian Survey* 21, no. 3: 879–900.

———. 1985. "Strategies of Policy Implementation: Policy 'Winds' and Brigade Accounting in Rural China, 1968–1978." *World Politics* 37, no. 2: 267–293.

———. 1995. "Developmental Communities on China's Rural Coast: The Impact of Trade, Investment, and Transnational Alliances." *Comparative Politics* 27: 253–274.

———. 1997. "Rural People, the Politicians, and Power." *China Journal* 38: 153–168.

———. 1999. "Undemocratic Capitalism: China and the Limits of Economism." *National Interest* 56: 63–72.

———. 2002. *Internationalizing China: Domestic Interests and Global Linkages.* Ithaca: Cornell University Press.

Web Sources

China Data Online, http://141.211.136.211/eng/Default.asp

Hechuan City government, http://hc.cq.gov.cn/index.asp

Zhonghua renmin gongheguo guojia xingzheng gongshang guanliju [China State Administration for Industry and Commerce], http://www.saic.gov.cn

Zhongguo laogong tongxun [China Labor Bulletin], http://www.chinalabour.org.hk

All-China Federation of Industry and Commerce, http://www.acfic.org.cn

Zhengzhou Municipal People's Government, http://www.zhengzhou.gov.cn

Zhongguo jinrong wang [China financial network], http://www.zhjrw.com

World Values Survey, http://www.worldvaluessurvey.org

Index